IDENTIFYING THE ENGLISH

Identifying the English
A History of Personal Identification 1500 to the Present

Edward Higgs

continuum

Continuum International Publishing Group

The Tower Building	80 Maiden Lane
11 York Road	Suite 704
London	New York
SE1 7NX	NY 10038

www.continuumbooks.com

First published 2011

British Library Cataloguing-in-Publication Data
A catalogue record for this book is available from the British Library.

ISBN: HB: 978-1-4411-8203-6

Typeset by Newgen Imaging Systems Pvt Ltd, Chennai, India
Printed and bound in India

Contents

List of Illustrations

1

Introduction

THE IDENTITY PARADOX

In October 2007 a junior official at the United Kingdom's HM Revenue and Customs (HMRC) sent the National Audit Office two compact discs via the courier company TNT. These contained the personal details necessary for the payment of child benefit to 25 million individuals. Items of information included names and dates of birth of citizens, and those of their children, their addresses, their National Insurance numbers and, where relevant, the details of the bank or building society accounts into which the child benefit was to be paid. In doing this the HMRC official ignored security procedures, and the two discs disappeared in transit never to be seen again. It was alleged at the time that this information might be worth £1.5 billion to criminals who could use it to impersonate millions of people, and so 'steal' their identities. Such personal details could be used to access bank accounts to remove money; to set up other accounts under assumed names; to buy goods on credit using another person's credit ratings, and so on. The following month this debacle led to the resignation of the chairman of the HMRC, a public apology to the individuals concerned by the British Prime Minister, and a significant decline in support for his government. Surprisingly little criticism was made of the courier company, perhaps reflecting the pro-business zeitgeist of the age.[1] Over the following months the list of public sector bodies that admitted to losing people's personal details expanded to include the Royal Air Force, Royal Navy, Ministry of Defence, Home Office, the police, NHS Trusts, the Driver and Vehicle Licensing Agency (DVLA), the Department for Work and Pensions, and local councils. Those affected include patients, taxpayers, welfare recipients, applicants for driving tests, students, teachers, job applicants, farm workers, prison staff and service personnel. The HMRC episode was thus anything but an isolated incident.[2]

I was subsequently invited to be interviewed on the issues raised by these events by the BBC Radio Four programme *Broadcasting House*, where I had to confess that the previous day he had himself been the victim of identity theft. When I used my debit card and PIN number to withdraw cash from an ATM (automatic teller machine) in Oxford, I discovered that my current account was unexpectedly overdrawn. Using the bank's internet site, which required the inputting of a user ID number, a password and items from a set of 'memorable information', I discovered that the day before 250 euros had been withdrawn from my account by someone using an ATM in Germany. I rang the bank's Fraud and Dispute Operations, identifying myself through my address and other personal details, and arranged to have the stolen sum reimbursed and the fraud investigated. Surprisingly the bank refused to tell me the results of this investigation 'because of the Data Protection Act', an obvious misapplication of that piece of UK legislation. This sorry tale exemplifies a curious paradox at the heart of personal identification in developed Western societies. On one hand, there are more and more means for people to prove who they are, and, on the other, personal identities have never seemed less secure, or been the focus of so much public anxiety.

In Western countries individuals are registered and recorded from birth to death, and at various points in-between. States and private organizations hold vast databases of information on identifiable persons, and have done so for most of the past century.[3] Citizens and consumers possess wallets that literally bulge with means of identification in the form of credit cards, drivers' licences, membership cards, and the like. These contain means of personal identification in the form of signatures, photographs, microchips that can be used in conjunction with PIN codes, and so on. According to APACS, the trade body for payment services, in 2006 there were 142.8 million payment cards in use in the United Kingdom – 69.5 million credit cards, 4.9 million charge cards and 68.3 million debit cards. These were held by 31.4 million people, just under two-thirds of the adult population, with an average of 2.4 credit cards and 1.6 debit cards per person.[4] In my case, there would appear to have been at least one other counterfeit card in the possession of someone in Germany. In addition, since the 1960s a whole new range of techniques has been developed to identify people from the measurement and analysis of parts of their bodies (biometrics) – retinal and iris scans, facial and hand geometry, voice recognition, and DNA profiles.

At the same time, however, identity fraud is said to cost the United Kingdom £1.7 billion (up from £1.3 billion in 2000–01), and to affect perhaps 100,000 people, per annum.[5] The 'criminalization' of the internet, as organized crime has taken advantage of the ad hoc and vulnerable nature of online identification systems, is said to be a fundamental threat to its credibility.[6] Official attempts to pin down the personal identity of individuals, both within the boundaries of states and when they move across them, have also become increasingly frantic and controversial. In Britain this can be seen in the fraught debates over the introduction of identity cards, and of the expansion of the fingerprint and DNA databases held by the police. In the wake of bombings by Islamic fundamentalists in New York, London and Madrid, the fingerprinting of travellers at airports has caused increasing unease. Such concerns reflect the manner in which everyone has now become a suspect, and the threats that intimate identification through the body presents to privacy and a sense of personal integrity. Perhaps inevitably debates often revolve around the spectre of the Big Brother State in George Orwell's novel *1984*. These concerns have led to the creation of a number of protest groups, such as NO2ID, which seek to prevent the spread of identification cards and of the 'database state' in general.[7]

One of the aims of the present historical study is to help to resolve this apparent contradiction between the expanded means of identification, and its apparent fragility, by showing how these two phenomena are actually intimately connected. The book will also examine the extent to which anonymity is actually preferable to identification, or even possible. It is certainly true that internal passports and identity cards were used by both Stalin and Hitler to create their own forms of totalitarianism. To be purged or sent to the death camps people had to be known and identified.[8] However, States have also used forms of identification to ensure that citizens are eligible for rights to benefits and to the vote without fear of impersonation, while private individuals have used seals and signatures for centuries to lay claim to real and personal estate.[9] The right to identification can thus be a right to be recognized. This can be seen in some contemporary developing nations where those who are not registered at birth lack access to basic social services and property rights, and where displaced persons without papers cannot move, work or, even, marry.[10] Although Orwell's *1984* described the dangers of total surveillance, it also showed how in a totalitarian society one has no identity, and can simply become a 'non-person' to whom all reference has been expunged.

TOWARDS A HISTORY OF PERSONAL IDENTIFICATION

Academic historians are, as everyone else, increasingly interested in the subject of personal identification, both for what it tells us about the individual, and about his or her changing relationship with the State and the society to which they belong. Here one should mention Jane Caplan and John Torpey's path-breaking collection of essays, *Documenting Individual Identity*, which covers a broad range of subjects from the identification of citizens in the French Revolution to the use of identity cards to organize genocide in Rawanda in the 1990s.[11] There are also important historical studies of specific technologies of identification, such as John Torpey's important work on the modern international passport system,[12] and Simon Cole and Chandak Sengoopta's separate, and equally impressive, studies of the development and spread of fingerprinting.[13] Members of numerous other disciplines, including political scientists, lawyers, criminologists, anthropologists and sociologists, are interested in how people identify themselves, or how they are 'pinned down' by states and private businesses. Most of these discussions of the subject lack a historical framework, although this is certainly not true of some of the pioneering sociological analyses of David Lyon.[14]

None of these authors has tried to produce an overarching theory of the historical development of the means of personal identification. In a newly emerging field of research, they are more concerned to document particular facets of the historical story, or to examine issues of contemporary relevance. However, their works do contain asides, or introductory observations, that hint at a broad set of assumptions about the development of the means of personal identification – a sort of shadowy 'meta-history'. There is a tendency to understand the development of identification in terms of the impact of increased mobility during the Industrial Revolution, which is associated in turn with urbanization and the assumption of increasing social anonymity. For example, in his innovative *Suspect Identities*, Simon Cole argues in a preparatory remark that:

> In general, premodern societies already had an effective method of personal, and criminal, identification: the network of personal acquaintance through which persons were 'known' in the memories and perceptions of their neighbors. Most people spent virtually their entire lives in the village, or region, in which they were born. . . . In village society, there was little need for a signature to verify the identity of a neighbor. If a signature was used, it was more a gesture of good faith than a test of identity. . . . In the wake of the industrial revolution, enormous numbers of people migrated from intimate rural villages to anonymous urban settings. Cities grew dramatically along with population density. The informal system of personal acquaintance and collective memory began to collapse.[15]

Hence, Cole hints, the need for new forms of identification, such as the fingerprint, to deal with the social problems connected to the rise of anonymity in society. Similarly, Chandak Sengoopta in his *Imprint of the Raj* argues that fingerprinting can be seen within the context of urbanization and movement:

> Nineteenth-century Europe was a haven for criminals. Life was becoming steadily more urban, anonymous and mobile – in the large cities, one could simply disappear into a milling crowd of individuals and take on new identities that the surveillance and policing methods of the time could not hope to detect.[16]

Caplan and Torpey, who are fully aware of the complexity of this history, also see the development of identification in the period of the French Revolution and its aftermath against 'the background of an increasingly mobile society in which older and more stable conventions of identification were dissolving'. However, they also see new forms of identification in terms of political developments associated with the creation of the modern nation-state, a theme to which the present work will return.[17] In works written by non-historians on the politics of identification, the lack of mobility in pre-modern societies, and so the absence of a need for formal means of identification, are taken as axiomatic.[18]

Some of these arguments draw, in part, on classical sociological concepts. As I have noted elsewhere,[19] sociology was born in the nineteenth century in the aftermath of the Industrial Revolution, and its pioneers – Durkheim, Marx, Spencer and Weber – were concerned with that momentous transition in world history, and with its social and institutional results. Understanding modernity, in the sense of grasping what makes the modern, industrial world different to societies in the past, is still a fundamental concern of historical sociology. In the Western social science tradition the emergence of industrial capitalism at the end of the eighteenth century is seen as resulting in key shifts – from status to contract, from mechanical to organic solidarity, and from the sacred to the secular.[20] It should not be a surprise to discover, therefore, that sociologically informed accounts of the development of means of identification implicitly regard the late eighteenth and early nineteenth centuries as a period of fundamental change.

The belief in increasing anonymity during the processes of industrialization and urbanization was given one of its classic formulations in Ferdinand Tönnies's *Gemeinschaft und Gesellschaft*. Originally published in 1887, this work contrasted the supposed communal life of the ancient rural community, the *gemeinschaft*, with forms of contractual association in modern urban society, the *gesellschaft*. In the *gemeinschaft* people supposedly worked together, and were bound by ties of kinship, tradition and the common tilling of the soil. The *gemeinschaft* was an 'organic' entity in which feelings of love, habit and duty were said to combine to create harmony, and where individuals were known to each other personally. In the modern *gesellschaft*, or so Tönnies argued, all are strangers to each other, and people are orientated towards the fulfilment of personal goals and the making of money. In this form of society, others become mere tools to personal gain in a market economy. The State then acts as a means of keeping individuals from each other's throats, and enforces the rule of capitalists over the discontented working classes.[21] The concept of a 'society of strangers' is also found in the work of the early twentieth-century sociologist Georg Simmel.[22] The vision of a mobile, anonymous, society is plainly one, or so it can be argued, in which new forms of identification become necessary to prevent fraud and to impose social control through the punishment of known deviants.

The discussions of political scientists regarding the development of modern identification systems for tracking and limiting the movements of migrants and asylum seekers is similarly couched in terms of the mobility of contemporary global society. According to Didier Bigo, for example, contemporary techniques of identification – passports, visas, identity cards – are a form of rhetoric, an illusion to give the impression that the nation-state still has control over population flows in an era of economic globalization, and of supranational political structures such as the European Union.[23] Students of migration and refugee studies, such as Stephen Castles, have also linked migration, security and surveillance.[24] Similarly, David Lyon has linked surveillance and mobility, arguing that, 'Mobility creates a world of nomads and unsettled social arrangements, so it is not surprising that in transit areas, such as airports, surveillance practices are intense.'[25] Certainly, international boundaries are one of the sites where the need to produce evidence of identity is today paramount.

Alternatively, David Lyon has seen identification in terms of 'modernity', for as he puts it in his *Surveillance Society*:

> The coming of modernity meant that individuals were granted an increasing range of rights, starting with civil rights before the law, and moving to the political rights of citizens and social rights to welfare. But to obtain these rights, bureaucratic structures required careful scrutiny of the grounds of entitlement, according to consistent rules. So people had to be registered, and their personal details filed, which of course paradoxically facilitated their increased surveillance.[26]

This is, however, somewhat problematic in the case of England. As will be discussed below, people had rights before the law from the medieval period, to welfare benefits from the sixteenth century, and some had rights to vote from the same period. All these required some form of identification, albeit at a local level.

An emphasis on the modern State as inherently driven towards increasing the regulation of individuals, and on its desire to pin them down for the purposes of control and moulding, can also be found in a wide range of texts influenced by Michel Foucault's theory of 'governmentality'. Foucault saw the eighteenth and early nineteenth century as a period when statesmen, experts and learned men began to think in terms of acting upon the population as a whole. The latter became an entity to be measured and manipulated in the interests of the State. Hence, the rise, or so the argument goes, of demography and statistics. But Foucault also saw the State as attempting to control individual bodies through administrative means for the purpose of creating 'bio-power'.[27] Bruce Curtis, writing about the nineteenth-century Canadian censuses, follows Foucault in seeing such activities as an attempt 'to tie individuals to places within an administrative grid and then to hold them steady so that they may become objects of knowledge and government'.[28] Some of these ideas have been applied directly to technologies of bodily identification in recent post-modernist critiques.[29] This is also a theme taken up by Anthony Giddens in his *The Nation State and Violence*, in which the rise of the modern nation-state is seen as co-terminous with industrial capitalism. It expands its power through an 'internal pacification' of society that involves the collection and storage of information to identify citizens. Indeed, Giddens goes still further and claims that 'identity cards, permits of all sorts, and other kinds of official papers' are a concentration of surveillance associated with totalitarian states. How exactly Giddens squares such statements with the existence of such forms of identification in most Western liberal democracies is left characteristically vague.[30]

The concentration here on identification as state control, and the emphasis given to techniques and technologies for identifying criminals in much of the literature on the subject, creates a relentlessly negative picture. Identification is understood as all part of 'Seeing like a State', in the pejorative sense given to that term by James C. Scott.[31] Surprisingly little attention has been paid to rather more positive form of identification, such as the identification of the corpse so that kin and friends can mourn their dead. Similarly, the way in which identification underpins property rights, or facilitates control by commercial organizations, has been relatively underexplored. In this context, why is there so much concern over state identification cards, while store loyalty cards are accepted wholeheartedly by the public with little comment?[32] In the present work these less negative aspects of identification will be given fuller consideration.

Standing somewhat apart from the emphasis on the modern period in the history of identification is the work of Valentin Groebner, who clearly shows the existence of official forms of identification in fifteenth- and sixteenth-century Europe. In the pages of his intriguing book, *Who are You?*, we learn about the officers of the Inquisition pursuing heretics with the latter's portraits painted on small linen cloths; of soldiers, city officials and beggars wearing badges of identification; of travellers with official letters of safe conduct; of pilgrims issued with health certificates; and of the attempts of Phillip II of Spain to use documents to restrict the passage of heretics, *moriscos* and Jews to the New World. As Groebner notes, the belief in the immediacy and emotional authenticity of this earlier period, and its supposed lack of documentation, reflects a certain strain of Romanticism that looks back to a supposed Golden Age in the past.[33] But Groebner also has a tendency to assume that the State's will to identify individuals is a constant, and has its origins in his period of study.[34] Hence, he argues, 'Our modern day passports and (if we are unfortunate) wanted posters continue the history of medieval seals, coats of arms, and documents as written evidence of identity.'[35] This allows him to jump from identification in Renaissance Europe to that in the contemporary world as if he is examining the same, or at least a continuous, process. Scott takes a similar line when he argues that the development of surnames in the medieval period reflects the need of the state to pin down its subjects.[36] But is this picture of historical continuity any more reliable than that of rupture during the Industrial Revolution?

Such questions have, to a considerable extent, dictated the overall structure and nature of the present book. In order to gauge the impact of industrialization on the means of personal identification used in society, the period of study chosen here is extremely long, stretching from the end of the Middle Ages to the present day. To make any sense of such a long period the research has to be, in the main, confined to one society – England – itself merely one part of a larger modern political entity, the United Kingdom. This means limiting the extent to which comparisons can be made between societies, something that has proved so important in other relevant studies. Such a narrow geographical focus is, quite frankly, a limitation of the present work, especially when identification often takes place when moving between countries, and identification technologies have international currency. Even then, much of the history presented of legal procedures, political theories, registration systems, taxation, welfare provision for the poor, military administration, penal systems, and so on, must be rather cursory, and, perhaps, to the expert eye somewhat misleading. As an initial survey, it has also had to be based, to some extent, on secondary sources. Hopefully the ability to ask big questions about identification over the *longue dureé* will compensate for some of these deficiencies. Certainly, the conclusion of this book is that neither the existing models of 'rupture' or 'continuity' across the Industrial Revolution adequately capture the history of identification techniques, at least in the English context. It is intended that the present work will provide a preliminary framework which will be a spur to further research.

A concentration on England is also justified because historically it was both the cradle of the Industrial Revolution, and the centre of the British Empire. If industrialization, mobility, urbanization and the birth of the nation-state were responsible for the growth of modern forms of identification, then one would expect England to show a precocious development in this respect in the late eighteenth and early nineteenth centuries. In addition, England's position in the nineteenth and early twentieth centuries as the centre of a vast political network stretching across the entire globe made it a central node through which identification technologies circulated. For example, a modern system for the civil registration of births, marriages and deaths was established in London in 1837,[37] and had already been copied in its rudiments in Tasmania in Australia by 1838.[38] Similarly, the principal origins of modern forensic fingerprinting lay in British India, from where it was introduced into England in the early years of the twentieth century.[39] From there it spread to the United States and other parts of the world.[40]

It should also be added that contemporary Britain is at the forefront of the development of identification technologies. DNA profiling, for example, was developed in the early 1980s by Professor Sir Alec Jeffreys at the University of Leicester's Department of Genetics, who used a chemical process to force long DNA strands to separate into shorter pieces at predictable but variable points. These could then be arranged by size to create a set of horizontal bars resembling a bar code.[41] In an analogous manner, iris recognition technology allows the identification of an individual by the mathematical analysis of the random patterns that are visible within the iris of the eye. The algorithms for iris recognition were developed at Cambridge University's Computing Laboratory by Dr John Daugman, and the system is currently being used to record foreigners entering the United Arab Emirates and elsewhere.[42] Britain has, of course, the somewhat dubious distinction of being the world leader in the use of CCTV for public surveillance.[43] One of the many mysteries of contemporary Britain is why a country that prided itself historically on leaving people alone should now be a world leader in their surveillance and tracking. Nor is this necessarily something foisted upon the British by a malign State. Opinion polls show that although in the abstract the British believe that more collection of personal data by the government is broadly a bad thing, a majority have supported mandatory ID cards, a universal DNA database and the proliferation of CCTV cameras.[44]

Another drawback to looking at such a long and complex history has been the inevitable need to reify entities such as 'the State' for ease of exposition. States are, of course, constellations of groups – political, administrative, professional – with differing, and sometimes conflicting, interests, strategies and competencies, all claiming access to power and authority. The 'State' is a site of contestation as much as a unitary institution with a single purpose. Differing governing administrations, and political parties, can pursue differing policies, as can differing sets of civil servants. However, there is a sense in which the governing institutions hold together in the British State, and there are recognized hierarchies of authority and power within it, while there is a definite Civil Society that lies outside the State. This is the rather loose sense in which the term 'State' is used in this book.

THE WHAT AND HOW OF IDENTIFICATION?

But before actually proceeding to the history of identification in England, some effort needs to be made to define what the term 'identification' will actually cover in the present work, and, perhaps just as importantly, what it will not.

First, it is necessary to distinguish mechanisms for identifying unique individuals, from those for identifying those individuals as falling into particular groups or sets. The distinction drawn here can be seen in the way in which a passport both identifies a particular person through a photograph and a unique passport number, but also that the person is a citizen of a particular country. In the same manner, in the Auschwitz death camp, prisoners were identified individually through the tattooing of unique numbers on their bodies, as well as being forced to wear coloured markers to place them into groups – yellow stars for Jews, pink triangles for homosexuals, red triangles for political prisoners, and so on. The Nazis used the latter to destroy all individuality but were also obsessed with the bureaucracy of pinning down their victims' identity administratively.[45] The bureaucratic banality of Hitler's regime almost seems to worsen the horrors of the Holocaust, if such a thing is possible.

These two ways of understanding identification have sometimes been conflated, perhaps necessarily, in historical accounts. This is especially the case in the literature on the early modern period. Valentin Groebner, for example, plainly recognizes the distinction to be made between what he describes as the identification of the 'second-person singular', and that which identifies people as falling into particular groups.[46] However, because of the sources he has to deal with, much of his *Who are You?* might be better titled *Which Group Do*

You Fall Into?, discussing as it does the wearing of badges to identify individuals as the bearers of public office, as pilgrims, as licensed beggars, as the members of particular armies, and so on. Similarly, Steve Hindle's fascinating essay, 'Technologies of identification under the Old Poor Law', refers to the use of badges in England to identify the poor as paupers under an Act of 1697, rather than that which distinguishes one pauper from another.[47]

It could, of course, be argued that one can identify an individual uniquely through an enumeration of all the various groupings to which he or she belongs. I, for example, am a member of (1) the set of all human beings; (2) the set of human beings called Edward Higgs; (3) the set of human beings born in Lancaster, England, on a certain date; and so on. But this becomes somewhat artificial, and there is a sense in which all individuals are unique biological entities which have had particular sets of experiences and memories. Conjoined twins are something of a problem here, although the ethical and emotional problems they raise are perhaps the exception that proves the rule. It is the means of identifying these specific organic bodies with a history that will be the main subject of this book, although in practice it is not always easy to make such distinctions. For example, in the early modern period, and among certain social groups, the entity that mattered was not the individual body but the biological lineage, or blood-line. It can certainly be argued that perceived membership of groups was more central to identity in that period, which helps to explain why early modern historians have concentrated on that form of identification.

In addition, although this book will mainly be concerned with how individuals were identified as individuals, it will not attempt to deal with the authentic 'self' in itself. It will leave to one side the vast and burgeoning philosophical literature on the concept of the self, and that on the history of 'self-identity' – how people in history have understood themselves.[48] In part this reflects the difficulty of coming to an adequate understanding of what the 'self' actually means in an historical context. Certainly, historians disagree when the 'modern self' can be said to have come into existence. For Dror Wahrman the 'self' became a stable identity, which could not be shed or manipulated, as a reaction to the instabilities of the American and French Revolutions.[49] But for C. B. Macpherson the possessive, individualistic self was a product of the seventeenth century, and Keith Thomas has recently argued that a sense of individuality becomes more visible at this time.[50] However, Alan Macfarlane would place the origins of forms of legal independence in the Middle Ages,[51] and a philosopher such as Charles Taylor might push the story back to St Augustine in the late fourth century.[52] Instead of the construction of this hypothetical 'self', what will be described in the present work are the techniques or performances that are used by individuals to prove they are a particular person. After all, such identification is a social process – one has to identify oneself to someone else. This does not mean that the routine use of such techniques does not influence how one understands oneself as a citizen, customer or outlaw, but that is not the prime focus here.

Perhaps one of the most fruitful ways to approach the history of such techniques of identification is through the writings of the great Canadian sociologist Erving Goffman. For Goffman, society is a system in which people play conventional roles, which others are taught to understand in certain ways, and to which they also respond in a conventional manner. As he argued in *The Presentation of Self in Everyday Life* in 1959:

> Society is organised on the principle that any individual who possesses certain social characteristics has a moral right to expect that others will value and treat him in an appropriate way. Connected with this principle is a second, namely that an individual who implicitly or explicitly signifies that he has certain social characteristics ought in fact to be what he claims he is. In consequence, when an individual projects a definition of the situation and thereby makes an implicit or explicit claim to be a person of a particular kind, he automatically exerts a moral demand upon the others, obliging them to value and treat him in the manner that persons of his kind have a right to expect.[53]

When one meets a stranger it is necessary to discover the facts of the situation. It is necessary to know who he or she is so that one can react in the correct manner. One has a right to react differently to a demand for money when the person making the demand is a beggar, rather than an income tax inspector. But it is not possible to know all the facts of the situation, so one has to rely on cues, tests, hints, expressive gestures, status symbols, and so on, as predictive devices. It is necessary for the person making an identity claim to present credentials, or to perform some act, or supply some information, which carries credence. One has to rely on the ability of the stranger to produce proof of who he or she is. The income tax inspector sends one a letter on headed notepaper, a beggar makes a rather different type of appeal, which conventionally involves a specific form of body language.[54] Identification, as the performance of claims, can, of course, take place in hyperspace as well as in the physical realm.

Often this process means proving that one falls into a particular status group – one is actually a tax inspector – but frequently it involves proving that one is a specific person to whom certain rights and obligations are attached. I am the Edward Higgs who owns certain property, or who has the right to vote in certain elections. The attachment of certain types of rights and obligations to particular bodies through social processes of identification is what creates their social persona, as juridical persons and as citizens. The term 'persona' originally referred to the masks that actors on the classical stage donned to play various parts in a play. The individual who fails to perform in the correct manner may be placed outside the body politic as a criminal, an 'outlaw', and has an identity forced upon him or her, usually through their body. Rather than performing an identity, they are marked on the skin, physically described in registers, or their bodily features are captured in various forms of database. Identification is something that others perform on them. Identity, in this sense, is not something that resides in the individual but in the social interactions in which they take part.[55] Alan Bennett, another Goffman enthusiast, tells us that, 'In Goffman what we do with words (or what we do with our hands and feet) is about what we are.'[56] This is very true but Goffman would also add that we have to make those signs in front of an audience, and what they do in response to our performances is also vital to the establishment of our social persona. The techniques and technologies for identification are thus not simply artefacts or objective activities; they have cultural meanings. One is often not simply identified but identified as 'something' – a property holder, a citizen, a criminal, and so on. What is identified is a 'personality', and this personality can do things even when the body has ceased to exist, as in the will of the juridical person expressed in testamentary documents.

Since people can take on different social roles – citizen, customer, property holder, and so on – the performances through which they identify these personalities can differ. When identifying themselves as juridical persons, who are able to claim the right to acquire and alienate property, individuals have historically used possessions they could produce, acts they could perform, or signs they could utter (e.g. the use of seals, signatures or of PIN numbers in electronic transactions). When identifying themselves as citizens, who can claim welfare benefits or the right to vote, they have used similar techniques but have also tended to be identified through the active recognition of the community. On the other hand, criminals, and other deviants, have historically been identified through the body, rather than via a performance, knowledge or a possession. There has been a marked difference between identification claimed by an individual, in order to obtain social or economic rights, and identification foisted on an unwilling individual for the purposes of social control. In the case of the human corpse, identification has always been via the crudities of the body – except in *Hamlet* the dead do not perform. This takes one into the world of the coroner's inquest, and of the forensic scientist, which will be considered in more detail below.

In one sense identification has also been historically gendered, in that women in the past were less able to own property or vote, and often received rights to welfare through their husbands. They had far fewer opportunities to perform an identification. However, when women did have such opportunities, they used the same methods of identification as their male counterparts. There do not appear to have been forms of identification that were specific to men, or to women for that matter. As women came to be enfranchised, and were more commonly the owners of property in their own right, so the methods of identification they used continued to be the same as those of men. The forms of identification that have been used to identify female criminals also seem to have been gender neutral.

For the purposes of this book, however, it is also necessary to look in a little more detail at what the creation and use of such techniques of identification have involved. The necessary performances cannot simply be in terms of an assertion to others that 'I am Edward Higgs', since anyone could do that. Identification would then become a tautology – 'I am I.'[57] Beyond immediate kin and community, where one is known via shared experience, the 'other' to which one performs often means an entity that exists over time and space, such as the State, or commercial organizations. Identification before such entities usually involves an act of authority – the State or company declares that one has proven to it in some sense that 'You are X.' Then a token of this identification is given to the person that can be compared to a stored version of that original act of identification at a different time or place.

A few examples may make this more easier to understand. A person applies for a driving licence and supplies information to the State to prove who they are (authoritative act of identification). The information is stored and they obtain a driving licence (the token), which can be compared to the results of the original act (in a database) if necessary. Again, a bank customer sets up a bank account and supplies details of him or herself to the bank (authoritative act of identification). The information is stored by the bank and they are given a credit card and a PIN number (tokens) that can be compared to the original authoritative data held by the bank when a transaction is made. In the case of modern biometrics, such as iris scanning, the body itself becomes the token – a person's iris is scanned and the information stored on computer databases (authoritative act of identification). Later the person has to present their iris (the token) to another scanner to compare it to the 'stored identity' on the official database.[58] Even forms of identification that involve objects or performances unmediated by such organizations, seals and signatures, for example, are in the last resort underpinned by courts or statute law. It is necessary, therefore, to explore here not only the use of tokens, such as passports, but also how one convinces a body such as the State that one is a certain individual to whom a passport can be issued. Such systems of identification are only as robust as the original authoritative act of identification, and the documents or other performances upon which it was based.[59] The use of tokens of identification, as a supplement to systems of registration, can turn a means of collecting data for statistical purposes into a means of identification. This is a level of identification that tends to be missing from the current historiography.

Another way of understanding this history of identification is to see it in terms of information flows. Signs are appended to documents, in the form of seals or signatures, to identify their authors. Personal information is supplied to state or commercial bodies for storage, and is then retrieved in response to the presentation of a token. Information in databases is compared to substantiate the identity of a person, and so on. The history of identification is thus the history of personal information, and the performances which govern its 'utterance', dissemination, storage and retrieval.[60]

THE STRUCTURE OF THE BOOK

The structure of the present book is mainly determined by chronology, and by an attempt to maintain a distinction between the identification of the citizen, of the consumer and juridical person, and of the deviant. The latter differentiation is not just a matter of exposition but reflects important distinctions in English law, society and political activity.

The next chapter looks at the subject of imposture, outlining the careers of three impostors taken from different centuries. Not only will this help to draw out some of the ways in which people at the time went about proving an identity, but will also raise questions about periodization, and of continuity and change in the field. Chapter 3 then begins the analysis of identification in early modern England by considering in some detail whether or not the country in this period was a face-to-face society. The answer is, typically, 'yes and no', although it was certainly not a *gemeinschaft* in the sense given to that term by modern sociologists. The substantive discussion of early modern identification follows in the next two chapters. Chapter 4 looks at property owners and citizens in the period, and covers a variety of identificatory techniques, including heraldry, seals and signatures. It also gives some consideration to the development of the surname from its origins in the early medieval period. Chapter 5 examines the identification of the pauper under the Old Poor Law, the treatment of the corpse in the coroner's court, and the identification of the criminal and the alien in the period from approximately 1500 to 1750.

Identification during the years of the Industrial Revolution, from 1750 to 1850, is the subject of Chapter 6. It examines whether the great changes in the economy and society, seen in this period, led to corresponding changes in the techniques for identifying citizens, juridical persons and deviants. The development of new forms of biometric and bureaucratic identification in the 100 or so years after 1850, a period that sees the creation of a 'dossier society' is then discussed. Chapter 7 looks at the identification of the criminal in the period 1850 to 1970, while Chapter 8 examines that of the citizen and the customer in the same period. The following two chapters, Chapters 9 and 10, take the story up to the present, emphasizing the shift from the dossier to the digital database in the 'Risk Society'. Chapter 9 looks at the treatment of the consumer, and the following chapter that of the citizen and the criminal. The convergence in the identification of these distinct personalities in the recent past is an important theme of these two sections. The book concludes with a short chapter that attempts to pull together the complicated strands of the history of identification in England over the past 500 years.

ACKNOWLEDGEMENTS

Numerous scholars, working in very different fields and historical periods, have helped to inspire the ideas and arguments used in this work, although they may not always agree with my own formulation and use of them. The members of the Identinet network, a scholarly grouping funded by the Leverhulme Trust and dedicated to the study of the history of identification, have helped to shape and expand my horizons. Special mention should be made here of Keith Breckenridge, James Brown, Valentin Groebner, Steve Hindle, David Lyon, Simon Szreter and John Torpey. I have also found the annual meetings of the Identification in the Information Society (IDIS) group, which brings together information scientists, workers in the commercial ID industries, lawyers, philosophers and the occasional historian, of great help. James Backhouse, the organizer of IDIS and genial host, needs to be thanked in particular. Colleagues at the University of Essex, including John Walter and Kevin Schürer, have made important contributions to my thinking. Keith Thomas was kind enough to suggest that I should consult Richard Cobb's *Death in Paris*. Last, but not least, I must thank Jane Caplan, my co-founder of the Identinet network, for her support and stimulating insights.

2

Three Rogues

IMPOSTURE AND IDENTIFICATION

In the previous chapter it was argued that what identification involves is a series of techniques used in certain social settings, rather than some unmediated grasping of the essence of another 'self'. Or in plainer terms, it is what one does, rather than what one is, that matters. One can, therefore, study identification from the history of impostures just as well, if not better, than from that of 'true' identifications. Imposture is when someone is discovered to have made a performance they were not entitled to make. Such imposture is, of course, profoundly unsettling for a whole social system based on the acceptance of roles and the social forms that flow from them, and on the assignment of those roles to specific individuals.[1] It is, of course, possible to claim that imposture is not the same as 'true' identification but then how does one know that such identifications are not simply successful impostures?

Recorded history is full of impostors, some reaching to the highest levels of society. According to the Roman historian Tacitus in ad 69 Greece and Asia Minor were terrified by a false report that the Emperor Nero had returned from the dead:

> The pretender in this case was a slave from Pontus, or, according to some accounts, a freedman from Italy, a skilful harp-player and singer, accomplishments, which, added to a resemblance in the face, gave a very deceptive plausibility to his pretensions. After attaching to himself some deserters, needy vagrants whom he bribed with great offers, he put to sea. Driven by stress of weather to the island of Cythnus, he induced certain soldiers, who were on their way from the East, to join him, and ordered others, who refused, to be executed. He also robbed the traders and armed all the most able bodied of the slaves.[2]

Given his actions, as well as his looks and dubious talents, one might have been hard pressed to tell the impostor from the 'true' Nero.

Similarly, in early seventeenth-century Russia there were a number of false Dmitri's who claimed to be the younger brother of Tsar Fyodor, the latter having been killed on the orders of Boris Godunov in 1591. In 1604 one of these impostors, a manservant to a Polish prince, won the backing of Poland through adopting Catholicism, and with the support of the Don Cossacks marched on Moscow. After the death of Godunov he was crowned Tsar, and reigned for some months before anti-Polish sentiment led to his downfall. In the past century there was the famous case of Anna Anderson, who from 1921 to 1970 claimed to be Anastasia, the youngest daughter of the late Tsar Nicholas II. She asserted, rather implausibly, that she had survived the execution of the entire Russian royal family in 1918. However, she was probably a Pomeranian factory worker, a claim now apparently substantiated by DNA analysis.[3]

The English throne has also long attracted such spurious claimants. In the early fifteenth century an individual called Thomas Ward of Trumpington was recognized by the King of Scotland as the deceased Richard II, who had been deposed by Henry IV in 1399.[4] During the reign of Henry VII, who also came to the throne after overthrowing his predecessor in 1485, there were at least two significant royal impostors. Ten-year old Lambert Simnel was crowned King of England in Dublin in May 1487, claiming to be Edward, Earl of Warwick, son of the late Duke of Clarence, and thus the male heir to Edward IV and Richard III. However, his rebellion in England was checked by his defeat and capture at the Battle of Stoke in June 1487.[5] In the following decade, Henry faced another impostor, Perkin Warbeck, whose story will be told in more detail below. A curious modern example of imposture was King Anthony (Hall), a policeman from Shropshire, who in the course of the 1930s conceived and developed the notion that he was the legitimate male-line descendant of Henry VIII. He used the soap-box to pursue his claims and issued a brief pamphlet that called for the recognition of ex-servicemen (such as himself); the confiscation of money held by banks; and the general principle that 'Government will keep out of business' and 'Business shall keep out of Government'.[6] His 'rival', George V, was worried by Hall's attacks on him as a 'pure bred German', perhaps understandably in the case of a sovereign who had changed the family name from Saxe-Coburg and Gotha to Windsor at the height of the Great War. George's private secretary supported the Home Office's proposals to prosecute Hall for using 'quarrelsome and scandalous language' liable to cause a breach of the peace.[7]

Even 'real' monarchs could have a very dubious right to the royal title. After defeating the Yorkist King, Richard III, Henry VII claimed the crown of England via his descent from John of Gaunt and Henry V's queen, but he was hardly a member of what one would today call 'the Royal Family'. The Earl of Warwick, the young son of George, Duke of Clarence, had a better title to the throne, and Henry was to execute him in 1499. Henry tried to create a genealogy supporting his claim, and that of the Tudor dynasty, that showed him descended not only from a long line of English rulers but also from the pre-Conquest Anglo-Saxon kings, and also of the kings of the Britons going back via Arthur to Brutus, the mythical founder of Britain, and thence to the Trojans, Noah, and Adam and Eve. To bolster these claims Henry called his eldest son Arthur, and ensured that he was born at Winchester, the supposed site of Camelot and the Round Table.[8] Henry's real claim to be King of England was based, of course, on faction, military success and persuasion. What was important was the power to act as a sovereign, and this meant getting others to respond to one as sovereign, rather than any simple abstract legitimacy.

However, imposture has not just been the preserve of royalty. There is, for example, the famous case of Martin Guerre in the village of Artigat in southern France in the mid-sixteenth century, described by Natalie Zemon Davis. Here a peasant from a neighbouring village, Arnaud du Tihl, is said to have impersonated Guerre, who was away at the wars, and to have lived with the latter's wife for a number of years. Falling foul of Guerre's family over some property, he was accused and tried as an impostor, and successfully defended himself until the real Martin suddenly appeared in court.[9] An even more bizarre example of imposture within living memory was the career of Wa-sha-quon-asin, or Grey Owl, who claimed to be the child of a Scottish father and an Apache mother, and who had emigrated from the United States to join the Ojibwa Indians in British Canada. He wrote numerous books and toured the British Empire in the 1930s promoting the cause of ecology before large audiences, which included the young Queen Elizabeth II. After his death in 1938 it was discovered that he was actually Archibald Belaney, the son of a farmer from Hastings in England, who had been fascinated by nature and native cultures from his early years, and who had emigrated to Canada in his teens. In some strange way his assumed persona was more authentic than his 'true' self, and he is seen today as a pioneer of environmentalism.[10]

What such examples of imposture often show is not only the triumph of fantasy over 'reality' but also the mechanics of how individuals went about proving a particular identity. In the rest of this chapter the careers of three impostors from differing periods of English history, Perkin Warbeck, the Tichborne Claimant and John Stonehouse, will be examined to see how they went about illicitly claiming an identity. They have been described here as 'rogues', although this reflected the fact that their impostures were discovered, and they suffered for it. This is also not an attempt to provide a history of changing forms of identification, but merely to raise some issues for more detailed consideration in subsequent chapters. However, the mechanisms of imposture in the late fifteenth-century and mid-nineteenth-century examples appear to have had more in common with each other than with those in the case from the late twentieth century. This, in turn, raises questions about the presumed rupture in forms of identification during the Industrial Revolution.

PERKIN WARBECK AND THE TRAPPINGS OF ROYALTY

Perkin Warbeck, the first of the 'rogues' to be discussed here, maintained that he was Richard, duke of York, one of the Princes in the Tower supposedly killed by their uncle, Richard III. Warbeck claimed that he was the King of England, as the rightful heir of the House of York, rather than the Lancastrian Henry VII. He was supported in this by the Holy Roman Emperor Maximilian I, by James IV of Scotland and by Margaret of Burgundy, the sister of Edward IV, and thus Richard's aunt. Margaret was the chief supporter of the adherents of the House of York in their efforts to overthrow Henry VII, but all Warbeck's supporters had dynastic or political reasons for wishing to undermine the Tudor monarchy. In the mid-1490s Warbeck travelled widely in the royal courts of northern Europe gathering support. His attempt to invade England in 1495 via a landing in Kent failed ignominiously, and he had to watch from his boat offshore as his small expeditionary force was butchered. He subsequently went to Scotland, where he married Catherine Gordon, a cousin of James IV, and accompanied the Scottish king on a border raid into Northumberland. Once again, he failed to attract popular support. In 1497 Warbeck landed in Cornwall, which had recently rebelled against Henry, proclaimed himself Richard IV and raised a ragtag army. His forces were met by those of Henry VII at Exeter, and before battle was even joined the pretender fled. He was subsequently captured, forced to admit that he was an impostor and held at Henry's court. In 1499 he and the Earl of Warwick were hanged, supposedly for renewed plotting against the King.[11]

In the confession he signed after his capture, and which was widely publicized in England and abroad, Warbeck admitted to being the son of a minor official from Tournai in Flanders. He was said to have travelled to Portugal and worked as a page at the royal court before sailing to Cork in Ireland in 1491 in the employment of a Breton silk merchant. Here supporters of the House of York were claimed to have persuaded him to pretend to be the surviving Yorkist heir to the throne.[12] Ireland, as ever, was the Achilles heel of the English monarchy, and Lambert Simnel had also been crowned there as King in 1487.[13] There are a number of problems with this account of Warbeck's life, and with many of the details of the confession.[14] Francis Bacon, writing in the early seventeenth century in his *The Reign of Henry VII*, notes a story of the time that Edward IV had been Warbeck's godfather, which gossip 'might make a man think, that he might indeed have in him some base blood of the house of York'.[15] Ann Wroe suggests that Warbeck could have been a royal bastard brought up in the household of Margaret of Burgundy.[16] At least one modern author actually goes further, and has claimed, perhaps somewhat improbably, that Warbeck was indeed Richard.[17] However, the truth about Warbeck's parentage, or whether or not Warbeck's confession is accurate, are really quite irrelevant here. What are important for the present analysis are the sorts of performances that might reasonably be expected to allow someone to claim a particular royal identity.

What first started Warbeck on his career of imposture was his outward appearance – he looked and acted like a prince. According to his confession, when he in Cork dressed up in his master's wares, 'They of the toun because I

Perkin Warbeck dressed as a prince of the House of York.
(Source: Wikipedia Commons)

was ariad with soom clothis of sylk . . . cam unto me and threpid upon me that I shuld be the duke of Clarence sone that was before tyme at develyn [Dublin].' He swore on a cross that this was not the case but he was soon approached by Yorkist exiles and persuaded to masquerade as one of the heirs of Edward IV, the Duke of Clarence's elder brother. Warbeck was subsequently sketched in his finery of silks and furs, with a badge and its pearl drops pinned to his hat, the very portrait of nobility.[18] This outward appearance of majesty was reinforced with the trappings of royal heraldry. In Antwerp, when he was staying in the court of Margaret of Burgundy, he displayed his arms on the House of the Merchant Adventurers were he was staying – an escutcheon quartered with the royal arms of England and France, the three lions and three lilies. The significance of this outward sign was not lost on Henry's local supporters, who pelted it at night with mud and filth. The pretender also sealed documents with a secret seal carrying the royal arms, and perfected the signing of letters with a royal monograph. Perkin/Richard's personal bodyguard in Flanders wore the Yorkist livery of murrey (mulberry) and blue, embroidered with the white rose of York. He himself became known simply as 'the White Rose'.[19]

To this was added the personal accomplishments necessary to pass Perkin off as an English prince. This was a period when personal behaviour, especially in the courtly households of Europe, was developing those aspects of the French *courtoisie* that set the gentle born apart from the rest of society. Farting, spitting and other bodily functions were becoming less acceptable in public for this class, and one can be sure that Perkin literally knew how to keep his nose clean.[20] In his confession he claimed that his Yorkist minders had 'agayn my wyll made me learn Inglysh & tawgth me what I shuld doo & saye'.[21] According to a contemporary, the chronicler Edward Hall, Perkin, 'kept such a princely countenance, and so counterfeit a majesty royal, that all manner of men did firmly believe that he was extracted of the noble house and family of the dukes of York'.[22] What was important here was the performance of an identity, which was, in some ways, its substance, since the English always appear to have been addicted to regal flummery.

But if Perkin had learnt to keep his bodily functions in check, that body was also one that needed to be displayed to, and recognized by, others. Margaret of Burgundy may have been self-seeking in her support of Perkin but she still found it politic to write to Isabella, the Spanish Queen, in 1493, claiming that, 'I recognized him (for the reason that I had once seen him in England) as easily as if I had last seen him yesterday or that day before that . . . this man is the one whom they once thought dead.'[23] She also claimed that she had

sent certain men who would have recognised him as easily as his mother or his nurse, since from their first youth they had been in service and intimate familiarity with

King Edward and his children. These men too with a most sacred oath affirmed that this man was the second son of King Edward. They cursed themselves with great oaths if he should turn out otherwise, and were ready to endure every torment and great physical pains of every kind.[24]

Richard of York was said to have three 'hereditary' marks on his body that could be recognized by anyone who had known him. Tanjar, a Portuguese herald who knew Perkin in Portugal, said that he had a mark under his eye, a slightly prominent upper lip and another mark on his chest, which made people think that he was the Duke of York.[25] Would-be supporters were invited to examine Perkin physically to reassure themselves, although not everyone was convinced in this manner. Henry VII certainly understood the importance of such forms of physical recognition, and tried after Warbeck's capture to prove to his own courtiers that the pretender was a commoner from Flanders by 'bringing people who knew Warbeck to court and threatening to bring his childhood friends from Tounai thither'.[26] Warbeck's supposed likeness to Edward IV may explain why the Spanish ambassador claimed that after his eventual imprisonment in the Tower of London on charges of treason, Warbeck had been facially disfigured.[27]

Bodily recognition was, of course, at the heart of the imposture of Martin Guerre a century later, although, once more, it could be inconclusive. Guerre's wife, Bertrande, supposedly accepted the impostor as her husband, while at his trial 30 to 40 people claimed that Artigat was Martin Guerre, including Martin's 4 sisters and his 2 brothers-in-law.[28] But some witnesses maintained that Martin had been taller, thinner and darker than the accused, had a flatter nose and more projecting lower lip, and a scar on his eyebrow that the accused did not have. The shoemaker claimed that Martin's shoes had been larger than the prisoner's based on the moulds he used to make them. But other witnesses insisted that Guerre had extra teeth in his jaw, a scar on his forehead, 3 warts on his right hand, and each of these was discovered on the body of the accused. It was only when the real Guerre physically appeared in court that the impostor was unmasked.[29] One of the themes of the present work is actually the indeterminacy of the body as a means of identification, and the more recent attempts to pin its identity down through scientific and bureaucratic means.

However, the identifiable body was also one that had to possess memories of lived experience. One of the reasons that Arnaud du Tihl was able to get away with his imposture was because he was able to pick up and deploy information that would have been known to Guerre. At his trial he could recollect what clothes individual guests wore at Martin's wedding, and details of his activities in France and Spain.[30] As Davis notes, Bertrande was unsure of the new Martin at first, 'Only after he had spoken to her in an affectionate voice, recalling what they had said to each other the first night of their marriage and reminding her of the white hosen he had left in a coffer the day of his departure, did she embrace him and say that his growth of beard made it difficult for her to recognize him.'[31] The new husband might, of course, have been an improvement on the old, and any husband was perhaps better than none.

In a similar manner, Perkin Warbeck had learnt, or been coached, in many of the details of Richard of York's life. According to Bernard André, in his contemporary life of Henry VII, Warbeck could:

> recall all the circumstances of Edward IV, and recited by heart all the names of his household and servants, as though he had been taught these and had known them from the time he was a little boy. In addition he gave details of locations, dates, and persons . . . He even (as fine player he was) fortified these facts with a veil of such deceit that . . . men of wisdom and great nobility were induced to believe him.[32]

Margaret of Burgundy explained to Isabella of Spain that she recognized Warbeck as the son of Edward IV by knowledge of:

> the private conversations and acts between him and me in times past, which undoubtedly no other person would have been able to guess at. Lastly [I recognized him by] the questions and conversations of others, to all of which he responded so aptly and skillfully, that it was manifest and notorious that this was he who they thought had died long ago.[33]

But perhaps such tricks depended on a willing suspension of disbelief. When Warbeck was captured, Henry VII proved that he was not Richard IV by asking him to identify people in the court who knew the son of Edward IV. According to Roger Machado, the Richmond Herald, Henry bade the prostrate Warbeck to rise and addressed him, 'We have heard that you call yourself Richard, son of King Edward. In this place are some who were companions of that lord, look and see if you recognise them.' Warbeck replied that he did not know any of them, and that he was not Richard.[34] In the final analysis a performance, however expert, only took one as far as the audience would allow.

THE TICHBORNE CLAIMANT AND VICTORIAN IMPOSTURE

While Warbeck threatened the throne of England, he appears to have been a rather colourless character. This could never be said of the impostor known as the Tichborne Claimant, who was one of the most outrageous rogues of the nineteenth century. He was a butcher from Wagga Wagga in New South Wales, Australia, who maintained that he was the baronet Sir Roger Tichborne, and thus the heir to the Tichborne estates in Hampshire.

The real Sir Roger had been born in Paris in 1829, the eldest son of the Catholic Sir James Doughty-Tichborne and his French-born wife, Lady Henriette Felicité. The two parents were estranged, and their son lived with his mother in France until the age of 16, at which point his father lured him to England on the pretext of his attendance at a funeral. Once in England he was sent to the staunchly Catholic Stonyhurst College, and in 1849 he joined the 6th Dragoon Guards in Dublin. The military life does not appear to have suited him, and he left the army in 1852 to take up a life of travel. In 1853 he departed for South America, and from Valparaiso in Chile he crossed the Andes, arriving in Rio de Janeiro in 1854. On the return voyage to England his ship, the *Bella*, was lost at sea with all hands, and on the subsequent death of his father the baronetcy and the Tichborne estates passed in due course to his younger brother.[35]

However, the Dowager Lady Tichborne refused to believe that her son was dead, and began placing advertisements in newspapers around the world offering a reward for information about him. She was disposed to believe that her son might be in Australia because in 1858 a former sailor, now a vagrant, appeared at Tichborne asking for alms. Henrietta quizzed him insistently about the *Bella*, and perhaps not surprisingly the tramp 'volunteered' the information that the crew of a ship by that name had ended up in Australia. When the wife of a lawyer in Wagga Wagga saw one of Lady Tichborne's notices, she recalled that her husband had been handling the affairs of a bankrupt local butcher, Tomas Castro, who had made vague allusions to property he was owed, and to a shipwreck in which he had been involved. The fragility and uncertainty of identity in Australia at this period made such claims possible.[36] In November 1865 Sir Roger's mother received a letter from a Sydney solicitor to the effect that a man fitting the description of her son had been discovered in the colony. Overjoyed, Lady Tichborne sent money for Castro to come to Europe, where she instantly recognized him, despite the lack of any obvious similarity to her son. Sir Roger had been a rather slight, willowy youth, while Castro was an enormous man of 25 stones.[37]

Castro, who came to be universally known as the 'Tichborne Claimant', or simply 'the Claimant', began to collect supporters, including intimates of the Tichborne family, members of parliament and businessmen. He also began to live the life of a baronet, eating prodigiously, wearing fine clothes, and engaging

ROGER C. TICHBORNE,
ALLEGED TO HAVE BEEN LOST IN THE "BELLA."

A somewhat effete Sir Roger Tichborne: 'Roger C. Tichborne alleged to
have been lost in the 'Bella'. (Source: Australian National Library,
PIC T3395 NK9595 LOC NL shelves 137)

in aristocratic pursuits such as shooting and fishing.[38] As in the case of Perkin
Warbeck, the appearance of gentility was part of its substance. To support the
Claimant's lifestyle, and the legal case to recover his rightful estate, 'Tichborne
Bonds' were sold, which promised repayment once the Claimant 'came into his
own'.[39] The trial to establish his inheritance and to eject the twelfth baronet, a
young child, began in the Court of Common Pleas in May 1871 and lasted 102
days. The case was a *cause celebre*, and the crowds of spectators were so large
that the trial had to be moved to the Court of Queen's Bench. The Chief Justice
presiding invited acquaintances and dignitaries to sit with him on the bench,
including the Prince and Princess of Wales, the American ambassador, and the
Emperor of Brazil. Although cross-examined by some of the finest barristers of
the day, the Claimant held his own until a crucial piece of evidence of identity
was introduced which undermined his case. The case lost, the Claimant was

PORTRAIT OF THE CLAIMANT
FROM A PHOTOGRAPH

A somewhat less effete Tichborne Claimant: 'Portrait of Arthur Orton, 1874'.
(Source: Australian National Library, PIC S10700 LOC 7810)

arrested and charged with perjury. His criminal trail began in April 1873, and lasted 188 days, with the presiding judge taking no less than 18 days to sum up. This was the longest criminal trial in English legal history until the 'McLibel' case of the 1990s. The Claimant would travel to court in a Wedgewood-blue brougham, and on a typical Monday morning during the hearings between 8,000 and 10,000 people would gather outside the court to catch a glimpse of him. In the course of the trial it was revealed that the Claimant was actually Arthur Orton, the son of a butcher from Wapping in London. Orton was convicted on 2 charges of perjury and sentenced to 14 years' hard labour.[40]

The aftermath of the trial was almost as remarkable as Orton's own career of imposture. His defence counsel, Edward Vaughan Hyde Kenealy, was a somewhat strange man. In 1867 he had published *The Book of God: The Apocalypse*, an unorthodox theological work in which he claimed that he was the 'twelfth messenger of God', and descended from both Jesus Christ and Genghis Khan.[41] During the Tichborne trial, Kenealy had abused witnesses, made outrageous allegations against Roman Catholics and showed disrespect to the presiding judges. His conduct of the case became a public scandal and, after rejecting his client's claim, the jury censured his behaviour. Kenealy subsequently started a newspaper, *The Englishman*, to support the Claimant, and to attack the judges in the trial. His behaviour was so extreme that in 1874 he was removed from the Bar. Never a man to admit defeat, Kenealy formed the Magna Charta Association and went on a nationwide tour to further the cause. In time the Association became a radical, working-class movement espousing a heady brew of anti-Catholicism, law reform based on hostility to the legal profession, and opposition to school boards, income tax, the Lunacy Laws, food adulteration, the Contagious Diseases Acts and compulsory vaccination, as well as urging the justice of the Claimant's cause. At a by-election in 1875, Kenealy was elected as the Member of Parliament for Stoke-upon-Trent with a majority of 2,000 votes. In the House of Commons, Kenealy called for a Royal Commission into the conduct of the Tichborne case, but lost a vote on his proposal by the impressive margin of 433 to 3. He gradually ceased to attract attention, lost his seat at the 1880 General Election and died in London of heart failure a few days later.[42]

Meanwhile, having served ten years in prison, during which he was a model inmate and even convinced some of his jailors of his identity as Sir Roger Tichborne, the Claimant was released in 1884. Playing to his obvious gifts as a showman he took up a career as a 'turn' in the circus, music halls and lecture theatres. He confessed to his imposture in a newspaper article, and then retracted, and died in poverty in 1898.[43] His funeral in London attracted a large crowd, and the 'twenty-stone lubble', as the *Pall Mall Gazette* described him in its obituary, was laid to rest in a coffin marked 'Sir Roger Charles Doughty Tichborne'.[44]

The manner in which the Claimant went about claiming to be someone he was not had some striking similarities to the imposture of Perkin Warbeck 400 years earlier. Much of the Claimant's case depended on personal recognition, above all that by his 'mother', Lady Tichborne. She had filled out a deposition to the effect that, 'His features, disposition, and voice are unmistakeable, and must, in my judgment, be recognised by impartial and unprejudiced persons who knew him before he left England in the year 1853.' Kenealy put considerable emphasis on this at the trial, adding melodramatically, 'gentlemen, sneer as you will at maternal and paternal instincts. I say that maternal and paternal instincts are ever-living and all-conquering in the human heart.'[45] Of course, maternal instincts could be wrong, and Lady Tichborne seems to have been extraordinarily keen to overlook the inconsistencies in the Claimant's story and behaviour. She ignored, for example, the Claimant's complete ignorance of French, despite this being the language of Sir Roger's youth.[46]

Unfortunately for the Claimant, the Lady Dowager died before he went to law but his legal team could call upon an impressive array of witnesses to 'prove' his identity. According to the *Pall Mall Gazette*:

> The world, in all probability, will be slow in producing quite such another example of the power of cunning stupidity as ARTHUR ORTON. Devoid of education, destitute of the smallest semblance of refinement, he held his own day after day against the ablest counsel of the Bar, and converted into passionate adherents, not only the mob, who regarded him unjustly deprived of his 'rights', but persons of position, and presumably, therefore, of reasoning faculties.[47]

His adherents included Andrew Bogle, an old Tichborne servant who knew Sir Roger well; Edward Rous, the owner of the Swan Hotel, Alresford, a short distance from Tichborne; Francis Baigent, the Tichborne family antiquarian; Edward Hopkins the family solicitor; J. P. Lipscomb, the family doctor; and members of Sir Roger's old regiment, who swore that they recognized their former fellow officer.[48] However, there were numerous other witnesses who failed to recognize the Claimant as Sir Roger, and still others who recognized him as Arthur Orton. These included Orton's former girlfriend, Mary Ann Loder.[49] As in the case of Martin Guerre, personal recognition was not a reliable form of legal identification.

There were plainly lots of differing reasons for misidentification in this case. Lady Tichborne was desperate to find her son, indeed perhaps any son, and she certainly had an animus against the Tichborne family.[50] Others were probably taken in by some superficial facial similarities between the Claimant and Sir Roger, and the former's accumulated knowledge of the latter's life and of the Tichborne heritage. Genealogical information and family history supplied by Francis Baigent was plainly of use here. For some even the slips and lacunae in the Claimant's knowledge was proof of his veracity– wouldn't a true impostor, they reasoned, have concocted a better story! Other backers had a financial incentive to see their man come into his own, especially given the amount they had invested in his aristocratic lifestyle.[51] For the supporters of the Magna Charta Association, the Claimant was an irresistible mixture of an anti-establishment (and anti-Catholic) figure, someone with a right to 'fair play', and at one and the same time a working man (a butcher), and a sporting lord.[52] It was just these contradictions within the popular mind that was to prevent any truly revolutionary, proletarian consciousness ever forming among the English working classes.[53] Fair play for an obese baronet was hardly the cry of the barricades.

As with Perkin Warbeck, the body of the Claimant, and there was certainly a lot of it, became a site for contestation over identification. For example, the Dowager Lady Tichborne claimed that her son had a lump behind one ear from a fall at the seaside, scars at his ankles where he had been bled during an asthma attack, and the distinctive mark of an 'issue' on his upper arm, all of which the Claimant was supposed to have.[54] In a more salacious vein, it was revealed in court that Sir Roger had a 'malformation', that is, he had a very small penis. Indeed, it transpired that in his Army days Sir Roger had been nicknamed 'Small Cock'. Edward Kenealy believed that this was why he had left England, and why the Claimant referred to himself as a 'Withered Leaf'. Dr David Wilson, one of the medical witnesses at the perjury trial, examined the Claimant to determine his physical attributes in this respect. Supposing that the member in question was merely obscured by the vast rolls of fat enveloping it, he had asked the Claimant to hold up his own stomach but, seeing him unequal to the task, had wedged the back of a chair under it. The doctor testified that he had seen the Claimant urinate and found 'the penis was absolutely out of view, and nothing whatever of it could be seen but the orifice from whence the stream issued.'[55] These shocking revelations led one contemporary balladeer to compose a popular song with the peerless refrain:

When the Jury said I was not Roger,
Oh! how they made me stagger,
The pretty girls they'll always think
Of poor Roger's wagga wagga.[56]

A box full of hair samples now held in the records of the Supreme Court of Judicature reveals another manner in which family resemblances were sought.[57] When the Claimant entered prison his hair was cut and it was found to have been dyed auburn, perhaps to conform to what he thought was Sir Roger's hair colour.[58]

The Claimant finally came unstuck, however, over the question of Sir Roger's tattoo. The history of the use of the tattoo in the West is long and complicated but has tended to be associated with the criminal or marginal. The Bible prohibited the use of tattoos, as did Koranic law, since the body was to be the temple of the soul.[59] On the other hand, the Greeks, Romans and Byzantines branded and tattooed slaves and criminals, and mutilated those unworthy to hold office.[60] In practice, tattooing in England appears to have been copied from the native peoples of North America and the South Seas in the eighteenth century, and become a popular cultural form among the bored and marginal. Male and female convicts en route to Australia tattooed themselves, as did the soldiers and sailors who guarded them.[61] The practice also spread to other 'marginal' groups such as the Royal Family and aristocracy, something that Arthur Orton discovered to his cost. Edward VIII and his sons, including George V, were tattooed, and one tattooist at the end of the Victorian period, Ted Riley, claimed to have tattooed the Grand Duke Alexis of Russia, Prince and Princess Waldemar of Denmark, Queen Olga of Greece, King Oscar II of Sweden, the Duke of York, Lady Randolph Churchill and the Duke of Newcastle.[62] It might come as no surprise, therefore, that Lord Bellew, Sir Roger's friend from Stonyhurst, remembered at the end of the Claimant's first trial that as a boy he had tattooed a heart crossed with an anchor on Sir Roger's inner left arm. However, this certainly was a surprise to the Claimant and his counsel, for Orton did not possess such marks, and it led to the collapse of his attempt to 'recover' the Tichborne estate. But even this was somewhat inconclusive since at the second trial for perjury, Kenealy forced Bellew to admit that his memory of the tattoo was imperfect – he was unsure which arm he had tattooed, or indeed what the tattoo illustrated.[63]

However, the Tichborne trials did see some attempts to pin down the body through the use of a technology, that of photography, although with little success. The real Sir Roger had posed at Santiago in Chile in 1853 for two daguerreotypes, and these were compared to the Claimant. Mrs Sherstone, the wife of an Army officer who had brought Sir Roger to their house, thought the 1853 daguerreotypes were a poor likeness, and noted, 'I very seldom see any likeness in photographs unless they are very good.' On the other hand, a former coachman to relatives of the Tichbornes, Thomas Muston, felt that the 1853 photographs had a strong resemblance to Sir Roger, but did not detect any resemblance in a recent photograph of the Claimant. It was only when he met the Claimant and noted his twitching eyebrows that he was convinced of his identity. During the trial, one of the Claimant's lawyers noted that photographs could be manipulated, 'photographers were able to place any face they pleased on any form they pleased.' But the Tichborne lawyers were able to show from the photographs that Sir Roger did not have ear lobes while the Claimant did. There was also debate over whether Roger Tichborne and the Claimant shared 'a large protuberance of flesh on the thumb', with Kenealy claiming that the photographs of Sir Roger had been doctored to hide this.[64]

Composite photography, involving the superimposition of images, was also used in the Tichborne case in 1873. William Matthew, honorary secretary of the rather grandly titled 'Bristol Science-Test Tichborne Committee', invented the Identiscope and its by-product, the Tichborne Photographic Blend. The Identiscope took two portraits and by 'geometric admeasurement' compared their subjects' features. Using the technique, Matthew overlaid a current portrait of the Claimant on Roger Tichborne's daguerreotype to reveal that the position and dimension of the features of the two were identical.[65] This was, of course, misleading if the Claimant was indeed Arthur Orton. Forty years later, Edward Kenealy's son Maurice again compared the photographs of Sir Roger and the Claimant in his *The Tichborne Tragedy, Being the Secret and Authentic History of the Extraordinary Facts and Circumstances Connected with the Claims, Personality, Identification, Conviction and Last Days of the Tichborne Claimant*, but in a somewhat inconclusive manner to the unprejudiced eye.[66]

Eventually Arthur Orton's imposture was unmasked, at least to the satisfaction of a court of law, but the cost had been prodigious, and the perceived threat to property rights extremely serious . This may explain why the Tichborne case led to greater severity in the legal treatment of impostors, since in 1874 Parliament passed the False Personation Act (37 & 38 Vict., c.36), whereby anyone 'falsely and deceitfully personat[ing] any person, with intent fraudulently to obtain any land, estate, chattel, [or] money', would be liable to life imprisonment.

JOHN STONEHOUSE AND IMPOSTURE IN A PAPER WORLD

Moving forward a century to the case of John Stonehouse, the last of the 'three rogues' to be examined in this chapter, one enters into a different world. This is not only because the late twentieth century produced so much more in the way of historical sources, some of them authored by Stonehouse himself, but also because imposture now meant the use of false official papers. England had become what one might call a 'dossier society'.

John Stonehouse was born into a family of trade unionists in Southampton in 1925. He joined the Labour Party at 16 before entering the RAF during the Second World War. He subsequently read economics at the London School of Economics and Political Society. Stonehouse was a keen advocate for the cooperative movement, and set up cooperative societies in Uganda in the early 1950s. He entered Parliament through a by-election in 1957 as an MP for the Co-operative Party, an affiliate of the Labour Party, eventually representing the constituency of Walsall North in the industrial Midlands. His parliamentary career in Harold Wilson's Labour government of the 1960s was worthy but hardly spectacular. He was parliamentary under-secretary at the Ministry of Aviation and for the Colonies (1966–67), Minister of Aviation (1967), Minister of State for Technology (1967–68), Postmaster General (1968–69) and Minister of Post and Telecommunications (1969–70). However, he was never in the Cabinet, and was dropped from the Labour government shortly before it fell in 1970.[67]

In the early 1970s Stonehouse set up a number of companies, mostly involved in the import–export business. The most important was perhaps the British Bangladesh Trust (BBT), which aimed to encourage trade between Britain and Bangladesh. Stonehouse claimed that this was an extension of his support for Bangladesh during its struggle for independence from Pakistan.[68] The BBT got off to a bad start because of an unfavourable article in the *Sunday Times* that accused the BBT of fraud for circulating a Bengali prospectus containing false statements. Stonehouse expected to raise £500,000 for the BBT from subscriptions but received only £15,000. He saved the company by throwing his personal and business resources behind the BBT, and borrowing from elsewhere. According to Stonehouse, in a somewhat bombastic vindication of his subsequent actions:

> I had saved the day but in the process I had shackled myself to the wheel of a chariot; and as the wheels turned the spikes dug into me, slowly draining me of blood, and preparing me for a final sacrifice at a Roman circus.[69]

With his business affairs going from bad to worse, his dealings being investigated by the police, and rumours circulating that he was a spy for communist Czechoslovakia, Stonehouse decided to fake his own death and start a new life. In *The Death of an Idealist*, written when he was subsequently awaiting trial for fraud, Stonehouse portrayed this as an existentialist crisis brought on by 'the cant and hypocrisy and humbug in English Society and politics'. This he claims led to a psychotic splitting of his personality:

> Although I did not fully recognise it at the time, I was operating on three levels. One, the imaged man: cool, calm and apparently in command of all his senses carrying on the life normally expected of him. Two, the original man, who carried all the heavy layers of the imaged man as a burden and despised this role, suffering deep torment as the desperation of his position became more evident. Three, the Phoenix man: a make-believe person who was uncluttered with problems and tensions and, through natural relaxation, gave comfort to the other two. The first two men had to die for the strain of living for them was too great. I wanted them to want to die. I wanted them to die. I wanted to die. There was no other way.[70]

This image of a deeply ill man is perhaps at variance with the coolly calculated manner in which Stonehouse went about creating an alternative identity for himself as 'Phoenix man'. In July, 1974, he contacted a hospital in his parliamentary constituency and asked for information about middle-aged male patients who had recently died, saying he had money available for their widows. He was given the names and addresses of five men, including those of Mr Donald Mildoon and Mr Joseph Arthur Markham. Stonehouse went to see the widows of the two men to gather information to support his forged applications for copies of their birth certificates. In the case of Markham, he used the birth certificate he had obtained to acquire a passport in Markham's name. On the backs of two passport photographs of himself, which he submitted to the Passport Office in order to obtain the passport, Stonehouse forged the signature of Neil McBride, MP, as his official 'recommender'. He then took out an insurance policy on his life for £125,000. Stripping cash from his companies he flew to Miami in November 1974, left his clothes on the beach, and disappeared into the sea. It was assumed that he had drowned, although he was actually on his way to Australia with his passport and visa in the name of Joe Markham, to start a new life with his secretary and mistress, Sheila Buckley.[71] Perhaps unsurprisingly, none of this was mentioned in *The Death of an Idealist*.

On the face of it, it is difficult to square such premeditation with Stonehouse's somewhat florid protestations of temporary insanity. Madness does not, however, preclude careful planning, and the junior defence counsel hired for his trial, Geoffrey Robertson QC, certainly thought that he was unbalanced. For Robertson, Stonehouse's flight was irrational, 'There should have been no great difficulty about leaving his wife for Sheila, his bankers would never have forced an MP into bankruptcy, and his creditors would have compromised.' His crimes were not committed before he ran away but in order to run away – hence taking the money, making the false statements to get a passport, and the insurance fraud to look after his family. Robertson believed:

> that he was mentally disordered, that his illness was triggered by mild reverses, and that it combined with a natural arrogance and self-regard to produce a state of mind which paid little or no attention to whether his behaviour was criminal.[72]

He gained support in these views from a report on Stonehouse by the great existentialist psychiatrist R. D. Laing, who came up with the sage diagnosis that:

> The mind temporarily 'boggles', the person 'cracks' in two or three, or even more, into multiple pieces – and dissociation, splitting, disintegration of the personality occurs. A man in public life begins to feel desperately trapped by the life he is in, and he reacts by acting out a weird death-rebirth fantasy.[73]

In this sense, Stonehouse's self-diagnosis of his condition in *The Death of an Idealist*, could be seen as proof of the theories put forward by Laing in the latter's *The Divided Self*.[74] But with someone so prone to self-publicity as John Stonehouse, it is perhaps unwise to speculate too freely.

Stonehouse's Australian career as Joe Markham did not last long. He had set up bank accounts under his new name in London, and had documentation and accounts transferred under that name to Australia. However, once there he took up a further 'parallel personality', that of Donald Clive Mildoon. This might well look like further evidence of conscious fraud, but Stonehouse argued that this was because the presence of John Stonehouse, 'was oppressive to me. I had to put a further barrier between him and myself'. He withdrew most of his cash from the Markham account at the Bank of New South Wales in Melbourne and opened an account in the name of Mildoon at the Bank of New Zealand round the corner. This was his undoing because a bank clerk at the Bank of New Zealand had seen him going into the Bank of New South Wales and had discovered that he was Markham in one and Mildoon in the other. The Victoria State Police, therefore, suspected Stonehouse of being involved in a bank fraud.[75]

When the Australian police first started following Stonehouse, they actually thought that he was 'Lucky' Lord Lucan, the aristocrat who had disappeared in November 1974 after his estranged wife's nanny was found murdered in Belgravia, London. As the police told Stonehouse after his arrest, 'You were such an English gentleman and we knew Lord Lucan was missing in England and wanted as a murder suspect.' Again, performance was an intrinsic part of identity, even if a mistaken one. But the idea that the 'toff' might have been Stonehouse seems to have dawned on the police, and they acquired a description of him from Interpol, including the fact that he had a scar at the inside of his right knee, which they used to identify him.[76] Identification, and misidentification, had become international, and based on the communication of stored data.

Much of the legal process that followed Stonehouse's arrest revolved around questions of identification. His Australian lawyers tried to prevent his extradition back to the United Kingdom on the grounds that:

> it is neither an offence in England, nor in Australia, to have more than one name, more than one surname. A person can use as many names, aliases, or *noms de plume* as he desires without committing any offence whatsoever.

The case of the UK authorities was, sensibly, that the purpose behind Stonehouse's changes of name was to perpetrate a fraud, and thus a criminal offence.[77] After failed attempts to gain asylum from Sweden and Mauritius he was deported back to Britain in June 1975. Stonehouse was charged, among other offences, with 'uttering' forged applications for certified copies of birth certificates and a passport, and with trying to swindle £125,000 from insurance companies by faking his death.[78] However, the charges relating to forging signatures to obtain birth certificates were subsequently dropped because it was discovered that at that time no signature was actually necessary on an application for a birth certificate.[79]

John Stonehouse at bay. (Source: Corbis Images UK Limited)

Stonehouse proceeded to make a complete hash of his attempts to defend himself and his reputation, perhaps adding substance to the claim that he was mentally unbalanced. At first he refused to resign as an MP, antagonizing the Labour Party and the press by publicly bewailing the decadence of contemporary Britain and the hypocrisy of his political colleagues.[80] His public standing was not improved by the publication before his trail of similar views in his apologia, *The Death of an Idealist*, the burden of which Geoffrey Robertson described as boiling down to, 'every good boy deserving a favour: he had been such a devoted public servant for twenty-five years that he was entitled to have a breakdown and start a new life.'[81] Three weeks before his trial in April 1976 he resigned from the Labour Party and briefly became the only MP of the English National Party, described by Robertson as:

> a collection of fairly harmless oddballs, who dressed up in Robin Hood costumes and held tea parties before jousting on the green sward – not much in evidence amongst the tower blocks of Walsall North, whose electors were now represented by the one MP who stood for Merrie England.[82]

Shortly before his trial Stonehouse sacked his legal team and undertook his own defence. This involved reading out a prepared statement from the dock for six days. This so annoyed the presiding judge that when he later joined the Royal Commission on Criminal Procedure he successfully lobbied for the practice of dock statements to be abolished.[83] It was perhaps no surprise that Stonehouse was sentenced to seven years imprisonment on charges of theft and false pretences, the judge concluding pointedly that, 'You are not an ill-fated idealist. You committed these offences when you intended to provide for your future comfort.'[84]

Stonehouse did not serve his full sentence, being released from prison in August 1979 on the grounds of ill health. He had suffered three heart attacks and undergone open heart surgery while in detention. He married Sheila Buckley in 1981, wrote a number of novels and made several TV appearances before dying of a heart attack in 1988.[85] The whereabouts of Lord Lucan are still unknown.

Although it would be foolhardy to try to write a history of identification from these three disparate case studies, they do exemplify some of the key ways in which people have historically been identified. Indeed, many of the techniques of identification discussed here are still of importance. In a seminal essay on the forms of identity used in modern electronic information systems,[86] Roger Clarke has identified a number of ways in which people can identify themselves, including the following:

1. appearance – or how the person looks;
2. social behaviour – or how the person interacts with others;
3. names – or what the person is called by other people;
4. codes – or what the person is called by an organization;
5. knowledge – or what the person knows;
6. tokens – or what the person has;
7. bio-dynamics – or what the person does;
8. natural physiography – or what the person is; and
9. imposed physical characteristics – or what the person is now.

Perkin Warbeck's imposture could be understood under the headings of appearance, social behaviour, names, knowledge and natural physiography. Much the same could be said of the Tichborne Claimant, although he came unstuck in terms of imposed physical characteristics, or at least his lack of them in respect of Sir Roger's alleged tattoo. In the case of John Stonehouse some of these headings were of less importance and what was crucial was his possession of tokens of identification in terms of birth certificates and passports. The passport would certainly have had a number code that would link him to information held by the UK Passport Office. He was eventually identified via a scar, information about this being held on an international database.

However, what the case studies discussed in this chapter have shown is the fragility of these forms of identification. Appearances can be deceptive, while behaviour, names, codes, knowledge and tokens can all be acquired illicitly. The case studies also show a shift from forms of identification based on immediate personal performances to impersonal, bureaucratic information systems. Warbeck and Orton had to continually perform an identity over a considerable period of time, while Stonehouse only had to perform a few acts of imposture before authority to acquire a new identity. Once given his tokens of identification, in the form of his birth certificates and passport, which he tendered to immigration officials on three continents, he was able to duplicate this act of identification with comparatively little effort. Identification has become easier, but it also becomes easier to steal an identity if one can acquire a suitable token, or the code that links the token to the information imbedded in an official system. Hence the increasing ease of identity theft. This, in turn, may help to explain the more recent emphasis on scientifically based forms of bodily identification which rely on measuring the unique physiognomy (Clarke's 'physiography') of individuals – fingerprints, DNA profiles, retinal scans and other forms of biometrics. Some elements of this can be seen in the use of photography in the case of the Tichborne Claimant but their full development has been a feature of the twentieth century.

But if the lives of the 'three rogues' discussed here give some hints about the nature of changing forms of identification, they do not necessarily explain those changes. Certainly they cannot be understood in terms of any simple equation of mobility with anonymity and a consequent need to pin people down. Given the difficulties inherent in travelling in the fifteenth century, Perkin Warbeck's movements between Flanders, Portugal, Ireland, the Netherlands, Germany, Scotland and England reveal him as being as mobile as John Stonehouse. Similarly, the story of the Tichborne Claimant spans three continents. One could argue, of course, that Stonehouse required a passport because he lived in an age of mass movement but, as will be noted below, the nineteenth century was also an age of extraordinary mobility. Hence the existence of an Australian Wagga Wagga to titillate the Victorian popular imagination. The reasons for the shift to bureaucratic and biometric forms of identification lie elsewhere, and will be one of the major themes of this book.

3

Early Modern England – a Face-to-Face Society?

ENGLAND AS *GEMEINSCHAFT*?

It was claimed in the introductory chapter that identification is the outcome of an individual's performance before an audience. That is, a set of things that he or she is expected to do in a particular social setting. If that is the case, then the nature of that social setting and the expectations held by the people in it are of crucial importance in defining what are acceptable techniques of identification at any point in time. So what was the nature of early modern England in this respect? It would be foolish, and unnecessary, to try to give here a potted history of the country in the years between, say, 1500 and 1750, especially since far better historians of the period have already produced excellent general introductions.[1] However, it might be appropriate to examine the applicability to early modern English society of the concept of the *gemeinschaft*, which, as already noted, has been used to frame the discussion regarding the history of identification in that period.

In his *Gemeinschaft und Gesellschaft*, Ferdinand Tönnies argued that the *gemeinschaft* was an organic entity based on the family, clan and neighbours. Thus, 'The relationship . . . between the community and its members, is based not on contracts, but, like those within the family, upon understanding.'[2] For Tönnies the 'main laws of gemeinschaft' were that:

> (1) Relatives and married couples love each other or easily adjust themselves to each other. They speak together and think along similar lines. Likewise do neighbours and friends. (2) Between people who love each other there is understanding. (3) Those who love and understand each other remain and dwell together and organize their common life.[3]

There are three types of *gemeinschaft*, 'closely interrelated in space as well as in time':

> The first or kinship Gemeinschaft signifies a common relation to, and share in, human beings themselves, while in the second one such a common relation is established through collective ownership of the land, and in the third the common bond is represented by sacred places and worshiped deities.[4]

In this form of face-to-face society there is, of course, no need for formal techniques of identification, for everyone is known and knowing, and trust is universal. But were all social interactions in early modern England of this type, or were there occasions when people had to prove their, or others', identity as strangers?

As Richard Smith has shown, Tönnies' understanding of pre-modern communities was derived, in part, from Sir Henry Maine's *Ancient Law: Its Connection with the Early History of Society, and Its Relation to Modern Ideas*, originally published in 1861.[5] Maine's belief in the early English community as the preserve of closely bound, and unchanging, family groupings were derived from his study of Indian village communities, and his interpretation of Roman law. This attempt to show that the liberty of the individual was not innate but an historical development was part of a conservative repost to both democracy and socialism.[6] Human rights are not innate but the product of institutions and history. This view of the Middle Ages can also be found in Jacob Burckhardt's *The Civilization of the Renaissance in Italy* (1860), in which he claimed that in the medieval period, man 'was conscious of himself only as a member of a race, people, party, family or corporation' – that is, only through some general category.[7] Maine's ideas regarding the binding of individuals to the communal soil in the ancient and medieval world were challenged at the time by the work of the historian F. W. Maitland, who saw medieval freehold property as being fully alienable by the tenant.[8] As already noted, this led Alan Macfarlane to push the concept of modern possessive individualism back into the English Middle Ages.[9] However, Maine's vision of rustic immobility survived to influence subsequent generations of historians and sociologists, and to migrate from an explanation of ancient and medieval society, to be applied to all pre-industrial societies.

MOBILITY IN EARLY MODERN ENGLAND

So prevalent was this assumption of immobility that when in the 1960s historians began to look at early modern English communities, and found high levels of population turnover, they were nonplussed. This discovery will ever be associated with the great historical demographer Peter Laslett, and his colleagues at the Cambridge Group for the History of Population and Social Structure. When they established that high rates of population turnover existed in seventeenth-century English parishes, Laslett commented at the time that his team thought this, 'So surprising . . . that we do not yet know quite what to make of it.'[10] In the case of Clayworth in Nottingham, Laslett compared two parish listings for the years 1676 and 1688, and found a turnover rate of 61.9 per cent – only 157 of the 402 persons living in the community in 1676 were still there 12 years later. Only 92 of the 244 who disappeared were recorded in parish registers as dying, so the rest most probably moved away. Parish listings of the inhabitants of Cogenhoe in Northampton in the period 1618 to 1628 showed a turnover of about 52 per cent, so Clayworth was not unique in this respect.[11] Such movements led Alan Macfarlane to claim, perhaps somewhat rashly, that, 'Any particular community in England in the past was probably no more isolated than a Chicago suburb or twentieth century Banbury.'[12]

Subsequent research has shown such lifetime mobility to be common in the early modern period,[13] and the phenomenon has been pushed back into late medieval England. According to Christopher Dyer, for example, of those giving evidence to church courts in late fifteenth-century Essex, 76 per cent had not lived at the same place throughout their lives. In the case of the manor of Kingston in the parish of Chesterton in Warwickshire, of the 15 family names mentioned in court rolls in 1387, 5 had departed by 1394, 7 more went in the period 1394 to 1426, and 4 between 1426 to1430, leaving only 2 long-standing families. Similarly, rentals of Ladbroke in the Feldon district of Warwickshire show that of the original 31 families of 1374, only 4 remained by 1457. Yet again, comparing the lists of taxpayers for the 1327 lay subsidy tax and the subsidies of 1524–25, a sample of Worcestershire villages shows only 8 per cent of the 1327 surnames surviving until the latter date.[14] Dyer sees this as an effect of the reduction of the population during the Black Death of the mid-fourteenth century. Land was plentiful in its aftermath, and could sometimes be acquired cheaply. This meant that peasants could build up holdings, or move to acquire the best property. They might have less of a desire to hold onto land, or keep it for their heirs.[15] Here Maitland's theories on the alienability of freehold land in the medieval period become important.

Population growth in the sixteenth and early seventeenth centuries, and the expansion of a nascent capitalist market in agricultural products, seem to have led to the concentration of land in fewer hands, and to the creation of a mobile 'surplus' population of agricultural labourers and farm servants.[16] According to Peter Clark:

First, migration was an almost universal phenomenon affecting the great mass of the national population. Secondly, most of this migrational activity involved what we might call 'circular mobility', with servants, apprentices, would-be spouses, and others out to better themselves, travelling fairly limited distances, to a neighbouring town or village, usually within any area defined by traditional notions of a sub-regional 'county'. Thirdly, there was a significant level of longer distance *subsistence* migration, involving mainly poor people, pushed by hardship on the road, often moving towards towns.[17]

Patricia Fumerton has claimed that the 'unstable working poor' – those 'most prone to periods of unemployment, multiple or serial employment, desperate indigence, and physical mobility' – constituted 30 to 50 per cent of the early modern population.[18] This instability was especially true of the rootless 'race' of itinerant beggars. According to John Taylor in his *The Praise, Antiquity, and Commodity of Beggary, Beggars and Begging* of 1621:

A Beggar lives here in this vale of sorrow,
And travels here to day, and there tomorrow.
The next day being neither here, nor there:
But almost nowhere, and yet everywhere.[19]

In such circumstances, one might imagine that early modern English men and women were constantly meeting strangers, who would need to be identified. As Dave Postles has shown, many marginal people did pass through communities unknown and unclaimed. He points to parochial burial register of St James' Church, Norton, in 1594 containing the entry, 'Pauper stranger, name and place of abode unknown, died at the home of James Bate, where he had been hospitably received'; or the entry in the register of St Mary, Dymock for 1616, 'A pore man being a Welshman & a beger his name not knowen'. Similarly, the burial register of Garstang, a parish in northern Lancashire, showed an extraordinary amount of anonymity in the late Elizabethan and early Stuart periods. Between 1571 and 1625, 14 burials were recorded as being only that of 'a poor man', and between 1595 and 1623 there were 8 burials of a 'poor woman'. From 1618 to 1638, the interment records gave no more detail than 'a pore child' in no fewer than 21 cases. The 3 entries reporting the burial of 'a pore cripple' may have related to disabled paupers being conveyed through the parish.[20]

English men and women were also increasingly urban dwellers. In very broad terms, the pre-industrial period saw movements of people from northern and western areas of England towards the south and east, often coinciding with migration to a town. In 1500 perhaps 3.1 per cent of the population of England and Wales lived in towns with over 10,000 inhabitants, but this had risen to 8.8 per cent by 1650, and to 16.7 per cent by 1750.[21] This rate of urbanization was exceptional in Europe, with over half of the Continent's total urban growth in the period 1600 to 1800 occurring in England.[22] Much of this expansion was in the metropolis of London, which in the later seventeenth century contained half a million people, or about a tenth of the population of England. Migration from the rest of the country to London absorbed about half of the total extra-metropolitan birth surplus.[23] Such long-distance migration into London was already a feature of the capital in the fourteenth century, when 52 per cent of migrants came from over 64 kilometres away.[24]

By the sixteenth century, London was already a city with a shifting, unstable population, where people could come and go anonymously.[25] In 1617 the Mayor of London no less came across a line of 'strangers' with 'bags and baggage by his door' on their way to an unknown destination.[26] Thomas Harman in his *A Caveat or Warening for Commen Cursetors Vulgarely Called Vagabones* of 1566, a titillating exposé of the supposed horrors of vagabondage, reveals how malfeasants could take advantage of this society of strangers. He describes the activities of a 'counterfeit crank', who begged in one part of town in filthy clothes covered in blood but lived comfortably in another part of town on his takings, 'having a pretty table, well stuffed, with a fair joint-table, and cupboard garnished with pewter, having an old ancient woman to his wife'.[27] We cannot say whether Harman was making all this up but the tale is evidence that such tricks of anonymity were not inconceivable in this period. Indeed, his story does seem to be based on a real beggar called Nicholas Blount *alias* Jennings.[28] By the mid-eighteenth century, Henry Fielding, the novelist and magistrate, could claim of the slum areas of London that

> had they been intended for the very purpose of concealment, they could hardly have been better contrived. Upon such a view, [London] appears as a fast wood or forest, in which a thief may harbour with as great security, as wild beast do in the deserts of Africa or Arabia.[29]

The anonymous city plainly predated the Industrial Revolution.

CREDIT AND TRUST IN A NASCENT MARKET ECONOMY

If early modern England could be an anonymous society, it could also be signally lacking in *gemeinschaft*-like love and understanding, especially where matters of credit were concerned. As Craig Muldrew has shown, credit arrangements were everywhere in England in this period. Due to the expansion of trade the demand for money was perhaps 500 per cent higher in 1600 than it had been in 1540, but the money supply had increased only by some 63 per cent. The difference had to be made good by borrowing, and by buying and selling on credit. Thus, a sample of 4,650 rural inventories for the period 1650 to1720 showed that 40 per cent contained some references to debts owed to the deceased, and the ratio for urban dwellers would probably have been higher.[30] The geographical reach of such credit arrangements was increasing in the period. Many were very local and informal, based on agreements made at one of the 760 market towns, located at intervals of a few miles from each other. However, the making of such transactions was moving out of official markets proper into private deal-making in inns and alehouses adjacent to markets, or in private houses, shops, or at the quayside.[31] Moreover, as the number of middlemen engaged in long-distance transactions between differing communities, and with London, increased, they came to use more formal, written means of credit.[32]

The increasingly technical nature, and sheer number, of credit agreements, often between relative strangers, created problems of trust. According to Muldrew:

> [A]lthough we will never know how many personal reasons early modern individuals might have had for breaking their agreements with each other, and how much dishonesty and fraud, the growth in the sheer complexity of obligations from the 1560s onwards meant that even the most careful and prudent person had difficulty keeping track of all of his or her obligations.[33]

The resulting crisis of trust was exacerbated by uncertainties surrounding the law of debt, and between 1700 and 1800 Parliament was forced to pass no fewer than 32 Acts to clear jails of debtors, or to improve the machinery to facilitate this.[34] There was also an increasing tendency for people to hold 'desperate' debts which were unlikely to be paid unless recourse was made to law.[35] As a result, a numerous and dense network of courts – borough courts of record, courts baron, hundred courts and county courts – developed to hear disputes over credit transactions,[36] and early modern property owners took advantage of them to an extraordinary extent. Muldrew calculates that by the late sixteenth century the amount of civil litigation in rural England might have been as high as 1,102,367 cases per year, one suit for every household in the country, although this level subsequently declined as households became more accustomed to dealing with large amounts of credit. In England and Wales in the mid-1990s the rate of civil litigation was only a quarter of this figure.[37] Shylock, in Shakespeare's *Merchant of Venice*, demanding that the forfeit for an unpaid debt should be 'an equal pound of your fair flesh, to be taken in what part of your body pleaseth me',[38] must have struck a chord with the original Elizabethan audience. The manner in which individuals identified themselves, and their will, in commercial transactions – their legal 'personality' – must have been of great import. Given this insecurity, the idea that pre-modern communities were, in the words of the sociologist David Lyon, based on 'trust emanating from "looking each other in the eye", and from the deal sealed with a handshake', appears somewhat naïve.[39] This appears to call into question the belief in a decline of trustworthiness during nineteenth-century industrialization.[40]

STILL A FACE-TO-FACE SOCIETY?

However, before one abandons the concept of the immediacy of identification in the early modern *gemeinschaft*, it should be noted that early modern England differed in many ways from today's anonymous society. For example, the shift from informal credit arrangements to formal instruments was a gradual one, and in the mid-seventeenth century, bonds still formed a minority of individuals' indebtedness.[41] Most people purchased on credit locally, since there were no national commercial organizations such as banks, or supermarket chains. Similarly, when people did move, they often did not move very far, their lifetime migration taking the form of a number of short steps. Thus, Lawrence Poos found that in fourteenth-century Essex people typically moved to and from communities in a radius of 10 to15 miles.[42] Evidence from Norfolk's midsixteenth-century quarter sessions courts relating specifically to servants shows that they rarely moved more than 20 miles between employers, or between home and employment, and this pattern was still found in the eighteenth century.[43] Even then farm servants were bound to their employers by a contract for a year.[44] Step migration was still the basis of much lifetime mobility in the nineteenth century, when Earnest George Ravenstein described it in his classic essay of 1885, 'The laws of migration'.[45]

In addition, mobility varied between region, class and time-period. The economic pressures that drove mobility in the early modern period were most powerful around London, and weakened the further one moved away from the metropolis. In Cumbria, in the very far north of England, small owner-occupiers do not appear to have been squeezed off the land, and there was more limited movement.[46] Economic change, enclosures and a fluid land market created opportunities for the rich, who moved to take advantage of them, and forced the poor into a life of rootlessness. However, the 'middling sort' may have been much more stable. Thus, in their examination of Terling in Essex in the sixteenth and seventeenth centuries, Wrightson and Levine found that the most fluid elements in village society were the gentlemen and great farmers, while the labouring poor were also subject to a very rapid turnover. It was the husbandmen and craftsmen of the parish who were the most stable element in society, those 'ancient' families who made up the parish elite.[47] Also, the population increase that was, in part, driving migration appears to have stalled in the mid- to late seventeenth century, only to resume in earnest a hundred years later.[48] Population movement declined in the intervening period, or at least tended to take place over shorter distances.[49] This meant that there might be places, social groups and years, for which the *gemeinschaft* model might make more sense.

It is also likely that although people in early modern England were very mobile over their life cycle, they were less so on a day-to-day basis. Very little work has been done on the history of this sort of mobility in the twentieth century, never mind in the early modern period.[50] Nevertheless, it would seem that the mass daily commute to work from the suburbs, or from satellite villages, into the centre of cities was a development of the nineteenth and twentieth centuries. This, and the replacement of localized forms of poor relief by the centralized Welfare State, may have helped to break down that extreme parochialism that Snell has detected in nineteenth-century parish communities.[51] However, not too much should perhaps be made of this, since, according to Colin Pooley, at the beginning of the twentieth century the mean commuting distance to work was only 4 kilometres, much of it still being done on foot, and only rose to 14.6 kilometres by the 1990s.[52] So many people may have been mobile but they may have stuck around long enough, and been present enough on a day-to-day basis, to become familiar to others, so obviating the need for formal means of identification.

It is also the case that although towns may have been growing in the early modern period, most people still lived in small settlements. Even in the larger towns the very exigencies of living cheek by jowl must have made anonymity difficult to achieve. When Richard Cobb examined the papers of the visiting magistrates to the Paris Morgue, he found that only a score or so of the 400 corpses received there in the years 1795 to 1801 went unidentified by neighbours or friends.[53] As he noted:

> Even a man who shoots himself behind a locked door is discovered, a few seconds too late, by his 24-year-old son, by the owner of the house and by half a dozen *voisins de palier*, as though his intended action, even its time and place – for there would be no doubt about the *manner*, the possession of the pistol being known by the whole house, the whole staircase, as an object too large to hide – had been known in advance.[54]

Through the work of historians such as Michael Anderson it has been established that in urban areas during the Industrial Revolution, migrants tended to live near kin who had already moved into the towns, or near former neighbours or countrymen who had already made the journey. This made sense in terms of taking advantage of networks of knowledge and mutual support, and led to the creation of the ethnic and regional ghettos of the great cities.[55] If this lack of anonymity was the case in the urban world of the late eighteenth and mid-nineteenth centuries, it was probably true of earlier periods. As a magistrate Henry Fielding may have found it difficult to identify the poor in Georgian London, but this does not mean that they were unknown to each other. Much the same could have been said of Londoners in the preceding century.[56]

It should also be noted that much modern identification takes place when individuals have to interact with national, or even international, institutions, whether commercial or state. The archetypal form of modern ID is the state passport, the national identification card, or the nationwide supermarket loyalty card. Given the distance, in every sense of the word, between the individual and the large, centralized bureaucracies that issue these tokens of identity, it is inevitable that the former should seem anonymous to the latter. But commercial and state institutions did not act at the level of the nation-state in the early modern period. Economic life was organized on the basis of networks of middlemen passing goods from hand to hand, and the circulation of credit documents in the other direction. The generalization of national oligopolies, whether in manufacturing, retailing or banking, was a feature of the twentieth century.[57] State institutions were similarly decentralized in the early modern period.[58] Welfare benefits, for example, were not paid out of central taxation by Whitehall departments of state but from a poor rate levied in each parish under the Poor Laws, and supervised by the local parish overseers of the poor.[59] Indeed, the Old Poor Law assumed that people lived in parish communities, and could prove that they had a 'settlement' – a right to relief based mostly on birth, or period of residency, in a particular place.[60] Those claiming welfare did not, therefore, have to deal with anonymous central bureaucracies to whom they had to prove their identity, but with the local worthies of the parish where they had lived for some time.

Policing was similarly decentralized, being based on the parish constable, and on watchmen in the towns. The medieval constable, a man appointed from within the community to carrying out the police duties of the office for probably no more than one year, increasingly became the executive agent of the manor or parish for which he was appointed. It was his task to make regular reports, or 'presentments' to the local court leet about felons, miscreants and nuisances. However, the medieval constable also acquired royal authority, and was responsible for maintaining the King' peace in his district. In the early modern period the parish constable came to be supervised by the local justices of the peace. Watchmen were local agents of law enforcement who had long been recruited by, and from among, urban dwellers. The Statute of Westminster of

1285 ordered boroughs to provide watches of a dozen men, while the smaller towns had to provide between four and six watchmen, depending upon their populations.[61] But these local officers were not part of a national, or even county, police force, nor had they any recourse to centralized information on criminals, such as modern fingerprint and DNA databases. Nor were they particularly involved with criminal investigations in the modern sense, which in the early modern period essentially involved the constable asking eyewitnesses for evidence. Alternatively, they, and the victims of crimes such as theft, kept their eyes and ears open for local people bragging, wearing new clothes, or other stolen objects, and organized searches of the local area.[62] In such circumstances the need for criminal identification was minimal, suspects were either known, or unknown (and, therefore, immediately suspicious).

If modern state and commercial entities now require citizens and customers to identify themselves, it may not be because the society in which they operate has become more mobile or anonymous. Rather the replacement of the decentralized State and economy of the early modern period, by large national and multinational institutions, has increased the distance between the individual and authority. The audience before which the individual has to prove his or her identity is now made up of the representatives of large anonymous organizations, rather than individuals with which they have lived for some time. As a consequence, he or she has to use more formal techniques to prove who they are.

CONCLUSION

As a result of this, admittedly cursory analysis, it is possible to come to a tentative, working hypothesis about the context in which identification was made in early modern society. On a day-to-day basis there was probably less need of formal identification than is necessary today, but that there were still plenty of 'comers and goers' in early modern England who needed to identify themselves to authority, or situations in which those with property needed to assert their legal personality. This meant that the techniques of identification of the period were not historically insignificant, and need to be examined in their own right. Nor, as will be shown, were they necessarily based on principles completely alien to the modern world. Indeed, there has probably been as much continuity as change in the history of identification in England.

4

Identifying the Great and the Good in Early Modern England

INTRODUCTION

In the early modern period, before democracy and market forces constructed individuals as citizens and customers with equal rights and obligations, there were some important differences between when, how and where various social groups identified themselves. The discussion of identification in the years between about 1500 and 1750 in this and the subsequent chapter will distinguish loosely, therefore, between the identification of the property owning classes, and of the poor and the deviant. The former identified themselves as citizens with political rights, and as juridical persons, while the latter were more frequently, but by no means exclusively, identified as welfare claimants and criminals. It would, however, be a mistake to make a watertight distinction between the two, since the poor were called upon to identify themselves as persons with rights and responsibilities within legal processes and contractual arrangements. In exceptional circumstances the poor could even be called upon to identify themselves in the political arena.

This chapter will attempt to describe some of the methods used to identify the property owner, and the poor when called upon to exercise their meagre juridical and political rights. The next will be concerned with the poor as welfare claimants, and with deviants, and other persons, beyond the law.

THE CONSPICUOUS IDENTIFICATION OF THE WEALTHY: CLOTHING

The rich and powerful in the sixteenth and seventeenth centuries, or so it has been argued, attempted to identify their status, position and lineage through

conspicuous outward signs. Clothes and heraldry, for example, were both obvious forms of social performance that were used in an attempt to project identity. Although these were not strictly forms of individual identification, the
close relationship between group identity and personal identity in the period
necessitates that they should be addressed first, before moving on to consideration of the juridical person. However, over time the social usefulness of such
forms of identification declined, or, perhaps more accurately, their limitations
became more obvious.

Clothes in early modern England certainly seem to have had a significance for
personal identification that is difficult to grasp today. Clothes, in some senses,
quite literally made the man (or woman), whether this was the monarch as he
or she put on the crown and coronation robes, the knight of the garter as he
donned his regalia, or the priest in his vestments. It is, for example, only when
one understands the role of vestments in investing their wearers with a certain
character that one can begin to understand the depth of feeling aroused during
the reign of Elizabeth I by Church of England priests wearing surplices and hats.
For Puritans these were indeed the very substance of the papist defilement of
the Church. This might also help to explain the care taken over the depiction of
items of clothing in the portraiture of the period, when the treatment of the likeness of the person at the same date was somewhat cavalier.[1] Such outward signs of
identity were plainly of great importance to impostors such as Perkin Warbeck,
and still later to the Tichborne Claimant. The role of clothing in signifying status
explains, in part, the passing of various Sumptuary Laws from 1337 onwards,
which attempted to restrict the wearing of certain types of fabric to particular
social groups.[2] In a proclamation of the reign of Elizabeth I, for example, it was
laid down that:

> None shall wear . . . cloth of gold, silver, or tinsel; satin, silk, or cloth mixed with gold
> or silver, nor any sables; except earls and all of superior degrees, and viscounts and
> barons in their doublets and sleeveless coats;
>
> Woollen cloth made out of the realm; velvet, crimson, scarlet or blue; furs, black
> genets, lucerns; except dukes, marquises, earls or their children, barons, and knights
> of the order;
>
> Velvet in gowns, coats, or outermost garments; fur of leopards; embroidery, pricking
> or printing with gold, silver, or silk; except baron's sons, knights, or men that may
> dispend £200 by year.[3]

The importance of clothing to status may also help to explain the comparative
ease with which the wealthy could disguise themselves by changing their garb.
Thus, after the Battle of Worcester in 1651, when Oliver Cromwell soundly

defeated the army of Charles II, the young royal escaped, having formed, in his own words:

> [T]he resolution of putting myself into a disguise, and endeavouring to get a-foot to London, in a country fellow's habit, with a pair of ordinary gray-cloth breeches, a leathern doublet, and a green jerkin . . . I also cut my hair very short, and flung my clothes into a privy-house, that nobody might see that any body had been stripping themselves.

His brother, James II (then Duke of York), had escaped to the Continent three years earlier dressed as a girl.[4]

In the eighteenth century, masked balls and the institution of the masquerade, are said to have allowed the rich to don disguise for the purpose of laying aside social and sexual conventions.[5] The latter can certainly be seen in the case of the young James Boswell, who on his arrival in London from Scotland in 1762:

> resolved to be a blackguard and to see all that was to be seen. I dressed myself in my second-mourning suit, in which I had been powdered many months, dirty busking breeches and black stockings, a shirt of Lord Eglington's which I had worn two days, and a little round hat with tarnished silver lace belonging to a disbanded officer of the Royal Volunteers. I had in my hand an old oaken stick battered against the pavement. And was I not a complete blackguard? I went to the Park, picked up a low brimstone, called myself a barber, and agreed with her for sixpence, went to the bottom of the Park arm in arm, and dipped my machine in the canal and performed most manfully.[6]

But these sorts of escapades show the limited ability of clothing to provide a stable form of identification – after all, both Warbeck and the Claimant were impostors, despite their finery. Just as the rich could dress down, so the lower orders could dress up (in all senses of the term). Daniel Defoe's Moll Flanders, in the book of the same name of 1722, realized that was possible to alter one's status with one's appearance. When one of her several husbands, 'a gentleman-tradesman':

> had a mind to carry me to court, or to the play, he might become a sword, and look as like a gentleman as another man; and not be one that had the mark of his apron-strings upon his coat, or the mark of his hat upon his periwig; that should look as if he was set on to his sword, when his sword was put on to him, and that carried his trade in his countenance.[7]

The establishment of a second-hand clothes trade in the late sixteenth century, which saw the development of the occupation of 'fripper', or 'fripperer', who sold recycled 'frippery', helped to undermine the status function of clothes.

This seems to have especially been a feature of London, a consequence of the development of 'the Season' in this period, when the wealthy flocked to the capital to be seen about the court and to take part in social activities. The imperatives of costly display meant that yesterday's fashions were passed on to servants and retainers, and quickly resold.[8] In any case, the English Sumptuary Laws lapsed at the beginning of the seventeenth century, and may have had as much to do with an attack on the sin of vanity, and on the import of foreign cloth and clothing, as with a defence of social status. Clothing as a means of social emulation, rather than of social segregation, undermined its use in the performance of identification.[9] However, as will be noted below, since people in the past had so few clothes, particular items of clothing could still be useful for describing specific individuals rather than their status.

THE CONSPICUOUS IDENTIFICATION OF THE WEALTHY: HERALDRY

If the elite found it difficult, or at times inconvenient, to signify their caste via clothing, they seem to have been more successful, and just as eager, to identify their lineage through the outward signs of heraldry. The life of the leading county elites revolved around the family – the basis of social life, county administration and of political activity. This can be seen in the diary for the years 1617 and 1618 of Nicholas Assherton of Downham in Lancashire, a member of a leading county family. Of the people he mentioned meeting, 30 per cent were kin, while those he mentioned without meeting, 40 per cent were his relatives. The more frequently he met or mentioned a person, the more likely they were to be kin, and his social life revolved around family gatherings, the most important being at Christmas. This was rather different to the 'middling sort', or the poor, who seems to have been far less dependent upon extended networks of kin.[10] For the aristocracy and gentry, lineage implied ancestral rights, property, honour and duty. Hence the importance of what Daniel Woolf has calls the 'tokens and symbols of lineage', such as heraldic arms and crests.[11] As already noted in the case of Perkin Warbeck, individuals could become synonymous with such devices.

The heraldic symbols of lineage can be found everywhere in the aristocratic world of Europe in the early modern period, and in this England was no different.[12] In the sixteenth century, arms and crests were increasingly used as domestic, ecclesiastical and civic decorations, adorning monuments, paintings, books, furniture, carriages, horses and buildings.[13] At Theobalds, Lord

Burghley embellished the hall with a huge map of England showing the estates and coats of arms of every prominent landowner in the country. Sir John Ferrers decorated the great parlour of Tamworth Castle with a frieze of shields tracing his ancestry back to the Conquest. Cuthbert, Lord Ogle, thought his pedigree in letters of red was a suitable decoration for the chancel wall of the church of St Andrew, Bothal, and by the end of the eighteenth century, 719 quarterings of the Grenvilles were depicted on the ceiling of the Gothic Library at Stowe.[14] Such symbolism was carried over into clothing through the institution of livery, whereby family retainers wore the heraldic emblems and colours of their masters. The outward symbols of lineage were present even at death, with hearses and horses emblazoned with arms, and flags carrying heraldic arms unfurled.[15]

So ubiquitous was the use of such symbolism to identify a person, or his and her belongings, that a writer such as Jane Austen could refer to it casually in her novels as late as the Regency period. Thus, in *Persuasion* (completed in 1816), when the Elliot sisters are at breakfast one morning in an inn at Lyme, they spy an impressive carriage, and are astounded to hear that it belongs to their cousin, Mr William Elliot:

> 'There! you see!' cried Mary in an ecstasy, 'just as I said! Heir to Sir Walter Elliot! I was sure that would come out, if it was so. Depend upon it, that is a circumstance which his servants take care to publish, wherever he goes. But, Anne, only conceive how extraordinary! I wish I had looked at him more. I wish we had been aware in time, who it was, that he might have been introduced to us. What a pity that we should not have been introduced to each other! Do you think he had the Elliot countenance? I hardly looked at him, I was looking at the horses; but I think he had something of the Elliot countenance, I wonder the arms did not strike me! Oh! the great-coat was hanging over the panel [of the carriage], and hid the arms, so it did; otherwise, I am sure, I should have observed them, and the livery too; if the servant had not been in mourning, one should have known him by the livery.'[16]

Their father, Sir Walter Elliot, of Kellynch Hall, in Somerset, was satirized by Austen as 'a man who, for his own amusement, never took up any book but the *Baronetage*',[17] but the joke might have been lost on many of her aristocratic contemporaries. This language of heraldry was so well known from the late medieval period onwards that it even allowed the *cognoscenti* to recognize visual puns. For example, Hans Holbein's *A Lady with a Squirrel and a Starling*, painted in 1527, has been plausibly identified as a portrait of Anne Lovell, wife of Sir Francis Lovell of East Harling in Norfolk. The starling may be a punning reference to the family seat, and the chained pet squirrel, nibbling a nut in the sitter's arms, a reference to a heraldic beast that featured in the Lovell coat of arms.[18] The lady here was perhaps being identified as the property of her husband as much as Mr Elliot used a crest to mark his horse and carriage.

The history of heraldry in England is, of course, a long and complex one. Heraldic arms in the modern sense were derived from the devices on shields used in the Middle Ages.[19] J. H. Round, the late Victorian and Edwardian medievalist, believed that they had assumed their modern form by the reign of King Stephen (1135–54),[20] and then spread down from the King, and his counts and earls, to the barons by about 1200, and to knights by 1250.[21] There is some debate over whether they were originally used to make members of the feudal host recognizable to their followers in battle. Certainly, the Marshal, and his senior colleague the Constable, seem originally to have had authority over the right to bear arms, and they were, in the main, military officers with authority over armies in the field.[22] However, the mud and debris of battle would probably have quickly obliterated the battered surfaces of shields, rendering such devices unrecognizable.[23]

Whatever their origins, so important were the rights to bear particular arms, and the estates that went with lineages, that they generated endless disputes and false claims.[24] The authority to regulate arms passed to the heralds, probably from the reign of Edward I (1272–1307), and there was a 'King of Heralds' from at least 1276.[25] The heralds originally appear to have been sent ahead of the court to proclaim tournaments. They also cheered combatants as they fought, and were expected to know their characters and histories, and they acted as masters of ceremonies to their lords and to the knights of their companies.[26] As such, they may have borne more than a passing resemblance to modern television football commentators. The heralds began to act as a court of heraldry, with the first Chapter, or Court, of the Kings of Arms and Heralds of England being held before Rouen during its siege by Henry V in January 1420.[27] Visitations of heralds to check on the lawful bearing of arms may go back to the thirteenth century but the first royal visitation commission was in 1530. The heralds were to ensure that arms were not borne by those:

> issued of vyle blood rebelles to our persone not heritiques contary to the faithe. But men of good honest Reputacyon, And all suche which shall be enoblished to have their armes registered in the Erle Marshalles boke.

Between 1530 and 1686, at intervals of usually about 20 years, the Crown would issue letters patent, notifying mayors, sheriffs and other county authorities that the Clarenceux or Norroy King of Arms intended shortly to make a visitation to their county, and directing those authorities to lend them assistance. The heralds were to correct or prohibit arms borne unlawfully, and to enter onto their rolls those that were borne lawfully, listing the descendents of those who bore them.[28]

The right to bear a particular set of arms depended upon the production of evidence. In order to authenticate arms, the heralds of the sixteenth and early seventeenth centuries looked not only at ancient documents but also examined monuments. Here they searched for coats of arms carved or painted on tombs or buildings, or set in stained glass, which could be used as evidence of ancient usage.[29] By the late seventeenth century at the latest, the heralds were collecting pedigrees, often based on the documents and artefacts held in muniment rooms of aristocratic families, or on research made in the official records in the Tower Record Office. According to Sir William Dugdale, Norroy Herald (1660–77) and Garter Herald (1677–86), the proof of rights to arms:

> is to be by Grant, or *prescription*, and if by prescription, it is to be shewed from some auntient Decree, sealed with an Impression of the Armes he pretends to, or some sculpture upon Tombes and Monuments, Armes in Glasse windowes, auntient paynted Tabletts, or some such Authenticque Testimoniall as may demonstrate that his lineall auncestors have made use of them above 80 Yeares last past at the least.[30]

Care had to be taken to distinguish between true and forged evidence, given the lengths to which some would go to prove a spurious pedigree. Thus, a fictitious claim of descent of the Wellesbournes of Buckinghamshire from Montfort Earl of Leicester was supported by forged medieval deeds and seals, and the placing in Hughenden church of a fabricated thirteenth-century knightly effigy.[31]

These activities linked heraldry to the development of antiquarian and archaeological studies, and the heralds began to produce the earliest published reference works for aristocratic pedigrees. William Camden, the local historian and archaeologist, was brought into the College of Arms as the Clarenceux Herald in 1597. Augustine Vincent, who came into the College of Arms as Rouge Croix in 1621, developed a close working knowledge of the medieval state records, producing manuscript extracts from the Patent and Close Rolls, Inquisitions Post Mortem, and the Plea and Fine Rolls, from which he compiled pedigrees. Dugdale's *The Baronage of England* was published in 1675 and 1676, although it had been in preparation since 1642. Many county histories from the early modern period grew out of genealogical and heraldic research, as did the *Victoria County History* in its original incarnation under Herbert Doubleday and William Page at the beginning of the twentieth century. Doubleday also published and co-edited the *Complete Peerage*, completed in 1959. Many early medieval historians, such as William Stubbs and Round, were genealogists – the latter publishing such works as *Studies in Peerage and Family History* (1901) and *Peerage and Pedigree* (1910). Similarly, some of the learned antiquarian societies, such as the Harleian Society, the Society of Genealogists, the British Record Society and the Pipe Roll Society, all had genealogical elements.[32]

However, as with clothes, heraldic symbolism gradually ceased to be an effective means of identification because, in part, it was increasingly emulated by non-aristocratic families. Quite modest landowners began to insist on flaunting coats of arms, as can be seen in the case of Samuel Pepys, the seventeenth-century diarist. The Pepyses were country people who, from the thirteenth century onwards had held land around Cottenham in Cambridgeshire, including the manor of Impington. In the seventeenth century the family also owned a yeoman's farmhouse in the village of Brampton in Huntingdonshire, along with 74 acres in the parish. But Pepys's father was actually a London tailor, and his mother the daughter of a Whitechapel butcher. However, Pepys was himself highly conscious of his lineage, as perhaps befitted a man on the make in Restoration England. Thus, on 10 February 1662 he wrote in his diary:

> Musique practice a good while, then to Paul's Churchyard, and there I met with Dr Fuller's 'England's Worthys,' [Thomas Fuller's *The History of the Worthies of England* published in London in 1662] the first time that I ever saw it; and so I sat down reading it, till it was two o'clock before I thought of the time going; and so I rose and went home to dinner, being much troubled that (though he had some discourse with me about my family and arms) he says nothing at all, nor mentions us either in Cambridge or Norfolk. But I believe, indeed, our family were never considerable.[33]

By the 23 March of the same year, reflecting his growing affluence and position, one can find the diary entry, 'This morning was brought me my boy's fine livery, which is very handsome, and I do think to keep to black and gold lace upon gray, being the colour of my arms, for ever.' By 23 October 1663 he was visiting the Mitre Inn in Fenchurch Street and 'saw some of my new bottles made with my crest upon them, filled with wine, about five or six dozen'.[34]

Heraldry had, of course, long begun its steady decline into decadence by this date. As early as the sixteenth century, the purveyors of illegal coats of arms were legion. In 1577 William Dawkyns was arrested for impersonating a Queen's officer, for selling coats of arms, and compiling false pedigrees. He was brought before Star Camber, and sentenced to be whipped and to lose his ears, as well as to be pilloried in every shire where he had transacted his 'noisome business'. However, even the official heralds were guilty of abetting forgeries. In 1616, for example, the Garter King at Arms and York Herald, the then senior officer of arms, was summoned before the Earl Marshall's commissioners and committed to the Marshalsea Prison for facilitating the granting of arms to 'Gregory Brandon of London, Gentleman'. Brandon turned out to be the common hangman of the City of London, and the Heralds' offence was compounded by the fact that they had not noticed that Brandon's new arms were a combination of the arms of the rulers of Aragon and Brabant.[35] By the late eighteenth and early nineteenth centuries the Heralds were providing pedigrees for the lesser gentry, and yeoman and merchant classes, based on probate records, parish registers and monumental inscriptions.[36] As with clothing, the power of emulation undermined social distinctions.

On the other hand, it has been argued that it was not so much the popularity of heraldry that was its undoing as a gradual lessening of the desire to identify oneself with military prowess. As Keith Thomas has pointed out, as the population at large became more civilian in the late seventeenth and eighteenth centuries, and as military affairs became increasingly the preserve of a specialized occupational group, aspiring to the trappings of marshal glory became faintly ridiculous.[37] It is rather difficult to imagine Beau Brummell donning spurs and cutlass, never mind a heraldic helm. This would help to explain the contemporary fears regarding the feminization of men and the masculinity of the female libertine.[38] Genealogy continued, of course, but was increasingly shorn of some of the heraldic symbols of the past. By the nineteenth century heraldry had become a somewhat dotty pastime for librarians, underemployed vicars and scholarly young women.[39] The resulting printed family trees still litter the British Library, the other copyright libraries and the holdings of the Society of Genealogists. However, the coat of arms had long since ceased to be the principal means of identifying oneself in the wider world.

IDENTIFYING VOTERS UNDER THE *ANCIEN REGIME*

Heraldry, and the claims to property and rights that went with lineage, depended on a mixture of communal knowledge and documentary proof of lineage, and both were also evident in the manner in which the owners of another form of property, the vote, were identified. Under the *ancien regime* this was, of course, the preserve of men. By the end of the seventeenth century the franchises in English boroughs were already determined by tradition. In a few places, such as Westminster, residence and the payment of rates conferred the right to vote, and as a consequence the electorate was large and constantly changing. In others the franchise was restricted to the owners of certain freehold properties, or 'burgages', to members of the corporation, and to the freemen of the town. In rural counties, the franchise was confined to those holding freehold property valued at 40s per annum. In smaller boroughs, with their small constituencies of perhaps 12 to 50 voters, a man whose predecessor in the possession of a property had been admitted to the poll was himself entitled to vote. Which properties conferred the franchise was general knowledge, and the electors were known to each other, and to the officers who conducted the poll. John Prest has argued that in many medium-sized boroughs the returning officer and his assessors would also have had little difficulty in establishing changes in the ownership of property though marriage, inheritance and sale, and what changes had taken place among the freemen through the coming of age, or the service of apprenticeship.[40] However, Derek Hirst has suggested that constant land transactions and the infrequency of elections may have made this difficult in practice.[41]

More formal record-keeping was being introduced, if haltingly, into the process of identifying voters in the early modern period. In 1711, in order to prevent corruption and fraud, it was enacted that people could not vote at an election for a knight of the shire unless they had been assessed to pay the land tax, and were shown on subsidy rolls as having actually paid it. Land tax assessors were henceforth responsible for keeping what was in effect a check-list of eligible voters. Although this system was abolished in 1745, it was reinstated in 1780.[42] However, the extent to which the subsidy rolls were a foolproof means of identifying electors is difficult to determine, since there appear to have been individuals in every county regarded as 'sufficient' freeholders for the purpose of an election, but not for the purposes of taxation, or for jury service.[43] In 1763 the so-called Durham Act (3 Geo. III, c.15) was passed, which prevented borough freemen of less than 12 months standing from voting. As a consequence, the mayor, or bailiff, of each borough was also to keep a book in which to enter the names of all citizens, burgesses and freemen entitled to vote.[44] As will be noted below, these traditional, communal forms of identification, were to have a surprisingly lengthy history.

THE JURIDICAL PERSON AND THE CITIZEN:
SEALS AND SIGNATURES

In the modern world it is frequently necessary for individuals, acting as juridical persons and citizens, to express their will on documents, or rather to indicate that a document is a valid and authentic expression of their will. This is usually done by a signature, and the person who signs the document can then identify themselves as the signatory by repeating the signature. Alternatively, an authoritative proof signature can be provided to an institution, such as a bank, which can then compare the signature on documents to the proof copy.[45] In the medieval and early modern periods, however, the signature shared this function with the seal, and was indeed for much of the time subordinated to the latter. Even when used, the signature was not necessarily the sort of sign manual in use today. A discussion of these techniques, and of the gradual emergence of the priority of the signature, helps to place the identification of the legal personality in a broader context, and to reveal its problematic nature. The modern phenomenon of identity theft plainly had its counterpart in older forms of forgery, although the two forms of imposture are by no means identical.

The seal is a very ancient form of personal validation. Minute stone or clay discs, engraved with straight lines or criss-cross patterns have been found in Mesopotamia from the period of the Hassuna culture of 6000 to 5500 BC. These amulets, probably worn on a string round the neck, may possibly have been impressed as a mark of ownership on lumps of clay fastened to baskets or jar stoppers, and were perhaps the first examples of press seals. Cylinder seals can be found in Iraq from the period of the Uruk culture of 3750 BC to 3300 BC.[46] The first evidence of such technologies of identification in Britain comes from the Roman period in the form of the seals or seal impressions of military units, urban authorities and even private individuals. The stamps that oculists used to mark medicinal preparations for the treatment of eye ailments with the name of the preparation, and the man responsible for making it, have even been used to plot the positions of local markets in Roman Britain.[47]

However, the English seal of the medieval and early modern periods almost certainly developed from the example of the pendant lead bulla used to seal papal documents from the sixth century onwards. The earliest English documents known to be authenticated by seals are writs of Edward the Confessor (1042–66), although there are earlier Anglo-Saxon references to them.[48] However, as Michael Clanchy has shown, seals were at first only one of the types of personal memento, or token, used to prove one's identity in the early Middle Ages – charters might be accompanied by swords, or knives, or personal objects that were associated with the person of the knight. Thus, a charter of 1151 for St Denys priory near Southampton has two parallel slits in it, through which the blade of the donor's symbolic knife was once fixed to the parchment. In the reign of Henry I, at the beginning of the twelfth century, the knife apparently had to be broken by a church or royal official as part of the ceremony of transfer. In addition, the priority of the written document over personal testimony seems to have been something that was only accepted in the early thirteenth century. In the twelfth century, to 'record' something meant to bear oral witness, not to produce a document. In Henry II's reign (1155–89), Ranulf de Glanvill's treatise *Tractatus de legibus et consuetudinibus regni Angliae* provides the text of a writ which orders a sheriff to have a plea 'recorded' in his county court, and then he is to convey this 'record' to the King's court by four knights. It is evident that the knights convey the record orally, as the parties to the plea are ordered to come to 'hear the record'. Only personal testimony carried proof. Fifty years later, by the time of Henry de Bracton's legal treatise, *De Legibus et Consuetudinibus Angliae*, the procedure for making a record of this type required the seals of the sheriff and of the coroners, which were obviously attached to the document. Only two knights, rather than four, were now required, since their word was now of secondary importance. The increasing bureaucratization of both government and the legal system in the Middle Ages meant, in the terms used by Clanchy, that identification and authentication moved from the world of the voice and memory to that of objects and written documents.[49]

Originally the seal impression seems to have been made by a seal matrix with a handle. Richard I (1189–99) appears, however, to have had a signet ring but their use was not common until the fifteenth century. Seals in medieval Britain were always impressed in coloured beeswax, usually red, green or brown, to which, in the later Middle Ages, resin was added. Seals might be attached to open documents by tags, or used to close documents, hence the distinction drawn between letters patent and letters close, and between the enrolled copies of such royal missives on the Patent and Close Rolls in the National Archives in London.[50]

The iconography and form of seals were plainly of great importance. They were often made of precious metals, and could be worn as pendant jewellery. Many early seals were made from Graeco-Roman gem stones, and the symbol of the king, later knight, on horseback may go back to Roman imperial iconography.[51] Seal matrices could have the power to represent the personality of their possessors – they were not necessarily simple utilitarian objects. Indeed, Brigitte Miriam Bedos-Rezak has argued that in the early medieval period the seal partook, in some sense, of the person of its owner. In early medieval debates about the nature of the Eucharist was developed the idea that reality was capable of being perceived through an iconic convention. The bread and wine were the body and blood of Christ – 'to be like' became 'to be part of'.[52] As a result, the impression of the owner's symbol in the wax of the seal could embody his person in the artefact. Seals could even speak in the first person with inscriptions such as TEGO SECRETA FRANGE L[EGE] ('I cover secrets. Break [me and] read'). The ability of the seal matrix to create its mirror image,

Medieval double seal and seal matrix of Joanna Plantagenet. About 1196–99
France, Silver. (Source: Wikipedia Commons)

and the person of its owner, in wax inevitably associated it with magic and the
occult.[53] Due to such considerations, and the manner in which sigillography
developed out of the heraldic concerns of the aristocracy, the literature on seals
has often concentrated on the iconography of seals, often to the exclusion of a
study of their actual use. However, many seals were not heraldic. Thus, out of
870 fourteenth-century personal seals from the series of ancient deeds in the
Duchy of Lancaster's records examined by Harvey and McGuinness, only just
over a third were heraldic in form.[54]

The lack of heraldic symbols was most common among the peasantry, whose
use of seals was widespread. For example, as early as the early thirteenth century an agreement was made by the earl of Chester and Lincoln with the men of
Frieston and Butterwick in Lincolnshire, which bears the seals of at least fifty of
the latter.[55] Most of these men were probably not technically serfs, but were certainly smallholders. Similarly, a large number of free tenants, including three
women, engaged in resisting an enclosure of common land on a Middlesex
manor in 1316, appended their seals to a document now held in the Middlesex
County Record Office.[56] Serfs were not supposed to have seals, but the 1285

Statute of Exeter required 'bondsmen' to have seals to authenticate their written evidence when they served on inquests for which there were insufficient freemen. According to Clanchy, by 1300 probably all freemen, and even some unfree serfs, would have had a seal.[57]

It seems probable that from the fourteenth century onwards plenty of small, ready-made seals were available offering a choice of devices from which the purchaser might choose. Some appear to have even had a space for a name to be engraved. Among smallholders, seals without heraldic devices or names were entirely normal, and the use of other people's seals not uncommon. The exchange of seals between generations and individuals probably meant that in the later Middle Ages the impressions of seals could not have been regarded as very reliable guarantees in cases of disputed authenticity. People found other methods for security, including the registering of documents in courts of law.[58] The act of sealing in the presence of others may have been more important to smallholders as a means of identification than the possession of the seal itself.[59] Such laxity may help to explain the not uncommon occurrence of forged seals. Bracton, along with other legal treatises, regarded the forgery of the seal of one's lord, as well as of the King's seal, as treason. A petition to Parliament in 1371 requested that the forgery of seals of private individuals should be made a felony. The appeal was unsuccessful, but the statute was finally passed in 1413 (2 Hen. V, c.3).[60]

The development of the signature in the medieval period was equally complex and problematic. In the twelfth and thirteenth centuries the signature, or sign manual, was not accepted by itself as a lawful symbol of authentication on a document. A Christian was required to either sign with a cross, indicating that he was making a promise in the sight of Christ crucified, or more commonly he affixed to the document his *signum* in the form of a seal. A signatory who put a cross on a charter would have also made a ceremonial sign of the cross across his body with his right hand touching his forehead, heart, left shoulder and right shoulder.[61] This did not apply if the signatory was a Jew, who could not, for obvious reasons, make the sign of the cross. There was no set signature in this period, and there is evidence of more than one document being written and witnessed by the same clerk but in differing scripts. Even his written name could be rendered in a different 'hand'.[62]

If a signature appeared on a medieval document it might not be that of the person who was acting through the document. Instead it might be the signature of a notary – an official who provided safeguards against forgery, usually by writing the document in his own hand and by appending to it his name and an individual *signum* which he drew with a pen. If a dispute over the authenticity of a document arose, the notary could be cross-examined. If he were dead, reference could be made to other documents signed by him, or to a register in which an exemplar of the notary's style and *signum* were recorded.[63] Notaries were appointed originally by the Church, and, after Henry VIII's break with Rome in 1534, by the Crown. However, such officials were a comparative rarity in common law England, being a more frequent feature of Roman law systems in France and the Mediterranean world.[64] As already noted, the English tended to have recourse to registering documents in courts of law, rather than with such independent scribes, perhaps reflecting the stability and centralization of courts in England from a very early date. Even then the activities of notaries seem to have been in decline in the seventeenth century.[65] What was important in legal terms was not the identity of the authentic self but official forms of authentication that created a legal personality.

The sign manual, or autograph signature, became more common in the later Middle Ages. It was used by Edward III as early as 1362, but probably only because it was the custom of the King of Castile to whom he was writing. Although the practice spread rapidly in England in the late fourteenth and early fifteenth centuries, even in the 1400s, when the sign manual was in common use, seals were still used on formal documents.[66] There were in addition other sorts of written 'signature', such as the royal monograph, and the jealously guarded identification marks, or monograms, which merchants used to mark their goods[67]. On the Continent, Albrecht Dürer even got an official ruling that banned all non-Nuremberg traders of prints from selling illegal reprints bearing his famous 'AD' monogram.[68]

Gradually a 'mixed economy' of forms of identification seems to have developed to identify the juridical person. Thus in 1509, Henry VII attested his will with his sign manual, his great seal, his privy seal, the signet that was kept by a secretary, and the privy signet with the eagle, which he kept himself.[69] By the seventeenth century, seals were often accompanied by signatures on documents, and the latter increasingly took precedence. Thus Charles I's death warrant was both signed and sealed by 59 commissioners, although one of the seals of the regicides (appropriately that of Oliver Cromwell) was actually used twice.[70] By the eighteenth century, the 'seal' was often reduced to an unstamped blob of wax that accompanied a personal signature for form's sake, although large formal seals continued to be used by the Crown, corporations and municipalities.

So why did the signature eventually replace the seal? Only some very tentative answers to this question are possible here, given the relative lack of research undertaken on the subject. It is unlikely, however, that this process can be

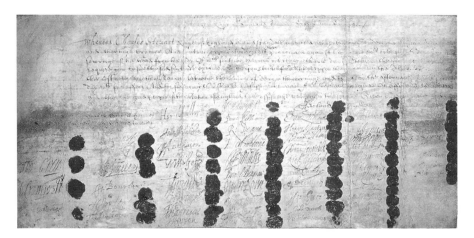

The death warrant of Charles 1, 1649, showing a mixture of seals and signatures.
Those of Oliver Cromwell are in the first row on the left, the third ones down.
(Source: Wikipedia Commons)

understood simply in terms of the replacement of one form of identification by one that was more generally acceptable. Indeed, it is a moot point whether the gradual replacement of the seal by the signature increased the number of people who could reliably identify themselves in the early modern period.

At the end of the thirteenth century, according to R. H. Hilton in his *The Decline of Serfdom in Medieval England*, while the whole of the body of customary tenants, or villeins, had been declared unfree, the proportion of free tenants was probably greater than in Domesday Book in 1087. Except for Leicestershire, where the proportion of sokemen or freemen was 28 per cent, the highest proportion of freedmen in 1086 was 4 per cent (Cambridgeshire). However, in the Hundred Rolls for 1279–80, covering the population of parts of Huntingdonshire, Cambridgeshire, Bedfordshire, Buckinghamshire, Oxfordshire, Warwickshire and Leicestershire, 40 per cent were free tenants. There were, of course, local differences – the figure was as high as 55 to 70 per cent in parts of Cambridgeshire and Bedfordshire, but as low as 20 per cent in areas of Oxfordshire. These counties were intermediate in social structure between East Anglia and Lincolnshire, well known for large numbers of free tenants, and the Western counties, also known for large numbers of slaves in 1086 and subordinate villains thereafter.[71] On the basis of these figures, and Clanchy's arguments respecting seal ownership, one might conclude that some 40 per cent of the peasantry had access to seals in the late thirteenth century. However, the widespread use of seals appears to have declined in the later Middle Ages, and the peasants who had them were probably those who had to authenticate documents more than just occasionally.[72] This may have been part of that process by which many small holders were converted into landless labourers in the centuries after the Black Death.

On the other hand, according to David Cressy, drawing on the ability of people to sign depositions in ecclesiastical courts, 90 per cent of men and 99 per cent of women were illiterate in 1500. These figures for illiteracy had declined to perhaps 55 per cent for men and 75 per cent for women by the time of the accession of George I in 1715.[73] In the period 1841 to 1845, when the Victorian General Register Office had begun to calculate the numbers of people who could sign the civil marriage register, just under a third of men and half of women were illiterate.[74] In so far as levels of literacy were determined by formal education, which depended on paying fees, it is probable that literacy in pre-industrial times varied by social and economic class, and also by place.[75] An analysis of wills and depositions undertaken by Wrightson and Levine showed that in Leicestershire in 1640, 55 per cent of yeomen were illiterate, but more than 80 per cent of husbandmen, and more than 90 per cent of labourers and servants, were unable to sign their names.[76] Cressy found similar class literacy gradients in his analyses of the diocese of Durham in the years 1561 to 1631, and of London, the City and Middlesex, in the period 1580 to 1700. Yet the ability to sign one's name was higher in all social classes in the latter urban metropolitan area than in the former rural diocese in the North.[77]

On this basis, therefore, of these very crude calculations, it may not have been until the eighteenth century that the proportion of Englishmen who could identify themselves with a signature exceeded the proportion of the male population who used seals in the late thirteenth century. Women's ability to use either form of juridical identification were, of course, more limited still. However, the two forms of identification are not strictly comparable because, as already noted, for many peasants the use of a seal for identification was dependent upon the presence of witnesses, just as was the use of a mark on a document by an illiterate labourer in the seventeenth century. All that one can say is that the history of personal identification in this period in not necessarily a linear one.

It is possible that the ability of the seal to 'embody' the person, as Bedos-Rezak has argued, may have declined in Reformation England along with the acceptance of other forms of embodiment, such as the Roman Catholic Church's belief in transubstantiation. The outward show of the sign was replaced by the signature which was supposed to reveal traits of character and penmanship – the inner man, rather than outward show. This might be seen as reflecting the emphasis of the Reformation on salvation though inner faith, rather than through outward show. However, similar developments were also going on in Catholic countries. Béatrice Fraenkel, discussing the development of the signature in France, has seen this development in terms of the 'importance progressively accorded to the singularity of the subject', and the development of individualism from the sixteenth century onwards. One might see this in terms of either the development of 'possessive individualism', or of the need of the State to individualize its subjects for the purposes of control.[78] According to Fraenkel, the signature, unlike the seal, was devoid of heraldic symbolism, and appeared to be less involved with the trappings of aristocratic lineage, the use of which was prohibited during the French Revolution.[79] Similarly, one might also see this in terms of the replacement of an aristocratic form of identification, the seal, by a form of penmanship associated with the vulgar commercial activity of accountancy, yet another sign of the 'rise' of the middle classes.[80]

It is difficult to see exactly how one could test such suppositions, especially since the 'rise' of the signature can be detected from the late medieval period. It might be more fruitful, therefore, to think of the alphabetization of the sign manual as part and parcel of a transformation of written culture from the late Middle Ages onwards. The period saw the multiplication of the forms and numbers of written texts; the appearance of printing; and changes in the status of writing, and of the function of documents. The late Middle Ages also saw the fixing of the inheritance of names, as will be discussed shortly.[81] The subsequent increase in the use of the signature might then be associated with the increasing requirement for literacy in the early modern period. This may have made it easier to replace the seal matrix, which was cumbersome to use and inconvenient if lost or damaged, by the quick and, literally, 'to hand' facility of the sign manual.

In the case of England some impetus may also have been given to the increasing use of signatures, and the decline of the seal, by the passing of the 1677 Statute of Frauds. This Act (29 Cha. II, c.3), said to be for the 'prevention of many fraudulent practices, which are commonly endeavoured to be upheld by perjury and subornation of perjury', laid down that:

1. certain conveyances of interests in land must be in writing and signed by the parties;
2. wills of real estate must be in writing signed by the testator;
3. no written will of personal estate could be revoked unless done so in written form;
4. declarations or creations of trusts of land or tenement must be in writing signed by the party creating the trust;
5. certain forms of contracts were unenforceable by action unless evidences by a note or contract in writing signed by the parties;

6. contracts for the sale of goods for the price of £10 or over were to be evidenced by either acceptance and actual receipt, or by a gift of something in earnest, or by part payment, or by a note or memorandum in writing signed by the parties.[82]

Although the provisions of this Act were mostly repealed in England in the nineteenth and twentieth centuries, the central idea that contracts should be written and signed found its way into the legal systems of the United States and of other former colonies of the British Empire. Here it has been a bug-bear to those who wish to develop online forms of contractual agreements.[83]

It has been suggested that the passing of the Statute of Frauds reflected the uncertainty of property rights after the upheavals of the Civil Wars, the Cromwellian dictatorship and the restoration of the monarchy, in the middle of the seventeenth century.[84] Alternatively, it might have been a reaction to the confusion over property rights after the Great Fire of London, when so many deeds had been destroyed. The general creation of written records would help to stabilize ownership without the creation, suggested by some, of a central registry. The latter was seen as a possible means of levying a land tax, or other forms of confiscation, and threatened the fees that lawyers could make out of the contemporary complexity of property rights.[85] However, the enactment of similar laws in France, Germany and Italy, in the same period may indicate other, still broader, forces at work here.[86]

It might be argued that since the lower orders in the early modern period had little property, they did not need to sign their names. However, this probably underestimates the extent to which even the poor were expected to engage with documents. As noted above, depositions in court had to be authenticated in some fashion, as did other documents, such as apprentices' indentures of servitude at the beginning of their yearly term of the contract. Similarly, under Hardwicke's Marriage Act of 1753 (26 Geo. II, c.33), entries in the parish registers relating to marriages were supposed to be signed by both the bride and groom. As already noted, however, many working-class men, and especially women, could only make a mark on marriage registers well into the Victorian period.

The taking of general oaths, an element of formal citizenship, was also a feature of the early modern period. Thus, in the aftermath of the Gunpowder Plot, anyone over the age of 18 suspected of being a Roman Catholic had to take an oath of allegiance to the effect that James I was the rightful King, and that the Pope had no right to depose him. It ended:

I do make this recognition and acknowledgment heartily, willingly and truly, upon the true faith of a Christian: so help me God. Unto which oath so taken, the said person shall subscribe his or her name or mark.[87]

During the Civil Wars, Parliament drew up the Solemn League and Covenant in September 1643 to secure the allegiance of citizens to the parliamentary cause. The Covenant, to be sworn by all males over 16 years of age, began:

> We noblemen, barons, knights, gentlemen, citizens, burgesses, ministers of the Gospel, and commons of all sorts in the kingdoms of England, Scotland and Ireland, by the providence of God living under one King, and being of one reformed religion . . . enter into a mutual and solemn league and covenant, wherein we all subscribe, and each one of us for himself, with our hands lifted up to the most high God, do swear, ...

Those taking the Covenant undertook to preserve the reformed religion, to extirpate Popery and prelacy (i.e. church government by bishops), and to defend the liberties of the kingdoms, to the 'encouragement to the Christian Churches groaning under or in danger of the yoke of Anti-Christian tyranny'.[88] Parliamentary commissioners, and ministers favourable to Parliament in south-east and central England, secured subscription to the Covenant. Although subscribing to the Covenant did not necessarily imply signing, or appending one's mark to it, this appears to have been how it was understood at the time.[89] At the Church of St Margaret's Lothbury in the City of London, for example, church wardens superintended the swearing-in of the parishioners. First the men of the parish 'with uplifted hands' swore, and signed the parish register. They were followed by the women of the parish, although the Covenant did not require this.[90] Plainly, signing, or at least making one's mark before witnesses, could be of fundamental constitutional importance.

However, the relative inability of most Englishmen to use a seal, or sign their name, in the early modern period, may have been a contributory factor to the very high levels of litigation noted in Chapter 3. Most of the vast number of credit transactions undertaken in the period were not written down but were witnessed orally by the neighbours and friends who were present. The procedure in the exchange of oral credit was ritualistic, and was already well established by the thirteenth century. Commonly a penny, or a larger amount, sometimes called a 'hansel', would be paid 'in hand' or 'in earnest' to set a seal on a transaction, and religious oaths were sworn.[91] This must have left considerable scope for disputes, and reneging on agreements. This may explain why more formal credit instruments – the bill obligatory, bill of debt or bond – were developed by merchants for long-range transactions. These were sealed documents which typically combined acknowledgements of debt, with an undertaking to settle them, and contained the names of the parties, the amount of the debt, the date or dates for repayment. Such documents were often assigned to others by endorsements on the back, so that the assignee took the place of the assignor, and the instruments became means of circulating credit. Moreover, merchants often acknowledged debts with 'bills of hand', or promissory notes, that were open documents and merely signed. Increasingly, the principal financial instrument used in inland banking was the inland bill of exchange – an unconditional order in writing, addressed by one person to another, signed by the person giving it, requiring the person to whom it was addressed to pay on demand, or at a fixed date, a certain sum of money to the bearer, or to a specified person. This usage can still be seen in the wording on the front of the modern British bank note, 'I promise to pay the bearer on demand the sum of . . .', with the signature of the chief cashier of the Bank of England.[92]

Despite the greater use of the signature in the early modern period, it was still possible to steal someone's legal identity through forgery. Indeed, the eighteenth century seems to have been as concerned by this threat to the identity of the juridical person as the public today is about 'identity theft'. The precise scope of what under the English common law was considered forgery was not generally agreed in the early modern period. However, a statute passed in 1562, 'An Act against forgers of false deeds and writings' (5 Eliz. I, c.14), prohibited the forgery of publicly recorded, officially sealed documents relating to the title of land. In a major expansion of the law's coverage, a legal decision of 1726 laid down that a false endorsement on an unsealed private document was indictable both under the Elizabethan statute and at common law (*Rex v. Ward*, 92 Eng. Rep. 451 (K. B. 1726)).[93] Writing half a century later, William Blackstone in his *Commentaries* pointed to several contemporary statutes relating to the forgery of bills of exchange (2 Geo. II, c.35; 2 Geo. II, c.22), and declared that 'there is now hardly a case possible to be conceived wherein forgery, that tends to defraud, whether in the name of a real or fictitious person, is not made a capital crime.'[94] The pillory, fines and imprisonment were the penalties in those rare cases that were not subject to capital punishment.[95]

Bank of England notes were a favourite target of the eighteenth-century forger, the most notorious examples perhaps being the work of Charles Price in the 1780s. Price not only engraved plates for reproducing the notes and the relevant signatures, but had his own paper works for producing watermarked paper. 'Old Patch', so called because of the eye-patch he wore as a disguise, was eventually caught, and hung himself in Bridewell Prison in 1786. His case was a *cause célèbre* of the period, and the subject of popular works such as *An Authentic Account of Forgeries and Frauds of Various Kinds Committed by That Most Consummate Adept in Deception, Charles Price, Otherwise Patch . . .*, published in the year of his death.[96] However, the demise of Patch did not staunch the flow of forged currency, especially given the Bank of England's increasing issue of paper money during the French Revolutionary and Napoleonic Wars.[97] In 1819 the issue of a one-pound note, consisting of a simple pen and ink inscription on ordinary white paper, led to a vast wave of forgery, and over the next seven years large numbers of forgers were arrested, and sentenced to death.[98]

A flavour of the precarious nature of identification via signatures in the late eighteenth century can be obtained from an examination of a few of the forgery cases brought to the Old Bailey. Thus, in April 1777 Mary Thomas was accused of forging a promissory note for the payment of £50 purporting to be drawn by Francis Tutte, a clergyman. Mary Thomas owed Thomas Blades, an upholsterer and cabinet maker of St James' in London, £100 for household furniture, and promised to give him £10 if he would discount the note for her. Blades suspected the note, 'there being so many forgeries about'. He showed it to a neighbour, Richard Atkinson, who confronted Thomas and 'told her he rather suspected it, because the signature of the note was not like the hand of a gentleman'. Thomas tried to talk her way out of this by claiming that, 'Gentlemen you know frequently write very bad; it is done in haste.' Anderson replied, 'Madam, you will pardon me, there is a deal of care taken in the writing of it; but it is done by a very bad writer; it appears to me to be the hand of a lady.' Seemingly, many women were not proficient signers, although they plainly recognized the importance of this technique of personal identification. Thomas was subsequently found guilty and sentenced to death.[99]

Similarly, in the trial of John Francis for forgery on 10 September 1783, a still more complicated chain of events was revealed. Francis knew that another John Francis was a carpenter's mate aboard *HMS Panther*, and that he was owed prize money – his share of the value of an enemy ship captured by the *Panther*. The first Francis forged a letter of attorney so that he could receive the prize money due to the second, signing the letter with his own signature. According to William Thomas, an attorney's clerk who had helped to draw up the letter of attorney, when he went with Francis to Mr Ommanney's counting house to hand in the letter (presumably Francis did not want to go in himself):

I told . . . [Mr Ommanney] . . . my business, he said, money due to John Francis, on board the *Panther*, why, he was paid two days ago; I shewed him the power of attorney, and he asked me where John Francis was, I told him he was at the door, I beckoned to him, and he came in; then Mr. Ommanney asked him if his name was John Francis, he said yes, was you carpenter's mate on board the *Panther*, he said yes; then Mr. Ommanney asked him where he was born, he said Bristol; upon which Mr. Ommanney said that would not do, for John Francis was born in Ireland. A seaman happened to come in, who had been on the *Panther*, and he said, he was not the John

Francis that was on board the *Panther*. I had turned my back, and was looking at the almanack, and the man slipped away, he was presently brought back.

When Ommanney was questioned by the court he noted that he had a John Francis on his books, 'Yes, there is such a name in my prize list, which is the proper man's signature.' The false Francis was thus caught out by not knowing the relevant information in the navy records (place of birth), having the wrong signature and through eyewitness testimony. Francis was also sentenced to death.[100]

Plainly, the replacement in the early modern period of the seal by the signature as the main form of validation for legal documents did not provide a foolproof form of identification for juridical persons. Just as new forms of documents and contracts have raised fundamental questions about identification online in the contemporary world, so the development of new instruments of commerce in the early modern period placed a strain on the techniques for identification. An important difference is, perhaps, that forgery was the early modern bank's problem, while contemporary identity fraud is now the problem of the customer of the bank. This shift, from ensuring identification as the responsibility of the vendor to the responsibility of the juridical person, is perhaps just one more example of the ability of commercial organizations to outsource their risk.[101] These developments will be considered in more detail in Chapter 9.

NAMES AND NAMING IN THE EARLY MODERN PERIOD

The signature as a form of identification presupposes fixed and stable names. Today the name is one of the standard means of linking people to databases and official documentation, and is always part of tokens of authoritative identification. Credit cards, driving licences, passports, identity cards, membership cards, and so on, almost always carry this indispensable item of identity. However, the use of fixed, two-part, names is actually rather unusual, since in many cultures names can change from context to context, and over time. Individuals can even have different names at each stage in the life cycle – infancy, childhood, adulthood, parenthood and old age – as well as in death. Fixed names, it has been claimed, reflect the influence of the State.[102] James C. Scott, in his widely acclaimed *Seeing Like a State*, has gone as far as to argue that the standard name underpins state control:

> The invention of permanent, inherited patronyms was, after the administrative simplification of nature (for example, the forest) and space (for example, land tenure), the

last step in establishing the necessary preconditions of modern statecraft. In almost every case it was a state project designed to allow officials to identify, unambiguously, the majority of its citizens. Tax and tithe rolls, property rolls, conscription lists, censuses, and property deeds recognized in law were inconceivable without some means of fixing an individual's identity and linking him or her to a kin group.[103]

Certainly, the *Song of the Husbandman*, probably of the early fourteenth century, depicts the beadles collecting taxes from the peasants 'by authority of an Exchequer writ', and telling them that, 'You are written in my list, as you know very well.'[104] However, the stabilization of the name in England has always been, in fact, rather precarious, despite the fact that its use in official systems dates back to the medieval period. Indeed, in England the insistence that people should have a fixed standard name had little basis in common law.

The development of the Christian/surname structure of modern English names was certainly a feature of the medieval period. In Domesday Book most subtenants did not have a second name, but by the twelfth century most of the elite, lay and clerical, did. At the old Anglo-Saxon capital of Winchester before the Norman Conquest, 55 per cent of the town's citizens did not have a second name. By 1100 to 1150, however, about 70 per cent of citizens had a 'surname', and a survey in 1285 showed only one person without a second name. Much the same could be said of the peasantry. In 1100 a list of the tenants of the Abbey of St Edmund at Bury St Edmunds shows that half had only a single name, yet a century later 69 per cent of the tenants had two. By 1300 the vast majority of people had first and second names.[105]

However, as Dave Postles has pointed out, before 1350 'surnames' among both men and women of the lowest social orders were really 'bynames' – ascriptions made by the local community. They were what people were called by their neighbours in the form of nicknames – not a personal affirmation of identity, or a state imposition, but communal ascriptions. These could be disciplinary and regulatory, to condemn transgressive acts, or to confirm marginalization, as well as to identify people.[106] It was not only the State that sought to control people. Such bynames in the early medieval period could be derived from various characteristics, as well as the usual place or occupational names. These included the following:

personal character, for example, Parlebien ('speak well' – loquacious as much as articulate), Sanscor ('heartless'), Maufesour ('wrong doer');
clothes, for example, Blakhod ('black hood'), Blakhat ('black hat'), Shorthose, PeDargent ('silver cloth');

bodily characteristics, for example, Burreheved (red-head), Beaupel ('fine skin'), Wythals ('white neck'), Belebuche ('fine mouth'), Hareberd ('grey beard'), Crocbayne ('crooked-leg');

crimes, for example, Coupgrayne ('cut corn'), Pickpese ('pick purse');

violence and anger, for example, Shakedager ('shake dagger'), Tempersnaype, Brekedore;

and sex and love, for example, Brekehert, Longtail, Strokehose, Swetabedde, Loveswete.[107]

Among the latter category one might include the highly suggestive name of 'Shakespeare'.

Far too many of such names given in documents seem to be too whimsical or personal to be created by bureaucrats, as Scott sometimes implies. R. A. McKinley suggests that emulation of those higher up in society, and the need to distinguish people as the range of possible Christian names declined sharply in the period, led to the adoption of nicknames as surnames by the lower orders themselves.[108] By the seventeenth century, for example, between one-quarter and one-fifth of all the male poor, that is those not paying the hearth tax, were called John, and many of the rest were called Thomas or William. These names made up between 40 and 50 per cent of the first names of such men.[109] However, the greater need for identification in official documents must surely have encouraged most people themselves to use their ascribed bynames as surnames, if only to avoid paying fines, or being taxed twice. Rather than being simply a 'state project' designed to control subjects, the surname may have had its origins in peasant society, and then been co-opted by the State for its own purposes. The shift from nicknames to family names may, of course, have reduced the ability of a woman to have a second name unique to herself, rather than depending on taking that of her husband.

In practice, records in the Tudor and early Stuart periods show that names were not always fixed, known, or given in a modern form. Postles, for example, points to the financial accounts of Ipswich of the 1560s, which frequently recorded payments to men called 'Palmer the plumer', 'Cutberd the scav-ell man', 'Martin the musician', 'Harpam the pynner', 'Smythe the laborer', 'Becket the carpenter', 'Clarke the mason', 'King the thatcher' and 'Smithe the brewer'. Similarly, when Thomas Ansloe of Liverpool was presented for baking without the licence or freedom of the town, the records qualified him as 'called otherwyse Thomas the Baker', presumably because he was usually so addressed by the local inhabitants.[110] The use of aliases was also not uncommon, and not necessarily suspicious. Some *aliases*, Postles argues, may have simply been variants of a surname: Thomas Caksey *alias* Coksey *alias* Cookes, of Rowley Regis, victualler; Laurence Conway *alias* Cowley, late of Yoxall, victualler; William Cutter *alias* Cutler, late of Sedgeley, collier; and Henry Kester *alias*

Christofer, of Swinford Regis, yeoman.[111] Such vagaries may not have caused as many problems to officers under the Crown, such as the constable or overseer of the poor, as Scott has suggested,[112] since they were members of the local community under the decentralized forms of English governance at this period.[113]

However, Catherine Cotterel 'alias Irish Kate alias Catherine Irise alias Twford', a 'person of light fame' indicted at the Old Bailey in January 1685 for stealing 15 guineas from a fellow servant, was probably using aliases for nefarious purposes.[114] Indeed, the London underworld of the seventeenth century seems to have been awash with roguish nicknames designed to obscure identities and crime.[115] Similarly, according to the Essex Session Rolls of Midsummer 1587, Enoch Garrett had visited the wife of a man called Church in High Easter, contending that her husband had sent him to collect money. Garrett had changed his name to John Wyllcocke. He had previously enacted the same subterfuge to extract money from Byrd's wife, declaring himself then to be named John Wawker. Reverting to John Wyllcocke, he illicitly collected rent in the district. For another fraudulent purpose, he used the name John Willson.[116] In these cases, the existence of enclosed communities may have made it easier for itinerants to assume new identities at will, rather than creating a face-to-face society where everyone was known. As with Perkin Warbeck, a name, whether official or unofficial, might be no guide to someone's 'true' identity.

However, changing one's name in England was not in itself a crime. As already noted in the case of John Stonehouse, English common law recognized that a person might take any surname he or she pleased, provided that this was not done for a fraudulent purpose, or in order to deceive and inflict pecuniary loss on another. As long as the person persuaded the public to adopt and use the name he or she preferred, a change of surname was perfectly legal, and this seems to be true of first names as well. Officially enrolling a change of name by deed poll enhanced the legal standing of the new name, but was by no means a necessity.[117] This was rather different to the situation in France, which saw a progressive rigidification of names in the modern period. As in England, French bynames were converted into hereditary family names in the later Middle Ages. Under the *ancien regime* it was possible in practice to change one's name, as long as it was not for the purposes of fraud, although the use of official names in documents, and the use of extracts from birth registers as a means of proving identification, created problems if one did so. During the Revolutionary and Napoleonic periods the French State moved to assert its control of the name. Various pieces of legislation laid down that no citizen could take a name other than his or her 'true' name, which was that which he or she received at birth. The name became an 'institution de police', and all public functionaries were prohibited from using names other than official ones in documents. Even today, change of name is only permitted in France via an official state procedure of authorization.[118] In the naming of citizens, as in so much else, one can see the French belief in an identity through the state, as opposed to the English belief in an identity outside the state. As will be noted below, however, the English practice of *laissez faire* in naming practices has shifted to a position nearer that of the French in the recent past.

At the beginning of the early modern period, the Christian/surname may have been given greater fixity through the introduction of parish registers. In 1538, Thomas Cromwell, Henry VIII's vicar-general, sent a series of instructions to the bishops of the Church in England. These included Protestant-inspired injunctions to parish priests on such things as the teaching of the rudiments of the faith to the people; preaching scripture; guarding against superstitious ceremonies; and the placing of an English Bible in each church. However, there were also instructions as to the keeping of registers recording the baptisms, weddings and funerals of men and women at which the clergy officiated. This was part of the process by which the medieval Catholic Church was brought under the control of the Tudor monarchs. The injunction respecting registration was repeated, and penalties for neglect introduced, by an Act of 1597 (39 Eliz. I, c.18). This also ordered that transcripts of the registers should be sent annually to a diocesan registrar. These 'bishops' transcripts' are now held at diocesan registry offices.[119] In theory, the registers preserved a record of the full names given to individuals at baptism and death. In December 1538, Cromwell was forced to issue a circular to justices of the peace denying rumours that parish registration was for the purpose of taxation. He stated that the real reason for its introduction was to aid the identification of juridical persons and citizen, or as he put it, 'for the avoiding of sundry strifes, processes and contentions rising upon age, lineal descent, title of inheritance, legitimation of bastardy, and for knowledge whether any person is our subject or no'.[120] Cromwell may have been being dishonest here, but given the turnover of local populations noted above it is difficult to see how the registers could be used for raising taxes.

Parish registration certainly placed individuals in their family and social settings. Juridical persons were, after all, not social atoms, since they often had property rights because of their lineage. Baptismal registers frequently mentioned the names of parents (or at least the father), and marriage registers the names of the bride and groom, and sometimes witnesses to the event. These records were essential for establishing the lines of descent upon which the right to bear arms, and the ownership of inherited property, depended. The first report of the Commission on Real Property of 1829 claimed, for example, that,

'Since the visitations of the heralds have ceased . . . [evidence of pedigree] . . ., as far as public documents are concerned, has depended entirely upon parish registers of marriages, baptisms and burials.'[121] Similarly, the 1833 Select Committee on Parochial Registration, whose deliberations led to the introduction of civil registration of births, marriages and deaths in 1837, saw parochial registration mainly as a means of underpinning property rights.[122]

Simon Szreter has argued that the relative security of property in England resulting from parochial registration facilitated the economic developments that are associated with the Industrial Revolution.[123] However, it does not appear that the registers and bishop's transcripts were always preserved properly,[124] or written up in times of crisis such as the 1640s and 1650s.[125] In addition, as already noted, names in England were not necessarily fixed. Nor was such registration unknown in Continental Europe. In 1563 the Council of Trent commanded all catholic priests to keep written records of all baptisms and marriages. In 1567, the Council of Constance obliged priests to keep detailed records of their parishes by entering baptisms, Holy Communions, marriages and deaths in separate registers. Confessions made before Easter were to be in a separate register. Two years later, the provincial synod required three general registers – the first to contain the names of all parish members, together with their ages and status; the second to record all decedents and those who had moved away; and the third to list all newborn babies and immigrants.[126] Nevertheless, the overall quality, and national and temporal coverage, of the English parish registers was such that they must have had an important impact on the fixity of property rights as Szreter suggests.

Nevertheless, the uncertainty over naming in England, led the Utilitarian philosopher Jeremy Bentham to advocate a radically new system in the early nineteenth century. Bentham was exercised by the need to 'facilitate the recognition and finding of individuals', since, 'Everything which increases the facility of recognising and finding individuals, adds to the general security.' However, he believed that in England, 'the indication arising from a name is vague; suspicion is divided amongst a multitude of persons; and the danger to which innocence is exposed, becomes the security of crime.' He advocated instead giving everybody a unique proper name made up of the family name, a single baptismal name, and the place and date of birth ('Edward Higgs Lancaster151153'). Moreover, alluding to the common practice of sailors printing their names on their wrists in case of shipwreck, he suggested that the entire population should have their names so tattooed. Bentham recognized that the English public would not stomach this, especially after the French Revolution, during which many persons owed their safety to disguise. However, he hoped that education, and the use of 'great examples' might bring people round. He hit on the visionary, or perhaps rather dotty, idea of getting the aristocracy to tattoo their titles on their foreheads, through which 'these marks would become associated with the ideas of honour and power.'[127] The thought of the members of the contemporary House of Lords so adorned is perhaps amusing, although perhaps less so in an age of DNA databases.

CONCLUSION

In his usual, idiosyncratic manner, Bentham's discussion raises some issues to which the present work will return. The first is the difficulty of identifying individuals in the absence of a unique identifier, which has led elsewhere to the development of such artefacts as the universal US and French social security numbers. Apart from the comparatively short periods in the twentieth century when it had a National Registration system, there has been no British equivalent for the general identification of the public. Why should this be the case? One might be able to explain the lack of such a requirement in the early modern context because of the localized nature of the state and market economy. There would be less likelihood of confusion over two 'Edward Higgs' in a parish (although they might be father and son[128]), than over the hundreds of citizens with such names who might exist in a national welfare system. However, this still does not explain the absence of a unique identifier in modern Britain. The second issue that Bentham's ideas highlight is the extent to which the English have always rejected the use of the body to identify 'respectable' citizens, at least until the last decades of the twentieth century. This appears to have been because identification through the body was associated with the 'non-respectable', the deviant, the foreign and the alien. The identification of the poor and the deviant in the early modern period is the subject of the next chapter.

5

Identifying the Poor 'Citizen' and the Deviant in Early Modern England

INTRODUCTION

The term 'citizen' is a very problematic one to use with respect to the poor in England in the early modern period, carrying as it does today the connotation of equal, and irrevocable, rights and obligations held by all at the level of the nation-state. The English poor were not 'citoyen' in the sense understood by the American and French Revolutions of the late eighteenth centuries. They were certainly not all eligible to vote in local and national elections, for example, and, as already noted, this was reflected in the means by which electors were identified. But people do seem to have believed that they had certain rights and liberties before the law, and processes such as the signing of the Solemn League and Covenant would have reinforced this. At a very minimum, they recognized the tactical efficacy of appealing to royal statutes or proclamations, which were of course read out in church, when protesting about the high price of bread, or 'popish plots', or in the defence of 'liberties'.[1] It was also believed by the poor that they had a 'right' to relief under the Poor Laws if they could prove that they belonged to a particular place, although this could be disputed by the local officials responsible for implementing the system.[2] It is in this more restricted, localized, and inconsistent, sense that the term 'citizen' is used here. As with the juridical person and the elector, the poor citizen in this period was not simply an abstract 'individual' by virtue of his or her existence, but was situated in a network of rights and obligations determined by place and custom. It was important to be not just 'Edward Higgs' but 'Edward Higgs of Lancaster'. However, the existence of such rights and obligations still required that citizens should be identified in some manner, and this was done through a mixture of communal knowledge and documentary proof. The deviant, on the other hand, was not a citizen, and was identified in a very different manner.

IDENTIFYING THE WELFARE CLAIMANT UNDER THE POOR LAWS

The 'Poor Laws' is a term that covers a series of parliamentary statutes passed from the early sixteenth century onwards that regulated the treatment of the indigent poor at the local level. In essence, the Poor Law system, as it was gradually elaborated over time, laid down that the 'respectable poor', who could prove that they had a 'settlement', or 'belonged', in a parish, should be given welfare relief paid out of a parish-based tax – the poor rate. People proved a settlement in a parish via birth, marriage, the ownership or renting of property, paying parish rates, or residence and employment in a place for a stipulated period.[3] Women, of course took their husband's place of settlement on marriage. However, the poor who wandered about the countryside without any fixed abode, or means of support, were stigmatized as vagrants, and could be sent back to their place of settlement, whipped, branded and even executed as deviants. The whole system was administered by the parish overseers of the poor, drawn from the wealthier inhabitants of the parish, and supervised by the gentry-magistrates, the justices of the peace.[4] The Poor Laws were merely one element in what might be called an early modern 'mixed economy' of welfare, taking its place alongside the support of kin, the 'kindness of neighbours' and the charity of the wealthy.[5] Indeed, up to the late Elizabethan period parish relief was still relatively small scale, generally unsystematic, and often confined to market towns and the larger rural parishes. Nevertheless it expanded over time, and the system was probably operational in about a third of England's 10,000 parishes by the 1650s, and was well on the way to universal implementation by the third quarter of the seventeenth century.[6]

Contrary to some accounts,[7] the Poor Laws did not stop migration, but allowed local communities, like so many miniature republics, to pick and choose who they wished to remain within their borders. Tolerant, even supportive, attitudes towards immigration prevailed in respect of artisans such a blacksmiths, wheelwrights and of apprentices in trades where there were shortages of local skills. Migration was accepted, and even encouraged, in the textile areas of Leicestershire and Gloucestershire, for example, and by the late eighteenth century increasing arrangements for the payment of relief to people with a settlement but resident outside the parish facilitated movement.[8] The 1662 Settlement Act (14 Cha. II, c.12) also spoke of the need to allow people 'to go into any county, parish, or place, to work in time of harvest, or at any time to work at any other work'. It was only those who were likely to become, or had become, a burden on the poor rates that were treated as deviant vagrants.

All these traditional and new forms of relief depended upon local communal knowledge. Indeed, those who drafted the Poor Laws assumed that English local communities were, or ought to be, *gemeinschaft*, with self-contained, settled populations that were intimately known to each other.[9] The 'deserving poor' had moral attributes that could be known intimately by the overseers of the poor, whose job indeed was to oversee. The recipients of relief had to be God-fearing, industrious and thrifty, sober, deferent and careful not to harbour potential charges on the Poor Law in their homes. Failure to adhere to these tenets of righteousness might mean the inability to get relief, or its removal. One had to perform the role of 'deserving' pauper, as well as prove one's entitlement through identification as a person with a settlement. Given that poverty was constantly changing over the life cycle – greatest when there were large numbers of young children and in old age – overseers had to maintain constant vigilance over the poor.[10] Paupers were often the neighbours, tenants and employees of the overseers and Justices of the Peace (JPs), so their family circumstances would have been known informally.[11]

Knowledge of the poor was also gained through the house visits recommended by published works such as *An Ease for Overseers of the Poore* (1601). As early as 1585, for example, the clergymen and 'ancients' of the town of Dedham in Essex made quarterly inspections of the households of those residents who were in poverty, to distinguish between 'the miserable estate of those that wante' and 'the naughtie disposition of disordered persons', and to make provision accordingly. Sometimes overseers drew up censuses or listings of the poor, supplemented by lists of immigrants, and of other strangers. *An Ease for Overseers of the Poore* actually provided a model for such a listing. For each household, overseers were to collect the following details: name and address of occupants; state of health; usual employment; weekly earnings; employment status; those fit for apprenticeship; those who boarded orphans and others; weekly allowances; and those licensed to beg. Such forms of local enumeration were carried over into the organization of the early nineteenth-century censuses.[12] But in general, most of these investigations into the circumstances and eligibility of the poor proceeded by oral interview, and so are lost to the historian's view.[13]

Information supplied by the poor during examinations into their rights to settlement undertaken by the overseers and magistrates could be veritable auto-biographies. In April 1809, for example, Henry Foulds was examined before a justice of the peace in Nottinghamshire:

> This Examinant, upon Oath, saith, That he is about the Age of Thirty Eight Years, and that he was born, as he hath been informed, and verily believes, in the Parish of Old Daulbey in the County of Leicester of Parents legally settled at Shelford in the County of Nottingham. That when about seventeen years of Age he was hired to Mr Simpson of Saxelby in the County of Leicester aforesaid for one year and served him accordingly. That at Martinmas following was hired to Mr John Cooper of Shelford aforesaid and served him Eighteen Moneths. That in the Month of December fol-lowing he went to Work at Grantham Canal. That in the year 1800 he went to Great Grimsby in Lincolnshire and Married Fanny his now Wife which gave him a Vote for Great Grimsby aforesaid, and there Rented a House. [14]

However, documentation also helped to underpin parts of this elaborate wel-fare system. The parochial registers provided information about baptisms, marriages and burials, which could be used to solve all manner of practical disputes about who had a settlement in a parish.[15] Steve Hindle notes that it was not unusual for differences between parishes over the identity of paupers, and who was liable to relieve them, to be settled by a search of the relevant parish registers. Thus, the protracted dispute over the maintenance of Jane Smith and her son Peter, which preoccupied the Prescot vestrymen and Lancashire jus-tices in the late 1640s, was only settled in 1649 when the churchwardens spent 8p on a journey to Farnworth 'to know the age of Peter Smith' by consulting the parish register.[16] As late as 1841, an overseer of Chewton Mendip in Somerset was writing to his opposite number in Daventry, with respect to an identifica-tion for settlement purposes, noting, 'Having examined some of the oldest and most intelligent inhabitants, they have never heard the name here, and having likewise referred to the Parish Registers, I find that there never was any entry of the surname Eales.'[17] In this manner, a system established to protect property rights expanded through 'mission creep' to become a crucial underpinning of welfare systems. As will be discussed below, much the same was to happen in the case of civil registration after it was introduced in England in the early nineteenth century.

Such documentary forms of identification were made mobile in the eight-eenth century in the form of the settlement certificate. This was a paper, signed by the magistrates, which named a migrant and indicated that he or she had a

Poor Law settlement in a particular parish. This guaranteed that the officers and ratepayers of the parish of settlement would relieve the pauper, whether that was in the parish of settlement itself or, increasingly as the decades passed, in the parish where the pauper resided. Settlement certificates were intended to be delivered to the parish officers as soon as a migrant came into the parish. Sometimes, however, paupers carried them with them to the new parish, showed the certificates to the parish officers, and then kept them themselves.[18] As late as 1818, for example, one finds John Hall writing a heartfelt plea to the overseers of the poor at Chelmsford, Essex:

> Sir
>
> My Present Occation Obliges me to Send you this Letter for I have No Work to do at this Time & I have Two Lads at home have Nothing To do and What to do We Cannot Tell So Sir I hope you Will take our Present Distress into Consideration for We Cannot Get Bread Sir I Am A Certificate Pirson to Chelmsford So I hope you Will Send a answer To my Petition or I Shall Be Obliged to go this Parrish for We are In Great Want Sir I am your Humble Petitioner John Hall.[19]

One could see this as a form of internal passport, although it was intended to aid migration, rather than to restrict it.

A somewhat different form of documentation was the 'beggar's licence', authorizing a person to beg within the parishes that made up a hundred or wapentake. These were mostly to be found under the Poor Law system prior to the 1601 Poor Relief Act (43 Eliz. I, c.2), and declined thereafter. Such documents identified an individual as a pauper, with the geographical and moral context that gave that status a meaning. The licence usually identified the individual and his or her parish; and provided a brief description of the reason for their poverty, and by implication the deservingness of their case. It then permitted him or her to 'aske gather receive and take the almes charetie [and] devocion at the house or houses of the inhabitants'. At the same time 'willinge and requiringe' householders and parish officers 'not to molest or trouble' them 'but to bestowe . . . such almes as in their discretion might seem good'. According to Hindle, the begging licence, remaining as it did in the hands of the poor person, conferred eligibility for, and arguably even entitlement to, the charity of his or her neighbours.[20] Linked to such licences were certificates allowing the unemployed, those left destitute by fire, shipwrecked sailors or maimed soldiers, to travel in search of jobs, home ports or places of settlement.[21] There were also a number of related documents that the non-elite were expected to carry around with them in the early modern period. The Apprentices Act of 1536 (28 Hen. VIII, c.5) exempted servants from its full rigor for one month after the end of their service but required them to obtain a testimonial stating the date of their departure. The 1562 Statute of Articifers (5 Eliz. I, c.4) provided that those who did not carry passports would be treated as vagabonds. An Act of 1572 stated that criminals leaving gaol were to have a licence from two justices of the peace permitting them to beg for their fees on their way home.[22]

Somewhat similar in form to the beggar's licence, but rather different in intent, was the vagrant's passport. Whereas the licensed beggar was in some sense seen as deserving, the passport-carrying vagrant was a deviant undergoing punishment. The passport ensured that those taken and punished as wandering vagabonds were returned to their place of settlement. According to Hindle:

> The pass took the form of a warrant, signed and sealed usually by two magistrates, giving the vagrant's name and parish of settlement; recording the location where he had been taken begging; and requiring the constables or tithingmen between that parish and the parish of settlement to conduct him on his way, relieving him as necessary as he passed. Finally it stipulated the period of time, usually a number of days, within which the journey should be made. The vagrant would be liable to punishment only if he exceeded the specified time period, or strayed from the appointed course.[23]

The vagrant was to show the passport to the constable of a parish en route to his or her place of settlement. The constable was supposed to conduct the vagrant to the next parish, relieving his or her needs as appropriate. He would then hand the vagrant over to the next relevant parish official, and endorse the passport. This, in theory, would continue until the vagrant was returned to his or her place of settlement, although many parish officials do not appear to have bothered to endorse the passport, or to have conducted the offender to the next constable.[24] In London in the 1630s, 6,000 printed passports were being issued to constables every year.[25] Here indeed was a form of identity document that was created to constrain migration, although paradoxically it did so through facilitating movement back to where people 'belonged'.

Inevitably, the existence of such documents, which could give unfettered authority to beg and move about the countryside, was an invitation to forgery. According to Hindle counterfeit passes could be purchased almost anywhere from itinerant forgers equipped with pen, paper, ink and the plausible, or actual, names of country magistrates. In Essex in 1581 it was reported that a forger called Davy Bennett could counterfeit any magistrate's seal:

> [I]f he seeth it in waxe he will laye it [a]fore him and carve it out in woode very perfitely, and so he will do theer handes for that he wryteth sundrye handes and hath most commonly about him a little bage full of counterfeit seales.[26]

Similarly, in early Stuart Wiltshire, Henry Taverner, who made counterfeit passports for himself and others, carried with him 'a note of the names of the knights & justices of peace of sundry counties to know whose names might fitly be used of the same counties in his counterfeit passes'.[27] In the reign of James I, two vagabonds claimed that there were at least half a dozen counterfeiters working between Bristol and Salisbury, or about one every 10 miles. At this period passports cost between 6d and 1s, and some beggars carried more than one. A man taken begging in Salisbury in 1620 had two, one saying he was from Colchester and the other from Fetter Lane in London, although he was actually from Wotton-under-Edge in Gloucestershire.[28] London in the early modern period was, as one might expect, awash with fake licences.[29] The widespread use of various types of forged documents to facilitate travel around Continental Europe during the Renaissance has, of course, been revealed recently by the work of Valentin Groebner.[30] Thomas Harman, the Elizabethan moralist and author of the anti-vagabond tract *A Caveat for Common Cursitors*, believed it axiomatic that many supposedly shipwrecked sailors using begging licences were in fact 'fresh-water mariners', whose ships 'were drowned in the plain of Salisbury'. He claimed that their documents, some adorned with counterfeit Admiralty seals, were mostly forgeries.[31] Harman fulminated against the 'abominable, wicked, and detestable behaviour of all these rowsey, ragged rabblement of rakehells'.[32] However, how far they were doing anything very different to the aristocrats and gentry who falsely embellished their own pedigrees is questionable.

Another subcategory of forged documents were the counterfeit characters that servants supplied to prospective employers when applying for work. So widespread did this practice become, that in 1792 Parliament passed the Servants' Characters Acts (32 Geo. III, c.56), which was intended to suppress the production of such documents by:

> evil disposed persons being or pretending to be the master, mistress, retainer or superintendent of such servants, or by persons who have actually retained such servants in their respective service, contrary to truth and justice and to the peace and security of his Majesty's subjects.

The Act introduced fines for such practices, which seems positively mild given the draconian measures taken against forgery in the same period, and survived on the statute books until as late as 2008.[33]

Whereas the licence and the passport identified the poor person as an individual within the Poor Law system, other methods were used to place him or her within the general category of paupers. Most conspicuous among these was the parish badge, often consisting of the initial letters of the parish of settlement in red cloth, and worn on the shoulder in conformity with the stipulations of the 1697 Poor Law Act (9 Will. III, c.11). Any pauper who refused to wear the badge was, in theory, either to have their relief withdrawn, or to be whipped and committed to the bridewell for three weeks' hard labour.[34] As already noted, Groebner has revealed that the wearing of badges was, of course, widespread in early modern Europe, adorning the clothing of the bearers of public office, pilgrims, beggars and the members of differing armies.[35] However, whether the institution of badging in many eighteenth-century parishes represented a recognition of deserving status, a sort of parish livery, or a mark of shame to deter recourse to the Poor Law, is difficult to determine. Presumably this differed from place to place, and at differing times, depending on the outlooks and actions of the local Poor Law officials.[36] The role of badging as an identifier of the morally reprehensible raises the whole issue of the use of the body and outward show to identify the deviant in the early modern period, a subject that will be dealt with shortly.

IDENTIFICATION OF THE CORPSE

Historically, it has not only been the living that have been identified in England. Even the poor subjects of the Crown have also been the objects of acts of recognition when dead, although in such cases their designation as being a particular person has inevitably been a somewhat passive one. Most bodies in the early modern period were identified by the family and friends present at the death. However, in cases of sudden, or 'unnatural death', the process of identification was associated above all with the ancient institution of the coroner's inquest. The office of the coroner had been established in 1194, and throughout the Middle Ages the coroner could be ordered by the King to perform almost any duty of an administrative or inquisitorial nature within his 'bailiwick', either alone, or with the sheriff. However, holding inquests upon dead bodies, both male and female, even if they only comprised decayed bones with no flesh on them, was the duty that exercised the medieval coroner most frequently.[37] In the later medieval period many of his other duties were taken over by the justices of the peace, and the coroner was increasingly restricted to holding inquisitions on the dead.[38] In order to put the coroner above bribery, the qualification for the post was theoretically the possession of sufficient land to enable the postholder to take upon himself the degree of knighthood. A borough coroner needed no such qualifications by estate, residence, or otherwise, as long as he was a 'fit person'.[39]

In the early medieval period the reason for setting up the coroners' courts seems to have been partly financial, and partly political. Relatives of the dead had to present Englishry, that is, they had to swear that the dead person was English, rather than a member of the ruling Norman elite. If they could not do so, then the men of the neighbourhood incurred a *murdrum* fine. Such presentment for Englishry was only abolished for all cases in 1340. It would seem that the inquest was also an opportunity, in the time-honoured manner of medieval England, for the coroner to practice extortion in one form or another.[40] This explains why at its inception the qualifications for the post were based on social position rather than medical or legal expertise. Gradually, however, the inquest came to serve primarily as a means of preventing 'foul play'. According to the late thirteenth-century statute De Officio Coronatoris (4 Edw. I, c.1), if someone was slain it was the duty of the coroner to enquire of local people, 'whether they know where the person was slain, whether it were in any house, field, bed, tavern, or company, and if any and who were there'. If slain, 'in the fields, or in the woods and be there found', the coroner was to inquire, 'if the dead person were known or else a stranger; and where he lay the night before'. It was the duty of the person finding the body, the 'first finder', to raise the alarm, and the local township had to guard the dead body until the coroner's arrival. On being notified of such a death it was the responsibility of the coroner to go to view the body, and to summon a jury of 12 to 16 men from the locality to meet on a certain day. The 'first finder' showed the naked body to the coroner, who had the unpleasant duty of feeling it to look for wounds, bruises or signs of strangulation. The jurors at the inquest had to identify the body, and determine if the death had been caused feloniously, by misadventure or naturally, and if feloniously, whether by homicide or suicide. On obtaining the names of those who had committed the homicide from the jurors, the coroner had to order their arrest.[41]

Identification was always a subordinate part of this process, but provided an important function in an age when the extensive ceremonies associated with death – the tolling of bells, embalming the corpses of the wealthy, 'watching' of the corpse (sitting up with it), winding the corpse in its shroud, processing to the grave, the wearing of mourning black, the giving of doles or dinners by the rich – had important social and psychic functions.[42] The legal identification of the corpse was especially important because the classic authorities of English Law – Blackstone, Hawkins, Coke and Hale – all agreed that, for the most part, there was no property in corpses. Certainly under English Common Law there would appear to be no right of relatives to the ownership of the deceased, and the court or state had the final say in the disposition of the cadaver.[43]

Since the identification of the corpse in the early modern period depended on the dead person being known by the local community, rather than through any forensic or expert evidence, when the dead person was a stranger, he or she had to remain 'unknown'. The displacement of communal knowledge in the processes of identifying the dead, and the increasing importance of scientific expertise, was a feature of the modern period, and the subject of later sections of this book. Thus, the coroner's roll for Nottinghamshire in January 1555 records the inquest verdict that:

> About 11 a.m. on 20 Jan. unknown men assaulted and feloniously murdered another unknown man, dragged hime to some water called 'a comen yssue' near 'leekeclose hedge' and put him in the water. They struck him on the back of the head, giving him a mortal wound 2 inches long, half an inch wide and 1 inch deep, and on the front of the head, giving him another mortal wound 3 inches long, 2 and a half inches wide and a quarter of an inch deep. Bartholomew Lynton of Winthorpe, shepherd, a man of good reputation and standing, was the first finder of the unknown man on 20 Jan.[44]

The 'unknown' corpse was most frequently a feature of inquests held in districts bordering the sea, or through which large rivers flowed. Thus, out of the 2,047 deaths listed in the coroners' records for the coastal Suffolk hundred of St Etheldreda in the period 1757 to 1858, 129 (6.3 per cent) were of unknown adults, and 24 of unknown children (1.2 per cent). Almost all the unknown adults were drowned bodies 'washed ashore', while the children seem to have been mainly the victims of infanticide.[45] At Lyminster in Poling Hundred, Sussex, in March 1620, the jury informed the coroner that:

> About 8 a.m. on 14 March a river near the sea in Lyminster, which ebbed and flowed into the sea, threw a man, unknown to the jurors, who was wearing only 'a shirt' of linen of no value, onto the bank of the river dead. When, where or how he came to his death the jurors do not know.[46]

Such bodies were, of course, often unrecognizable through decomposition. This explains why fishermen wore tokens of their home parish to identify them – name-and-parish pendants, guernseys and garments with patterns unique to a particular community, and boots marked with initials. However, as already noted in Chapter 3, parish registers from inland places could also contain numerous references to the burial of 'unknown' strangers.

DEVIANTS

If juridical persons and the citizenry mainly identified themselves through the community and documentation, early modern deviants had identity ascribed to them through the marking of the body, or through the dissemination of information via official and commercial channels. In the latter case, the identity of the deviant was written on paper, in the former those in authority wrote an identity on the very skin of the wrong doer. As Michel Foucault argued in *Discipline and Punish*, the early modern criminal was not a person, he or she was a body that had rebelled against the authority of the sovereign. This 'outlaw' was to be physically punished in revenge by the State, rather than imprisoned. However, just as punishment was through the criminal body, so was identification.[47] As noted when discussing Sir Roger Tichborne's tattoo, the Christian West has always tended to regard the marking of the body for the purpose of identification as indicating infamy, drawing in part upon the biblical injunction in Leviticus 19.28, 'Ye shall not make any cuttings in your flesh for the dead, nor print any marks upon you: I am the Lord.' The Devil was, of course, supposed to identify the bodies of his followers with witches' 'marks', or 'teats'.[48]

It should not be surprising, therefore, that branding and ear-boring, as a means of marking the deviant status of the criminal, had been statutory punishments in England from at least the late fourteenth century. A labour statute of 1361 declared that fugitives were to be branded on the forehead with 'F' for 'falsity'. The Vagabonds Act of 1547 (1 Edw. VI, c.3) ordered that vagrants should be branded with a 'V' on their breast. Ear-boring was introduced in 1572, when a statute was passed requiring all vagabonds to be 'grievously whipped and burned through the gristle of the right ear with a hot iron'. By an Act of 1604, incorrigible rogues were to be 'branded in the left shoulder with a hot burning iron of the breadth of an English shilling with a great Roman "R" upon the iron'.[49] Suspect criminals were invariably stripped and searched for such marks on their bodies.[50] Such marking of the skin might be associated with other forms of mutilation. Thus, the seventeenth-century Puritan William Prynne, who was punished for writing pamphlets against Archbishop Laud, had his ears cut off and his nose slit, as well as being branded with 'SL' ('seditious libeler') on his cheeks.[51]

Similarly, convicts at the Old Bailey who successfully pleaded benefit of clergy, or were found guilty of manslaughter instead of murder, were branded on the thumb (with a 'T' for theft, 'F' for felon or 'M' for murder), so that they would be ineligible to receive such leniency again. The branding was a public affair, and took place in the courtroom at the end of the sessions in front of spectators. For a short period, between 1699 and January 1707, convicted thieves were branded on the cheek in order to increase the deterrent effect of the punishment, but this rendered them unemployable, and the practice reverted to branding on the thumb.[52] Such methods of criminal identification were also exported to the British colonies. The colonial East Jersey law codes of 1668 and 1675 laid down that a letter 'T' should be branded on the hand for burglary, and 'R' on the forehead for a second offence. Similarly, 'A' for adultery was also used as a mark in Puritan New England.[53] However, in line with the general shift noted by Michael Foucault from punishing the body to punishing the mind,[54] such disciplinary practices began to be phased out in the late eighteenth century. Branding as a punishment for those receiving benefit of clergy in England ended in 1779, and the last convict sentenced to branding at the Old Bailey received the sentence in 1789.[55] Much the same happened in France, where branding was outlawed in 1832, but seems to have already fallen out of use by at least 1809.[56] The practice was also being abandoned in Prussia and Austria in the early nineteenth century.[57]

As will be noted in the next chapter, as the marking of the body to place it into a deviant category declined, so the description of the individual deviant came to be given greater prominence. Identification shifted from being an outward categorical sign, to become a flow of unique information. This was to be an extension of the way in which, as already described, much detection had always been undertaken locally by the victims of crimes themselves, either through personal enquiries, or through the ancient institution of the hue and cry. This procedure had been instituted in 1285 by the Statute of Winchester (13 Edw. I, cc.1 and 4), which stipulated that anyone, either a constable or a private citizen, who witnessed a crime should cry out, and that others hearing the cry should join in the pursuit of the criminal. The hue and cry had to be kept up against the fleeing criminal from town to town and from county to county, until the felon was apprehended and delivered to the sheriff. By the early seventeenth century the physical pursuit across parish and county boundaries had often been replaced by the bureaucratic procedure of the issue of a written warrant of hue and cry to be circulated among law enforcement officers. Constables' accounts for Manchester in the period 1612 to 1631, list on average 12 issues of such warrants per year.[58] In London at the same date, court books were full of descriptions of wanted criminals.[59] Sir Francis Bacon claimed that the use of warrants was directly responsible for the rise in the number of thefts in the early seventeenth century, claiming that 'now hue and cries are of no consequence, only a little paper is sent up and down with a soft pace, whereas they should be prosecuted with horse and foot and hunted as a thief'.[60] The written warrant, designed to be passed from hand to hand, necessitated the introduction of the prose description of the wanted person.

By the late eighteenth century, the circulating warrant of hue and cry seems to have been in decline,[61] although standard formats could still be found in published works such as Richard Burns' *The Justice of the Peace, and Parish Officer* of 1770. This contains a draft 'Warrant to levy hue and cry on a robbery having been committed' to 'all constables and other officers, as well in the said county of Westmorland as elsewhere, to whom the execution hereof doth or shall belong'. It gives the name of the issuing justice of the peace and his place of jurisdiction, and describes the crime. The warrant then goes on to describe one of the men:

> [A] tall, strong man, and seemeth to be about the age of . . . years, is pitted in the face with the small pox, and hath the scar of a wound under his left eye, and had then on a dark brown riding coat, &c, and did ride upon a bay gelding with a star on his forehead . . . [The constables are commanded] . . . forthwith to raise the power of the towns within your several precincts, and to make diligent search therein, for the persons above described, and to make fresh pursuit and hue and cry after them from town to town, and from county to county, as well as by horsemen, as by footmen . . .

and bring them before the justices.[62]

IDENTIFYING THE ALIEN

Yet another group of people who were treated with suspicion by the English were, of course, foreigners or 'aliens'. The attitude of the Crown to such persons oscillated in the course of the medieval and early modern periods. The twelfth-century laws of the merchants of lower Lotharingia indicate the sorts of restrictions that foreign merchants laboured under in early medieval England. They were controlled in the way they could approach the port of London; how they could enter the port; the way they could unload their goods; what they could buy; and the procedures via which they could go outside London to trade. They were also not allowed to stay in London for more than 40 days. Although other foreign merchants might have had better terms, they were still restricted in their activities and length of sojourn.[63] In addition, the 1215 Lateran Council of the Church imposed new restrictions and disabilities on Jews in all countries, including the requirement for them to wear a yellow badge wherever they went, and in 1290 Edward I expelled all the Jews from England.[64] However, a charter of 1303, the Carta Mercatoria, relaxed the controls over many foreign merchants, and they could now trade in cities without restrictions on lodging, or 40 day time limits. During the reign of Richard II at the end of the fourteenth century, the distinction made was not between English and foreigner but between those who were loyal to the Crown and did homage, and those who did not. The foreigner was given full liberties as long as he swore fealty to the Crown, and dissociated himself from his countrymen.[65] However, in the Tudor and early Stuart periods, foreigners still faced numerous restrictions on their ability to work and trade. They were unable to own, inherit or bequeath real property; they could not bring legal actions related to real property; they were unable to vote or hold office; and they were required to pay double taxation. These disabilities were similar to those of the reign of Richard III, but were reimposed by statutes of 1523, 1529 and 1540.[66]

Such practices inevitably led to the compilation of documents listing aliens. One might note here the lists of the alien religious paying taxes to the Crown in the reign of Edward I and Edward III, and the lists of aliens paying the alien subsidy taxes granted by Parliament in 1440, 1442, 1449, 1453 and 1458.[67] In October 1571 Lord Burghley, Elizabeth I's Secretary of State, had directed an examination of all 'strangers', covering London (with 4,631 strangers), Colchester, Harwich, Ipswich, Yarmouth, Norwich, the Cinque Ports, Southampton and Boston.[68] In 1621 a commission was set up to study the statutes relating to aliens, and complaints from the English that they were being evaded. In July 1621 directions were given that the Commissioners should make a yearly account of all aliens resident in England. Restraints were put on those involved in the retail trades, and they were to submit to restrictions as to the number of servants and apprentices they could employ. Nevertheless, aliens had to pay the same taxes as English members of companies.[69] Similarly, the records of the Stuart secretaries of state in the State Paper Office contain a listing of French and other refugees who in 1622 were resident in St Martin's-le-Grand in London, or who were engaged in various stated trades in Canterbury, Maidstone, the Cinque Ports, Norwich and Colchester. Various lists were also created under Orders in Council of those Huguenot refugees who came into the country in the period 1678 to1688 during the 'troubles' preceding and immediately following the revocation by Louis XIV of the Edict of Nantes, which had granted the French Protestants a degree of toleration.[70] From a very early date, therefore, aliens were being recorded and listed, although one might query the actual effectiveness of such forms of identification. In this the English were doing nothing usual for the period, and still more elaborate forms of documentation for the recording of aliens could be found in Continental Europe.[71] As will be noted below, the penal nature of the treatment of aliens continued into the modern period, and spawned a whole array of identification techniques.

DISGUISE AND SUBTERFUGE AMONG THE POOR
IN EARLY MODERN ENGLAND

Given the importance of local familiarity and outward show in practices of identification, it should come as no surprise that bodily disguise played a signal role in those situations in the early modern period in which authority and status were contested. Modern protestors still attempt to disguise themselves in order to hide their identity from the police or security services, although their efforts seldom show the sort of symbolic inversions that were so frequent in the earlier period.[72] As already noted, the rich used disguise to subvert status, but poor used it to subvert power.

The tendency in the period to see binary opposites in everything, especially Good and Evil, or God and Satan, meant that the possibility of inversion was ever present.[73] Such inversions could act as a release valve for the pent-up emotions generated by the strict enforcement of social and political hierarchies, and were institutionalized in the concept of 'misrule', in which conventional forms of identification could be subverted, at least for a set time. Thus, the 'Lord of Misrule' or the 'Master of Revels' mocked established heraldry – George Ferrers, Henry VIII's Lord of Misrule had his own coat of arms (a hydra) and his own crest (a holly bush). He made state entries into London dressed in purple trimmed with ermine and braided with silver. Oxbridge colleges and wealthy collegiate churches had the 'boy bishops' – children dressed as ecclesiastics. In around 1500, Kings' College had a boy bishop dressed in a white wool coat, a scarlet gown with its hood furred with white ermine, fine knitted gloves, gold rings, a crosier, and a mitre of white damask with a rose, a star, and a cross embroidered upon it in pearls, and in green and red gems.[74] Part of this practice of inversion was, of course, transvestism. Much cross-dressing took place on the stage but there was also transvestism practiced at the Maytime revels, with men dressed as 'May Marions'. Cross-dressing was also used to ridicule and discipline disorderly neighbours, part of the tradition of charivari or 'rough music'. Women dressed as men to travel, serve in the army or navy, to meet or accompany a lover, or to avoid sexual attentions.[75]

As Ronald Hutton has shown, early modern England was replete with festivals and seasons when disguise was accepted and even encouraged. 'Mummers', 'maskers' and 'guisers' were a feature of the Twelve Days of Christmas. They appeared in dramatic performances at the royal court and in great households, and passed through the streets of towns on their way to private fancy-dress parties. Similarly, morris dancing seems to have originally been performed by men blacked up to look like Moors – hence, possibly, the name. The London

Midsummer Watch in the early sixteenth century involved dressing up, morris dancers, naked boys dyed black to represent devils, the King of the Moors clad in black satin robes and mummers 'with visors and hats'. In the larger towns they were a problem for law and order 'because the combination of dark evenings and the presence of many people in disguise afforded marvellous opportunities for street criminals to escape unrecognized'. Between 1400 and 1560, London, Bristol, Chester, and probably other towns, forbade anybody to walk about masked during the Christmas season.[76] The wearing of false beards and wigs by London criminals can also be found in the early sixteenth century.[77]

Many of these traditions of inversion and disguise declined with the imposition of Protestant discipline after the Reformation. However, they reasserted themselves on subsequent occasions when authority was challenged. This can be seen in E. P. Thompson's examination, in his book *Whigs and Hunters*, of the origins of the 1723 Criminal Law (or Black) Act (9 Geo. I, c.22). This mandated the death penalty for 'the more effectual punishing wicked and evil-disposed persons going armed in disguise, and doing injuries and violences to the persons and properties of his Majesty's subjects'. The Act's preamble noted that:

> [S]everal ill-designing and disorderly persons have of late associated themselves under the name of Blacks, and entered into confederacies to support and assist one another in stealing and destroying of deer, robbing of warrens and fishponds, cutting down plantations of trees, and other illegal practices, and have, in great numbers, armed with swords, firearms, and other offensive weapons, several of them with their faces blacked, or in disguised habits, unlawfully hunted in the forests belonging to his Majesty, and in the parks of divers of his Majesty's subjects.

Thompson saw this as part of a long struggle between people living in the royal forests against the restrictions placed upon them by the forest laws, which prevented them from using the resources of the land. The blacks were also opposed to the corrupt administration of the forests by Sir Robert Walpole and his Whigs cronies.[78]

The first official notice of the 'blacks' was in March 1720 when a proclamation was made against night hunting in disguise in Windsor Forest. Fourteen men on horseback, armed with guns, together with two men on foot with a greyhound, had coursed red deer in the late afternoon in Bigshot Walk, with their faces blacked, and some with 'straw hats and other deformed habits'.[79] The blacks even had a leader, 'King John', who in January 1723, on learning that a proclamation against the blacks was imminent, let it be known that he intended to answer it publicly near an inn on Waltham Chase. According to the *London Journal*, 'But fifteen of his smutty tribe appeared, some in coats made of skins, others with fur caps, &c. they were all well armed and mounted, and at least three hundred people assembled to see the Chief Black and his mock negroes.'[80]

Such practices of disguise in order to confuse the authorities continued into the late eighteenth and early nineteenth centuries. Thus, in 1773 when the American colonists wanted to protest about the landing of tea by the East India Company in Boston, they disguised themselves as Mohawk Indians in order to tip the offending beverage into the dock.[81] In Australia the early bushrangers – convicts who had escaped into the bush to prey on farmers – blacked up their faces with charcoal, just as the Waltham blacks had done earlier in England.[82] Similarly, on the outbreak of the Rebecca Riots in South Wales in June 1839, in protest at the high tolls on the roads, a crowd of 300 to 400 men descended on the toll gate at Efail-wen, some with blackened faces and others dressed in women's clothes. After driving away the special constables, they smashed the gate with sledge hammers and dismantled the toll house within a yard of the ground. The leader of the rioters was addressed as Becca – hence the Rebecca Riots. Similarly, in December 1842 a crowd in women's clothing, and armed with scythes and guns, entered the village of St Clears and destroyed all the toll gates there. In June 1843, rioters, again all in female clothing, some masked and others with their faces painted, destroyed the gates at Llanfihangel-ar-arth. Finally, in June 1843, 300 men on horseback and 2,000 on foot marched through Carmarthen led by a man in women's clothing with long ringlets of horsehair.[83] Authority could be mocked by such disguise, at the same time as the rioters' identities were obscured.

CONCLUSION

Plainly the identification of individuals in early modern England, especially those on the move, could depend on official documentation. These depended, in turn, on acts of official, authoritative ascriptions of identity – an official recognized a person as a certain individual, and created a paper token of that identification. To a certain extent, therefore, it is incorrect to see identification based on information systems as something peculiar to modernity,[84] or even post-modernity.[85] Yet in many cases personal knowledge of a person and their circumstances was what counted, rather than central state systems, or expert knowledge. In addition, there is comparatively little evidence that the period saw the creation of the two stage information systems of identification that are seen today. A token of identification was created but there was no database of information held by the central state to which it could be compared in cases of dispute. Where officials did hold the records, as with parish registration, there was no general issue of tokens of identification, such as baptismal certificates. This may all help to explain, in part, why forgery was so successful in the period, and why the physical inscription of a deviant status was written on the body of the felon for all to see.

The period after 1750 saw the significant changes in the nature of English society that have been described as the Industrial Revolution. As already noted, these, in turn, are said to have created the conditions for new forms and methods of identification based on the State. So did this period see the replacement of the community by the State as the means of identification, and did the latter come to depend on central record-keeping and scientific expertise? This is the subject of the next chapter.

6

Identification in the First Industrial Nation, 1750–1850

THE NATURE OF THE NEW INDUSTRIAL SOCIETY

England in the late eighteenth to mid-nineteenth centuries was a very odd place indeed in global terms. It is certainly true that historians have recently poured cold water on the notion of a sudden 'Industrial Revolution' in the period, preferring to see the economic growth in these years as but a slight acceleration of previous rates. N. F. C. Crafts, for example, estimates that the rate of growth of national product per head in 1700 to 1760 was 0.31 per cent per annum, while the figure for 1780 to 1801 was only slightly higher at 0.35 per cent.[1] Similarly, Tony Wrigley and Leigh Shaw-Taylor have calculated that the proportion of the population employed in secondary industries, such as manufacturing and construction, actually declined slightly over the period of the classic Industrial Revolution, with a stronger growth in services.[2] In some sense, British manufacturing has been in decline since the eighteenth century. Nevertheless, the early nineteenth century saw the rapid decline of agriculture from perhaps 35.9 per cent of the occupied population in 1801 to 15.1 per cent in 1871.[3] The population more than doubled in these years from just under 9 million, to just over 22 million, and while in 1801 one-fifth of the population lived in cities and town with 10,000 or more inhabitants, this figure had grown to a half by the census of 1851. In this half-century the rate of urbanization in England and Wales was over twice that of the United States, and over three times that of either Prussia or France.[4] The expansion of some of the new industrial towns of the Midlands and North was astounding. The population of Birmingham, for example, grew from 71,000 at the beginning of the nineteenth century to nearly a quarter of a million 50 years later, while a town like Blackburn in Lancashire could grow from a modest 12,000 in 1801 to a large city of 129,000 by the end of the century.[5] It was not the increase in manufacturing that was novel but its concentration in towns and its dependence on steam. England had become the world's first urban, industrial society.

Much of this urban expansion was the result of internal migration to the towns from the countryside.[6] To this vast movement must be added the waves of foreign migration experienced by England in the nineteenth century. There were, for example, huge movements of the Irish into Britain in the wake of the Potato Famine of the late 1840s. Such migration led to the establishment of large immigrant populations in English cities. According to the 1861 census, out of a population of 20 million, England and Wales contained 600,000 people born in Ireland, 169,000 born in Scotland, and 150,000 persons born in the British colonies or foreign countries, many of the latter being in London.[7] Many of these would have had children recorded in the census as being born in England, so the ethnic immigrant population was in fact much larger than these figures suggest. The country was not to see in-migration like this again until the early twenty-first century.

Many foreign migrants were also moving through England on the way to somewhere else. Thus, much of the European emigrant population of the newly independent United States passed through English ports such as Liverpool and London. In 1842 nearly 200,000 people were emigrating to the United States via Liverpool, something like half of all migrants leaving Europe. Between 1830 and 1930 over 9 million people sailed from the Lancashire port bound for a new life in the United States, Canada and Australia.[8] Of course, some would-be Americans never made it across the Atlantic, and created foreign enclaves in England, such as the Little Italy's of Manchester and of Holborn in London.[9] Such families were later to form the 'Ice Cream Dynasties' that enlivened the street fare of Victorian cities. Along with such migrants came asylum seekers, such as Karl Marx, who created a radical diaspora in the heart of British Empire.[10] Many of these migrants became British citizens, although many did not bother, or like Marx had their applications for naturalization turned down.[11]

Contemporaries believed that new and momentous changes were taking place. For Friedrich Engels, yet another radical migrant, in the 1840s:

> A town, such as London, where a man may wonder for hours together without reaching the beginning of the end, without meeting the slightest hint which could lead to the inference that there is open country within reach, is a strange thing.[12]

He found the 'brutal indifference' of the people who crowded about him without even a glance in each other's direction, and the 'unfeeling isolation of each in his private interest', both repellent and offensive.[13] For Engels, of course, this was a result of the expansion of the capitalist system, and held within it the seeds of its own overthrow in the alienation of the industrial proletariat. Engels saw this in a positive light as the inevitable transcendence of a rotten system, but others saw the threat much more negatively. For example, Joseph Fletcher, the early nineteenth-century schools inspector and statist, looked with horror on the working populations of the large industrial cities:

> Here, brought into close neighborhoods, and estranged from the influence of superior example, they are subject to temptations, hazards, and incitements far beyond those which approach the rural cottage; ignorant and largely depraved, they are likewise capable of combination; and combined, they form bodies little prepared to stoop to the exigencies of a reeling alternation of prosperity and adversity; to say nothing of all the evils which improvidence and heathenism pour out upon themselves.[14]

Contemporaries were also shocked by the apparent rise in the numbers of paupers, and of the number of crimes committed, which led to the increasing rigours of the New Poor Law of 1834, the establishment of uniformed police forces, and the expansion of prisons.[15] In the background lurked the ever-present fear of revolution, and of political radicalism.[16]

As already noted, the anonymity and novelty of such large cities can be overdone, but the period of the Industrial Revolution certainly seemed one of alarming portents to middle-class contemporaries. One would have expected, as some historians and sociologists have suggested, to have seen marked changes in the techniques for identifying individuals in society, and especially the intrusion of the central state into such practices. However, although there were some significant innovations in the period, state identification was, on the whole, the dog that did not bark. Social control appears to have been imposed through other means, and indeed it can be argued that some forms of state identification actually declined in England in the late eighteenth and early nineteenth centuries. The case of the Tichborne Claimant in the early 1870s discussed above shows the difficulties in attempting to identify someone that still existed at the end of the period covered in the present chapter.

IDENTIFICATION OF THE JURIDICAL PERSON

Probably the most important innovation with respect to state-facilitated forms of identification in this period was the replacement of the dispersed system of parochial registration of baptisms, marriages and burials, by a more centralized civil system for registering births, marriages and deaths. This subsequently led to the issuing of birth certificates, which became, in time, general all-purpose tokens of identification sponsored by the state, both in Britain and in the wider Empire. Thus, when Rudyard Kipling came to write his great Indian novel *Kim* at the end of the Victorian era, he supplied his young hero with a leather amulet case slung round his neck, which contained his father's certificate of membership of the Freemasons, and his own birth certificate. These his father had proclaimed 'in his glorious opium-hours, would yet make little Kimball a man'.[17] However, the English system of civil registration was, in many ways, a continuation, and perfection, of the older parish-based arrangements, and its initial purpose was to improve the identification of the juridical person who could hold and alienate property. It was only later that the system became a means of proving an identity to the State, and commercial companies and even then, as already noted in the case of John Stonehouse, birth certificates might be used to claim an identity that was not one's own.

As discussed above, the effectiveness of the system of parochial registration was increasingly being brought into question in the late eighteenth and early nineteenth centuries. The Select Committee on Parochial Registration, which reported in 1833, found that many of the parish registers of the Church of England were in a poor state of preservation. The growth of Nonconformity meant that the many dissenting property holders who were unhappy to register the baptisms and burials of their kin in such documents further undermined coverage. The cost, and on occasion impossibility, of proving one's lineage through the parish registers, created insecurity of title to property. This was seen as a serious problem given the increasing complexity of commercial transactions, and newly developed types of property, witnessed during the Industrial Revolution. If parochial registration had laid the foundation of economic growth, as Simon Szreter suggests, it was now seen as a hindrance to it.[18]

Attempts at improving the situation began as early as 1812 when Parliament passed 'Rose's Act', or, to give it its full title, *An Act for the Better Regulating, and Preserving of Parish and Other Registers of Baptisms, Marriages and Burials in England* (52 Geo. III, c.146). The intention of the Act was to 'greatly facilitate the proof of pedigrees claiming to be entitled to real or personal property, and be otherwise of great public benefit and advantage'. The main result of this legislation was the introduction of standardized, printed forms of parochial registration of baptisms, marriages and burials. However, the original Parliamentary Bill for this Act was more extensive in that dissenting ministers were to send 'memorandums' detailing baptisms they had performed to the local Anglican minister. It also proposed the setting up of registries in London and York (to cover the archbishoprics) to hold the parish registers. It was intended that they should have 'Registrar-Generals' who could make copies of the entries. The more elaborate parts of the proposal fell through because the Anglican clergy objected to performing a time-consuming civil function; dissenters disliked the dependence on the Anglican vicar; and the powers to be given to the clergy to ascertain facts about vital events were seen as too inquisitorial.[19]

A number of other proposals and Bills were subsequently introduced to set up more centralized systems of registration but none was successful until the passage of the 1836 Registration Act (6 & 7 Will. IV, c.86). This has often been seen by historians in terms of the production of medical and demographic statistics, but the principal origins of the new system lay once more in the protection of property rights. Under this Act the whole of England and Wales was divided into registration districts based on the Poor Law Unions and registrars were appointed to each of them. These local officers were to record, and issue certificates of, birth, marriage and death, the latter including cause of death. They also sent copies of the certificates to a central General Register Office (GRO), which created indexes of these and made them available to the public at a central site at Somerset House in London. A Registrar General for England and Wales was appointed to head the GRO, and to supervise the local registration system.[20]

The new civil system still depended, however, on the local community for its information, since parents registered the birth of their children, both male and female; brides and grooms signed the marriage register; and the next of kin, or neighbours, registered the dead, with cause of death being supplied by the local doctor. As in the case of parochial registers, the issue of birth certificates by the new, central GRO was seen, at least at first, in terms of the production of pedigrees. In the *Twenty-Second Annual Report of the Registrar General for 1859*, for example, the second Registrar General, George Graham, noted that in that year there were 4,110 successful searches in the registers at the GRO – 1,662 births, 1,866 deaths and 582 marriages. Of such searches leading to the issuing of certificates, the 'greater number ... are for legal purposes, and are applied for by solicitors'. In turn, such successful searches were only 1 in 5 of all searches.[21] By 1866 the GRO was issuing just over 10,000 certificates a year, and this figure had doubled by 1875.[22]

Civil registration gradually expanded into the rest of the then United Kingdom. In Ireland arrangements were introduced by the government in 1845 to allow the registration of non-Catholic marriages, and for the appointment of registrars, who were also given the power to perform civil marriages. In addition, a Registrar General of Marriages was appointed, and given responsibility for the central collection and custody of marriage records. In was not until 1863, however, that a complete Irish civil registration system was in place.[23] The introduction of civil registration in Ireland had been delayed by the opposition of the Roman Catholic Church, and something similar happened in Scotland. Here the opposition of the Protestant clergy, and of the kirk session clerks, held up the introduction of civil registration till the passing of the 1854 Registration (Scotland) Act (17 & 18 Vict., c.80).[24]

The new civil system spread just as quickly to some of the farthest reaches of Britain's white dominions, at least for white settlers. Compulsory civil registration began in Tasmania as early as 1838 under 'An Act for Registering Births Deaths and Marriages in the Island of Van Diemen's Land and its Dependencies' (2 Vict., No. 8). Births, marriages and deaths were to be registered in a 'General Register Office' to be established in Hobart Town, and a Registrar of Births Deaths and Marriages was to be appointed. Western Australia followed suit in 1841, South Australia in 1842, Victoria in 1853, Queensland in 1855 and the Northern Territories in 1870.[25] Compulsory civil registration of births, deaths and marriages commenced in New South Wales on 1 March 1856, under the 1855 Marriages Act (19 Vict., No. 30) and the 1855 Registration of Births, Deaths and Marriages Act (19 Vict., No. 34). An office of Registrar General was also established there, and the colony divided into registration districts. The purposes of registration appear to have been both public and private: the provision of statistical data to government and the public, and the creation of authentic legal records for proving descent and identity.[26] New Zealand introduced the registration of European births, marriages and deaths in 1838 but only made it compulsory in 1856. Maori registration, however, did not become compulsory until just before the First World War.[27] In Canada civil registration records began in Nova Scotia in 1864, in Ontario in 1869 and in British Columbia in 1872.[28]

In an age of information spread by international postal and telegraph systems, far-flung British colonies could import the latest techniques for identification from metropolitan England. Indeed, civil registration could be more easily introduced here than in Scotland and Ireland, because the colonies represented a clean slate. The lack of existing parochial systems of identification, or for recording property rights (those of the aboriginal peoples were easily ignored), meant that new identification systems could be introduced with minimal opposition. England had become a node in a complex interchange of technologies of imperial identification. In this case it was exporting techniques, but early in the next century it was to become an importer of new methods of identification elaborated elsewhere in the Empire.

Whatever its broader economic significance, the development of the birth certificate gave little security in terms of identification in day-to-day commercial transactions. As Margo Finn has argued, although chequebooks, backed up by archives of specimen signature in banks, allowed elite Victorian consumers to pay on the spot, or by post, cash payments of credit accounts in person remained a standard retail practice. Even the supposed retailing revolution of the 1850s onwards, involving the development of cooperatives, multiples and departments stores, did not entirely replace the older personalized forms of shopping on credit. As a consequence, references to 'money hunting' expeditions undertaken on foot, horseback and by train, continued to fill the diaries and memoirs of tradesmen in the nineteenth century, along with references to debtors going into hiding, or moving address in the night. County court statistics, for what they are worth, show rising levels of debt disputes, from nearly 400,000 in 1850 to over 1,140,000 by 1900.[29] Commerce was still awash with insecurities, including the dangers of impersonation and fraud.

Despite this problem of bad debt, retailers did not turn to the State for protection but formed their own private protection societies. As early as 1776 the London Guardians, or the 'Society for the Protection of Trade against Swindlers and Sharpers', had been established in the Metropolis to pool information about fraudsters.[30] There was also a 'United Society of Merchant Tailors for the Protection of Trade against Frauds and Swindlers' active in London at the beginning of the nineteenth century.[31] Similar societies grew up in commercial and industrial centres in the provinces. The Liverpool Guardian Society for the Protection of Trade, for example, was set up in 1823, and the Hull Guardian Society for the Protection of Trade held its first meeting in 1828.[32] By 1854 the Leicester Trade Protection Society had connections with affiliates and agents in 469 towns at home and abroad, and there was a National Association of Trade Protection Societies (NATPS) coordinating the work of provincial organizations from 1866 onwards.[33] Similar bodies were also established in the United States, such as the Mercantile Agency set up in New York in 1841, which amassed vast amounts of information from local agents from all over the Continent on the character and credit-worthiness of businessmen. One of its field agents in Illinois in the 1840s and 1850s appears to have been a young prairie lawyer by the name of Abraham Lincoln.[34]

In the early days such associations, as with many Victorian middle-class gatherings, were as much social clubs as commercial organizations. When the Preston Guardian Society for the Protection of Trade held its anniversary dinner in 1850, it was described by *The Preston Guardian* as 'of the most *recherché* description'. The gathering involved numerous toasts, the singing of songs ('Happy are we, a'thegither', 'The morn was wet', 'Remember, oh remember'), and a recitation by Mr J. Parker titled 'The Arab's farewell to his steed'.[35] In a much more practical manner such societies also produced weekly, fortnightly or monthly circulars describing swindlers active in their area. These provided a wealth of information on the personal qualities and practices of suspect customers. The *City of London Trade Protection Circular*, for example, described Adrian Beaumont, alias Barlowe, as 'of gentlemanly deportment, highly accomplished in painting, music, and most of the fine arts, and . . . accompanied by his wife, sister, and a little boy of . . . rather delicate appearance'. In 1883 the *Credit Draper's Gazette*, described Edward Roe, once a lamp-cleaner, as a 'stiff, bowlegged man' and 'used to a bit of tinkering when near Sheffield five years ago'. By combining their own private records of recalcitrant debtors with published press reports of local bankruptcies, insolvencies and county court litigation, guardian societies amassed a wealth of information on consumers, which were made available to subscribers. This network spread as the societies were integrated. A year after beginning to conduct business the NATPS claimed to have received 75,000 credit enquiries. The National Association developed a 'Telegraphic Code' to encourage the rapid exchange of information on debtors via the telegraph, with differing keywords, 'safe', 'good', 'with care', and so on, defining levels of credit worthiness.[36]

Two important facets of this development should be noted. First, the reduction of identification to the amassing and circulation of information that was to become increasingly important to the mechanisms for identifying the honest, as well as the dishonest, consumer. Secondly, the development in this period of techniques of identification based on private associations and civil society, rather than via the State.

IDENTIFICATION OF THE DEVIANT

Similar patterns can be found in the late eighteenth and early nineteenth centuries in respect of the identification of the deviant. Just where one might expect to find the State taking the lead, civil society turned to its own resources. It is true that in 1771 John Fielding, the blind London magistrate and brother of Henry Fielding, took the logical step of bringing together the descriptions of wanted criminals found in the warrants of hue and cry into a single publication, which could be circulated to justices throughout the country. In that year he began publishing the *Quarterly Pursuit* and the *Weekly or Extraordinary Pursuit*, which later became the *Hue and Cry*. Fielding was in correspondence with magistrates all over London and the provinces, and asked them to send him details of criminals at large. He collated these and sent the results to the magistrates on a weekly and quarterly basis, and the information collected on criminals was to include 'an exact description of their persons'. The first *Quarterly Pursuit* contained the descriptions of 36 'offenders at large', including:

> Benjamin Bird, a tall thin man, pale complexion, black hair tied, thick lips, the nail of his forefinger of his right hand is remarkably clumsy, comes from Coventry, and is charged with several forgeries, the last at Liverpool.
>
> John Godfrey, pretends to be a clergyman, middle-sized, thin-visaged, smooth face, ruddy cheeks, his eyes inflamed, a large white wig, bandy-legged, charged with fraud at Chichester.
>
> William Thompson, by trade a butcher, about five feet five inches high, pale complexion, effeminate voice, light curled hair, flat nose, the end of which curls up, charged with felony in Westminster.[37]

In this manner the body of the criminal, and his or her identification, was again converted into a flow of information. At the same time as the locus of punishment was passing through confinement in prison from the body of the criminal to his mind, so the identification of the criminal was passing from the external marking of his or her body to the creation of descriptions of that body. However, it is doubtful if these official publications were that effective since the descriptions were often subjective (what exactly did 'pale' mean?), and they did not circulate among the general public. This led the Home Office to declare in 1827 that, 'As a means of communication and publicity, the present *Hue and Cry* is evidently useless.'[38] Given the concentration of the early uniformed police on deterring crime through their physical presence, and their relatively poor training and education, one can understand this failure to develop sophisticated criminal identification systems.[39]

From the late eighteenth century, annual registers of men and women indicted for criminal offences in the county of Middlesex began to be compiled by the Home Office, and this spread to other counties in the first decade of the next century. Prisons and the new uniformed police forces also began to keep their own registers. These all contained some minimal descriptions of prisoners and criminals – name, age, height, the colour of eyes and complexion, and so on.[40] For example, the Newgate Calendar carried such information in the period 1790 to 1805, although the range of descriptive information then contracted.[41] However, these cannot have been of much use for the active

apprehension of criminals. Instead, in the late eighteenth-century official systems for disseminating deviant identifications were increasingly supplemented
by the private use of newspapers, and other printed artefacts. This reflected the
rapid spread of printing in the provinces, as well as improvements in postal,
coaching and carrying services, and in the road network itself. Thus, although
there were no provincial newspapers in 1700, there were about 35 in 1760, and
100 by 1808. In 1729, the *Leeds Mercury*, the town's only newspaper, carried 12
crime advertisements, but during 1784 it, and the *Leeds Intelligencer*, carried 77.
In the latter year, 15 per cent of these adverts included descriptions of wanted
individuals. Associations for the prosecution of felons were set up, and subscribers could use these to place adverts and make rewards.[42]

Such advertisements could also be a means of finding missing persons.
In 1821, for example, the *Liverpool Mercury* carried an extremely florid, and
lengthy, description of one who had 'strayed from his friends':

> [A] middle aged man, of Irish extraction, about five feet eight inches high, a bald high
> forehead and pale complexion, with a sort of *theatrical* strut in his gait, and who may
> be further recognised by the following particulars: – he has a natural mark or mole on
> the forehead, the exact resemblance of a *rat*, which he is very careful to conceal with
> a richly embroidered cap, having a tassel and curiously wrought bells on the top....
> should he see a decent well-dressed female in the street insulted with abusive language
> by some sparks of fashion flushed with the juice of Bacchus, it is ten to one he presently
> mounts up on the top of a barrel, into a window, or some other elevated situation, and
> commences a speech, in which he assures a crowd of bye-standers that this lady has
> long been his most particular friend and acquaintance, for whom he entertains the
> most greatest possible esteem, and that she is the most glorious, elegant, and accom-
> plished creature in the universe.[43]

Such prolix prose was, of course, the exception rather than the rule.

In addition to newspaper advertisements, printed handbills could often provide a much deeper, and clearly targeted, penetration of the potential audience
at the local level, especially in rural areas where the circulation of newspapers
was limited. In London, where literacy was high from an early period, parishes
were printing 'tickets' as early as the early seventeenth century to track down
missing persons.[44] Such handbills could often go into much more detail than
most newspaper advertisements to aid identification. Thus, a veritable pamphlet of seven pages printed in Ireland in the mid-eighteenth century, sought
the apprehension of

> DIONYSIUS, a brawny, strong-bodied jolly-looking Man, about Five Feet Nine inches
> and a half high; had on a Coat of Parsons Blue, lined with Black, Waistcoat and

Breeches of the same, and a Grey Bob Wig; speaks loud and fast, is a notorious Lyar, a profane Swearer, and has much the Air of a Rogue, by a remarkable Squint or back Look, such as is observed in Horses that are vicious and apt to recalcitrate.[45]

It is interesting here, as with so many descriptions in the pre-modern period, that clothes and habits seemed as important as the body in identifying people. Dionysius was plainly a striking man but many people did not have truly distinguishing marks, or could only be described conventionally. Inevitably clothes were used as important distinguishing signs, especially when the poor had so few clothes to wear. However, even clothes were of limited use. Certainly, the ubiquity of second-hand clothing worn by the corpses in Richard Cobb's Paris Morgue at the end of the eighteenth century made any attempt to use dress to identify specific individuals difficult. Even laundry marks could be misleading – 'a man with the initials A.M.L. has a shirt marked in blue DD; another, with the initials C.L.A., has a shirt marked F.B. and slippers marked E.B.; a 61-year-old *rentier*, P.F.G., has a shirt marked B, and so on and so on.'[46]

Such descriptions could work, at least some times. Thus, in September 1819, Mary Ridding, aged 20, was tried at the Old Bailey for kidnapping Benjamin Schrier, the 14-month-old child of John and Grace Schrier, of Bancroft's Place, London. John Schrier, who was constable of the night at Mile End, Old Town, had travelled to Birmingham 'Owing to a letter I had received', and his colleague, Martin, had gone before him and apprehended Ridding, who was staying with her sister-in-law there. Martin described the confrontation in his evidence:

One of them said, 'How do you know it to be your child?' I pointed to a mole on the right arm – they said that I might have discovered that since I came; I do not know whether it was she or her sister. After I had pointed out two or three marks, I described one on the leg; the same answer was made. I said I had brought them something to assure them it was mine, and produced a printed bill with a description of the child. The prisoner then put her hands together, made some confession, and said she had been deceived or taken in, and that the child had been put into her arms.

Ridding was found guilty, fined one shilling, and confined for one year in the House of Correction.[47]

It could be argued that these privatized forms of criminal identification merely reflected the bureaucratic limitations of the English State in this period. However, it should be noted that government bodies were quite able to create and manipulate large amounts of data when required, as can be seen in the case of the GRO's handling of civil registration and its organization of the decennial censuses from 1840 onwards.[48] Similarly, both the War Office and Admiralty created extensive records describing members of the armed forces from at least the late eighteenth century onwards. Here is perhaps evidence of the impact of mobility on the need for forms of identification, since Britain's military were the basis of her global expansion in the period. If soldiers could desert in India, or sailors jump ship in the West Indies, it was necessary to have systems of identification to track them down. However, this was mobility at the behest of the State rather than mobility caused by economic and social change.

The army began to produce 'description books' from the 1760s, compiled by regiment or depot, giving soldiers' names, heights, and descriptions of complexion, colour of hair and eyes, and notes on distinguishing marks. They appear to have been designed as a means of preventing fraudulent claims of service, which could be used to claim pensions. These books may also be linked in some way with the registers of deserters that can be found for the early nineteenth century, and which give physical descriptions. These descriptions were also published in the *Police Gazette*, the successor to the *Hue and Cry*.[49] The Militia, a voluntary part-time force for home defence based on the counties, also created vast amounts of data, although at a local level. Although Anglo-Saxon in origin, it ceased to be summoned after the Civil Wars but was revived in 1757, when the Militia Act (31 Geo. II, c.26.) established Militia regiments in all counties of England and Wales. The Yeomanry (cavalry) and the Volunteers were introduced later. In 1808 a further force, the Local Militia, was formed, although by 1816 the Local Militia and the Volunteers had been dissolved. A form of conscription was used for the Militia, and each year, the parish was supposed to draw up lists of adult males, and to hold a ballot to choose those who had to serve in the Militia. The Militia lists (of all men) and the Militia enrolment lists (of men chosen to serve) should, at least in theory, provide complete and annual censuses of all men aged between 18 and 45 from 1758 to 1831. The surviving lists, mostly held locally, and sometimes incomplete, can be very informative, even giving details about individual men and their family circumstances.[50]

Naval captains were also supposed to keep description books containing information on the physical appearance of every man on board ship. They did not return these to the Admiralty but descriptions of deserters were taken from them and used to compile published 'Run Lists'.[51] The Admiralty records in the National Archives certainly contain description books for Royal Marines going back to the 1750s.[52] The introduction of continuous service in the mid-nineteenth century led to increased pay, paid leave and improved sick pay, and ratings who served 22 years in the navy became eligible for a long-service pension. Service records were then introduced, partly to calculate eligibility for pensions, and partly to prevent the sort of impersonation that was noted above in the case of John Francis. Such records included for each rating the date and place of birth, a physical description, date on entry into the navy, names of ships served in, dates of individual entries and discharge, ratings held, date of pension and date of death if in service. By the First World War theses records contained official number (introduced in 1873), name, age, height, chest measurement, hair, eyes, complexion, wounds, and scars or marks. After 1875, lists of deserters from Royal Naval vessels, together with details of rewards for their capture, can also be found in the *Police Gazette*. These gave name of ship deserted from, date of desertion, rating, age, where born, physical description and details of ships previously served on.[53] In addition, the Register Office of Merchant Seamen, set up in 1835 to keep records of potential recruits into the Royal Navy, introduced a register ticket system for each member of the mercantile marine. The details registered for each seaman included their ticket number, name, rank and a simple description – height, complexion, hair and eye colour. The 'ticket' could, of course, act as a token of identification.

In their Empire the British were again quite capable of creating extensive systems for the identification of their deviant countrymen. This is seen perhaps most clearly in the treatment of convict populations in the militarized colonies of Australia in the early nineteenth century. On arrival in Australia convicts were stripped and examined, and an extensive description taken down of features, scars, tattoos, hair colour, eyes, teeth lost, appearance of nose, ears, chin, mouth, and height and weight.[54] In Van Dieman's Land (Tasmania), Sir George Arthur, the lieutenant governor from 1823 to 1837, ordered the compilation of the 'Black Books', which contained the name, physical description, sentence, details of transportation and labour assignment, jail and surgeon's reports, conduct and punishment records of every convict. This enabled Arthur to introduce a calibrated system of rewards and punishments in an attempt to reform prisoners. His successor, Sir John Franklin, proposed in 1837 that all convicts assigned to free colonists as labourers – including domestic help – should wear a distinguishing patch, or badge, on their clothes. This was perhaps a colonial echo of the badging of Poor Law paupers in England and Wales. However, the governor, Sir George Gipps, was reluctant to apply this idea in New South Wales because he feared the reactions of rich colonists who 'did not want the splendour of their flunkies' uniforms dimmed by this mark of infamy'. Under the Australian assignment system of labour, every convict when off his master's property for any time or reason had to carry and show on demand a written pass that stated his name, where he had started from, where he was going, and the precise number of days and even hours he was to be on the road.[55] In addition, frequent musters, household searches and censuses created a form of population register, which helped control the convict population.[56]

Such record-keeping enabled detailed descriptions of escaped convicts to be produced for wanted posters. Thus, that for Charles Stagg, a 23-year-old labourer from Norwich who ran from the Tasmanian Seven Mile Creek probation station in March 1843, enumerates his tattoos, which included the initials of most of his family as well as of his own sweethearts:

> Mary Stagg, Thomas Stagg, crucifix, 5 dots, shoe, crucifix, WS, man with stick, HK, dog, Gwynson, X Mary Robinson, Liberty, bracelet on right arm, Eliza Smith, O Sun and blue marks and rings all over right hand; man and woman, two men fighting, TS WS LS LHHS 1842, anchor, MSCS on left arm, blue dots and rings on fingers of left hand, H Stagg, William, crucifix, sun and moon on breast, ABCDEFGH on left arm, large scar on upper right arm.[57]

Plainly Stagg was either a very large man, or this represents a high density of distinguishing marks. It is unlikely that such a comprehensive system of identification could be found in early nineteenth-century England. It could be argued, of course, that transportation to the colonies obviated the need for such systems within the metropole.

The relative lack of state identification systems in England during the period of the classic Industrial Revolution can also be seen in the treatment of aliens, or rather in the manner in which the identification of aliens came and then went. As with the military and transported convicts, the English could create extensive systems of surveillance and identification in times of crisis, but could relax them afterwards. Thus, the outbreak of the French Revolution in 1789, and the subsequent wars between France and England, led to a fear that foreign aliens would introduce dangerously radical ideas, such as democracy, into the realm. This led to the passage in 1793 of a Regulations of Aliens Act (33 Geo. III, c.4). Under this new law all foreigners coming to Britain had to register with customs officials, and the masters of ships had to declare the number, and details, of aliens aboard their ships. The Act, and another law introduced in 1798, established a system for registering aliens, who were required to sign declarations at ports of entry into Britain. Aliens already living in Britain, and those arriving after January 1793, had to give their names, rank, occupations and addresses to a magistrate. In March 1797, the Home Secretary sent round a circular asking for details of those who had arrived since May 1792, and householders who had taken in migrants as lodgers had to give details to local officials. In order to leave London, aliens had to obtain passports from the Secretary of State in London, and they were forced to stay either in the ports where they had first arrived, or in certain inland areas. A Superintendent of Aliens was appointed in 1793, and his government department became known as the Aliens Office. It was concerned with the registration of migrants and issued directions to local agents, mayors and local officials on the detention or expulsion of migrants, and made enquiries about the character of foreigners seeking to be naturalized.[58]

The 1816 Regulation of Aliens Act (56 Geo. III, c.86) led to the creation of a central system of registration. Every alien on arrival was issued with a certificate, showing the name of the ship on which he or she arrived, and his or her own name, description, place of departure, destination and profession, with space for references and remarks. Unless he or she was a servant, each immigrant was to produce the certificate within one week to a magistrate or a justice of the peace, and copies of the entries on the certificates were to be sent both by the port, and by the magistrate or justice, to the Secretary of State in London. Yet another Registration of Aliens Act (7 Geo. IV, c.54) was passed in 1826. Aliens were now required to send to the Secretary of State, or to the Chief Secretary for Ireland, a declaration of their place of residence every six months, and the clerk at the Aliens Office was to send in return a certificate. Migrants were no longer required to produce their certificates to a magistrate or justice of the peace but they were to produce them at the Aliens Office if residing within 5 miles of the City of Westminster, or to make a declaration in writing if they were not. They were also required to make a declaration before leaving the country and, for the first time, they were required to produce police registration certificates.[59]

However, despite suggestions to the contrary,[60] much of this draconian system was, in practice, dismantled by the 1836 Aliens Act (6 & 7 Will. IV, c.11). Masters of ships and migrants still had to make a declaration on arrival, and aliens were still given a certificate, copies of which were sent to the Secretary of State in London. They were also still required to produce a police registration certificate but it was no longer necessary for them to visit or send a written declaration to the Aliens Office, and the declaration they made on leaving the country was in future to be made at the Customs Office at the port of departure. An alien living in England no longer had to report his address every six months, and he or she was in future to become exempt from the provisions of the Act after three, rather than seven, years.[61]

From this date there was no central system to keep track of the whereabouts of aliens after they had stepped off the quay, and no attempts appear to have ever been made to check the lists submitted by masters. From the 1860s until May 1890 the resulting lists were only collected by the Board of Trade for

London, and partially for Hull, and one or two other ports. Indeed, Robert Giffen, the head of the Commercial and Statistical Department of the Board of Trade, was unaware of their existence in 1888. Aliens were supposed to state whether or not they were en route to other countries, but this stipulation was meaningless. When, at the beginning of the twentieth century, the Board of Trade examined lists of emigrants, it discovered that in 1902 alone, 7,983 aliens had left England who were not stated to be en route. For all practical purposes, the central identification and control of aliens had ceased by the mid-Victorian period.[62] Aliens only risked repatriation if they fell on hard times and had recourse to the local Poor Law authorities, or charitable bodies such as the Jewish Board of Guardians.[63]

This rescinding of alien controls was part of general movement across much of Europe in the mid- to late nineteenth century to relax passport and visa requirements.[64] But whereas many Continental countries moved to replace external passports with internal forms of registration and travel documents,[65] England adopted a system of *laissez faire* in which the movement of aliens was, to all effects, free. Of course, this also applied to British citizens as well, who did not require a passport to leave the country and return to it in this period. If, as John Torpey argues,[66] modern nation-states have an in-built desire to achieve a 'monopoly of the legitimate means of movement', then Victorian England appears a particular oddity.

In sum, it can be argued that the period of the classical Industrial Revolution does not see the general expansion of state-sponsored forms of identification for deviants. The State was quite capable of doing so when it came to military personnel, when convicts were under military rule in the colonies, or when England was at war. But internally, and in peace time, the State appears to have been happy to leave the tracing of deviants to private individuals, or, in the case of aliens, to abandon it altogether.

IDENTIFICATION OF THE WELFARE CLAIMANT AND THE CITIZEN

The absence of new forms of state identification in this period can also be found in the case of citizens, despite some radical changes to the basis of their rights and obligations. The Poor Law system, for example, was changed significantly by the passage of the 1834 Poor Law Amendment Act (4 & 5 Will. IV, c.76). The Act established a Poor Law Commission to oversee changes to the national operation of the Poor Law system. These included the combination of small parishes into Poor Law Unions and the building of workhouses in each union for the provision of poor relief. The Amendment Act did not ban all forms of outdoor relief; it was only 'discouraged'. But by the 1840s, at least in theory, the official method of relief for the poor was for them to enter a workhouse. Many workhouses functioned as little more than prisons, and married couples and their children were normally separated upon entry. In conformity with the concept of 'less eligibility', conditions in the workhouse had to be worse than those that could be obtained with the wages paid by the worst job outside the workhouse. This principle existed to deter people from claiming poor relief altogether.[67]

But these changes did not lead to a major change in the nature of identification techniques, or to the expansion in the use of official, paper-based tokens of identity. In general terms, the use of settlement certificates in the Poor Law system actually seems to have been in decline in the late eighteenth and early nineteenth centuries, just when one might assume that increased mobility, urbanization and anonymization, would make the requirement for official forms of identification all the more necessary. The 1795 Relief of the Poor Act (36 Geo. III, c.23), for example, described the use of settlement certificates as 'very ineffectual', and only a small fraction of those examined in rural parishes seem to have possessed them.[68]

Indeed, the elaboration of the New Poor Law could be seen as circumventing the need for innovation in this field. According to Keith Snell, and contrary to the accepted historical orthodoxy and the policy of the Poor Law Commission, outdoor relief in the parish still dominated the Poor Law after 1834. The workhouse was a threat to cow the poor but most of them still received relief outside it. Over the whole period from 1834 to 1929, after which the Poor Law system tended to fall into disuse, normally over 80 per cent of poor relief was out relief. Again, following Snell, it was only in London and the urban areas of the North and Midlands that workhouse relief predominated. The continuation of outdoor relief in the countryside, Wales, and many small towns, meant that the parish overseers still needed to have personal knowledge of the poor.[69] On the other hand, in the large urban areas where the workhouse was the main form of relief, the 'workhouse test' obviated the need for any detailed knowledge of the poor. If a family presented themselves for relief at the workhouse, they were automatically assumed to be in the direst extremities of want. This was confirmed by Henry Longley, an inspector of the Local Government Board (which took over the oversight of the Poor Law system in 1871) when he appeared in front of a parliamentary select committee in 1873. He was asked:

> Have not the guardians in the country a large amount of personal knowledge of the poor, which is wanting in the guardians of the metropolis?

Yes, I think that in some cases that is so. There are three or four unions or parishes in the metropolis in which the guardians have a surprising knowledge of the poor, considering the extent of the unions, but, as a rule, they have not anything like the knowledge which the country guardians have.

Not having that knowledge, they are obliged to use the workhouse as a test to prove the necessity of the applicant?

I think the effect of their want of knowledge is that they rely more upon the relieving officer than they otherwise would.[70]

Indeed, it was lack of identification in the workhouse that was at the heart of *Oliver Twist*, Charles Dickens' classic condemnation of the New Poor Law published in 1838. Oliver's mother, whose name no one knows, is found on the street and dies in the workhouse just after Oliver's birth. The child spends the early years of his life being badly treated there, and is eventually apprenticed to a local undertaker, Mr Sowerberry. Being abused once more, Oliver runs away and walks to London. Here he joins Fagin's gang of infant pickpockets, and is horrified when he sees them 'swipe' a handkerchief from an elderly gentleman. Oliver runs off, but is caught and narrowly escapes being convicted of the theft. Mr Brownlow, the man whose handkerchief was stolen, and an archetypal Dickensian man of heart, takes the feverish Oliver to his home and nurses him back to health. Brownlow is struck by Oliver's resemblance to a portrait of a young woman that hangs in his house.

Meanwhile, Fagin and a mysterious man named Monks are set on recapturing Oliver. It is revealed that Oliver's mother left behind a golden locket in the workhouse when she died. Monks obtains this token of identification, and destroys it. Oliver is seized by Nancy, an ex-pupil of Fagin pretending to be Oliver's sister, and returned to a life of crime. But he is shot while being forced to burgle the home of Rose Maylie and her elderly aunt. The Maylies take Oliver in, and, perhaps inevitably, he is again nursed back to health. Mr Brownlow, subsequently reunited with Oliver, confronts Monks, who is using a false identity, and wrings the truth about Oliver's parentage from him. It is revealed that Monks is Oliver's half-brother. Their father, Mr Leeford, unhappily married to a wealthy woman had an affair with Oliver's mother, Agnes Fleming. Mr Brownlow, by an extraordinary stroke of good fortune, happens to have been Mr Leeford's best friend, and the portrait that resembles Oliver is, in fact, of his mother. Monks has been pursuing Oliver in the hopes of ensuring that his half-brother is deprived of his share of the family inheritance, and Brownlow forces Monks to sign over Oliver's share. Moreover, by another, somewhat inexplicable, twist of fate, it is discovered that Rose is actually Agnes's younger sister, hence Oliver's aunt. Mr Brownlow adopts Oliver, and they and the Maylies retire to a blissful existence in the countryside, and, no doubt, live happily ever after.

It is undoubtedly foolish to rely on a work of fiction, and one with such an improbable plot, as evidence of the role of identification in the workhouse system. Paupers were certainly identified in workhouse day books, accounts and admission registers, although not necessarily described,[71] and the Poor Law union would no doubt have advertised Oliver's description in the local newspaper as a runaway apprentice.[72] However, it is perhaps significant that Dickens could weave his plot around the issues of identification, disguise and mistaken identity, indicating that for contemporaries the 'spike' was a place where identities were lost, or confused, rather than a site of new identification techniques.

Just as welfare claimants were identified in the traditional manner within the community, so were Victorian voters. Under the 1832 and 1867 Reform Acts (2 Will. IV, c.45; 30 & 31 Vict., c.102) there were property qualifications for the vote. The £10 householder franchise was introduced in boroughs, and town clerks had the responsibility of drawing up lists of freemen. These lists were displayed on the doors of every church and chapel, and objections could be made to the names, appeals being heard by revising barristers. In counties, electors had to approach the overseers to have their names put on the lists, and overseers could examine their qualifications, and objections could still be made. Annual registration of voting involved the posting up of lists of voters which members of the public could vet. The overseers of the poor were the registration officials, and so used the poor rate books to identify qualified persons, since those holding property had to pay the rates. The 1867 Reform Act gave lodgers paying rent of £10 the vote but they were not on the rate books, so they had to make a claim to the registration officer. Their name on the list of voters could again be challenged by other voters or claimants, although the voter could appeal to a revising barrister's court.[73]

The system was very complex, and 'personation' thrived because of the careless way in which the electoral lists were maintained, and the fact that one person might appear several times on the lists for as many qualifications as he possessed. This was despite the fact, or perhaps because of it, that nearly a third of the 82 clauses of the 1832 Reform Act (2 & 3 Will. IV, c.45) dealt with voter registration. Under the Act, at the time of voting, the returning officer could ask:

'1. Are you the same Person whose Name appears as *A.B.* on the Register of Voters now in force for the . . . [county or borough]'

'2. Have you already voted, either here or elsewhere, at this Election for the . . . [county or borough of . . .]'

'3. Have you the same Qualification for which your Name was originally inserted in the Register of Voters now in force for the . . . [county or borough of ...]'

Voters were then asked to swear an oath, 'You do swear that you are the same Person whose Name appears as *A.B.* on the Register of Voters now in force in the . . . [county or borough].' The Act also indicated, 'And if any Person shall wilfully make a false Answer to any of the Questions aforesaid, he shall be deemed guilty of an indictable Misdemeanor, and shall be punished accordingly.'[74]

Despite this, the system could be circumvented easily. In the election of 1886, for example, Benjamin Stubley attempted to vote for his father, James, who was on the electoral list in Deptford. His application for a ballot paper was queried by a 'personating agent' (presumably from one of the political parties), who was standing besides the clerk to the vestry of St Pauls, Deptford, who was acting as returning officer. When he was confronted Stubley claimed, 'I have done it before, and no notice has been taken of it. I thought that I could do it for my father.'[75] Such confusion offered the electoral agents of political parties numerous opportunities for sharp practices, since the chance of disenfranchising an opponent, or obtaining a vote for a non-qualified voter, was too tempting to be resisted. This, in turn, led to the development of local party machinery to take advantage of the system.[76]

As with so many other aspects of identification during the Industrial Revolution, techniques were used to identify voters that would have been familiar in the seventeenth and early eighteenth centuries.

IDENTIFYING THE DEAD

If Oliver Twist had died on one of his criminal escapades, there would, no doubt, have been a coroner's inquest on his body. It is unlikely, however, that any new technology of identification would have been applied to his corpse, and that Monks would have achieved his aim of consigning his rival to oblivion. Identification of the corpse was indeed part of the nineteenth-century inquest, but it was still generally understood in terms of identification by the community in the form of the jury. According to John Jervis', *A Practical Treatise on the Office and Duties of Coroners* of 1854, during the inquest, 'The Christian name and surname of the deceased, either his real name or that by which he is usually known, must be stated, if it be known.' However, 'If the name of the deceased be unknown, he may be described in the inquisition as a certain person to the jurors unknown.'[77] No mention was made of the use of expert testimony to identify the corpse.

Medical experts were only just beginning to intrude into the courtroom by the mid-nineteenth century, and then only fitfully. Edinburgh University had established a chair in 'Medical Jurisprudence and Medical Police' in 1807, and a similar post was established in Glasgow in 1839.[78] Non-professional positions were subsequently established in London, at Guys and Charing Cross Hospital. One of the first textbooks on forensic medicine, George Male's *Epitome of Juridical or Forensic Medicine* appeared in 1816.[79] The earliest recorded use of dental evidence in a court of law was also in Scotland, in a case of June 1814. This involved the prosecution of Dr Granville Sharp Pattison and Dr Andrew Russell, partners in, and lecturers at, the College Street Medical School in Edinburgh, for snatching bodies to dissect before their students. The evidence in the case included the teeth of a head found bubbling in a tub of water over a fire in the process of being defleshed, said by one James McGregor to be that of his sister, Janet McAlister.[80] But when Alfred Swaine Taylor, a lecturer on Medical Jurisprudence and Chemistry at Guy's Hospital in London, published his *Elements of Medical Jurisprudence* in 1836, he included nothing on identification. His fourth edition of 1852 merely contained a brief mention of using fractures of bones to identify the dead from skeletons, and the example of the instep of a child being used for identification in a case of infanticide.[81]

Doctors might be called upon to determine the cause of death of a corpse but were not to the fore in questions of identification. Thus, in 1828 a fisherman from Barking in Kent found a dead man floating down the Thames. The jury on viewing the corpse found:

> The throat was cut from one ear to the other in a most dreadful manner, and several of the front teeth had been knocked out. There were also marks of violent contusions on the head and on the left arm, and the latter was broken near the wrist. A cord was tied round the waist of the deceased, to which was attached a stone of about eight pounds' weight.[82]

Mr Deacor, a surgeon, gave evidence but only as to the likely cause of death – the injury to the throat. When it came to questions of identification, however, the inquest looked solely at the evidence of the man's clothing. His shirt and shoes were marked 'W. M.', and it was noted that the waistcoat and trousers had pieces cut out of them where identification marks might have been. Despite this, after an 'animated discussion', the jury returned a non-committal verdict:

> That the deceased was found, on the 7th of September inst., dead, and floating in the river Thames, with his throat cut, and a stone tied to his body; but whether he died of the said cut, or by drowning, or by his own hands, or by the hands of any other person, there is no evidence before the Inquest to prove.[83]

There was thus no appeal to forensic science, or any recourse to police records, few of which would have existed at this date anyway.

Even if doctors had wished to apply forensic techniques to the identification of corpses, they would have been restricted by the lack of suitable facilities in which to perform autopsies. Public mortuaries seldom existed, and bodies awaiting inquests were often stored in barns, or locked rooms in taverns. Hence Charles Dickens could claim in his novel *Bleak House* that, 'The coroner frequents more public-houses than any man alive. The smell of sawdust, beer, tobacco smoke and spirits is inseparable in his vocation from death in its most awful shapes.'[84] Even when public mortuaries were established in the early nineteenth century, rather than being examined for identification, bodies would be more likely to find their way into the hands of the dreaded 'resurrection men', who procured dead bodies for anatomists and medical schools such as that run by Sharpe and Russell. In Edinburgh and Aberdeen public mortuaries were established for the unidentified or unclaimed dead, and one of their primary functions was the apparently innocuous acquisition of corpses for dissection.[85] Liverpool also had a mortuary in Princes Dock in the early nineteenth century run by the towns' Dock Committee. This was mainly for people pulled out of the water, although later provided a service for the whole city. Before that a room in the lower part of the parish church of St Nicholas was used. It was to the latter that the bodies were sent that had been raised by resurrection men from a local churchyard, and found in a cellar of a 'young gentlemen's boarding school' in Hope Street in 1826, 'salted and ready for shipment to the dissecting rooms of Edinburgh and Glasgow'.[86]

The 1832 Anatomy Act (2 & 3 Will. IV, c.75) provided that a person 'lawfully in possession' of a body might permit it to undergo anatomical examination provided that no relative objected. Anatomists were given legal access to corpses that were unclaimed after death, in particular of those who died in prison or the workhouse. Workhouse mortuaries were thus used as staging posts for the 'unclaimed' poor dying in the community. Of course, the last thing that those involved in this noxious trade were interested in was the identification of the dead person.[87] It is perhaps ominous that Dickens' *Oliver Twist* ends with a description of the tomb of Oliver's mother in a quiet country church yard but notes that it is a tomb without a coffin.

CONCLUSION

In general terms, therefore, the industrialization model of modern identification is not very helpful in explaining what was happening to practices of identification in England in the period 1750 to 1850. The State does not appear to have developed new techniques to suppress deviancy in an increasingly urbanized and anonymous society. Civil registration was introduced to underpin property rights, rather than to pinpoint deviants. Commercial fraudsters and criminals were identified most effectively in private systems of identification, rather than by the State. In the Poor Law, documentary forms of identification declined, or were circumvented by the 'workhouse test'. Voters and the dead were identified in this period much as they had been in early centuries. If this is true of the First Industrial Nation, is the industrialization model very illuminating?

When state-mediated forms of identification did develop in this period, it was more likely to be associated with militarization than with industrialization. Hence the development of identification by dossier in the armed forces, merchant marine and Militia, and the enhanced bureaucratic systems for pinpointing aliens during the French Revolutionary and Napoleonic Wars. The demise of the latter in the long period of the mid- to late nineteenth century, when England had few Continental entanglements is suggestive. Also of interest here is the elaboration of extensive systems for identifying English convicts in the highly militarized conditions of the early Australian colonies.[88] Rather than thinking of the development of identification as a function of the needs of Society, in some vague sociological manner, it might be better to think in terms of the specific needs of commercial organizations, and of the State itself. The latter should be seen, at least in the late eighteenth and early nineteenth centuries, in terms of military preparedness rather than in controlling internal deviancy. The emphasis on understanding the State's development in terms of its own needs, especially in a situation of interminable international conflict, rather than in terms of the State as an organ servicing Civil Society, is congruent with much recent sociological theory. For scholars such as Michael Mann, Anthony Giddens, Christopher Dandeker and Michel Foucault, the State needs to be seen as an entity in its own right, pursuing its own interests within a broader context of global state interactions.[89]

In the next one hundred years, however, the British State did begin to elaborate more extensive systems for identifying its citizens, and its deviants, within the British Isles. In the next few chapters the reasons for this shift will be explored in detail in terms of the rise of total warfare, and rise of the total welfare with which it was linked.

7

Towards the 'Dossier Society': Identifying Deviants in England, 1850 to 1970

INTRODUCTION

If one wished to look for a period of innovation in the history of identification in England one would not look to the years of the 'classical' Industrial Revolution, but at the century or so after 1850. However, there was as much continuity as change in this period, and, on the whole, the earlier distinctions between the identification of the juridical person, the citizen, and the deviant were maintained. The juridical person was identified through his or her acts; the citizen via the community or documentation; and the deviant via the body. It has only been in the very recent past that such distinctions have begun to be blurred, or indeed effaced.

Within these broader continuities, however, there were structural changes that introduced significant innovations, including the increasing centralization of the State, the consolidation of capital that expanded the scale of commercial organizations, and the intrusion of science into everyday life. The expanding scale of both State and Capital meant that identification through the community and documentation came to mean identifying oneself to central bureaucracies, and was increasingly in terms of large, centralized databases. Identification became more formalized, and involved interactions within larger geographical and temporal frameworks. At the same time, the application of new, scientific forms of identification to the body transformed the identification of the deviant and the dead. Ultimately these technologies depended yet again on the creation of large, centralized databases. Identification of the deviant increasingly came to depend on information systems, a tendency that has been taken even further in the period since 1970. This is part of what Ericson and Shearing have described as the 'scientification' of police work. However, they tend to think of this in terms of contemporary technologies such as CCTV, wiretaps, tape recorders, computer profiling, breathalysers, and so on, but the process plainly goes back to innovations in the late nineteenth century.[1] Haggerty and Ericson have also argued that the recent past has seen a concern with transforming the body into information, so that it can be rendered mobile and comparable. However, this is something that goes back much further, and also had its origins in the late Victorian period.[2]

The following examination of identification in the period 1850 to 1970 will be in two parts. The present chapter will deal with the deviant, and the following chapter with the identification of the juridical person and the citizen. This is mainly for ease of exposition, since one of the principle issues to consider with respect to the juridical person and the citizen is why the new bodily forms of identification being applied to the deviant were not also applied to them. The telling of this latter story also depends on some prior knowledge of the history of criminal registers, fingerprinting, and other means of deviant identification. It is also necessary to keep the criminal separate because this separation reflects a shift in the manner in which society was understood in this period. The histories of the identification of those within and without the constitutional pale also have differing chronologies. The 'heroic' age of innovation in the history of criminal identification lies in the late Victorian and Edwardian periods, while that for identification of the juridical person and the citizen lies slightly later in the early twentieth century.

A NEW CRIMINAL CLASS?

Contrary to the argument that the development of new forms of bodily identification was a reaction to a general loss of trust in an urbanized 'society of strangers', it could be argued that this actually served to draw a line between the 'criminal classes' and the rest of respectable society. Rather than all the lower orders, the 'respectable' and 'vagrant' poor alike, lying outside the political nation, the former were being incorporated into it in the late nineteenth century. The criminal was now outside the pale, and understood in terms of a deviant class, or even as a biological subpopulation. The distinction between the criminal who was subject to new forms of bodily identification, and the respectable citizen who was not, helped to reassert trust in those within the political pale. This process of differentiation can be seen in the elaboration of the concept of the 'habitual criminal' epitomized by the passing of the 1869 Habitual Criminals Act (32 & 33 Vict., c.99). This set up a Habitual Criminals Register at Scotland Yard, later transferred to the Home Office, to record details of all persons convicted of crime in England. This was so that if they reoffended they could be placed under police supervision for seven years, in addition to any other sentence that might be passed on them. The 'habitual' came to be seen as a class apart,[3] and one to be placed outside the political community along with other incompetent social groups such as the mentally defective, and, of course, women.[4]

Neil Davie has recently gone as far as to claim that, 'There is a strong case for arguing that to all intents and purposes British criminology was born in the space of a few short months in 1869 and early 1870.'[5] This, and the concern over the habitual criminal, he puts down to the ending of transportation of criminals to Australia in November 1867, which meant that the British public 'were no longer separated from their most dangerous criminals by a comforting stretch of salt water'.[6] However, this particular conjuncture, seems unlikely to have been crucial since transportation had effectively stopped decades before – in 1840 in the case of New South Wales, and in 1853 in that of Tasmania.[7] A more likely catalyst for the desire to mark and segregate the habitual criminal can perhaps be found in the passage of the 1867 Reform Act (30 & 31 Vict., c.102), that began the process of giving the English working man the vote. According to both José Harris and Keith McClelland the politics of the Act involved the drawing of cultural and political distinctions between forms of working-class masculinity – between a sober, respectable and independent manhood, and 'rough' men.[8] This distinction was summed up by the radical liberal politician John Bright in Parliament in 1867:

> At the moment, in all, or nearly all boroughs, as many of us know sometimes to our sorrow, there is a small class which it would be much better for themselves if they were not franchised, because they have no independence whatsoever, and it would be much better for the constituency also that they should be excluded, and there is no class so much interested as having that small class excluded as the intelligent and honest working men. I call this class the residuum which there is in almost every constituency, of almost helpless poverty.[9]

The concept of a deviant 'residuum' was one that haunted Europe in the late nineteenth century, and was given physical, biological substance in the work of the Italian criminologist Cesare Lombroso. For Lombroso the criminal represented a throwback to an earlier, savage stage in human development, for as he somewhat luridly argued:

> Thus were explained anatomically the enormous jaws, high cheek bones, prominent superciliary arches, solitary lines in the palms, extreme size of orbits, handle-shaped ears found in criminals, savages and apes, insensibility to pain, extremely acute sight, tattooing, excessive idleness, love of orgies, and the irresponsible craving for evil for its own sake, the desire not only to extinguish life in the victim, but to mutilate the corpse, tear its flesh and drink its blood.[10]

Lombroso believed that the development of the individual in the womb recapitulated the history of the species, and thus criminality could be seen as a form of immaturity.[11] In this he was working within the biological theory of foetal recapitulation popularized by evolutionary biologists such as Ernst Haeckel.[12] Early British criminologists, such as Sir Edmund Du Cane and Henry Maudsley, followed Lombroso in seeing the criminal as a degenerate type.[13] Similarly, the Scottish prison surgeon J. Bruce Thompson could write in 1870 that habitual offenders were 'a criminal class distinct from other civilized and criminal men'. They lived and intermarried among themselves, he argued, and inbreeding transmitted criminality to their children.[14] These ideas merged imperceptibly with the British belief in the existence of criminal races within the British Empire as a whole.[15]

However, this argument should not be taken too far. Later Victorian criminologists disliked Lombroso's dogmatism, as well as his lack of clinical experience, or scientific case notes. Rather, they were concerned to differentiate between environmentally and biologically determined criminals. The former could be redeemed and made into respectable citizens, while the latter (a comparatively small number) were irredeemable.[16] This distinction shaded into that found in the report of the Troup Committee on the Identification of Habitual Criminals that claimed in the early 1890s, that:

> If a distinction be made between a 'professional' criminal – the man who has deliberately adopted a career of dishonesty or violence as a means of obtaining a livelihood – and the man who only lapses into crime occasionally and, as it may be said, under the stress of circumstances, it is clear that the travelling thief or burglar belongs almost always to the former rather than the latter category.[17]

At much the same date, Charles Booth, the social investigator, was making similar distinctions within his survey of working-class London, *Life and Labour of the People in London*. At the very bottom of London's population he placed a Class A of hereditary 'occasional labourers, street sellers, loafers, criminals

and semi-criminals', that was distinct from other strata of the working population who were poor because of competition and irregular wages.[18] Ambivalence
over the respective roles of nature and nurture in criminality was a widespread
feature of European thought at this time.[19]

IDENTIFYING THE CRIMINAL BODY AS SURFACE

Whether or not the criminal was a biological, rather than a social, entity, the
Victorian penal system had a new incentive to identify the deviant, and so differentiate him or her from the respectable. However, although the criminal
was still identified using the body, there was a shift from identification *on* the
body, to identification *through* the body. As already noted, the physical marking of the deviant body through mutilation or branding had died out by the
early years of the nineteenth century. Despite suggestions as late as the 1860s
that such methods should be reintroduced to identify the habitual criminal,[20]
identification of the deviant increasingly meant the generation, storage and
retrieval of information about aspects of the criminal body.

This shift could be understood in terms of broader changes to the manner in which the body was conceived in the nineteenth century. In the early
modern period the body was conceived in Galenic terms as a unique balance
of the four humours, and illness was the outward manifestation of imbalances
therein. The role of the physician was to look for outward symptoms, or signs,
of these inner imbalances, and to attempt to intervene to rebalance the system.
Increasingly in the modern period, however, biomedicine came to understand
the body as a series of systems that could be examined through internal examination and measurement. Disease was then reconceptualized as the impact on
these differing systems of external pathogens, or a degeneration of the former.
This historical model of development was given its classic form in some of the
early works of Michel Foucault, especially his *Naissance de la clinique – une
archéologie du regard médical* (1963), and *Les mots et les choses – une archéologie
des sciences humaines* (1966).[21] By analogy, the criminal body ceased to be the
bearer of marks, and became a collection of systems to be measured.

At first, however, rather than biometrics, the new criminal information systems merely attempted to consolidate forms of description and registration.
As already noted, prisons and police forces had long been creating registers of
criminals of both sexes, and both the Habitual Criminal Registry, and the later
Metropolitan Police Convict Supervision Office set up in 1880, maintained
similar registers for criminal identification. The latter contained physical

descriptions, and records of 'distinguishing marks'.[22] Criminal identification was becoming a matter of centralized information systems. Since the criminal population was no longer to be transported to the Australian colonies, the military systems of bureaucratic identification that had been elaborated there in the early nineteenth century were repatriated to the centre of empire. On this basis it could be argued that it was actually a decline in the mobility of criminals that led to the creation of new forms of deviant identification in England, rather than increasing movement or anonymity. Criminals exported to Australia could be ignored, habitual criminals at home could not.

The photographing of male and female convicts as part of this consolidation of registration began early in England. The Birmingham police may have started taking photographic portraits of criminals in 1850, and the Bristol prison governor James Anthony Gardner was using photography in 1852.[23] Photography in prison registers spread rapidly thereafter.[24] Under the 1871 Prevention of Crimes Act, photographs of convicts were also sent by prison governors to the Habitual Criminals Registry, which held 34,000 portraits by 1888.[25] The use of photography was also developing in French and German policing at about the same date, although the New York Police Department held 450 ambrotype photographs as early as 1858.[26] In 1876 Dr William Matthews, in his graphically titled *From Chili to Piccadilly with Sir Roger Tichborne. The Santiago Daguerreo-Types and the London Photographs Compared. Identity Demonstrated Geometrically, etc.*, used a type of composite photography to blend photographs of Sir Roger Tichborne and the Claimant. As his title reveals, he showed, at least to his own satisfaction, that they were one and the same person.[27] This sort of work was taken further by Sir Francis Galton, the great Victorian polymath, who superimposed photographs of certain sorts of criminals in an attempt to reveal ideal criminal types.[28]

However, despite the publication of alphabetical registers of habitual criminals giving names, 'distinctive marks' and descriptions, such aids to identification were infrequently used by the police. This was because the information they contained could not be easily retrieved. In practice, one needed a name to use the registers properly, which somewhat undermined their use as a means of identification. The published registers were only for prisoners released in one year and did not, therefore, contain all habitual criminals; few marks were really distinctive; and the registers were published up to 20 months after a convict's release – the period when he or she was most likely to reoffend.[29] In addition, sepia photographs could not easily be classified and indexed, especially by colour of eyes or hair, and the whole collection might have to be searched manually to find a particular individual. In practice, people could look alike, easily disguise their appearance, 'mug' in front of the camera, or change as they grew older.[30]

The problems of using registers of this type meant that many policemen preferred to rely on personal recognition. Convicts released on licence had to report to the police every month which meant that the police acquired some skill in facial recognition. It was also the practice to house all prisoners remanded in London in Holloway Prison, where they were inspected three times a week by police officers and warders from all divisions of the Metropolitan Police. If the criminal was unknown to the police in one division, he might be recognized by those from another. This was considered by the police as being a very effective method of identifying repeat criminals. In 1883, for instance, 1,826 repeat offenders were identified by this exercise, 1,711 in 1888 and 1,949 in 1893. However, each successful identification cost an average of 90 hours of detectives' time, which made this a costly procedure.[31]

Moreover, the use of such subjective methods could lead to serious miscarriages of justice, as in the notorious case of Adolf Beck. In 1877, a conman known as John Smith was convicted of theft after approaching successive women 'of loose character' claiming to be a nobleman. He would invite them to become his mistress, install them in a house in St John's Wood, and then disappear after stealing his victims' money or jewellery. Smith was sentenced to five years' imprisonment. In 1895, another of Smith's victims encountered Adolf Beck, a businessman, in the street and denounced him to the police as the man who had tricked her. Beck denied the charge but was identified as Smith not only by several other women but also by the police constable who had originally arrested Smith in 1877. Sentenced to seven years in jail, Beck was treated as a repeat offender. He petitioned the Home Office several times but only in 1896 did officials examine Smith's records. They then discovered that the prison doctor had reported that Smith was circumcised, while Beck was not. So Beck's previous conviction was struck out but his current conviction was left untouched. He was released in 1901, but was arrested yet again on a similar charge in 1904 and convicted once more. The judge, evidently suspicious, postponed sentence, and in July of that year Smith was arrested for acts that were committed while Beck was still in prison. This led to Beck's release and pardon, and he was awarded £5,000 as compensation. A committee of enquiry investigated the whole sorry affair, and concluded that evidence of identity based solely on personal recognition was unreliable.[32] The use of bodily similarities to identify individuals bears similarities to the case of the Tichborne Claimant, while the fallibility of personal recognition recalls that of Martin Guerre.

Similar issues arose in respect of the long and controversial history of identification parades. One of the first recorded instances of the use of such parades in England was in the case of the public protests at Queen Caroline's funeral procession in August 1821. The Queen, the estranged wife of George IV, was an icon of radical discontent in the troubled years between the end of the Napoleonic Wars and the passage of the 1832 Reform Act.[33] On her death the Prime Minister, Lord Liverpool, refused to allow her body to be conveyed through the City of London for fear of rioting, and had it escorted by the Life Guards who had orders to remove the body from the country to Caroline's native Brunswick. The soldiers opened fire when demonstrators erected barricades in Oxford Street, and killed two men, Richard Hanney and George Francis. The whole of the 1st Regiment of Life Guards was paraded and examined by witnesses, under the supervision of the Bow Street magistrates, who picked out individual soldiers. But the identifications did not lead to prosecutions because the soldiers denied involvement to the inquest jury, who eventually returned a verdict of 'murder by an officer to the jury unknown'.[34] Metropolitan Police orders of 1860 began the regularization of the identification parade, and detailed Metropolitan Police regulations concerning them were commended to all chief constables in 1905.[35]

However, there were still continued problems with identity parades, and two cases of mistaken identity leading to wrongful convictions – that of Luke Dougherty for a robbery from a supermarket in Sunderland in 1972, and of Laslo Virag, who was convicted of theft from parking metre boxes in Liverpool and Bristol in 1969 – resulted in the establishment in 1974 of the Devlin Committee on Evidence of Identification in Criminal Cases. Devlin concluded that modern research showed that visual ID, either at parades, or in the dock, was unreliable, and concluded that, 'the power of the average witness to recall accurately is very limited.' In a draft letter to the Chairman of the Bar Council the Committee went even further and declared that in the case of dock identification, 'All evidence suggests that it is nearly valueless.' The problems with such identifications were actually increased in cases where witnesses were shown photographs of the accused beforehand. Devlin recommended identity parade identification should always be corroborated by other forms of evidence.[36] The identity parade came to be seen as irredeemably subjective, although their use and reliability as a form of identification is still being debated by modern forensic psychologists.[37]

Similar problems were discovered with the use by witnesses of Identikits to build up likenesses of criminals. The Identikit, an extension of earlier verbal descriptions and line drawings, was developed by Hugh C. MacDonald, the chief of the Civilian Division of the Los Angeles Police Department. In 1940 he was in Europe investigating cases where criminals had taken advantage of the wartime movement of people to commit fraud, or evade detection. To save time, rather than sketching descriptions he developed a set of different noses, eyes and face shapes, on transparent plastic sheets that could be built up into complete faces. With the Townsend Company of California he produced a commercial system including 525 coded and numbered transparencies, with 102 pairs of eyes, 32 noses, 33 lips, 52 chins, and 25 moustaches and beards. The codes meant that faces could be transmitted over the wire without the police having to send whole graphics. The first case in London where an Identikit was employed was in 1960, when one was used to apprehend the killer of Elsie Batten, stabbed to death in an antiques shop off the Charing Cross Road. By September 1969 there were 42 Identikit systems in use England and Wales, with between 2,500 and 3,000 pictures produced annually. The Identikit was replaced in the 1970s by the Photo-Fit system invented by Jacques Penry. This was a kit containing the facial features of five groups of people photographed front on, which were updated annually. It contained about 200 forehead/hair-styles, 100 pairs of eyes, 90 noses, 100 mouths and 75 chin/cheek sections, as well as hats, moustaches, age lines and chinagraph pencils for additions.[38] In the late 1980s this was replaced in turn by the computer graphics system E-FIT (Electronic Facial Identification Technique).[39]

However, a report by the Home Office Police Research and Development Branch in 1969 saw a number of problems with the Identikit system:

1. it needed to be used soon after a crime lest the witness's memory was contaminated by delay, or by further stimuli in the form of looking through photograph albums;
2. the Identikit needed to be kept up to date with changes in fashions in hairstyles and in different countries;
3. it seemed to be more effective with women and children than with men.[40]

The Photo-Fit system, with its annual updates, was intended to solve some of these problems. However, the Devlin Committee had doubts about its effectiveness. Research undertaken at the University of Aberdeen showed that subjects performed rather poorly in constructing a Photo-Fit likeness, even when the original was in front of them. In tests the number of correct identifications using the system was just one in eight, and the production of photofits in actual criminal investigations only led to positive identifications and arrests in 5 per cent of cases.[41]

CREATING THE FIRST CRIMINAL DATABASE:
ANTHROPOMETRICS

The problem with many of these subjective forms of identification was that they depended upon someone interpreting whether a particular criminal in the flesh was one and the same as the criminal recorded in registers. Did they look the same as a photograph; what was a 'fair complexion'; were the distinguishing marks the same; was this the tattoo recorded in the register; and so on? Increasingly, from the late nineteenth century onwards, the solution to this dilemma was to make the flesh of the criminal the token of his or her identity. Aspects of the body – its measurements, the structure of skin, its genetic coding – became the data held in registries, which was then compared to the flesh of the criminal. The forms of subjective identification of the criminal so far described became supplementary to these more objective database systems that have been built up since the end of the nineteenth century.

The first attempt to create an information system that identified the individual criminal objectively, and that allowed systematic retrieval, was anthropometrics. This was the system of identification through bodily measurement developed by Alphonse Bertillon in France in the 1880s.[42] Alphonse was the son of Louis-Adolphe Bertillon, one of the pioneers of nineteenth-century social sciences such as demography and anthropology. As such Alphonse grew up in a home filled with anthropometric measuring tools, which were used by his father to make 'scientific' observations of the bodies of 'savages' and people of other races. The assumption underlying these inquiries was that human attributes – intelligence, savagery, race, ethnicity, heredity, evolutionary history, and so on – were manifest in the measurable features of the body, especially in the dimensions of the skull.[43] Such anthropology had an obvious racial aspect both in Europe and in the colonies of European empires.[44]

Bertillon Junior was plainly something of a misfit, and did not settle down to a formal education, or a career. He was expelled from the Imperial Lycée at Versailles in 1870 for carrying out cookery experiments in his Greek classes. He had installed a spirit lamp, chocolate and a miniature saucepan in his desk, which inevitably caught fire.[45] Through contacts made during his medical and statistical work for the Paris municipality, his father was able to get him a job in the Parisian Prefecture of Police in 1879. Bertillon's clerical work brought him into contact with the Prefecture's collection of convict photographs. The French had been collecting pen portraits of criminals since 1819 in the 'redaction du bureau des prisons',[46] and photography had been used in sections of the Paris Prefecture from as early as 1872, with suspects photographed unsystematically from various angles and with various degrees of expertise. The photographs were then catalogued by name alone, and so could not be used when the criminal unsportingly gave a false name, something that Bertillon noticed when filing the photographic forms.[47] As he put it in his *Identification Anthropometrique* of 1893:

> On avait cru un moment, il y a trente ans, que la photographie allait donner la solution de la question [of the identification of criminals]. Mais la collection des portraits judiciaires ainsi rassemblés ne tarda pas à attaeindre un nombre si considerable qu'il devint matériellment impracticable retrouver, *de découvrir*, parmi eux, l'image de'un individu qui dissimulait son nom.[48]

However, he noticed from the photographs that the bodily measurements of no two individuals were exactly alike. Bertillon saw that he could apply the measuring techniques that his father had taught him to criminals, but rather than using them for the purpose of classifying humanity into groups, he could isolate individuals from each other, and show them to be in some respects unique.[49]

The anthropometric technique that Bertillon developed involved elaborate measurements of parts of the body of a criminal, both male and female. These were recorded on a card along with carefully controlled discursive descriptions of features and distinctive marks, and a photograph. The measurements were used to classify individuals and to allow for easy retrieval of information when they were remeasured at a later date, but it was the peculiar marks and the photographs that were then used for identification.[50] In addition, the precise descriptions and standardized abbreviations formed the basis of Bertillon's 'portrait parlé', via which a trained operator could transmit via the telegraph a usable physical description of a criminal to another operator entirely in words, numbers and coded abbreviations.[51] The identification of the deviant was thus reduced to standardized information which could be stored in an information system, retrieved at a later date and transmitted over distances. In this manner identification ceased to require 'co-presence' between the authenticating identifier and the identified, who could now be widely separated in time and space.[52] MacDonald's Identikit system plainly drew on these aspects of Bertillon's work.

Anthropometrics was widely adopted by the police in France, and was introduced into the Metropolitan Police in London in the 1890s. Moreover, anthropometrics could be used for other purposes than criminal investigation. In 1896, for example, Bertillon was called upon to photograph and measure the bodies of the crew and passengers of the *Drummond Castle*, a ship en route from South Africa to London, that struck the Pierres Vertes off Ushant. Of the

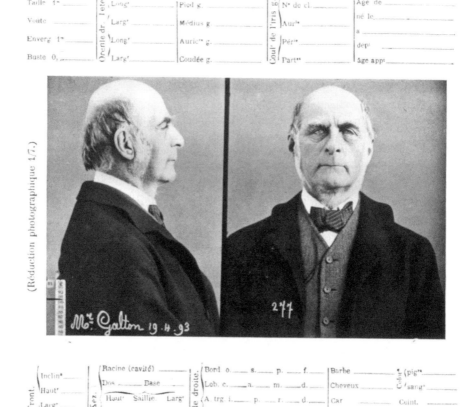

Photograph and Bertillon record of Francis Galton (age 73) created upon Galton's visit to Bertillon's laboratory in 1893.(Source: Karl Pearson's *The Life, Letters, and Labours of Francis Galton*, vol. 2, ch. 13, plate LII).

53 bodies recovered, Bertillon was able to describe 27, and 10 were identified from his descriptions.[53] 'Bertillonage' appeared to hold out the possibility of a standardized and reliable method of general identification.

FINGERPRINTING AND THE ADVENT OF MODERN CRIMINAL IDENTIFICATION

However, although Bertillonage allowed the criminal identity to be reduced to a code that could be retrieved from within an information system, it had serious drawbacks as a forensic technique for the British police. These included the requirement for costly instruments that required calibration; training for operatives on the decimal, rather than imperial, scale; the possibility of error in transcribing measurements; the time taken to perform measurements (in triplicate); and the complicated procedure for searching through records.[54] Moreover, in May 1888 anthropometrics was criticized theoretically, rather than on practical grounds, by Sir Francis Galton in a Friday Evening Discourse at the Royal Institution titled 'Personal Identification and Description'. Galton had two main objections, first, that Bertillon divided physical characteristics such as the width of the head, and the length of the middle, or little finger, into large, medium and small, for classification. Galton saw this division as arbitrary because Bertillon was dividing a continuously varying characteristic into three discrete, discontinuous groups. Also, Bertillon ignored the possibility that body parts were correlated – that, for example, long feet and long middle-fingers usually go together. At the end of this talk Galton first suggested in public that fingerprinting – 'those fine lines of which the buttered fingers of children are apt to stamp impressions on the margins of books they handle' – might be a better method of personal identification.[55]

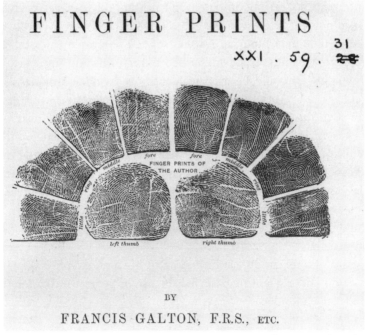

Francis Galton's fingerprints. (Source: Title page of Francis Glaton's *Finger Prints* (1892))

Fingerprinting was actually a very ancient technique of identification. Archaeological evidence from seventh-century China shows fingerprints embossed on clay seals that were used to sign documents, and the practice may have been as old as the Han dynasty (202 BC–AD 220). In 1303 the Persian historian Rashid-al-din, reporting the use of fingerprints as signatures in China, declared, 'Experience shows that no two individuals have fingers precisely alike.'[56] Closer to home, in 1691 a group of 225 citizens living near Londonderry sent two ambassadors to petition William III for compensation for losses they had suffered during his recent conflicts in Ireland with James II. The citizens promised to pay their ambassadors, if their negotiations were successful, one-sixth of the amount granted by William, and 'signed' the covenant to this effect with their fingers.[57] However, the first systematic modern use of fingerprinting for forensic purposes was actually in Argentina, where Juan Vucetich, a Croatian-born anthropologist and police official, introduced his own system in the early 1890s.[58]

The story of forensic fingerprinting in England and its Empire revolves around the activities of four men, Sir William Herschel, Henry Faulds, Sir Francis Galton and Sir Edward Henry. Herschel was a British civil servant in India who used fingerprints for identifying 'native' Indians in the 1850s and 1860s, although his various initiatives do not appear to have survived after he returned home.[59] Interest in the subject in England was revived by a letter published in 1880 in the journal *Nature* from an obscure medical missionary in Tokyo, Henry Faulds. Faulds described fingerprints and suggested various ways in which they could be used to identify individuals uniquely.[60] In the 1880s Faulds tried to get the Metropolitan Police interested in using fingerprints for identification purposes but with little success.[61] He also wrote to Charles Darwin about his ideas, who, characteristically, claimed that ill health prevented him from corresponding further and passed Faulds' letter on to his cousin, Francis Galton. Galton subsequently downplayed Faulds' contribution to the development of fingerprinting, and gave the credit for the technique's development to the more establishment figure of Herschel. This led in turn to an acrimonious debate between the three men over their respective contributions to the field.

In a series of publications, culminating in his monograph *Finger Prints* of 1892,[62] Galton laid a scientific basis for the use of fingerprinting for the purposes of identification by:

1. showing that an individual's prints persisted over time;
2. giving an argument based on probability for the near-uniqueness of prints; and

3. showing that fingerprints were heritable but not to a degree that would preclude identification between siblings.[63]

He also devised a scheme of classification to permit the filing and retrieval of prints. However, Galton had to admit before the 1893 Troup Committee on the Identification of Habitual Criminals, that although he had managed to classify fingerprints into broad categories, he had not devised a working method of subclassification, which would allow a practical means of retrieving individual records.[64]

The creation of a fully effective means of classifying fingerprints was the achievement of Sir Edward Henry when Inspector-General of Police in the Bengal in the 1890s, although he may merely have been taking credit for the work of his Indian subordinates. The verbose title of his monograph describing the new system, published by the Indian authorities in 1896, *Bengal Police: Instructions for Classifying and Deciphering Finger Impressions and for Describing Them with Sufficient Exactness to Enable Comparison of the Description with the Original Impression to be Satisfactorily Made*, reveals the centrality of information retrieval in his method.[65] Henry subsequently introduced the new system into the Metropolitan Police when he became Assistant Commissioner in charge of CID at Scotland Yard in 1901.[66] On the recommendation of the 1900 Belper Committee on the Identification of Criminals, fingerprinting replaced anthropometrics as the principle means of criminal identification.[67] As with anthropometrics, criminal identification was reduced to information that could be stored, retrieved, and subsequently transmitted over the telegraph in coded form.[68]

The Henry system of fingerprinting came to be increasingly imbedded in the work of the British police. A small police laboratory was set up on Cardiff in 1902 with fingerprints and photography as its basis, and the West Riding of Yorkshire set up a fingerprints registry in 1907.[69] From England the new technology spread throughout the Empire, and beyond. Canada, for example, moved quickly to embrace fingerprinting for criminal identification. It was pioneered there by Inspector Edward Foster of the Dominion Police, who had been sent to guard an exhibit of Canadian gold at the 1904 Saint Louis World Fair, and attended a talk on fingerprinting by John Ferrier from the Metropolitan Police. Foster subsequently became head of the Canadian Criminal Identification Bureau in 1910.[70] Fingerprinting also came into the United States via contacts with Scotland Yard. Henry DeForest, the chief medical examiner of the New York Civil Service Commission visited New Scotland Yard in 1902, and a year later the New York State Bureau of Prisons sent two representatives to London, who brought back a copy of Henry's *Classification and the Use of Finger Prints*. In addition, John Ferrier remained in the United States after the 1904 World Fair to train identification clerks in the Henry system.[71] Similarly, Inspector John Tunbridge of the Metropolitan Police CID, with whom Henry Faulds had corresponded unsuccessfully, became Commissioner of Police in New Zealand in 1897, and subsequently introduced the fingerprint system there.[72] Fingerprinting was thus a technique that circulated round the Empire, with London acting as a nodal centre of dispersion, in much the same way as civil registration had spread some 60 years before. However, in the case of fingerprinting England was as much importing knowledge as originating it.

Francis Galton believed that fingerprint evidence could be evaluated by untrained laypersons, and that experts would only be needed to interpret blurred prints. Nevertheless, courts in England were soon calling upon fingerprint experts to give expert testimony in court.[73] However, compared to their American colleagues, British fingerprint specialists erred on the side of caution. In Britain fingerprinting was not originally a very scientific activity, being carried out by police officers or clerks trained via manuals and apprenticeships. This explains the high number (16) of points of similarity between prints for a positive identification required by British fingerprint experts in order to maintain confidence in their methods.[74] By contrast the Americans relied on fewer points of similarity, and preferred to leave identification up to the judgement of the fingerprint professional. North American fingerprint examiners were preoccupied with being perceived as scientists, and they soon established a number of professional bodies – the International Association of Criminal Identification (IACI) in 1915, and the International Association for Identification (IAI) and the International Society for Personal Identification (ISPI), both in 1919.[75]

The spread of fingerprinting through the British Empire would have some far-reaching consequences for the future cohesion of that geopolitical colossus as a result of its introduction into the South African pass laws. This system had its origins in the eighteenth-century Dutch Cape Colony, in which a regulation of 1760 required that any slave moving between town and country had to carry a pass authorizing his journey, and signed by his owner. Thus, when the British took control of the Cape during the Napoleonic Wars, a system of passes already existed for the non-white population. Pass laws were amended and new ones were introduced at the Cape in 1809, in the Transvaal in 1844, and again in 1867, 1874, and 1883. The purpose of these laws was to control the movement and labour of native peoples, both for work in urban

also began to set up a series of regional forensic laboratories, the beginnings of the modern Forensic Science Service. The East Midlands Forensic Science Laboratory in Nottingham was, for example, established in 1936 to undertake various types of analysis:

Chemical – identification of blood, stains, poisons, dust;

Physical – ultraviolet, infrared photography, handwriting, typewriting and print;

Biological 'identification of blood species, blood groups, spermatozoa, and so on, hairs, fragments of plants, insects, and so on.[86]

The Home Office publication of *Scientific Aids to Criminal Investigation: Forensic Science Circulars* began in 1936, and such guides soon began to be circulated in Britain, the Empire, and internationally.[87] The caseload of the Metropolitan Police Laboratory subsequently took off during the Second World War, with 260 cases in 1936, 165 in 1940, 400 in 1945, and 855 in 1951. There was also a similar expansion in the Forensic Science Service and regional services, whose overall budget increased from £58,000 in 1940 to £662,000 in 1946. The expansion of the forensic services in the postwar period appears to have reflected the greater prestige of science as a consequence of the War, and the advances made in scientific techniques. The police also had a greater familiarity with what science could do for them as more police came to be trained at Hendon. British forensic science began to be professionalized in the late 1950s and early 1960s with the establishment of the Forensic Science Society and the British Academy of Forensic Sciences. The first number of the *Journal of the Forensic Science Society* appeared in 1960.[88]

This forensic service pioneered the development of techniques that would pave the way for the later introduction of technologies such as DNA profiling. Identification of the deviant was passing beyond recording the surface of the body to concern itself with bodily fluids. This is seen most obviously in the development of blood group serology, based on the work of the Austrian Karl Landsteiner in the first decade of the twentieth century. However, many of the problems with the technique were not overcome until the discovery of the Rh blood groups in the 1940s, and the practical developments associated with blood transfusions for troops during the Second World War.[89] Serology inevitably became involved in the seamier side of police work. Thus, in the return of work at the West Midlands Forensic Science Laboratory, Birmingham, for the quarter ending 30 September 1938 is a sad note that on 9 July in Oxford:

A girl, aged 9 years, stated that she slipped in a stream, and made one of her socks wet, whereupon a man put the sock into his pocket 'to dry it'. The girl complained that he then indecently exposed himself and indecently assaulted her. Dr Webster examined the girl's clothing and found many large stains upon the knickers, from two of which he recovered human spermatozoa. He also found human spermatozoa on the child's dress. The accused asked at the Police Court that the group of the seminal stains should be compared with his blood group. The test was carried out by Dr Webster, who found that the seminal stains were caused by someone with group 'A' and the blood of the accused was also group 'A'.[90]

In the same year Webster was also undertaking private work in Birmingham to prove paternity of a child through examining the blood groups of a man, a woman and her infant son.[91] Thus, modern identification was returning to an examination of lineage, although in a rather grubbier manner than that ever envisaged by the medieval Court of Heralds.

ALIENS IN THE DOSSIER SOCIETY

Given the increasing desire in the late Victorian and Edwardian periods to use techniques and technologies of identification to demarcate the boundaries of the respectable political nation from the criminal, it should come as no surprise that much the same happened with respect to the identification of the alien. The centrality of politics in these developments, rather than the imperatives of mobility, can be seen even more clearly than in the case of the habitual criminal.

The Victorian policy of relatively lax controls on aliens in England came to an end in 1905. The Aliens Act of that year (5 Edw. VII, c.13) empowered immigration officers chosen from among the customs inspectors to examine and reject aliens considered undesirable – the diseased, insane, criminal and the putative public charge.[92] The 1905 Act was less than watertight since it only related to aliens travelling in steerage or in boats with 20 or more aliens – it could be evaded in theory by choosing a boat carrying 19 aliens or less, or travelling first class. The 'posh' and the careful could slip through the net. However, since the shipping companies could be fined for bringing in 'undesirables', there may have been screening even before aliens got on board ship.[93] Shipping companies were being turned into agents of the State, much as airlines have been co-opted in the contemporary world to control movement. The 1905 legislation appears to have been introduced by a Conservative government concerned to attract working-class voters, especially in the East End of London, who were opposed to the immigration of Jews fleeing persecution and poverty in Eastern Europe. This needs to be seen in the context of the competition in the Edwardian period between the Conservative and Liberal parties, and the recently founded Labour Party, for new voters in an emergent mass democracy.[94] As with the local xenophobia associated with the decentralized polity of early modern England, so the creation of national citizens' rights created a desire to defend the national patrimony. Much the same was happening in other European countries, such as France, at the same period.[95] As Adam McKeown has noted the link between white democracy and immigration controls can also be found in the British dominions.[96]

The First World War further developed this policy of exclusion. In a world in which mass, democratic societies were being mobilized for total warfare, all aliens were potential, or presumed, enemies. The Status of Aliens Act (4 & 5 Geo. V, c.17), passed the day after war was declared, ordered the registration with the police of all aliens over the age of 16 years. The requirement for aliens to register with the police was renewed by the 1919 Aliens Restriction (Amendment) Act (9 & 10 Geo. V, c.92). The legislation gave the State powers to require aliens to give the police detailed particulars including name, address, marital status, employment or occupation, including employer's name and address, a photograph, and to pay a registration fee. A registered person was also required to inform the authorities of changes of address, marital status, nationality, and of employment or occupation. In return the individual received a police certificate of registration. The information on the certificates included full name, date of birth, date of arrival into the United Kingdom, employment history, address, marital status, details of any children and date of naturalization, and they usually bore at least one photograph. Each alien was also issued with a six-digit number, linked to their registration data. For the first time in history, the government had some reasonably accurate information concerning migrants in terms of numbers, places of residence, occupations and race, while aliens had to have 'papers'.[97] Political exigencies had created a new surveillance society.

CONCLUSION

The identification of the deviant in the century after 1850 reveals increasing centralization, bureaucratization and the use of scientific techniques. But above all, it saw the association of these new forms of identification with the creation of information systems and databases. These processes would be taken much further in the period after 1970 with the advent of the electronic computer in government and commerce. There are certain features of this process, however, that should be noted. First, it cannot be explained simply in terms of increasing mobility and anonymity. More important was the creation of a new type of nation-state based on mass democracy in which the respectable voter was to be distinguished from the criminal and the alien. Secondly, the identification of the deviant was still in terms of the body, although the official gaze passed from applied 'marks of Cain', to the skin as an organ of the body, and even to its internal constituents. In the same period, however, the identification of the respectable still revolved around earlier methods – possessions, abilities, documentation and communal knowledge. This will be the subject of the next chapter.

8

Towards the 'Dossier Society': Identifying Citizens and Customers in England, 1850 to 1970

The identification of the juridical person and of the citizen in the years 1850 to 1970 may have involved similar principles to that of earlier periods but, as already noted, it took place in a rather different context. The central State grew in importance compared to local authorities, and even to civil society. This was partly due to the decline of the local community – there are simply not enough people at the lower level willing to take on the sorts of responsibilities that had been undertaken by local magistrates, overseers of the poor and local constables, in the early modern period. But the rise of the central State in Britain had also something to do with processes of globalization and imperial decline. At the end of the nineteenth century, Britain probably had the most decentralized state in Europe, so it's subsequent loss of imperial hegemony undermined faith in local initiative. 'National efficiency' seemed to require central, rather than local, activity.[1] This can be seen in the gradual withering of the local Poor Laws, and their replacement by central forms of welfare, such as old age pensions (1908), National Insurance (1911), and in the postwar Welfare State.[2]

This new centralized welfare provision, and the vastly expanded system of personal taxation that supported it, created novel problems of identification since there was a dissociation in time and space between the welfare claim and the decision to grant it. How in the absence of personal knowledge was the central bureaucrat to know if claimants were who they said they were? What new 'performances' were necessary to convince central bureaucrats of one's identity? This new, more interventionist State was also one that discriminated by age, placing obligations on individuals, families and employers not to employ children before a certain age, to send their children to school at another, and which granted benefits to the elderly when they reached a particular birthday. As a consequence, individuals had to prove their dates of birth with increasing regularity.[3]

In the period 1850 to 1970, the size and scale of commercial organizations were also increasing.[4] This could be seen, for example, in the retailing sector, as department stores, cooperative associations and multiples began to encroach on the corner shop.[5] How was the commercial bureaucrat to check the identity and probity of the individual asking for credit? Moreover, a new philosophy of management based on system and efficiency was developing in these large organizations, in which the collection, analysis and communication of corporate information came to serve as a mechanism for managerial coordination and control.[6] This movement of 'systematic management' was also associated with changing technologies within the office – the development of the file, the typewriter, carbon paper, early duplicators and mechanical calculators for accounting purposes.[7] Such developments were eventually to have important implications for the development of institutions, and of systems for identifying customers and creditors, yet this was perhaps a matter of scale rather than of kind in this period. For the middle classes the signature was still the fundamental basis of identification in commercial transactions, and in many interactions with the State.

FINGERPRINTING AND THE CITIZEN IN THE NASCENT WELFARE STATE[8]

The reaction of the State to the crisis of identification in the new Welfare State was halting, and inconsistent. The Treasury in central London became increasingly interested in the identification of those receiving welfare benefits in the years immediately prior to the First World War. In 1914 a Treasury Committee on the Periodical Identification of Government Pensioners had been set up, made up of representatives from state bodies that paid pensions to their ex-employees, such as the War Office, Admiralty, Board of Customs and Excise, and Post Office. The Committee expressed itself satisfied with existing departmental arrangements for preventing fraud via the periodic scrutiny of claimants, which was mainly undertaken through the personal interviewing of samples of pensioners to check their identity and eligibility.[9]

However, the introduction of old age pensions in 1908, and of unemployment and health benefits under the 1911 National Insurance Act (1 & 2 Geo. V, c.55), made the Treasury profoundly uneasy. How could the State guard against impersonation and fraudulent claims by the 'great unwashed', who the Treasury viewed with intense disquiet? As a Treasury official noted in a memorandum of 1920:

> Fraud – which was not unknown before the war – may very likely in a few years time become widespread, particularly in view of the greater value of the present pension: and the problem of detecting fraud has clearly assumed proportions for which previous methods are quite inadequate.[10]

The Treasury had returned to the subject of the identification of pensioners during the First World War, after receiving a memorandum from the Chief Commissioner of Medical Services at the short-lived Ministry of National Service. In a covering letter to his memorandum of April 1918, the Chief Commissioner declared that given the proposed payment of war pensions to large numbers of demobilized fighting men, 'a simple and certain method of identifying the discharged Soldier, Sailor and Marine is absolutely necessary in the interests both of the individual and the State: the only method which possesses the required qualifications is Finger-Print'.[11] The Treasury forwarded the memorandum to the War Office, who turned down the idea, on the grounds that it:

> has always been ruled that it was not possible to enforce such a system at a time when the Army was a voluntary organization, and, until it has been decided whether the Military Forces of the Crown are to be maintained on a voluntary or compulsory basis when the present war is terminated, it is not considered advisable to re-open the matter.[12]

This is perhaps a rather odd argument given that the British Army had been largely a conscript one since 1915.[13]

In 1919 the Treasury was asked by the Public Accounts Committee of the House of Commons to produce a report 'showing the means which have been devised to guard against fraud by pensioners'. As a result the Treasury sent out a circular letter to departments asking what they did about identifying pensioners, and how they would feel about the use of fingerprinting for this purpose.[14] The resulting replies showed that some minor departments were in favour of the proposal. The Ministry of Pensions, however, was opposed to the idea, and the War Office was again adamant that 'they could not agree to finger-prints of soldiers being taken during their service'.[15] By early 1921 the Treasury had reluctantly come to the conclusion, 'that it is not possible to introduce at present a system of identification by means of finger prints'. Instead it proposed, in line with the system already introduced for ex-government employees, that all departments should review 20 per cent of pensioners annually by question-naire and interview to ensure 'identification, and assurance of their contin-ued eligibility for pensions'.[16] However, much to the Treasury's annoyance, this procedure does not appear to have been followed by other government depart-ments, probably because of the extra workload it would involve in the postwar period of financial restraint known as the 'Geddes Axe'.[17]

This rejection of fingerprinting as a means of identifying the citizen would have disappointed the Victorian pioneers of the technology, all of whom saw the technique as a way of protecting property rights. In this they were inevita-bly influenced by the case of the Tichborne Claimant. Henry Faulds, for exam-ple, witnessed the huge crowds outside the Old Bailey waiting to hear the latest news in the Tichborne case as he was preparing to sail to Japan in 1873. He later claimed that, 'From that time the question of identification as a pressing scientific problem in medical jurisprudence was never long absent from my mind.'[18] Similarly, in an article in 1891 quaintly titled 'Identification by finger tips', Francis Galton pointed to the Tichborne case, warning that in the absence of sure means of identification, 'some alien scoundrel from foreign parts may assert himself to be the long-lost rightful claimant to an estate held in previous security by others on the supposition of his decease'.[19] William Herschel like-wise wrote to an official in India, noting that if there had been fingerprints of Sir Roger Tichborne in existence, then 'the whole Orton imposture would have been exposed to the full satisfaction of the jury in a single sitting by requiring Orton to make his own mark for comparison'.[20] In India, Herschel had used fingerprints as a means of identifying people for a whole range of civil purpos-es.[21] Juan Vucetich had also hoped to establish a national fingerprint registry in Argentina to allow citizens to identify themselves, and so protect themselves and their honour from 'simulation'.[22]

But in England, as already noted, the use of the body for the purposes of identi-fication, and of fingerprinting in particular, was associated with criminality. This was recognized by the Chief Commissioner of Medical Services when he suggested the introduction of fingerprinting for discharged soldiers in 1918. The British public, he noted, had a 'sentimental' objection to the proposal because it was so accustomed to associate fingerprinting with 'the identification of members of the criminal classes that public opinion would be offended and scandalized by it appli-cation to the discharged soldier and sailor'.[23] However, placing his faith in the pro-verbial common sense of the ordinary Englishman and woman, he went on:

> This objection is a real and serious one, but it can hardly be doubted that it can be
> overcome if resolutely and tactfully faced: public opinion in this country is amenable

to reason, and once convinced of the urgent necessity for the adoption of the measure as the only means of protecting the honest man, who has a claim on the country, and exposing the rogue who has none, it would accept with equanimity and approval so simple and effective a procedure.[24]

Somewhat more practically, however, the Ministry of Pensions was 'of the opinion that its adoption would be unpopular and would tend to produce hostility to the department initiating the practice' because of the fingerprint system's criminal associations.[25]

The similar position taken by the War Office in 1919 reflected its own experience of dealing with popular 'common sense'. In 1859 the Army had started vaccinating recruits on the inner part of the arm in order to identify deserters but, as an army memorandum later noted, 'the experiment gave rise to discontent and was abandoned three years later'. In 1869 a proposal to 'cup or cross cup' men discharged as disabled was rejected. In 1887 the Military Attaché in Paris brought to the War Office's attention the anthropometric system of identification developed by Bertillon. However, the War Office declined to introduce the system because the body parts of young army recruits were still growing, it was expensive to implement, and because 'of its supposed prejudicial effect on recruitment'.[26] In 1902 the Secretary of State for War set up a Committee on Identification by Fingerprints to consider whether the system could be used in the British Army. The Committee, which included the Army's Adjutant General, and the ever hyperactive Sir Edward Henry from the Metropolitan Police, concluded that 'some slight feeling, especially in Ireland, and to a certain extent in the public press, may be manifested against applying to His Majesty's soldiers a system at present limited in this country to criminals'. As a result, the Committee concluded that, 'Military opinion is unanimous that its application to all recruits on enlistment would have very prejudicial effect on recruiting', and the proposal was rejected.[27]

In addition, the association of fingerprinting with the identification of colonial peoples, just when the English were exhibiting one of their periodic bouts of hostility towards aliens, may have tainted it with a racial overtone. In India the British regarded all native peoples as essentially untrustworthy, if not downright criminal by birth.[28] As Thomas Babington Macaulay put it somewhat glibly:

> What horns are to the buffalo, what the paw is to the tiger, what the sting is to the bee, what beauty, according to the old Greek song, is to woman, deceit is to the Bengalee. Large promises, smooth excuses, elaborate tissues of circumstantial falsehood, chicanery, perjury, forgery, are the weapons, offensive and defensive, of the people of the Lower Ganges.[29]

The use of the body to identify Indians via fingerprinting should be seen in this context. Similarly, Francis Galton early experiments with fingerprinting reflected his belief that they would reveal inborn racial or criminal characteristics.[30] He also thought that the technique would be useful:

> in our tropical settlements, where the individual members of the swarms of dark and yellow-skinned races are mostly unable to sign their names and are otherwise hardly distinguishable by Europeans, and . . . are grossly addicted to personation and other varieties of fraudulent practice.[31]

Such associations would hardly endear the technique to 'respectable' Englishmen being inculcated with the notions of their country's unique forms of political responsibility and liberty. It should be noted, moreover, that the English were not alone at this time in this rejection of the fingerprinting of citizens. At almost the same date in France a newly introduced 'Identity Card of the French' was being rejected by the populace because the fingerprint it carried associated ordinary citizens with criminals.[32]

COMMUNITY AND DOCUMENTATION IN THE IDENTIFICATION OF THE CITIZEN, 1850 TO 1970

After the failure to introduce fingerprinting for civil purposes, the central State in England fell back on the traditional sources of identification for welfare claimants and citizens, the community and documentation. However, these means of identification were given a new, bureaucratic form. Indeed they came to be embedded physically in paper forms. Communal means of identification were carried over into the 'recommender system'. This involved some person with semi-official status in the local community countersigning the application forms of claimants to vouch for their identity and the information they supplied. For example, in order to determine claims under the 1908 Old Age Pensions Act, pensions officers were advised to obtain references from former employers, and 'respectable people on whose word reliance can be placed'. They could fall back on 'poor law officials, ministers of religion, clerks to the justices, petty session clerks, collectors of rates, police officials, shopkeepers, or officials connected with friendly and other provident societies, or with trade unions.'[33] Claimants for unemployment benefits under the 1911 National Insurance Act would also have their original applications sent back to previous employers for verification.[34] In the aftermath of the Great War, the widows and dependents of soldiers also had to have the forms by which they claimed allowances countersigned by local worthies.[35]

By the 1930s those claiming pensions from the Ministry of Pensions had to obtain a 'life certificate' proving their identity, which was to be attested by the usual officials or professionals – a minister of religion, a magistrate, a physician or surgeon, an officer of HM forces, a secretary of a friendly society, a postmaster or mistress, a police officer, a civil servant earning more than £200 a year, a solicitor, a bank manager, an accountant, a headteacher, or a chief area officer of the Ministry of Pensions.[36] This procedure seems to have developed out of the system of identification papers held by military pensioners in the late nineteenth century.[37] Life certificates were still being used for the dependents of soldiers who died in the Second World War.[38] In the interwar period, a similar range of communal elites was expected to countersign passport applications, and to sign the back of photographs forwarded with the applications to the Foreign Office.[39]

It was recognized from a very early date that there were problems with the recommender system. As early as the 1880s impecunious military pensioners were discovered to be pawning their life certificates. Pawnbrokers made the soldiers advances of cash, let the pensioners redeem their certificates after they had claimed their pensions, and then took a cut of the latter. In 1886 the clerk to the Chatham magistrates wrote to the War Office indicating that 'placards are placed in the windows of the lenders, drawing the attention of Pensioners to the fact that immediate advances are made to Pensioners.'[40] There was always a danger that life certificates could fall into the wrong hands. As a result of such concerns, cross-checking on the identity of pensioners who had served in the Army might also include asking for the provision of information that only the real pensioner would know. In the aftermath of the Great War 'test verifications' were carried out periodically on selected pensioners, during which they were asked where they were stationed at the time of Victoria's first and Diamond Jubilees, at the time of coronations, and at the declaration of the war or Armistice; who their commanding officer was; and when they went from the barracks to the railway station 'which way did you turn'.[41] The answers could then be checked against their service record.

Reference to official and semi-official documents was also introduced at an early stage in the nascent Welfare State. Pension officers assessing old age pensions in the years before the First World War were instructed to use the following hierarchy of documents to determine the identity and age of claimants:

1. 'acceptable as sufficient' – certificates of birth or baptisms;
2. acceptable only if (1) attempted and unsuccessful – certificate of service in the armed forces; certificate of membership of a trade union or friendly/provident society; certificates of marriage; entry in a family Bible; insurance policy;

3. not sufficient but no need for a pensions officer to appeal if a pensions commit-tee grants a pension – entries in Poor Law documents; statements by employ-ers, acquaintances; 'circumstantial evidence, and evidence not of a documentary character'.[42]

By 1912 mid-nineteenth-century census returns held at the Public Record Office were being used to check the age of those old age pension applicants who had been born before the introduction of compulsory birth registration in 1874.[43] Similarly, when applying under the Widows', Orphans' and Old Age Contributory Pensions (Voluntary Contributors) Act of 1937, applicants had to give proof of age in the form of a birth or baptism certificate, and, in their absence, a marriage certificate, an insurance policy, a certificate of military service, apprenticeship papers, a naturalization paper, a vaccination paper, or a certificate of admission to a trade union or friendly society.[44]

However, it was not until the aftermath of the Second World War that the Treasury began a concerted campaign to encourage the use of documenta-tion for identification rather than the recommender system. For example, in a memorandum of 1952 the Treasury suggested the abolition of the recom-mender procedures for passports, since the Passport Office had no idea if the signature of the recommender was genuine, or even if the recommender had much knowledge of the applicant. Instead it advocated the production of a page from a savings book with signature, a driving licence or paid cheques. If these were not available then two or more gas, rates or electricity receipts, insur-ance policies, a medical card or a letter from a government office, could be produced, and all to be supported by a ration book or birth certificate. At the time the Foreign Office dug in its heels and retained the recommender system, much to the Treasury's disgust, but it was plain in which direction the wind was blowing.[45]

By the early twenty-first century the documentary technique of identifica-tion had generally superseded the recommender system, with modern ben-efit offices requiring a vast range of documents for checking, including the following:

Valid passport/ID card
Two or more passports if of dual/multinationality
Home Office documents
Work permit
Letter from employer/contract of employment
Evidence of actively seeking work
Payslips

Mortgage/rental agreement or letter confirming where residing
Marriage/birth certificate/deed poll
Student loan documentation
Certificate of incorporation
Memorandum of association
Articles of association
Stock transfer form
Schedule D Taxation form
Services contract
Invoices
Letter from accountant
Letter from clients
Letter from college, including details of type and length of course and weekly hours
Student ID card
Full driving licence.[46]

Many of these documents can, of course, be cross-referenced with each other, and with the electoral register, that great fall-back for all official forms of identification. A similar range of documents could also be found being used to identify taxpayers.[47] Individual identification no longer depends on the personal knowledge of the community but upon one's own knowledge, or the possession of documentation that could be linked with official or commercial information systems. The British State has thus tended to rely on dispersed, rather than centralized information systems for identification.

IDENTIFICATION AND REGISTRATION IN WAR AND PEACE

Running in tandem with these evolving forms of welfare identification there was also a shift in state registration, in all its manifestations, from facilitating individual action to providing means of control by State and commerce. However, the use of registration for these purposes had limits that reflected a belief in the importance of preserving a space in which the respectable citizen was to be autonomous, or at least self-directing.

This development can be seen in the case of civil registration, and the issuing of birth, marriage and death certificates. As already noted, civil registration had originally been established to enable individuals to protect their property rights. This helps to explain why civil registration was not at first enforced by fines, which were only introduced by the 1874 Births and Deaths Registration Act (37 & 38 Vict., c.88). By 1877, however, Major George Graham, the Registrar

General, was noting in his *Annual Report* that besides their use for pedigree purposes:

> A considerable number of applications for birth certificates are made by candidates for civil service clerkships, for boys about to be apprenticed, and for boys about to be employed as messengers, etc. for post office purposes.[48]

This reflected, no doubt, the restrictions placed on the employment of children under a certain age by the Factory and Education Acts. Graham also noted that although:

> With respect to deaths, very few escaped civil registration, and the chief defect was the want of accuracy in the information supplied for record of persons 'present at death' and 'in attendance' during fatal illness. Many mistakes were consequently made as to the exact number of Christian names, the precise spelling of surnames, the age, the occupation of the deceased, and the cause of death; occasioning necessarily much trouble to the Bank of England, insurance offices, friendly societies, clubs, etc., and to everybody who had occasion to use certificates of death.[49]

The development of registration certificates as a general means of identification was already foreshadowed here, and came into its own in the more centralized welfare systems of the twentieth century. As with parochial registration before it, the uses of the civil registers seem to have expanded through 'mission creep'. As already noted, the GRO certainly experienced a rush of men and women during the First World War requiring birth, marriage and death certificates to prove entitlement to war pensions, or eligibility for service in the military and in munitions works.[50] Thus, the birth certificate became a standard means of identification in the postwar Welfare State, although the activities of an imposter such as John Stonehouse revealed its limitations. Hence the official demand today that original certificates should be proffered, rather than copies. The birth certificate did not actually prove identity in any concrete sense, it was an object that could be produced when called for. It did not contain biometrics, nor was it often cross-referred to the original registration entries. In a sense it operated in the same manner as the anonymous seals of peasants had in the late Middle Ages, as part of a performance.

Much the same could be said of that other standard form of official recording, the electoral register. The late nineteenth- and twentieth-century legislation on voting and electoral registers merely strengthened and elaborated the system established in the early nineteenth century, although the system was gradually being extended to women as well as men. Under the 1918 Representation of the

People Act (7 & 8 Geo. V, c.64) every local authority was now to have a registration officer who was responsible for drawing up the electoral register. He was to 'make the necessary enquiries and to prepare the electors list'. The latter were to be published, and objections could be made against individual names. In order to prove age and nationality the registration officer could demand a birth certificate, a certificate of naturalization or ask for a statutory declaration. For this purpose people could obtain birth certificates at a reduced fee of 6d. However, the 1947 Committee on Electoral Registration concluded that under the 1918 system people were being omitted from the electoral roll, and that a periodic house to house canvas of electors ought to be introduced.[51] This was then instituted under Section 5 of the 1948 Representation of the People Act (11 & 12 Geo. VI). However, the use of the household, rather than the individual, as the unit of electoral enumeration left the system open to abuse. One solution to these problems was, of course, to create a central register of all individuals and their addresses, and this was in fact briefly achieved under the national registration system during the Second World War. This became a 'civilian residence register', which was to be the basis of voting, with ID cards having to be produced at polling stations.[52] For a time the relationship between the individual citizen and the State had become a direct one, unmediated by the community or family.

However, although the British national registration systems of both World Wars do indeed show the possibilities of using registration to identify and control individuals, they also reveal the inability, or unwillingness, of the British State to pursue this strategy to its ultimate conclusion. The carnage of the trenches in the First World War led to the introduction of a national registration system to manage the conscription of citizens into the military and other war work.[53] This was based on a census of the country carried out by the GRO, which was to act as the national registration authority. Men and women were given certificates, containing their address, to show that they had been registered, and had to inform the authorities if they moved house, upon which they were issued with a new certificate. This document contained no forms of individual identification – it identified the act of registration, not the person who had registered. The whole system was kept up to date through the imposition of fines for non-registration, and through the activities of 'revisers', who were to visit houses checking on their occupants.[54]

There were proposals after the War that the registration system should continue during peacetime, but these soon foundered. The system was expensive to run, and smacked too much of 'Prussianization' for senior civil servants.[55] As early as 1915, for example, Sir Sylvanus Vivian at the National Health Insurance Commission was noting that:

> no system of legal obligation and penalties, even if an individual were aware of them, will induce or compel the general population to take steps which from their point of view are difficult and complicated, and the point and importance of which they cannot realize. This is not due to any lack of patriotism or of respect for the law, but has its cause deep down in the genius of the nation, the freedom of its private life from bureaucratic incursions, its unfamiliarity with and distaste for formalities or procedure and 'red tape'.[56]

Vivian was responsible for food rationing during the First World War, and was familiar, therefore, with the problems created by the National Registration system. Registration certificates could be stolen and used to gain extra ration books; individuals or families could get multiple ration books by registering under differing names; and a householder could simply overstate the number in the household and so get extra rations.[57] In 1919 Vivian became the head of the GRO, and was to remain so until the end of the Second World War.[58] When he came to plan a new National Registration system in the late 1930s, as another war loomed, he decided to tie the system more closely into rationing. Although the original identification of citizens for registration, and the issuing of identity cards, was again done by a census, the rationing system was to help maintain the Register. To get a ration book it was necessary to show an ID card, and the former would be sent to the address on the latter. There was thus a means of checking on changes of addresses, and picking up men and women who had not been caught by the census.[59] The thoroughness and universality of the resulting identification system exceeded that created in the totalitarian regime of Nazi Germany, in which the carrying of ID cards was only made effective towards the end of the War.[60]

During the Second World War there were different types of card for differing groups:

1. a standard blue card carried by the majority of the population, which gave individuals a number, and carried a signature but no other form of identification;
2. a green card, which carried a photograph, information on distinguishing marks, height, and place and date of birth, and had to be vouched for by a local 'public figure' – the recommender system once again. This was issued, at the behest of the security services, to people who had to have access to restricted areas – docks, airfields, public utilities, large industrial concerns, and so on;
3. a pink card distributed only to senior government officials, civil servants and serving officers.[61]

The limited information on the blue card was designed as a safety feature by Vivian. If a card was lost, a form had to be filled out to get a new one, and the information on the form could be compared to the more extensive data on the National Register.[62] Although established originally for the purposes of conscription and rationing, mission creep meant that the Register was soon used for administration in many other fields – health, insurance, immigration, voting, policing, refugee control, mercantile marine identification, internment, pensions, population statistics, birth, death and marriage recording, and so on. The favourable treatment given to those who held green cards led other people to seek them, and to even affix photographs to their blue cards.[63]

Citizens were being sorted here by risk, and this has led one scholar to see this in terms of 'social sorting', in which individuals in the twenty-first century are often treated differently according to their recorded social background.[64] However, sorting during the War was more by function than by socio-economic status. Moreover, there were limits to the reach and reliability of the National Registration system. According to Vivian, police access to the Register was only in cases of serious crime, or matters 'affecting the national security'. Assistance to the police in other cases was limited lest such access 'made the Register unpopular and prejudiced compliance with its obligations'. The Registrar General resisted attempts to use the register to trace income tax and rate defaulters, or the missing husbands, 'in accordance with the policy of avoiding a course which might antagonise the general public'.[65] It was not even necessary for citizens to use the name they had given at registration in their day-to-day life. In keeping with the traditional legal position with respect to the use of names in England, there was a conscious official decision to allow the use of aliases.[66]

Above all, the whole system of National Registration and ID cards was abandoned in 1952. This was mainly because a system that encroached on individual autonomy, and that associated the respectable citizen with the criminal, was only acceptable in a national emergency.[67] As the *Daily Express* put it in 1945:

> Except as a wartime measure the system is intolerable. It is un-British . . . It turns every village policeman into a Gestapo . . . It can put the law-abiding citizen in the same row of filing cabinets as the common thief with a record.[68]

Jon Agar sees this attitude as 'snobbish' but it plainly reflected a deep-seated belief in the boundaries of the State, and the 'proper' way in which the respectable should be identified in England.[69] The English reluctance to have ID cards, which mystifies many Continental Europeans, has always been predicated on the idea of liberty as freedom *from* the State, rather than *through* a State that enforces a constitution enshrining rights. The replacement of a Labour by a Conservative government in 1951 was also an instrumental factor in the demise of the ID card, since the concept of the National Register has always been associated with the statist policies of the former.[70] The defeat of the Labour government in 2010 led to the abandonment of the latest proposals for ID cards under the 2006 Identification Cards Act (2006, c.15).

However, even when the National Registration system was abandoned in 1952, the National Registration number survived within the NHS, voting registration and the National Insurance system. Similarly, information contained in the National Register was passed to specific government departments – the security services, the Ministry of Labour, the Ministry of Pensions, the GPO, Civil Defence, the Inland Revenue and the Board of Trade.[71] The State was gathering, and continues to gather, databases of information relating to individuals that only require a single common identifier to link them all together.

PASSPORTS: THE EPITOME OF STATE CONTROL?

As already noted, the modern passport system has been seen as a cornerstone of the nation-state's control over the mobility of its own subjects. However, in practice England only instituted mandatory passports for its own citizens in the twentieth century, and this was as much to comply with foreign requirements as for its own needs. After all, passports were to be shown to the officers of foreign states as much as to British officials. The passport was also a liminal document; it was required at the border but had little significance within England, at least until the very recent past.

Before the First World War it was not mandatory for those travelling abroad to apply for a passport. The monarch in early modern England had the right to control the movement of his or her subjects overseas, and records of applications for and grants of permission to leave the kingdom are to be found among the records of Chancery and the Exchequer in the National Archives in London. During the eighteenth and nineteenth centuries, passports were issued more frequently, although it was only in 1846 that regulations relating to applications for passports were first formulated. Possession of a passport, however, was confined largely to merchants and diplomats, and the vast majority of those travelling overseas did so with no formal documentation.[72] Even then, a grand British Foreign Secretary such as Lord Palmerston could refuse to attach a *signalment*, a written description of the passports holder, to the official passports he issued.[73] This exclusivity was reflected in the fee of £2 2s 6d paid for passport in the early nineteenth century, a sum far beyond the level that an ordinary person could afford. In 1851 the fees were reduced to 7/6d, including stamp duty, and in the first month under the new system the number of passports issued 'leapt' from 41 to 111.[74] This was hardly a system of mass documentation and control.

England's *laissez faire* policy on passports for its own citizens foundered during the global conflict of the First World War, when all foreigners, and some British subjects, came to be seen as potential enemies or fifth columnists. In November 1915 an Order in Council was issued to amend the Defence of the Realm (Consolidation) Regulations of 1914 (5 & 6 Geo. V, c.8). Among the amendments made was the addition of a requirement that:

> A person coming from or intending to proceed to any place out of the United Kingdom as a passenger shall not, without the special permission of a Secretary of State, land or embark at any port in the United Kingdom unless he has in his possession a valid passport issued to him not more than two years previously, by or on behalf of the Government of the country of which he is a subject or a citizen.[75]

In 1915 a one-page British passport folding into eight with a cardboard cover came into use. In addition to the photograph and signature, it contained a description of the male or female holder and was valid for two years. In the aftermath of the War this regulation stayed in force, as all Western countries erected passport systems to control their boundaries. After the International Conference on Passports, which took place at Paris under the auspices of the League of Nations in October 1920, a model form of passport opening like a book, containing a fixed number of pages, certain items of personal description and a photograph of the holder, was adopted by most of the League's member states.[76]

This was plainly a key change in the forms of identification, that ended an era of free movement. As the Legal Committee of the Council of Europe concluded in the early 1950s, because of passport restrictions, 'despite the remarkable technical achievements of the twentieth century, the journey from Paris to London by rail and sea could be done in less time at the beginning of the century than in 1953'.[77] However, for the vast majority of the population who never travelled further than the British seaside this hardly mattered, and as a consequence the passport was not a common possession until the dawn of package holidays in the 1960s and 1970s. The passport then came to be included in the range of documents that could be used to identify citizens for welfare and other purposes, although it was never used to control internal movement as in the Soviet Union.[78]

DRIVING LICENCES AND THE CRIMINALIZATION
OF THE CITIZEN

One significant exception to the general reluctance of the British State to create general registries of its citizens can be found in the introduction of drivers licences under the 1903 Motor Car Act (3 Edw. VII, c.36).[79] This established the system whereby all drivers of cars have driving licences that can be revoked or suspended for traffic offences. The passage of the Act can certainly be seen in terms of the threat to the concept of community presented by the individualism of the Edwardian motorist. Frequently the assumption was made that the motorist was an urban dweller on a spree, running down pedestrians, and invading the countryside in a cloud of dust. Added to this individualism was the anonymity of drivers, who might speed through two or more counties in a day, evading the hapless police on foot or bicycle.[80] The anonymity of motorists was heightened by the protective garb they wore. According to the Earl of Wemyss, 'Men went about in goggles and in a ghastly sort of headgear too horrible to look at, and it is clear that when they put on that dress they meant to break the law.' In the committee stage of the Bill there was an unsuccessful attempt to get the wearing of such attire made a criminal offence.[81] Could these concerns even be seen as a faint echo of the eighteenth-century Black Acts?

There was indeed a sense in which cars, and the motorists who drove them, were outside society, and thus a threat to law and order. As the poet A. J. Munby put it in his 'London Town' of 1909:

> Hark! To the hideous roar of the ugly implacable monsters
> Forging in frantic speed, each with the other at war;
> Howling and growling and hoarse, in the riot of insolent triumph,
> Deaf to authority's voice, reckless of order and law.[82]

The citizen, when a motorist, was seen as a proto-deviant, and thus liable to be registered and identified. At first there were, of course, very few motorists but as car ownership expanded more and more people were added to the registry eventually held by the Driving and Vehicle Licensing Agency. This registry was one of the first datasets added to the Police National Computer when that became live in the early 1970s.[83]

FORENSIC IDENTIFICATION OF THE CORPSE, 1850–1970

If the identification of the live citizen showed, on the whole, continuation with the past, his or her identification when dead saw more profound changes. Most people who died at home or in hospital, or whose bodies were in a recognizable condition, could still be identified by kin and neighbours. But in the case of disasters, and bodies subject to the coroner's inquest, new procedures began to intrude. First, by the late twentieth century the body was more likely to be identified through the application of science, and, secondly, this was more likely to take place in a specially designated place, the mortuary. These two developments reinforced each other since the mortuary allowed the proper application of science to the identification of the corpse, and the mortuary was increasingly, although not entirely, a medicalized space. The changes that had taken place can be epitomized by looking at the treatment of disaster victims at the beginning and end of the period under consideration here.

On 5 September 1887, poor design led to the Theatre Royal at Exeter being destroyed by fire, and 127 people were known to have lost their lives. This was the worst theatre disaster in British history. The local innkeeper opened his stable yard for the reception of the dead, and when that became overcrowded, bodies were laid out in his stables. Only 68 of the bodies recovered were recognizable, and the rest had to be identified, where possible, by any of their belongings that had survived the fire. The identification of the dead in the yard began the following morning with police admitting relatives a few at a time. The fire had been so fierce that there was often little left to identify – a few scraps of scorched and burnt clothing, watches, rings, a bead reticule with the beads partly melted, and so on. A coroner's inquest was set up, and the first thing that the coroner's jury did was to view and try to identify the remains in the inn yard. When the dead were buried on 8 September, the coffins of the identified victims bore a brass plate giving their name and age, but many of the other bodies had been reduced to charred bones. These were placed in coffins containing several sets of remains, which were labelled, 'Five unidentified persons', 'Seven unidentified persons', and so on. The forms of identification used here were traditional, and often ineffective.[84]

In 1967, when a Canadair C-4 Argonaut aircraft owned by British Midland Airways crashed near the centre of Stockport after engine failure, with the deaths of 72 of the 84 passengers on board, the approach to identification was very different. The coroner's jury were not involved in the identification of the dead, since under the 1926 Coroners (Amendment) Act (16 & 17 Geo. V, c.59) they no longer had to 'view' the bodies of the dead. Their role was now to weigh the evidence supplied in court, including that from medical experts.[85] In the case of the Stockport disaster the dead were examined by members of the Accident Investigation Branch of the Department of Trade and Industry, which included a pathological team, as part of its investigation of the accident. The inclusion of a pathological team was in accordance with a recommendation made by the International Civil Aviation Organization in 1961.[86] In his report on the disaster, the Chief Constable of Stockport concluded that, 'visual identification in cases where the next of kin is not very familiar with the deceased and in cases where gross disfiguration by burning or injury has occurred, is of little value', and several wrong identification were made. He laid the greatest stress in the process of identification on pathological and dental evidence, and the collection of medical and dental records.[87]

A few years later when the Nypro Chemical Factory at Flixborough exploded in 1974, with 28 dead and 36 injured, the authorities did not rely primarily on next of kin for direct identification. Instead each body was numbered by the pathological team, and a standard form was created for each corpse with various headings for different kinds of identification – odontology (teeth), fingerprints, tattoos, clothing, property, visual or osteology (historic bone injuries). The next of kin were only involved once removed in the process. Thus, 'Body No: 0921', or 'Tony', was identified as a control operator with two young sons on the basis of his dental records by an oral pathologist. The role of his wife was reduced to identifying her husband via a 'short sleeved orange "T" shirt, one brown safety boot (left), blue underpants and a cream coloured sock'. The body also had her name tattooed just above its left wrist.[88] The confrontation of loved-ones and the community with death and the dead in disasters had been reduced to a somewhat pathetic vestige as the English 'way of death' became increasingly impoverished. The diminishing importance of the community and kin in identification was also found in cases other than where people had died in disasters. In the early 1970s the Committee on Death Certification and Coroners found that in London less than half of all identifications for inquest purposes were performed by relatives or close friends of the deceased, although this rose to about 75 per cent in the rest of the country. Of all those who identified bodies, two-thirds were upset at having to do so, although most attached importance to the body being identified by a close relative.[89]

The intrusion of experts and science into these procedures had, however, been a slow and gradual one. As already noted, the fourth edition of Swaine Taylor's *Elements of Medical Jurisprudence* in 1852 contained only a brief mention of the use of fractures in bones to identify the dead from skeletons, and of how the instep of a child was used for identification in a case of infanticide. However, in his *The Principles and Practice of Medical Jurisprudence* in 1865, Taylor had begun to talk about identification using teeth, fractures, deformities and hair. The third edition of this work in 1883, perhaps inevitably, mentioned tattoos in the context of the Tichborne case. By 1910, when Fred J. Smith published a sixth edition of Taylor work, as *Taylor's Principles and Practice of Medical*

Jurisprudence, there was now a whole section of 120 pages on 'Identification of Living Persons and Human Remains, Blood and Semen'. The dead were now to be identified by complexion, 'likeness of features', occupation marks (e.g. calluses on a bricklayer's hands), race, deformities and birthmarks, fractures of bones, 'clothes, jewellery, and articles in the pockets', 'Bertillon's measurements' (already said to be superseded by fingerprints), by 'Galton's thumbmarks', stature and weight, teeth, scars and tattoos, and hair.[90]

By the interwar period, however, forensic science could achieve remarkable feats of identification, as was seen in the infamous Buck Ruxton case. Ruxton was a Parsi from Bombay, who had changed his name from Bukhtyar Rustomji Ratanji Hakim, and in 1930 had moved to practice medicine in Lancaster in Lancashire. He was reputedly a diligent doctor, well respected and popular with his patients, and lived in a large house in Dalton Square with his common law wife, Isabella Kerr, and their three children. Emotionally unstable and obsessively jealous, Ruxton became convinced that his wife was having an affair, and throttled her to death in September 1935. In order to prevent their housemaid, Mary Jane Rogerson, from discovering his crime before he could dispose of the body, he suffocated her too. Ruxton systematically tried to make the corpses of his wife and maid unrecognizable by draining them of blood, and removing anything that could identify them – eyes, prominent teeth and birthmarks. He dismembered the bodies and scattered the remains over a wide area of northern England. Ruxton had, however, somewhat foolishly wrapped some of the remains in a newspaper that was a local edition limited to the Morecambe Bay area adjacent to Lancaster. The neat way in which the body had been dismembered and the teeth removed raised suspicion that it had been done by a medical man. This led the police to Lancaster, where Ruxton's wife and servant had been reported missing. The case became a cause-célèbre, with the dismemberment of the bodies a sensational feature of media stories. A workman by the side of the Glasgow to Carlisle road discovered a bundle of newspapers and joked to his mate, 'Be careful, we might find a piece of Mrs Ruxton'. The parcel contained a foot.[91]

The bodies of the two women were identified by John Glaister, Professor of Forensic Medicine and Public Health at Glasgow University, and senior medico-legal examiner in Crown cases for Glasgow and Lanarkshire. Glaister led a team that included other pathologists, two dental experts, radiographers, and photographic and fingerprinting experts from the Edinburgh and Glasgow police. The dismembered parts of the two unfortunate women were reconstituted, and identifications were made on the basis of age, stature, hair, the eyes and complexion, teeth, the length of neck, vaccination marks, fingers and nails, scars, birthmarks, bunions on the feet, the size and shape of the feet, the form of head and face (involving the superimposition of photographs of the victims' faces on those of the skulls), breasts, the condition of the uterus after child birth, fingerprints, and so on.[92] Ruxton was found guilty of murder, and despite a petition urging clemency, he was executed at Strangeways Prison in Manchester in 1936. As late as the 1960s Buxton's house remained empty, and children would not dare to cross the northern side of Dalton Square in Lancaster where it lay.[93]

However, the development of such medical expertise in the field of identification does not necessarily mean that it was used extensively in the coroner's court. Thus, when a coroner in Cheshire wrote to the Home Office in 1900 stating that 2 skeletons had been found 'in a cottage now in course of demolition' at Knutsford, and asked if an inquest was required, a Home Office official replied that it was a matter for the coroner's discretion but that there did not appear to 'be any need for an inquest in the circumstances as stated'.[94] Despite pressure from the medical profession, the coroners remained a largely lay body, and in the mid-1930s, 268 coroners were barristers or solicitors, 4 had no professional qualifications, and only 37 were medical practitioners.[95] As late as 1957, a legal textbook such as W. B Purchase's *Jervis on the Office of Duties of Coroners*, a revised version of the original publication by John Jervis in 1854, contained very little on identification. The assumption appears to have been that identification would be made by lay witnesses, rather than by doctors, or by technical procedures.[96] By the 1986 version of *Jervis*, however, there was a distinct section on identification that went into considerable detail on the use of more scientific methods when identity could not simply be 'established from visual inspection of the deceased by relatives, friends or associates'. Indeed the assumption now was that such visual identification would be unreliable 'since such inspection may be unpleasant and distressing for those concerned and they may pay too little attention and make an error'. This echoed the views of the Chief Constable of Stockport a generation earlier. There was now a whole list of suggested ways of proving identity, which resembled those used at Stockport and Flixborough:

1. personal items – clothing, bank and credit cards, jewellery and keys, laundry marks, watchmakers' marks, hospital appointment cards, and so on;
2. facial reconstruction;
3. height and weight;
4. abnormal physical structures – rheumatoid arthritis, healed fractures, tattoos, comparisons of x-rays;
5. race;

6. age;
7. identification by dental records;
8. hair analysis;
9. sex;
10. fingerprints;
11. handedness
12. serology – blood groups and DNA.[97]

By this date new forms of identification, such as facial reconstruction, were also being introduced into forensic science.[98]

As already noted, the application of new forms of forensic identification was facilitated by the development of public mortuaries, where bodies could be examined in more suitable conditions. However, the development of such facilities was again a long, drawn-out process. The 1866 Sanitary Act (29 & 30 Vict., c.90) had allowed any nuisance authority to 'provide a proper place for the reception of dead bodies'. This was extended by Section 143 of the 1875 Public Health Act (38 & 39 Vict., c.55), that laid down that:

> Any local authority may provide and maintain a proper place (otherwise than at a workhouse or at a mortuary) for the reception of dead bodies during the time required to conduct any post-mortem examination ordered by the coroner or other constituted authority.

According to Viscount Cross, when introducing the second reading of the Bill in the Lords, this was 'to do away with that which is undoubtedly a disgrace to a great city like London, namely the existence of underground rooms such as are to be found at the present moment, and which would not be tolerated in any other civilised country'.[99] However, the 1875 Act was not passed to facilitate post-mortems, but to remove possible sources of infection from the home.[100] The dead were 'nuisances', rather than fellow citizens. In the early 1890s, J. Neville Porter, writing in *The Sanitary Record*, still regarded most mortuaries as 'ill-lighted, badly ventilated, dirty and quite unfit for the purposes for which they are provided'.[101] As late as 1894 a South Staffordshire publican was suing the local constabulary for loss of trade, which he attributed to noxious fumes emanating from a decomposing body left for six days in his pub's club room. The judge upheld the suit, remarking in his summation that 'some people imagined (erroneously) that because a public house was open to every member of the public lawfully frequenting it, a dead body could be taken there.'[102]

The gradual introduction of air-conditioned facilities, as used in the Paris Morgue from the 1880s, allowed bodies to be kept longer, and decent facilities began to be attached to hospitals.[103] However, in the mid-1930s the Departmental

Committee on Coroners reported that many local authority mortuaries were still ill-equipped and poorly designed, one facility consisting, 'of a slab in a shed used to house a steam roller, and where there are no facilities for cleansing bodies'.[104] Even as late as the early 1970s one witness before the Committee on Death Certification and Coroners could still claim that in small urban districts local authority mortuaries were:

> Small, poorly lit, wretchedly ventilated, freezingly cold in winter, malodorously warm in summer, often without refrigeration or proper working surfaces and with their woefully inadequate Victorian plumbing in a permanent state of semi-occlusion from the anatomical debris of decades, these buildings still stand in council yards, by sewage works and rubbish tips all over the land, the subject of prying curiosity of agile children and awkward silences at local council meetings. Next to public conveniences, to which many of them bear a curious and revealing architectural resemblance, they are usually the smallest buildings erected and maintain by the local authority and one cannot help but feel that their size accurately reflects the interest taken in them.[105]

Yet again, the lack of respect shown to the dead almost seems part of the English horror of death in a post-religious age.

IDENTIFYING THE MISSING AND THE FOUND

Similarly, the lack of respect shown to the living might also be part of the reason for the huge numbers of people who go missing in Britain every year. Recent estimates of the annual number of missing person reports made to the police in the United Kingdom range from 100,000 to 250,000. Each year 1 in 9 young people under the age of 16 in the United Kingdom run away from home, or are forced to leave, and stay away over night. In a recent survey the reasons for adults going missing in Britain were:

64 per cent 'decided' – relationship breakdown; escape from problems (finance, violence or arrest); to commit suicide; linked to mental health;
19 per cent 'drifted' – lost contact after moving away on foreign travel; transient life style (drug, alcohol, mental health problems);
16 per cent 'unintentional' – dementia, accident, miscommunication;
1 per cent 'forced' – victim of crime, forced apart by other factors.[106]

The 'missing' here are seldom the victims of murder, and seldom receive the sort of attention given to the victims of atrocities and mass killings in some other parts of the world.[107] The identification of the missing has never really got beyond the registry stage of description, and mass biometrics to help trace them, although suggested, have never been introduced.

The development of official registry systems for missing persons began in the Victorian period, although, as already noted, private circulation of descriptions goes back into the eighteenth century. On 14 May 1894, Frederick Pople of the Salvation Army Factory Battersea wrote to the Local Government Board about his wife. They had both attended the casual ward at Marylebone Workhouse one night but she had been discharged before him the next morning, and had disappeared. She was 'very weak-minded and childish', and Pople was worried that she had been 'decoyed away for some evil purpose by the other female tramps'. He described her, perhaps aided by a Salvation Army officer, as:

> Charlotte Pople, aged 24, 4 feet 10 inches high, rather stout, fair skin, brown hair and eyes, walks very badly as if crippled. Native of Bristol. She was wearing a black mantle trimmed with lace and beaded drab skirt, black stockings, laced boots, black straw hat. She has the marks of recent vaccination, about six weeks old, on left arm.

A subsequent Metropolitan Police superintendents' conference was told that Charlotte had actually remained at the workhouse for several months after she had gone missing without her whereabouts being ascertained by the police. This led to the introduction of registers of missing persons at institutions in London such as hospitals, workhouses, lodging-houses, casual wards and shelters.[108] A special form for reporting missing persons was developed to collect appropriate information, including name, address, age, height, features (complexion, hair, beard, whiskers, moustache, eyes, shape of nose, shape of face, build), 'marks and peculiarities', occupation, dress, jewellery worn and remarks.[109] Similar procedures presumably existed in provincial forces at this date.

The London police did much the same when they found dead bodies, with standing orders from the Edwardian period stating that, 'When dead bodies are found, and are not immediately identified, a description of the body, dress, and all other particulars, is to be circulated in printed information, and form 68 is to be posted forthwith on the notice boards at all stations.'[110] Photographs of the dead were also to be taken in lifelike and 'natural' positions, although this was difficult with swollen bodies recovered from the Thames, or where rigor mortis had set in. In such cases, clothing removed for post-mortems could not always be replaced.[111] At the same date, detailed descriptions of the dead were also circulated throughout the country via the *Police Gazette*, although these might not have been out of place in John Fielding's publications over 200 years before:

> 14th inst., at Hyde Park, with a bullet wound in the head, the body of A Man, aged about 35, length 5ft. 8in., complexion fair, hair (slightly bald on top) and moustache

light, slight scar left of head, mole left cheek and right of nose; dress, light covert coat, 'L. Cohen, 266, Mile End Road', on tab, brown vest, grey tweed trousers, blue and red striped Oxford shirt, white flannel shirt, 'W. Prince, shirt maker, 158 and 160, Green Street, N.E.' thereon, brown merino pants and socks, black hard felt hat, button boots; in pockets, a white bone handle pocket knife, 4 keys on a split ring, latch key, and a red and white pocket handkerchief; a 6-chamber revolver was found by the side.[112]

By the late 1930s the Metropolitan Police had introduced a 'Findex' system, via which elements in descriptions could be searched 'by semi-mechanical means'. This involved punched cards with holes corresponding to sex, age, height, colour of eyes, characteristics ('hunchback', 'cretin', 'truss'), birthmarks, and so on.[113]

The setting up of a national missing persons bureau was suggested in 1953 but rejected on the grounds of expense, and although the idea was resurrected in the 1960s it was not until 1994 that the Police National Missing Persons Bureau (PNMPB) was established.[114] However, the resulting clearing house for information does not receive details of all persons who disappear, since the police try to balance the right of the individual to go 'missing', with their well-being, and the needs of their relatives and friends. In 1997, for example, the Metropolitan Police received 32,314 reports of people under the age of 18 running away. However, only 2,197 missing persons regarded as 'vulnerable' were reported to the PNMPB. The police response to such cases involved questioning the informant about the nature of the disappearance and the person missing; obtaining a photograph; getting lists of associates; checking if the person was in custody; checking police indexes on domestic violence, child protection and community safety; consulting local social services 'At Risk' registers; checking local hospitals; circulating description to police patrols; searching the immediate area; and making appeals to the public. Perhaps 71 per cent of people reported to the Missing Persons Bureau are traced each year, but over a quarter are not, and the vast number of people who walk out of the door of their own free will are never seen again.[115] This is hardly the picture of an overbearing Big Brother State drawing on a vast web of databases and surveillance techniques to identify and pin down errant individuals.

It is perhaps in the context of missing persons that one should view Francis Galton's proposals to create a national fingerprint agency, and similar concerns have led to calls for the establishment of a general DNA registry in the recent past. However, the nearest that the United Kingdom has got to developing a general system of identification for the dead has been the use of 'dog-tags' during wartime. The military dog-tag, at least in the form that it is known today, seems to have originated in the United States. During the American Civil War, when there were large numbers of fatalities, and decomposition and disfiguring injuries were common, remains were not easily identified. During the late nineteenth century, therefore, it became common practice for American soldiers to wear metal identification tags so that they could be recognized if they fell in battle. In 1906, the US War Department instituted the policy that all servicemen should wear metal identification tags.[116] The British Army followed suit soon afterwards. Army Order 102 of 1913, relating to the 'System of recording and notifying casualties in war', laid down that the pay books of serving soldiers, 'with the identity disc of each man attached', were to be kept in bundles ready for rapid issue on mobilization.[117]

The World Wars of the twentieth century were, of course, conflicts in which the whole population had to be mobilized, and in which civilians as well as soldiers could die in horrendous circumstances. This created appalling conditions for those responsible for identification. A memorandum from a Metropolitan Police inspector at the West Ham Station, K Division, regarding an air raid on 19 March 1941, described how at the Municipal Baths Mortuary in Romford Road police constables worked:

> with the mortuary men, heedless of time and food and in the stench of flesh and blood, classifying and taking descriptions of the mutilated human remains and fragments of bodies and limbs until all but three bodies had been identified. I can think of no more gruesome or unthankful task than that which these men were asked to perform and the difficulty experienced can only be realized when I say that of the 204 bodies received, more than 100 of them were in such a mutilated condition that in the majority of cases the identification was established by clothing and effects.[118]

This was, of course, long before 'trauma counselling' had been developed. It is not surprising, therefore, that the extension of tagging to the Home Front had already been considered. In August 1940 an air raid on a Croydon factory killed 80 workers, of whom 36 could not be identified, and this led to discussions within the Ministry of Home Security about the issuing of dog-tags to civilians. But there were plainly practical problems. The ever sensible Vivian at the GRO thought that they would be difficult to distribute. Many people would forget to wear them, especially in bed, and, perhaps inevitably, suspicious civil servants thought that the discs would be abused. It was believed that they would be left at the site of air raids so that people could disappear, claim insurance money, or escape wives and creditors.[119]

Plans for civilian dog-tags were resurrected in the age of nuclear warfare. In 1953 the Stationery Office told the Home Office that it could not see how it could produce an identification disc with some degree of 'flame retardancy' unless it was metal. Fortuitously, a Civil Defense Technical Bulletin from the United States of October 1953 indicated that metal tags had survived atomic weapons tests in Nevada. Unfortunately the process of their production would be expensive and lengthy. According to a Home Office memorandum, produced in response to the work of a gruesomely titled Working Party on Disposal of Civilian Dead in War, such tags would cost £2.65 million, and would take 10,000 persons working in 1,000 centres 20 weeks to produce.[120] This seemed a rather leisurely procedure at a time when a surprise Soviet attack was expected. Even more grimly, a minute of 22 February 1955 noted that such proposals needed to be viewed:

> in the light of the scale of casualties expected from a hydrogen bomb explosion and the fact that all plans have now to be related to a short war of great intensity from the outset. The first of these means that the help which can be given by identity discs for determining the numbers of dead and satisfying relatives' inquiries, etc., is only marginal to the problem of casualties. A very high proportion in the close vicinity of ground zero will disappear without trace.[121]

Identification is only possible if there is someone left to do the identifying – there has to be an audience for which that identification has any meaning.

IDENTIFICATION IN THE CREDIT ECONOMY

Given the changes and innovations that were beginning to affect the identification of the deviant and the citizen, the means of identifying the juridical person and the consumer appear oddly conservative in the century down to the 1960s. The British were rather backward in terms of bank use, and in 1967 only 28 per cent of over-sixteens had a bank account, less than in other advanced industrialized countries. People were still, on the whole, paid in notes and coins in brown envelopes.[122] Even then, this was something of an innovation, since H. G. Wells remembered that in his youth in late Victorian Kent:

> Bank of England notes were dealt with very solemnly in those days: the water-mark was scrutinised carefully, and the payer, after a suspiciously penetrating look or so was generally asked to write his name and address on the instrument.[123]

Wells was from the lower middle classes, and anonymous financial systems were even less developed among the working classes. Down into the postwar period face-to-face forms of credit arrangements continued in many working-class communities, especially in the North. Female 'street' lenders worked with neighbours, while credit was offered by small shopkeepers, and through club or check trading. These were dependent on the agents of bodies such as the Provident Clothing and Supply Company, or of the Great Universal Stores Ltd making door-to-door collections.[124]

In such conditions, identification still depended on personal acquaintance, the credit histories held by trade protection agencies, or the specimen signatures held by banks. However, the 1960s were to see the start of a financial revolution that was to transform the way in which people interacted in the British economy, and this, in turn, had a fundamental impact on how they identified themselves as juridical persons and customers. In time this would also have important knock-on effects on how they were to identify themselves as citizens. This development will be a key theme of the next chapter.

CONCLUSION

Overall, the identification of the 'respectable' in the period 1850 to 1970 showed important changes, but also many continuities with the past. Despite attempts to introduce biometrics into the identification of the citizen in a period of increasing distance between State and individuals, state officials recognized that this ran counter to deeply help beliefs about the distinctions to be drawn between those inside and outside the political pale. Instead the British State bureaucratized traditional forms of identification based on kin and community, via the use of forms and procedures. Civil and electoral registration evolved new functions but continued to be based on pre-existing practices. National Registration briefly created new, centralized forms of identification during wartime, but did not become a permanent feature of British life. Registration did contribute to the creation of the modern 'database State', although this process was already under way. Even the development of the modern passport during the First World War probably had very limited impact internally within the country.

The identification of the dead citizen was another matter, and here it is possible to see the introduction of biometrics, and other forms of scientific identification. Increasingly kin and community were being edged out of the process by officials and experts, especially in cases where bodies were horribly disfigured. The English were increasingly protected, and indeed wished to be protected, from the full obscenity of violent death. Nevertheless, this process only went so far, and the medicalization of the coroner, of identification in his or her court, and of the mortuary, had distinct limits. The coroner's inquest remained on the whole a legal process, rather than a scientific procedure. Similarly, the methods for locating missing persons continued to rely on methods that the Fieldings would have recognized in Regency England, and were not centralized. The dog-tag found a place on the battlefield but not on the Home Front, even as the distinction between the two was being effaced. Similarly, the identification of the customer and the juridical person built upon techniques and technologies developed in preceding centuries.

Rather little of this smacks of a revolution in identification in the aftermath of industrialization. If people were becoming anonymous it was not because of urbanization and mobility, but because of the changing scale and nature of the State and commercial businesses. But even then the limits of identification techniques, and the continuity of traditional methods, are striking. However, from the 1970s onwards new technologies, new ways of conceptualizing the relationship between State and citizen, and new ways of doing business, changed radically the forms of identification. Indeed, what was actually being identified changed in the process.

9

Towards the 'Digital Person': Identifying the Consumer in England, 1970 to the Present

INTRODUCTION

As in the Cold War, ordinary citizens and consumers often feel themselves bemused bystanders in the contemporary world, while the struggle between public bodies, private companies and identity fraudsters, which can affect their interests intimately, is fought out around them. Part of the reason for this sense of helplessness is that identity increasingly resides in databases of information held by the likes of government departments and agencies, banks, supermarkets and credit reference agencies. The citizen or consumer has to present a token, or some information, a performance that will allow him or her to prove that they are the double of the digital person maintained by these organizations. The power and authority to say who someone is has passed from individuals, or the communities in which they live, to State and commerce. This means that the imposter who has stolen, guessed or manufactured such tokens, or informational keys, becomes the person he or she imposes upon. Identity can be stolen. In the past it was always possible to forge a signature, or persuade a community that one was someone else, but these acts were always open to contestation and negotiation. But when someone uses someone else's debit or credit card with the correct PIN, at that point in time there is no possibility of debate, they are that person. In a certain sense, therefore, the State and commercial organizations have created the conditions in which citizens and customers have been put at risk. In addition, while forgery was the commercial organization's loss, the financial risk of 'identity fraud' has been passed to the customer in one of those slights of hand so familiar in the contemporary 'service' economy. Identification is increasingly for the benefit of the State and commerce rather than for that of the individual.

The following two chapters will, therefore, be mainly about the use and development of databases in identification over the past 40 years. The present chapter will examine the identification of the consumer, and the next chapter the identification of the citizen and the deviant. Much prominence has been given in other accounts of contemporary identification to the development of biometrics, and these will be covered in Chapter 10 as well. However, as already noted, all biometrics are essentially information systems – the features of parts of the body are reduced to information that can be stored, accessed and compared to other body parts at other times and places. This has been the case ever since the development of Bertillon's anthropometrics in the 1880s.

Bertillon's system depended, of course, on the manual measurement and retrieval of information, but the machine-readable database was already being developed at much the same date. Punch-card tabulators were invented by Herman Hollerith to tabulate the 1890 US census, and were introduced into England and Wales in 1911 for the decennial enumeration of that year.[1] However, the period covered by the present chapter is dominated by the Information Revolution associated with the electronic computer, which has allowed a proliferation and merging of databases of information that had previously been too complex and extensive to analyse easily. The 1970s saw an enormous expansion of information and communication technology (ICT) in government in terms of data processing to reap economies of scale. Large computer systems were installed at the Department of Health and Social Security's (DHSS) central offices as Newcastle, the Driver and Vehicle Licensing Authority (DVLA) at Swansea, the central Passport Office at Peterborough and at the Inland Revenue's PAYE processing installation at Reading. In the fiscal year 1995–96, central UK government spent £2.3 billion on ICT, and local government over £1 billion.[2] Similar sums were also being invested in the private sector in the same period, although whether all the benefits have been passed to consumers is another matter.

Identification has also become as much about the assignment of risk to individual bodies, as about the social creation of distinct personalities. This can certainly be seen in some State practices of identification, but also in the activities of commercial organizations, such as credit reference agencies. According to Ulrich Beck, we now live in a 'Risk Society' in which, rather than being concerned with present discontents, societies and governments are obsessed with future risks – the problems of aging populations, the impacts of climate change, the threats presented by globalization, and so on. Rather than planning

one of the lowest to one of the highest levels of indebtedness in the world, well ahead of those in Continental Europe.[13] The working classes, who had always been in debt, now borrowed from the banks and building societies, and they were joined in this by the middle classes. The growth in financial transactions meant that in the 1960s there was an annual 5 per cent increase in the number of cheques and other paper instruments being cleared through the London Clearing House. By the mid-1970s it was feared there would soon be a billion cheques going through the UK clearing system, and it was necessary, therefore, to move to electronic systems before paper-based clearing collapsed.[14]

Banks were also said to be eager to introduce new services to ward off competition from the Post Office Girobank, which had been set up in 1968 by the Labour government of Harold Wilson. Wilson believed that a more democratic system of banking based on post offices would make good a perceived lack of financial services offered to working-class families by the commercial banks.[15] The latter also felt that they had to improve efficiency in the aftermath of a report by the Prices and Incomes Board on the level of bank charges to the public.[16] In addition, services to bank customers were under pressure in the 1960s because industrial action by trade unions, such as the National Union of Bank Employees (NUBE), had forced the banks to restrict the hours they opened. The ending of Saturday opening, just when customers wanted to use their accounts for shopping, was seen as especially serious.[17] All these pressures encouraged the banks to introduce innovative ways to allow people to handle their accounts, and in the process to off-load handling costs onto their customers and retail outlets. Key innovations included the development of credit and debit cards, electronic point of sale (EPOS) systems and of the ATM, the 'cash machine'. These systems took advantage of the new digitized banking system, and led to the issue of tokens of identity in the form of cards, backed up by either signatures, or secret keys such as PIN numbers.

Credit cards originated in the United States, where as early as 1915 'shoppers' plates' were being issued by a small number of hotels and department stores. By issuing these cards, the traders concerned undertook to allow their customers, upon presenting the cards, to purchase goods or services on credit from their own outlets. The next big development was arguably the creation in the United States in 1949 of Diners Club by Frank McNamara and Ralph Schneider. This organization, the symbol of which would identify its members as entirely creditworthy, persuaded hotels and restaurants to supply goods and services on the presentation of a uniform card held by each member. The organization took upon itself to repay the debt, and would then look to the card holder to pay the bills incurred. The first members were friends and acquaintances of

McNamara and Schneider, and the first affiliated establishments were hotels and restaurants in New York. American Express, a US rival to Diners Club, set up offices in the United Kingdom in 1963, and the British bank Barclays introduced its own credit card, the Barclaycard, in 1966.[18]

Such cards were originally part of a paper-based system. An applicant applied for a card at Barclays or participating banks, and after review and acceptance of the application, his or her details were input to computer, and the customer was sent a card with an embossed account number. The cardholder normally signed a Barclaycard sales voucher, which was in triplicate or quadruplicate. The sales voucher was then imprinted with the embossed details on the Barclaycard via a specially provided press. The trader checked that the card had not expired; that it was not subject to a card lost or cancelled warning notice; that the sum was not above the 'floor limit' (in which case he or she might have to ring Barclays for authorization of the transaction); and that the signature on the voucher corresponded with the authorized signature on the card. One copy of the voucher went to the cardholder, and another to Barclays to bill the cardholder and to refund the vendor.[19] This was, in some sense, an extension of the 'travel credit card' that had already been issued by the National Provincial Bank in the 1960s for use by cardholders when signing cheques at participating branches.[20] However, the development by IBM in 1965 of a magnetic strip on which data could be stored in binary form for electronic reading, transformed the 'plastic card' into a true digital artefact.[21] This allowed the 'dematerialization' of the payments system when EPOS technology was introduced in the late 1970s.[22]

The machine-readable card also allowed the development of the ATM. The cash-dispensing machine, which was a substitute for branch counter services, was conceived by John Shepherd-Barron, the managing director of De La Rue Instruments, a company that transported Barclay's cash. The company also made and supplied dispensing machines of various sorts. When Barclays first introduced their 'Hole in the Wall' in 1967, customers applied in advance for vouchers, which could then be used to withdraw cash from the ATM. The system was later reconfigured to accept electronically readable debit cards. Shepherd-Barron originally based the PIN number used in such machines on his six-figure army service number, later reduced to four digits because his wife told him that she could not remember any more.[23] Other banks followed suit, although the extent to which these were at first anything more than an advertising ploy is a moot point. A popular story among bankers at the time was of how one major UK bank overcame its ATM's teething troubles. When the bank's new machine was installed in Victoria, London, it refused to function. Not wishing to lose face, the bank put one of its employees behind the machine to operate it as though it were working normally until an engineer could mend it. Hence, when a customer inserted his card, the employee waited a suitable length of time before requesting the PIN, then waited again before requesting the amount of cash required, and finally returned the card through the slot and dispensed the cash. Customers were reported to be 'very impressed' with the efficiency of the new service.[24]

The use of 'plastic' expanded rapidly. By 1972 there were 1.7 million Barclaycard holders. In that year, other banks, including Lloyds, Midland and National Westminster, launched the rival Access card, and two years later linked it internationally with Mastercard.[25] By 1977 there were nearly 350,000 trade outlets in the United Kingdom where credit cards were likely to be accepted, and approximately 7.5 million credit cards were issued. In 1996 there were 560 credit cards and 550 debit cards per 1,000 people in the United Kingdom, and 42 per cent of the population held at least one card.[26] Similarly, in 1974 there were 14,908 branches of banks and no electronic ATMs, but by 1999 there were 11,044 branches and 17,892 ATMs. At first the use of cards was a middle-class phenomenon. Thus, in a survey of the use of consumer credit carried out by the Office of Fair Trading in the late 1980s, 32 per cent of respondents used credit cards, and 37 per cent had done so in the past 5 years, but the former figure fell to only 11 per cent of those earning less than £5,000.[27] But by the end of the century their use was widespread among all social classes, and in 2009 the UK Payments Council, a trade body setting standards in the field, was envisaging that cheques would be phased out by 2018.[28] Internet banking, in which the bank customer uses passwords and secret keys to access and manipulate their own accounts online, is a still more recent development. However, the Nottingham Building Society had introduced a form of online banking in conjunction with Prestel as early as 1983.[29] Here the physical token of the card is replaced completely by the information it contains. Online banking is, of course, part of the ongoing strategy of commercial organizations to outsource their handling costs to customers, something pioneered by the supermarkets.

Such an expansion in the use of tokens of identification inevitably led to problems of fraud, although some bankers were somewhat tardy in understanding the risks involved. On their introduction credit cards could be seen as 'fraud-free' because goods could not be bought if the transaction was greater than the cash limit on the card.[30] Similarly, one correspondent in *The Banker* in 1974 even went as far as to declare jauntily:

> The main problem posed by such [ATM] machines is not, apparently, security, but the difficulties facing a customer holding a briefcase, and umbrella, whilst trying to insert his Cashpoint card and tap out his code number.[31]

However, the banks were increasingly uneasy at dealing with their new working-class customers, as opposed to City workers. As *The Banker* noted in 1973:

> Until fairly recently banks served a rather privileged section of the community – the same section as, rightly or wrongly, shopkeepers deferentially expected to be honest. The expansion of the market has been accompanied by an increase of dud cheques and a greater degree of suspicion on the part of shopkeepers. The thirty pound guarantee which goes with the cheque card, but not with the Barclaycard unless presented directly to a bank, gives full reassurance to the shopkeeper that the cheque will be met.[32]

By the early 1980s figures quoted for the UK credit card fraud ranged from £18 million a year for cheque guarantee cards, to about £35 million for fraud losses for all types of transaction cards. Figures from individual banks and credit card operators gave plastic card fraud losses ranging from 0.2 per cent to 0.5 per cent of turnover. Out of 7 million Barclaycards issued each year in the same period about 200,000 went astray, and of these 7,000 are used fraudulently.[33]

In the early twenty-first-century identity theft is a fact of everyday life for millions of people around the world, including the present author. Calculating the levels of such fraud is difficult, and the official estimates have been much disputed.[34] However, according to the US Federal Trade Commission, in September 2003 almost 10 million Americans had been the victim of some form of ID theft within the previous year. It was estimated that a victim typically spent over 2 years, and close to 200 hours, in repairing the damage that the identity theft had caused.[35] In the United Kingdom, a Cabinet Office study estimated that in the financial year 2000–01, identity fraud totalled at least £1.3billion. The Association for Payment Clearing Services (APACS), the body that deals with fraud relating to bank and credit cards, estimated that all credit card crime had grown from £95 million in 1998 to £411 million in 2001 and that it would increase further to £650 million over the following 4 years.[36] CIFAS, the UK fraud prevention service, calculated that identity theft had risen from 20,000 cases in 1999 to 137,000 in 2005.[37] Nevertheless, the relative extent of such fraud can be exaggerated. For the private sector it has been estimated that although around 1 to 2 per cent of transaction value is lost through fraud, only about 3 to 5 per cent of such fraud is identity fraud.[38] This does not seem a very high level, although identity fraud can plainly have a disastrous impact on individuals.

Identity theft can operate in numerous ways – 'shoulder surfing' at ATMs, 'phishing' emails to trick people into providing account details, doctoring EPOS readers to record information, hacking into computers to record online transactions, and so on. Some of this fraud has become highly organized. According to a report by Symantec, a web security firm, in 2009 British bank account details were on sale online for as little as £5 in 'cyber-crime supermar-kets'. The UK bank account details were most often sold via instant-message groups, or web forums on the internet, that were live for only a few days or even hours.[39] However, one international forum, dubbed somewhat grandiloquently 'Darkmarket', ran for 3 years, and involved fraud totalling millions of pounds before it was shut down by the police. Nearly 60 people were subsequently arrested in Manchester, Hull and London, as well as in Germany, Turkey and the United States. Described by the Serious Organised Crime Agency as 'a one-stop shop' for criminals, entrance to Darkmarket was strictly by invitation only. It gave criminals access to a wide range of valuable personal information, such as the data held on the magnetic strip of an ordinary credit card, for as little as £1. One of its customers had spent as much as £250,000 on personal information in a 6-week period.[40] At the other end of the spectrum was the 14-year-old boy in Auckland, New Zealand, who in the 1980s used a cardboard lollipop packet to make a fictitious deposit of £340,000 in a cash dispenser of the country's biggest building society. During the next three weeks he was said to have withdrawn £700, 'before he got nervous and told his teacher'.[41]

Numerous solutions to such problems were suggested in the pages of maga-zines such as *The Banker* in the early days of banking automation, including the holographic scanning of the signatures of card holders etched onto their cards.[42] However, the insertion of machine-readable photographs on cards smacked too much of national ID cards, and fear of alienating customers made the proposal's adoption impracticable.[43] A solution to some of these systemic weaknesses was the introduction into the United Kingdom in 2003 of Chip and PIN, which combined a smart card with a PIN number.[44] However, such cards had been introduced into France in the mid-1980s, but the British banks con-sidered them too expensive to introduce at that time. They were not prepared to spend £80 million per annum to solve a problem that cost them, or more to the point their customers, £40 million. As one financial commentator noted at the time, 'The [British] banks will not do anything unless they are raped.'[45] Such fraud was running at nearly half a billion pounds per annum in 2001 before financial institutions took action.[46] British banks were slow to solve a problem that their own innovations had helped to create.

CREDIT REFERENCING IN THE DIGITAL AGE

If financial institutions in England were tardy in introducing means of protect-ing their customers from fraud, commercial organizations were somewhat less reluctant to protect themselves from credit risks.

In 1970 the two main credit reference agencies in Britain were British Debt Services (BDS) and the United Association for the Protection of Trade (UAPT). The BDS has 8 million items of information recorded on file under a time limit of seven years covering the whole of the United Kingdom. In that year it anticipated that it would handle 4 million enquiries, and would recover £2 million. Its central register contained information on known debtors, including county court judgements, trade information, bankruptcy proceedings, deeds of arrangement, bills of sale, court decrees, information on estates sequestered and trust deeds granted, and change of address. The company maintained a library of 'voters rolls', which it claimed, 'enables users to confirm the residential stability of their credit applicant at low cost and without delay'.[47] It also employed ex-police officers, no doubt for their proverbial tact, to visit houses to make 'status enquiries' for the verification of personal details.[48]

The UAPT, on the other hand, carried out work for the old National Association of Trade Protection Agencies, which had originated in the nineteenth century. Rather than having a central register, it was a much more decentralized organization based on 35 local offices. In these local branches was information on cards relating to 14 million people, and about 10,000 additional items were added to them each day. Outside London the UAPT's branch offices organized cards by name, but in London this was only done by street. The UAPT received some 300,000 enquiries a month.[49] Identifying individuals in the UAPT's records was plainly a somewhat hit-and-miss affair. Thus, the official Crowther Committee on Consumer Credit discovered in the early 1970s that the UAPT had objected to a clause in a proposed Consumer Credit Bill under which individuals could ask for information on their credit rating when a precise name and address was given in the request. The UAPT claimed that:

> If a Mr. David Jones of an address in Cardiff asks what is on file, the credit reference agency may tell him, in all good faith, that they have nothing on file although in truth they have information about him relating to a previous address in Cardiff (dated, say, 4 years previously) together with information about him in the Liverpool area where he resided until recently. The Cardiff area was said to have 20,000 Jones's on file, including 500 David Jones, 350 D. Jones and 200 'Jones (no initials)'.[50]

These organizations were subsequently out-competed by new companies coming into the British credit referencing market from somewhat different backgrounds. Equifax, for example, started out as the Retail Credit Company in the United States in the nineteenth century providing credit references to grocers in Tennessee. It computerized its records in the 1970s, and then moved into

Europe in the early 1990s.[51] One of the other big agencies in the contemporary British market, Experian, grew out of the mail-order business. In 1981 there were 4.8 million agents of mail-order companies, and this number reached 7.4 million by the 1990s, although a large number of these were personal shoppers. Mail order covered 5.7 per cent of non-food retail sales in 1965, and 9.2 per cent in 1979. One of the largest of these companies was The Great Universal Stores Limited (GUS), which had been founded in 1900 in Manchester by George Abraham and Jack Rose. Its credit scoring subsidiary, CCN, was set up Nottingham in 1980, and began by providing computerized credit referencing for GUS, as well as making handsome profits selling data to GUS's catalogue rivals. CCN later became Experian and demerged from GUS in 2006.[52] Other mail-order firms had already shown the way in computerizing personal data. Thus, Littlewoods, a now defunct mail-order firm based in Liverpool, bought the entire electoral register in 1971 and downloaded 16 million names from it onto computer. An individual's absence from the register raised problems with their ability to acquire credit.[53] Credit reference agencies now aspired to capture the entire population, rather than just problem consumers, as everyone became a potential risk.

A modern credit reference agency such as Experian holds a range of related databases of information on consumers, including the following: a postcode address file; the electoral register; information on aliases and associations; data on county court judgements, bankruptcies, administration orders and voluntary arrangements; previous searches made as the result of credit applications; telephone numbers; information from CIFAS relating to potentially fraudulent dealings; repossessions made by mortgage lenders; addresses from which individuals have recently set up a postal redirection; data on high risk individuals who appear on official sanction lists, such as the Bank of England Sanction File, the Politically Exposed Persons File (PEP) and the list from the US Treasury's Office of Foreign Assets Control (OFAC); and information about consumers who are in arrears on credit contracts, or who have moved without leaving a forwarding address.[54] Such agencies are increasingly becoming part of the State's armoury against identity fraud, and now receive death registration data directly from the GRO in order to prevent the identities of the dead being used to gain credit.[55] John Stonehouse would have found it more difficult to assume the identity of dead constituents in the twenty-first century. Experian holds information on 45 million UK consumers, and processes more than 1.5 million credit reports each week.[56] The databases of Equifax cover a similar number of people, and hold over 300 million credit agreement records.[57]

In the United Kingdom, a firm such as Experian provides information to over 100,000 organizations active in financial services, retailing, home shopping, telecommunications, the media, insurance, the automotive industries, leisure, charity, property, as well as to utilities. The company also claims that it 'helps public sector organizations make better decisions around policy formulation and efficient service delivery'. So important has credit referencing become, that Experian and Equifax now sell consumers the ability to view their own credit ratings and details, so the latter can check that they are correct.[58] Once again, commercial functions, in this case the maintenance of databases, are partly outsourced to the public. To prove identity, an individual has to supply information such as their name, gender, date of birth, postal and e-mail addresses, and credit card details.[59]

Of course, the extent to which such databases actually relate to individuals, rather than to bundles of risks associated with certain consumer profiles, is an interesting question. This is because an individual's credit-worthiness is established, in part, by the area in which he or she lives, as well as by their personal characteristics. In the early 1990s, the Office of Fair Trading (OFT) noted the development of such 'red-lining' in British credit rating agencies, although this was plainly a much older practice. The postcode in which consumers lived was given a weighting according to the number of county court judgements in that postcode. This was supplemented by 'geodemographic' information on the type of housing, composition of households, age, occupations, and so on, drawn from the census. The OFT thought this was acceptable as long as red-lining did not outweigh all other characteristics in the scoring system.[60] This form of 'social sorting'[61] is still practiced today by credit agencies such as Equifax and Experian.[62]

CONSUMER PROFILING IN THE RETAIL ECONOMY

It would, however, be misleading to see the profiling of individual consumers as something that they necessarily regard negatively. This can be seen most clearly in the development of customer profiling in the retailing sector. In the 1980s, the State's provision of data for retail planning, such as the census of distribution, was curtailed, and retailers had to fall back on their own resources.[63] The period saw the development of the store loyalty card, through which the customers of supermarkets provide the latter with personal details about themselves, which the supermarkets find useful, and receive an identification card in return. In the case of the contemporary Sainsbury's Nectar Card one has to supply information on name, date of birth, gender, postal and e-mail addresses, a password, and a memorable key word.[64] The loyalty card, which carries the usual strip incorporating customers' digitized identification details, is run through the store's EPOS systems when they pay for their goods at the till, and in return they receive points, or free gifts. In so doing, customers once more do the stores' work for them by identifying themselves, and providing data about their lifestyles. The data on purchases collected by the EPOS system also enables the supermarkets to control their inventories. Loyalty schemes not only identify individuals via the information the card holders supply, but use geographical information systems (GIS) to combine it with a number of different sorts of area information, including census data, postcodes, electoral role information, credit data, information on court judgements respecting bad debts, details of motor vehicle ownership, lifestyle data, transactional data, geographical information, and so on.[65] Thus, the supermarket card databases are similar to those found in credit reference agencies, although they are source of opportunity for customers, rather than an indicator of risk.

Supermarkets have used store loyalty card data to capture larger market shares. Tesco's Clubcard, for example, was launched in 1995, and helped that store move away from treating customers on mass, and to build an apparently more personal, individual relationship with them. The company changed the way in which shoppers thought about the supermarket chain – Tesco's mission statement at the time being to 'Continually increase value for customers to earn their lifetime loyalty'. Of course, such card schemes do not actually allow supermarkets to deal with customers as individuals, but by facilitating an ever finer segmentation of the customer base into more specific groups, they allow firms such as Tesco to give customers the impression that they were being treated on a one-to-one basis.[66] Customers in Tesco's databases were originally segmented into 'cost-conscious', 'mid-market' and 'up-market' segments, which were, in turn, segmented into 'healthy', 'gourmet', 'convenience', 'family living', and so on. These subsegments were then segmented further and communications tailored to each. By early 1996 Tesco had analysed their customer database and identified 12 different segments, each of which was targeted differently. By late 1996 there were 5,000 different versions of the Tesco magazine being sent out, and by mid-1998 there were 60,000 different market segments, each targeted with a different version of the magazine or 'offer'. Tesco's Clubcard programme had 10 million active households by 2005, and sent out 4 million unique quarterly mailings. Tesco reaped the rewards of introducing the store card by moving from being number two to number one grocer in the United Kingdom.[67]

By the late 1990s there were 150 retailer card-based schemes nationwide in the United Kingdom, with some 40 million cards in circulation.[68] In 2003, approximately 80 per cent of the UK population were participating in such loyalty programmes.[69] This data collection and profiling is, once again, a form of 'social sorting', that affects individuals through narrowing access to goods and services, or placing them in social categories that can be seen as problematic. Plainly, 'cost-conscious', that is poorer, customers will receive information about a narrower range of products from the supermarkets, and if they happen to live in a poor area their local shop in the chain (if they have one) may stock fewer products as well. However, this is more an example of placing people into groups than identifying them as specific individuals.

Nevertheless, the information collected by commercial organizations could potentially be used to develop intimate profiles of their customers. This is shown by an experiment in which two researchers were given access to 2 years' worth (1998–2000) of loyalty card data for a customer, dubbed by them 'Brenda', who used a loyalty card issued by a large British supermarket. Over the 2-year period Brenda used the card on 243 different days, spending £2263.25 in total. She undertook 1,551 product purchase transactions, resulting in 1,667 items being purchased, and her mean spend was £9.31. She made very few purchases on a Sunday in the first year, although this became more frequent later, and the researchers queried whether she was religious, or had other commitments. She bought savoury items, chocolate and snacks, which led the researchers to ask if she was 'a greedy and indulgent person', or just buying for others. She wore contact lenses, and used lip salves to ward off cold sores. She bought blemish concealer and Clearasil, so had spots, or was buying these for a family member so afflicted. From the size of her tights she was plainly a 'large woman', and she had long hair because of the hair and pony tail grips she purchased; and so on.[70] The combination of probable facts about Brenda, and surmises about characteristics which she may, or may not, have had, indicates the potential here for intrusive and problematic surveillance.

Similar data collection, and profiling, is undertaken by direct marketing companies. Direct marketing began in the United States in the early 1920s – General Motors, for example, began to target owners of 2-year-old Fords (who frequently did not purchase a Ford as their second vehicle), and sent them a brochure on GM vehicles. In 1996, 77 per cent of US companies used some form of direct mail, targeted e-mail or telemarketing, and the sale of mailing lists alone (not including the sales generated by the use of such lists) generated revenues of $3 billion a year. The average US consumer is today on about 100 mailing lists and is included on at least 50 databases.[71] Similar listings can be found in the United Kingdom. Thus, Whichlist.com has a consumer master list of 37 million records, and can break down families into specific groups, as given below:[72]

Code	Affluence	Life Stage	Additional Information (Examples)
BW11	Prosperous	Young families	Employed full time in finance and business service with high incomes.
CY23	Comfortable	Empty nesters and seniors	Retired Christians living in semi-detached houses with moderate mail-order use.
DX40	Striving	Older families	Employed in manufacturing, construction and retail. Have no qualifications and read popular newspapers.

The collection of consumer information is now being automated through the use of computer cookies, which have been described by Daniel J. Solove as 'high-tech cattle-branding'. When a person visits a website and downloads a webpage onto their computer, a small text file is saved on their hard drive, which includes a unique ID code. When they visit the website again, the site looks for the cookie, recognizes the user, and locates the information collected on the user's previous surfing activity. This information is shared with other sites, so that when someone goes online a programme such as DoubleClick, for example, accesses the cookie on their computer, looks up its profile on that person, and determines what advertising they should receive.[73] DoubleClick is now owned by Google, the largest search engine in the world, and ubiquitous on UK personal computers.

This degree of information collection, profiling and tagging of individuals seems almost Orwellian but has raised little opposition. After all, the individuals so identified receive special offers and a jaunty magazine, or the ability to buy 'on tick', rather than Big Brother's bullet in the neck. Members of the public are generally content to provide copious amounts of information to commercial organizations because they do not see problems, only advantages, in the transaction. Similarly, members of the public, especially the young, seem only too happy to publicize information about themselves on commercial internet networking sites such as Facebook, MySpace and Bebo. This is despite the possibility that this information can be used by criminals to steal their identities. Thus, a survey undertaken by Equifax revealed that of those using social networking sites, 87 per cent gave their full name, and 38 per cent their date of birth, on their profile. The same survey showed that 27 per cent of those using such sites place their educational history online, and 26 per cent do the same with their work history. Nearly a third of social networkers used no privacy or security settings on their personal sites.[74] Modern Britons want privacy, and yet broadcast their personal details with seeming abandon. It is as if the performance of identity has been dissociated from any sense of the audience that performance reaches.

CONCLUSION

In the long history of the identification of the individual in England, the role of commerce has been somewhat secondary. The almost imperceptible shifts in the identification of the juridical person and consumer, with the replacement of the seal by the signature, has seemed rather uninteresting compared to some of the innovations introduced by the State. Yet in the late twentieth century, many of the most far-reaching changes to identification technologies were introduced by commercial organizations.

This shift from State to commercial forms of identification has hardly been commented on, and for much of the population the latter have been welcomed, or at least accepted. Despite the manner in which commercial data gathering can adversely affect one's standard of life, the intrusive levels of surveillance created, and the way in which the commercial risks of impersonation have been passed onto the consumer, such systems have not created popular movements of resistance. However, when the State is collecting such information for the purposes of identification, the public are far more wary. This undoubtedly reflects the increasing tendency of the State to collect information on everyone to prevent risks, and the long association of such surveillance in England with the control of deviancy. As the present work has shown, 'respectable' citizens in England have long assumed that they should have a space in which they are relatively anonymous, and free of state interference. Until recently the British State agreed – at least to the extent that it was wary of maintaining a single, unitary system of identification such as a national register. The partial undermining of this assumption, and its effects, are the subject of the next chapter.

10

Towards the 'Digital Person': Identification in the Digital Database State, 1970 to 2010

THE DEVELOPMENT OF THE DIGITAL DATABASE STATE

As with commercial organizations, the modern British State has become increasingly dependent on databases for its activities. Although, as already noted, the State has long been collecting information about its citizens, this process accelerated with the advent of computing. In the late 1970s the official Lindop Committee on Data Protection found at least 38 computer datasets in government departments that held information on more than 1 million identifiable individuals,[1] and such databases have been growing ever since. In 1978, for example, the Lindop Committee found that the Department of Health and Social Security (DHSS) had 45 million computer records relating to national insurance contributions, while 7 years later Campbell and Connor claimed that it held 54 million such records.[2] Of course, the expansion of information technology in this field has not necessarily been driven by any sinister desire to create a police state but by considerations of efficiency and economy.[3] Such technologies enabled government departments to undertake their traditional functions – paying benefits, preventing fraud, creating statistics – at lower costs, through removing clerical error and reducing staff.

The Lindop Committee was set up as a reaction to public concern over the scale of state information gathering, and its work contributed to the passing of the 1984 Data Protection Act (1984, c.35). However, the range and complexity of such government datasets are still of concern today. Thus, a recent report produced for the Joseph Rowntree Reform Trust claimed that of the 46 government databases it assessed only 6 had a proper legal basis for any privacy intrusions, and were proportionate and necessary in a democratic society.

The report considered nearly twice as many were almost certainly illegal under human rights or data protection law, while the remaining 29 databases had significant problems, and should be subject to an independent review.[4] One of the concerns of the report was the way in which individuals were profiled as risks, rather than identified as having done anything illegal. For example, all children referred to a Youth Offending Team as potential offenders were assessed using the ONSET profiling tool, and the assessment stored on RAISE, or a similar system. RAISE holds information on those who have offended, as well as those 'likely' to offend. ONSET examines a wide range of factors in the child's life and looks for signs of social exclusion, such as being a victim of bullying, living in poor housing, or in a household with a low family income. Unless the ONSET system indicates that the child is at low risk of committing crimes, they will be referred to a preventive scheme such as a Youth Inclusion Programme (YIP), or to a Youth Inclusion and Support Panel (YISP). The authors of the Rowntree report were concerned that such children might be stigmatized by ONSET, since if they come to the attention of the police they might be more likely to be treated as suspects rather than as victims or witnesses.[5]

With the establishment of information networks across government, data sharing and data profiling have become easier, and much more common. The DHSS and the Inland Revenue, for example, began sharing information in the 1970s and 1980s. The Inland Revenue collected national insurance contributions from employers on behalf of the DHSS, while the DHSS notified the Inland Revenue of any taxable benefits it paid.[6] Data sharing also means that the State eliminates the cost of collecting the same, or similar, information more than once.[7] By the end of the 1980s, the technical means of such sharing were improved through the creation of a Government Data Network connecting the DHSS, Customs and Excise, the Inland Revenue, the Home Office and the police.[8] By the end of the twentieth century a government department such as the DSS supplied personal information to, among others, the Inland Revenue, Customs and Excise, the Home Office, the Department of Health, the Department of Employment, the National Audit Office, the Legal Aid Board, the Post Office, police forces, local authorities, banks, building societies, grant maintained schools, and so on. It was also involved in the trading of personal data.[9] A Cabinet Office's report of 2002, *Privacy and Data-Sharing: The Way Forward for Public Services*, advocated more data sharing within government, as a way of providing 'joined-up and personalised public service delivery', or at least services that were cheaper.[10]

However, the problem with this 'way forward' is that there has to be at least one unique variable that is common to each of the sets of personal information

1 million irises, and now 'enrols' about 600 new ones a day. It is reported that some 7 billion iris comparisons are performed daily at the 27 air, land and sea ports of entry into the country. Over a period of four and a half years the system caught some 50,000 people trying to enter the UAE using false travel documents.[19]

Such developments have led to a vast growth in the commercial biometrics industry. In 1990, 1,288 units of biometric hardware were sold worldwide but this had increased to 115,000 units by 1999. In the late 1980s the International Biometrics Association was established in the United States, and the Association for Biometrics was established in the United Kingdom in 1991, and subsequently spread throughout Europe.[20] According to the International Biometrics Group, the worldwide biometrics identification market totalled US$1.2 billion in 2004, and will reach US$5.7 billion by 2010, an annual compound growth rate of 40 per cent.[21] The British State began to copy such innovations, and to buy its technology from Digimarc, IBM, Sagem Sécurité, Thales, and the like. In the late nineteenth and early twentieth centuries, state officials such as Bertillon and Henry designed and introduced fingerprinting and identity cards systems; in the early twenty-first century the State purchases systems created by commercial organizations.

DNA PROFILING

The development of the United Kingdom's National DNA Database (NDNAD) shows both the potentiality of the new biometrics for crime detection, and the more expansive way in which the British State can come to understand risk. The process of DNA profiling or 'fingerprinting', which maps the unique repetitive sequences on an individual's DNA strings and stores it digitally, was first developed by Professor Sir Alec Jeffreys at Leicester University in 1984. Although the technique was the product of 'blue skies', rather than applied, research, Jeffreys immediately saw the forensic possibilities of the technique, as well as its use in the testing for paternity, immigration disputes and conservation biology. He patented the discovery, and the company Cellmark Diagnostics, an affiliate of ICI, was granted a licence to exploit the technology for paternity testing.[22] In a letter to the journal *Nature* in 1985, Jeffreys argued that the method would, 'revolutionize forensic biology particularly with regard to the identification of rape suspects'.[23]

Although DNA was described by Jeffreys and others as genetic 'fingerprinting', it differs in some important respects to the older technology. First, DNA does not 'identify' people; it can only give a 'match probability' – given the genetic make-up of the population, the frequency of a given profile genotype can be calculated. This can then be converted into a 'likelihood ratio' – how much more likely it is that the DNA at a crime scene comes from a particular person than not. The probability here depends on how complete a DNA profile can be obtained.[24] DNA profiling is a question of probabilities and risks. Secondly, the presence of DNA at a crime scene does not necessarily prove that a person was there – DNA may be found on a hat, but how many people have worn the hat?[25] Thirdly, DNA can be used to identify lineages, as well as individuals, so that the probable presence of a person at a crime scene can be inferred from the similarities between their DNA, the DNA recorded at the crime scene, and that of a relative whose DNA is held by the police. Unlike heraldry, the DNA profile is a form of pedigree that is not necessarily sought after, although it has been used to build on the ability of serology to prove kinship and paternity. In a certain sense, therefore, DNA undermines identity as an individual attribute. This decentring of identity as biological descent has also been reinforced by the rise of popular genealogy in the recent past. The population, as well as the State, see themselves as biological lineages. This return to the past in the 'hi-tech' forms of identification might also be seen in the electronic tagging of offenders, which has similarities to branding and badging.[26] Lastly, and even more controversially, DNA can be predictive, through inferring aspects of an individual's 'genetic ancestral origins', and thus some aspects of their likely physical appearance. The Forensic Science Service (FSS) now offers an 'ethnic inference service' of this kind, described as, using computer software called ALFIE (allele frequency for the inference of ethnicity) to predict the ethnicity of an individual by comparing differences said to exist between five 'ethnic groups'.[27] Lineal identity shades off into racial identity in a manner that would have gratified Sir Francis Galton.

The first practical application of the new technology was not actually in criminal forensics but to prove that a young Ghanaian immigrant was the son of a woman resident in the United Kingdom, in order to prevent his deportation.[28] However, in 1987 a mass DNA screening by police of men in Leicestershire led to the identification of Colin Pitchfork as responsible for the rape and murder of two girls. The technique was able to show that a young man who had confessed to one of the crimes was not guilty, while Pitchfork's attempt to avoid giving a sample, by asking someone else to impersonate him, was his undoing.[29] The taking of DNA samples, especially through mouth swabs, is far simpler than the taking of blood, semen and urine samples, the procedures for which had made mass identification through the body extremely difficult in the past.[30]

The practical success of the technique led to the FSS and Home Office taking over the new technique for criminal investigation and immigration control purposes.[31] Some of the enthusiasm of the police and FSS for DNA profiling perhaps reflected a desire to rescue the reputation of forensic science from the low point that it had reached in the late 1880s and early 1990s. The revelation of a number of miscarriages of justice in cases relating to terrorism and serious offences against the person, including the trials of 'The Birmingham Six', 'The Maguire Seven', 'The Guildford Four', 'the Tottenham Three' and the case of Stefan Kiszko, had shaken faith in police procedures. In addition, between 1981 and 1992 recorded crime had risen by over 70 per cent, while clear-up rates had fallen from 41 per cent in 1979 to 27 per cent in 1992.[32] It was necessary to show that the forces of law and order had the weapons to fight an apparently ever rising tide of disorder, while making British justice seem less fallible.

As with much scientific police work since the nineteenth century, the successful application of DNA techniques required the creation of a database of genetic information to which crime scene data could be compared. By 1988 the FSS was already considering the possibility of establishing a DNA database, and in February 1994, the Home Secretary, Michael Howard, announced the 'first step' towards a national DNA database with the decision to support the FSS and the Metropolitan Police Forensic Science Laboratory in a pilot study of the IT, scientific and policing implications of collecting, processing and storing samples on a database.[33] NDNAD was established in April 1995, and was the first of its kind in the world. There followed a gradual expansion in England and Wales of the legal framework under which DNA samples could be taken. The 1994 Criminal Justice and Public Order Act (1994, c.33) gave the police greater powers to obtain and retain samples, and made specific provisions for the speculative searching of profiles derived from these samples. The 1996 Criminal Procedures and Investigations Act (1996, c.25) widened the powers of the police to search speculatively samples taken from those arrested, charged or informed that they would be reported for a recordable offence. The 1997 Criminal Evidence (Amendment) Act (1997, c.17) extended the powers of the police to take samples without consent from a limited category of prisoners convicted before the 1994 Act. The Criminal Justice and Police Act of 2001 (2001, c.16) extended the powers of the police to retain and search the samples and profiles of those not convicted of a recordable offence but who were only charged. Finally, the 2003 Criminal Justice Act (2003, c.44) extended police powers to taking samples from those in police detention following their arrest for a recordable offence.[34] The scope in England and Wales of police powers in this respect was more extensive than in most other countries in Europe that had adopted the same technology.[35] As a result of police enthusiasm, and of their increasing powers, the NDNAD grew at a furious pace. In 1995–96 the profiles of 35,668 people were loaded onto the database but this annual figures had risen to 508,663 in 2004–05. Between 1995 and 2006, 3.9 million subject profiles were added to the NDNAD, and 3.8 million of these were retained as of 31 March 2006.[36]

As with fingerprinting, England acted as a point of dissemination of the new technology of forensic identification. Thus, in 1993 the FBI implemented CODIS, a national programme in the United States to help federal, state and local law enforcement agencies develop a DNA database; to improve DNA forensic analysis methods; and to develop means of using DNA to identify missing persons, or human remains from mass disasters.[37] The US Department of Defense also began collecting blood and tissue from every person in military service in 1992 to act as genetic 'dog-tags'.[38] By 2002 Interpol found that of the 46 countries in its European Region, 26 had set up a DNA database.[39] However, the United Kingdom's forensic DNA database remains the largest of any country, with 5.2 per cent of the UK population on the database in 2008, compared to 0.5 per cent in the United States.[40]

There was a particular acceleration in the growth of the NDNAD in the early years of the twenty-first century, when the then Prime Minister Tony Blair introduced an expansion programme, hailing, 'an acceleration in the high-tech drive against crime, with the major expansion of the police DNA database used to hunt down criminals'. He made a firm commitment to utilize this 'vital weapon in the law enforcement arsenal' through creating, by 2004, a database containing what he described as, '3 million suspect samples – virtually the entire criminally active population'.[41] The Home Office subsequently described the database as containing 'the profiles of the majority of the known active offender population'.[42] The problem with this statement was, of course, that the NDNAD contained a large number of profiles that related to persons in England and Wales who were not actually convicted of any crime. Thus, early in 2006 the government admitted that out of 3,457,000 individuals on NDNAD, 1,139,445, or nearly a third, had no criminal record.[43]

The argument was made that some of those on the NDNAD who had no criminal records were actually criminals, and would commit crimes in the future. Thus, in the case of R v. Marper and S (2004), in which men charged but not convicted of an offence attempted to get their profiles removed from NDNAD, it was asserted by the Law Lords that, 'The more complete the database, the better the chance of detecting criminals, both those guilty of crimes past, and those whose crimes are yet to be committed.'[44] The population on the NDNAD was thus seen as one at, or presenting, risk. To the untutored eye this sage legal pronouncement might seem to indicate a belief that 'there is no smoke without fire', and to place all those on the database under suspicion. This was certainly the belief of the European Court of Human Rights, which ruled unanimously in 2009 that in the case of these men, 'the retention [of DNA profiles] in question constituted a disproportionate interference with the applicants' right to respect for private life and could not be regarded as necessary in a democratic society.'[45] Critics of the wide powers of the police to collect and retain DNA samples in England and Wales pointed to the situation in Scotland, where samples and profiles taken from suspects, must be destroyed following a not-proven or not-guilty verdict in court. However, the Police, Public Order and Criminal Justice (Scotland) Act 2006 (2006, asp 10) does allow the police to retain, for a limited period of time, samples and profiles taken from suspects arrested or detained but not subsequently convicted, provided that criminal proceedings have been instituted against them for sexual or violent offences.[46] The announcement by the incoming Conservative/Liberal Democrat administration in May 2010 that it would restrict the scope of the NDNAD by adopting the Scottish arrangements for data retention appears to mark the limits of the growth of the database. However, one awaits the first case when someone removed from the database commits a serious crime to see how far this is a permanent reverse.

Another criticism of the NDNAD is that it is discriminatory, in that some groups are disproportionately present within it. Thus, profiles are held on nearly four in ten black Englishmen under the age of 35 – a much higher proportion than is typical of any other ethnic group.[47] This has led some, such as the Appeal Court judge Lord Justice Sedley, to argue that the NDNAD should cover the entire population, and in this he appears to be supported by the majority of the British population.[48] Such views are a striking departure from the public's traditional antipathy towards criminal databases covering the general population, and to their identification via the body. This transformation of a nation of citizens into a nation of suspects, to which populist governments have responded, is perhaps one of the most striking shifts in the nature of Britain in the recent past. This is even more remarkable given that the contribution of DNA profiling to the detection of crime has been relatively small. While 1,388,894 of the crimes recorded in 2002–03 were detected by the police, only 21,082 of these are described in official statistics as having been detected through the use of DNA profiles. Thus, Home Office figures show that 'DNA detections' comprised only 1.6 per cent of all detections.[49] As Lynch, Cole, McNally and Jordan have argued in their recent *Truth Machine*, the symbolic certainty of detection through DNA analysis, which gives the public something comforting to hold onto in troubled times, is perhaps more important than the technique's actual usefulness.[50] Indeed, it is now claimed that the fictional portrayal of the 'infallibility' of DNA profiling in films and television dramas has led to juries, especially in the United States, having unrealistic expectations of forensic evidence.[51]

Of course, such popular support for DNA databases might be tempered by a realization of the extent to which the NDNAD is accessed by the police forces of other countries. The harmonization of international DNA databases is being encouraged by Interpol, which has invested heavily in the development and implementation of its own cross-national register of profiles. Members of Interpol can currently submit and search profiles on a limited database, the majority of profiles being currently supplied by the United Kingdom and Croatia. A European DNA Profiling Group was formed as early as 1988, in order to promote international standards in DNA profiling, and the European Network of Forensic Institutes has also pursued an agenda for DNA profile sharing within the European Union. One result of this has been the Council Resolution of the European Union (2001/C 187/01) on the exchange of DNA analysis results between member states. This outlines procedures for the exchange of DNA profiles by police forces for the purposes of criminal investigations across the European Union.[52]

ALIENS AND CITIZENS IN A WORLD OF GLOBALIZATION

The collapsing of distinctions between the 'ins' and 'outs' of the British polity can also be seen in shifts in the identification of migrants, whether 'aliens', or British citizens. As noted in previous chapters, in the twentieth century, aliens in England had to have registration cards that identified them in ways that only applied to the native population in wartime. By the beginning of the twenty-first century such cards contained a photograph of the migrant, as well as various security features, such as fluorescent numbers and symbols, to ensure that the card was genuine.[53] Migrant workers from outside the European Union were also one of the first groups to receive the national biometric cards established under the 2006 Identity Cards Act (2006, c.15), which contained a digitized fingerprint.[54] As will be described in the next section, the New Labour government planned that such ID cards would be extended to the whole population in due course. Some of the features of the aliens' registration card had already been extended to British citizens with the introduction of the new photocard driving licence in 1998. This was a card, very similar to the later proposed ID card, that contained the driver's details, a photograph and a unique identifier based on the name and date of birth of the licence holder.[55] This was introduced to conform to the European Council Directive 91/439/EEC on driving licences of 29 July 1991.[56]

At the same time, the make-up, and procedures for acquiring a British passport, become more complex. In addition to the usual need for a countersignature from local worthies, as of 2009 a person applying for their first passport had to attend an interview. No doubt reassuringly, according to the Passport Office this will be 'conducted in a friendly manner and will consist mainly of asking applicants to confirm facts about themselves, which someone attempting to steal their identity may not know'. In preparation for the interview the Passport Office will check details on the electoral roll and address histories to create a 'biographical footprint', to which the passport applicant will be asked to respond.[57] If one wants to obtain a first passport with a name other than that which appears on a birth certificate it is now necessary to produce documentation to prove the change of name – something of a departure from traditional common law practice.[58] The UK passport itself now contains a facial biometric in order to conform to the requirements of the International Civil Aviation Organisation (ICAO).[59] In May 2003, in line with US initiatives, the ICAO published new standards for MRTD (machine readable travel documents), which introduced biometric technologies in order to facilitate global interoperability in border-control identification. Under these standards, the face has been selected as the primary biometric, in the form of a high-resolution digitized image, which will be stored on a contactless chip.[60] However, the Conservative/ Liberal Democrat government that came to power in 2010 has blocked proposals to add fingerprints to the next generation of British 'e-passports'.

The overlap between the treatment of foreign migrants and of British citizens travelling abroad can also be seen in the establishment in 2006 of the Identity and Passport Service, which brought together the issuing of identity cards, passports, and the civil registration of births, marriages and deaths. In addition, the distinction between migrants and British citizens is being effaced with regard to the requirement to produce 'papers' to obtain employment. The 2006 Immigration, Asylum and Nationality Act (2006, c.13), consolidated the legislation relating to the employment of adults 'subject to immigration control'. It gave the Secretary of State the power to fine an employer if he or she employed such a person who did not have a right to work in the country. However, UK Boarder and Immigration Agency guidelines issued in 2008, when the 2006 Act came into effect, noted that employers would be excused from penalties if they checked the identity documents of workers before they took up employment.[61] Moreover, in order to avoid racial discrimination, because 'many people from minority ethnic groups who live in the UK are British citizens', the guidelines suggest that all potential employees should be treated in the same manner.[62] The documents necessary to show that a prospective employee has a right to work in the United Kingdom includes a UK passport, or a combination of something showing a National Insurance number and name, such as a P60 tax document, and an original UK birth certificate.[63] If the documents provided had different names, because of change of name on marriage, divorce, or through change of name through deed poll, then supplementary documentation, such as original marriage certificates, need to be produced.[64] What this means in practice is that everyone, migrant or British citizen, needs to have 'papers', and the requirement is most onerous for women who may change their name through marriage – racial discrimination appears to trump sex discrimination. Everyone in Britain is now 'subject to immigration control', and the freedom to use whatever name one chooses has been circumscribed through a bureaucratic decision. The requirement to produce a copy of a passport countersigned by a solicitor when remortgaging a house, in order to prevent money laundering, is yet another example of the creeping necessity of the British to produce 'papers' on demand.

THE RETURN OF THE NATIONAL ID CARD?

The proposed National Registration system under the 2006 Identity Cards Act cut across many of the traditional features of identification in Britain. The Labour government's proposals involved the creation of a central National Register, and the issuing of ID cards containing digitized biometrics to everyone aged 16 and over.[65] The creation of a centralized information system to store identification data was a departure from the usual British decentralized systems of identification. Similarly, the creation of a single means of identification, and the use of biometrics, to identify citizens, juridical persons and criminals, collapsed distinctions that the present work has shown have existed for centuries. So how, and why, had this shift come about?

At one level one can explain this in terms of the statism inherent in Labour Party thinking over a long period. Fabian socialists supported the extension of the First World War registration system; the Attlee government of the postwar years maintained the Second World War registration system till its electoral defeat in 1951; and New Labour continued this tradition by seeking to establish a new national registration system.[66] On this reading, the drive to centralize identification depended on a Labour administration and would not survive the establishment of Conservative administration. However, this explanation is perhaps too glib. After all, the Conservative administration of the 1990s had attempted to introduce a voluntary identity card scheme, in the face of Labour Party opposition.[67] Similarly, the Conservative Party supported, in principle, the first ID Card Bill introduced into Parliament by New Labour in 2004,[68] so their opposition to the 2006 Act may have been more tactical than principled. In addition, the drive to introduce biometric ID cards is something that can be found in many countries throughout the modern world.[69]

The Conservative/Liberal Democrat government's decision to abandon the introduction of ID cards in May 2010 appears to return the British identification status quo to its traditional position. But how far this is actually the case needs to be seen. Will another terrorist strike put ID cards back on the political agenda, or will other forms of state ID, such as the passport, come to be used as a de facto ID card? It may not be the actual ID card itself that is important, but the number of points at which British citizens are expected to produce official 'papers' of some sort. On the other hand, and more intriguingly, the new administration's decision to enlist credit reference agencies in a campaign against benefit fraud may indicate the creation of a new, privatized, National Registration system.[70] Such an approach would fulfil Sylvanus Vivian's criteria for an effective system of state surveillance – that it should be linked to the provision of something that people want, credit in this case rather than rations during the Second World War. But what controls and democratic oversight will there be over the new system? Is a privatized ID system used to stigmatize the poor any better that a national registration that covers everybody?

Of course, one should not assume that the introduction of similar technologies across the globe has to reflect the same forces at work. So how, therefore, might one understand the specific reasoning behind the proposals to introduce identity cards into Britain under the 2006 Identification Cards Act? According to the British Home Office, when proposing their introduction, ID cards would

1. help protect people from identity fraud and theft
2. ensure that people are who they say they are
3. tackle illegal working and immigration abuse
4. disrupt the use of false and multiple identities by criminals and those involved in terrorist activity
5. ensure free public services are only used by those entitled to them
6. enable easier access to public services.[71]

On the face of it, this is an odd list. Item 2, for example, seemed to summarize some of the other items. Since it would not have been compulsory to carry the card, it is difficult to see how the proposed system could have achieved item 1 directly. Given the ability to forge documents, items 3 and 4 might not have been achieved, and ID cards would not have prevented criminal acts perpetrated by British citizens with valid documentation. ID cards could only reveal illegal migrants once they were already in the country, so did not tackle 'immigration abuse' directly. It is true that the increasing salience of terrorism influenced by Islamic fundamentalism has reinforced the requirement to underpin the security of the United Kingdom's borders, and to disrupt the use of multiple identities by terrorists, and this might have been facilitated through the introduction of identity cards. Both were advocated in the UK government's 2009 strategy for countering international terrorism.[72] However, the actual incidence of attempts to infiltrate the United Kingdom with false documents is arguably quite low. Thus, the number of entry documents at UK ports of arrival detected as being counterfeit in 2000 was just 0.006 per cent of the total.[73] Of course, the entry of just one Al-Qaeda terrorist into the country on false documents could be seen as one terrorist too many. Nevertheless, how exactly such measures were to prevent acts of terrorism by British-born citizens influenced by Al-Qaeda, and who have perfectly adequate UK identification documents, was left somewhat vague.

The State's concerns over illegal immigration and terrorism certainly reflect a widely held belief that Britain is under siege. However, as Didier Bigo has pointed out, it is difficult to see how frontier controls can work given the massive movements of people for economic purposes due to globalization, and in which employers collude. The development of international obligations, whether within the European Union, or at the level of the United Nations, has undermined the ability of a nation-state, such as the United Kingdom, to control population flows.[74] As with the 1905 Aliens Act, this has led to demands for measures to impede inward migration, including increasing support for withdrawal from the European Union, and from international obligations with respect to asylum seekers.[75]

However, rather than trying to understand New Labour's proposed introduction of ID cards in terms of identity theft, deviancy or migration, one might be on firmer ground looking at items 5 and 6 in the Home Office list above. New Labour's concern with identity may have reflected its preoccupations with the relationship between the citizen and the State. This can be seen as a purely negative lack of trust in the population. The British State has continued to fret about the extent of possible fraud in the welfare systems. In the late 1990s the

Department of Social Security (DSS) calculated that welfare fraud could be as high as £7 billion per annum, if all suspicion of fraud was included. Some of this was put down to the lack of a legal requirement for those claiming income support to prove their identity, and a legal obligation to do so was introduced.[76] The House of Commons Social Security Committee was also concerned in the late 1990s about the 18 million National Insurance numbers that were inactive due to death and emigration, and the 76,000 blank birth certificates that were missing through theft.[77] By 2000, the DSS was making a more modest estimate of between £2 billion and £4 billion a year for social security fraud and error. Although the proportion of this fraud that depended on false identity is difficult to determine, the Department could point to the example of an organized gang that adopted the identities of 171 people from the Irish Republic, and used these to make a string of false claims in the United Kingdom, leading to an overpayment in excess of £2 million.[78] The Cabinet Office's stated solution to such problems was to increase checks against government and private sector databases, the sharing of information between them, better physical scrutiny of documents, increasing use of risk assessments and profiling of applicants, and a switch to the use of photographs and biometrics in identification. The British State no longer trusts its citizens, hence its increasing desire to pool information in order to profile them to establish risks.[79] This is, in fact, a strategy that the British State has been pursuing since the 1980s.[80] Such sharing, of course, requires common identifiers that could have been provided by a National Register.

Similarly, the system of compiling the electoral register by household enumeration, rather than by individual registration, may have undermined that other facet of citizenship, the right to vote. By the beginning of the twenty-first century, research in London suggested that in some areas of the Metropolis up to a third of eligible voters might be unregistered, and that the registers might contain much inaccurate information. The system appeared to be vulnerable to 'personation' and fraud, in much the same way as it had been in the nineteenth century. This is especially serious as governments try to encourage participation in elections through the increased use of postal voting. In Northern Ireland the Electoral Fraud (Northern Ireland) Act 2002 (2002, c.13) has changed the system of household registration to one based on the individual. Citizens have to register themselves giving signatures, dates of birth and their National Insurance numbers, the latter being checked against Department for Work and Pensions records. When presenting themselves to vote Ulster electors have to present photographic ID – a driving licence, passport or an electoral ID card.[81] Similar procedures are to be introduced into the mainland United Kingdom within the next few years.[82]

At the same time, New Labour's drive to create a positive relationship between the State and its citizens was predicated on turning citizens into consumers of the State. As the then Prime Minister Tony Blair put it in another Cabinet Office report of 2005:

> The future of public services has to use technology [*sic*] to give citizens choice, with personalised services designed around *their* needs not the needs of the provider. Within the public services we have to use technology to join up and share services rather than duplicate them.[83]

'E-government', through which citizen-consumers interact with the State online was, in turn, seen as requiring the 'management of identity', through which

> government will create an holistic approach to identity management, based on a suite of identity management solutions that enable the public and private sectors to manage risk and provide cost-effective services trusted by customers and stakeholders. These will rationalise electronic gateways and citizen and business record numbers. They will converge towards biometric identity cards and the National Identity Register.[84]

The perception of citizens as risks, and the solution as lying in identity management, is here explicitly taken from the commercial sector, from which most of the technology for doing so was also to be derived. This brings one back to the development of the commercial databases described in the last chapter. The British State increasingly models itself on the supermarket and the credit reference agency, rather than upon relationships within the classical Liberal polity. Blair, it can be argued, saw the ID card as essentially the state equivalent of the Tesco Clubcard, which enabled that retailer in the 1990s to remodel its relationship with its customers by appearing to treat them as individuals rather than en masse. This was perhaps the ultimate conclusion of the Labour Party's long attempt to come to terms with the consumer society that began in the 1950s in the revisionism of Tony Crosland's *The Future of Socialism*.[85] In this business model there was little room for privacy, only risk assessment. The problem was, of course, that the British public associated state ID with wartime emergencies, and with the identification of the criminal, Johnnie Foreigner, and subject races, rather than with supermarket free gifts and bonus points.

CONCLUSION

Written contemporary history always runs the risk of becoming anachronistic, given the speed with which political events can overtake it. Time will tell if the effacing of distinctions between citizens, consumers and deviants described in this chapter is merely a passing phenomenon. However, in an age of mass insecurity and political popularism, the desire to pin down the identity of individuals is hardly likely to decline. Of course, how that could be done might vary between political parties, and New Labour's attempts to create a single, enforceable identity system might be replaced by a system of multiple, but interlinked, forms of ID. However, any British government will be under pressure from other governments, international bodies and commercial vendors of identification systems, to conform to global trends. In the nineteenth century the British could dictate international norms but this is hardly the case in the twenty-first century. The past distinctions between the identification of citizens, consumers and criminals, that the English developed and maintained over centuries may never fully be resurrected.

11

Conclusion

This book began with a paradox – that the modern proliferation of sites and techniques for personal identification has been accompanied by an increasing sense of identity insecurity. Hopefully the present work has shown that the paradox can be explained if we see that the expansion in the number of sites of identification, especially those involving the creation of database systems, is one of the principal reasons for the rise of identity theft. In former periods individuals had greater control over their own identity, especially as a juridical person or consumer, because they asserted or proved it through things they possessed or could do. But as seals and signatures were supplemented, and increasingly superseded, by forms of identification dependent upon supplying information to be compared to that held in commercial or official registries and databases, so individuals began to lose control of their identity. Individuals ceased to be their own 'identity providers', and came to depend on a multiplicity of external agents – banks, building societies, credit agencies, supermarkets, online retailers, employers, mobile phone companies, and so on – for proof of identification.

In a sense, people no longer had a social identity, except that which their digital, database *doppelgangers* gave them. Individuals could no longer assert an identity; they have to claim it from institutions, which can increasingly impute an identity to them. In the past this tended to be the fate of the deviant, not of the citizen, or juridical person. People's identity could be stolen because it had already been appropriate by the State, and increasingly by commercial organizations. Identity passed to such bodies, while at the same time they shifted the risks associated with identity theft to private individuals. As already noted above, this was a process that preceded the development of the modern digital computer, but has been greatly accelerated in the Internet Age. However, it is difficult to imagine the general public foregoing the advantages of virtual exist-ence in order to prevent their identities being compromised.

Going back to the discussion of Goffman's performance model of identifica-tion, what has essentially happened is that the audience that accepts the indi-vidual performance has been automated. Actual human interaction has been lost as what counts for a successful performance of identity has been reduced to a set of digital algorithms and 'significant' information held on a database. This explains part of the frustration of dealing with processes of identification. It is, in part, this process rather than simple mobility that explains the contem-porary sense of anonymity – our social audience is not even human.

It might be possible, theoretically, to simplify the current chaos of differing cards, PIN numbers, passwords and 'significant information', that everyone has to remember, or carry around with them, if dedicated 'identity providers' were developed. These might maintain an individual's identity, and then authenticate him or her as a particular person when they dealt with 'service providers', such as a bank or an online retailer. They would then have only one body to deal with in respect of identification, and one set of cards, passwords, PINs, and so on. However, this might only mean people putting all their eggs in one identity basket, and if their identity was stolen from the identity provider the potential loss might be enormous. But at least there would only be one problem to fix, and losses could be covered by a single insurance policy. However, the question of who carries the liability for losses may prevent the development of such solutions.

Anonymity is hardly an option in contemporary society. Given that a per-son's social identity is based on being a consumer, a juridical person or a citi-zen, with all the rights and obligations these personalities carry, it is difficult to see how they can avoid identifying themselves to others. They may not want to identify themselves to a bank, or to a government department, but then how do they claim a welfare benefit, or pay a third party via the bank? How can they refuse to identify themselves but then demand that others identify themselves when they interact with them? Identification is what makes people 'significant others' in a mass human society – indeed it could be argued that it is part of the performances that create their social selves. As long as the institutions of pri-vate property, and of citizenship are accepted, it might then be possible to argue about the circumstances and frequency with which individuals have to identify themselves, and the consequences of doing so, or failing to do so, but that is a somewhat different issue. In the words of Scott, Tehranian and Mathias:

> unless one wishes to make an ethical-philosophical case that no state ought to have
> such panoptic powers – and hereby commit oneself to foregoing both its advantages

(e.g. the Centre for Disease Control) as well as its menaces (like fine-combed ethnic cleansing) – one is reduced to feeding Leviathan and hoping, perhaps through democratic institutions, to tame it.[1]

But more fundamentally, official and commercial identification is essential to social recognition, and something that many in developing nations seek avidly.

The introduction to *Identifying the English* also noted that many historians and sociologists have tended to explain the development of forms of identification in terms of either the mobility and anonymity caused by the Industrial Revolution, or as an inherent feature of modern 'governmentality' – the need of the modern State to pin people down for the purposes of control and exploitation. These are often put together in the argument that the modern State extends its powers to ensure social control in a society of strangers brought on by the mobility and urbanization associated with industrialization. Still others have claimed that governmentality, stretching back into the medieval period and beyond, has always been what states do.

However, the story revealed in the present work does not fit easily into these ways of understanding the development of the forms of identification. The chronology in England cannot be mapped easily onto a sociological model that posits a sudden rupture during the Industrial Revolution of the late eighteenth and early nineteenth centuries. In the case of the juridical person, the great shift from the seal to the signature took place in the early modern period, and from the signature to the world of digital ID in the late twentieth century. Civil registration does date from the 1830s but was really only an extension of the parochial registration of the 1530s. Similarly, the identification of the citizen, including that of the welfare claimant and of the elector, has always been based on community recognition and documentation since the early modern period. This may have been bureaucratized in the 'recommender system', or converted into data profiling, in the twentieth century, but is still recognizable today. The identification of the corpse was only revolutionized in the twentieth century with the development of more scientific forms of analysis. Lastly, the key innovations in the identification of the criminal, including anthropometrics and fingerprinting, were features of the late Victorian and Edwardian periods. England may, of course, be the exception that proves the rule here, and historians of other societies will certainly indicate if this is the case. However, if England, the 'First Industrial Nation',[2] is such an exception to the industrialization model of the 'Identification Revolution', then is it a model that can be easily generalized?

Of course, one might try to save the industrialization model by arguing that the Industrial Revolution was, in fact, part of a much longer, drawn-out, process going back to the breakup of feudalism in the late medieval period. This would certainly fit the more recent downgrading of the impact of the classic Industrial Revolution on England, and the older tradition, typified by Karl Marx,[3] in which the Industrial Revolution was prepared by earlier agricultural and financial 'revolutions'. England in the early modern period was certainly undergoing significant economic and social changes that increased mobility and anonymity in the period before 1760. But extending the concept of the Industrial Revolution in this manner rather dilutes its analytical usefulness, turning it into part of a vague 'modernization theory',[4] and makes it difficult to conceptualize adequately the key changes of the late nineteenth and twentieth centuries.

Also, this positing of a long, drawn-out process of development, driven by social and economic forces working over half a millennium, ignores the periods of retreat in the development and deployment of forms of identification, at least on the part of the State.

Counter-intuitively, in the late eighteenth and early nineteenth centuries there seems to have been a relative decline in state-imposed forms of identification. As already noted, the practice of branding deviants, and the use of warrants of hue and cry, seem to have been on the wane by 1800. In the late eighteenth century, official systems for disseminating deviant identifications were overshadowed by the private use of newspapers, and other printed artefacts, for the same purpose. The use of settlement certificates in the Poor Law system seems to have been in decline in the late eighteenth and early nineteenth centuries. The New Poor Law established in 1834 did not rely upon documentation or identification to control the population but the 'workhouse test'. The increased control and registration of aliens during the French Revolutionary and Napoleonic Wars lapsed in the postwar period, and the use of passports to control movement in and out of the country declined in the Victorian period. This was despite the vast numbers of foreigners who were entering the country to take up residence, or en route to the United States or British Empire. Even in the twentieth century, the British State showed itself unable to sustain national registration systems and ID cards outside wartime, and was unwilling to use the new biometrics system of fingerprinting to identify citizens as opposed to criminals.[5] The current expansion of identification, the particular forms and techniques used, and the surveillance these allow, are not inevitable, or potentially beyond control.

As the recent decision of the Labour administration of Tony Blair not to restrict the migration of hundreds of thousands of east Europeans into Britain has shown, States do not have to respond to population mobility by introducing new forms of control. However, the problems that this caused for the Labour Party among many of its core supporters in the 2010 election reveals that population movements and anonymity are not, of themselves, the key to understanding the development of modern forms of identification.[6] What seems to be crucial is political practice, and the relationship between the State and citizens. The late eighteenth-century decline of branding can be seen in terms of a shift in how the State understood the population – as minds to be moulded rather than as subject bodies to be physically controlled and punished.[7] Civil registration was part of the creation of a bourgeois polity in the aftermath of the 1832 Reform Act, which gave the middle classes and nonconformists the influence to underpin their property rights. The Habitual Criminals Registry, and the development of early criminal biometrics (anthropometrics, fingerprints), were, arguably, a feature of a period of political reform, which led to a desire to distinguish the degenerate residuum from the respectable working classes. The origins of the 'dossier person' lay in the welfare reforms of the Edwardian Asquith government of the early twentieth century, which in the aftermath of the 1885 Reform Act tried to attract the working-class voter to the Liberal Party. The restrictions on aliens in the 1905 Aliens Act, and in subsequent immigration legislation, represent an attempt by political parties to attract working-class voters. ID cards and passports come out of total war and the mobilization of citizens by modern states for international conflict. The twentieth-century conflicts over ID cards can be understood in terms of a confrontation between a neoclassical liberalism that sees freedom as independence *from* the State (within certain defined bounds), and a statism that sees freedoms as provided *through* the State. This highlights that the State is as much a site of contestation as a monolithic entity, something that has perhaps been glossed over in the present work. The increasing lack of trust between State and citizens has also fuelled the development of the digital dossier society. Similarly, modern changes in the relationship between the capitalist organization and the consumer have been driven by a desire by the former to change its relationship with the latter, as much as by any demographic trends.

This is not, of course, an attempt to deny the importance of social, economic and demographic factors in the history of identification. Rather, it is to argue for greater attention to the way in which these forces are utilized, handled or mediated by institutions such as the State and capitalist enterprises. What interests do they serve, why do they choose particular strategies to serve them, what compromises do they make, and what are the constellations of forces that can form, limit or forward their plans? States can limit their identificatory ambitions, or simply not be interested in identifying the 'missing' at all. Understanding the specific history of identification only in terms of the onward march of some post-modernist 'will to power',[8] or the operation of vast social and economic trends, leads to fatalism and undermines choice.

Of course, the extent to which the English, or British, can now control the forms of identification they need to perform is a moot point. Pressures to extend the use of biometrics in passports may come from foreign governments and international regulatory bodies. Commercial vendors of new forms of identification, who have taken over from the servants of the State as the locus of innovation in the field, are always on hand to provide biometric solutions to the commercial and political perceptions of risk. Above all there are the vagaries of 'events' – a terrorist attack, or a moral panic over paedophiles – that may overwhelm attempts to limit the scope of identification in society. Once the registry, or database, is seen as the default means of risk management, is the creation of numerous 'Little Brothers' inevitable, and is this any better than a single national registration system? Or will the system of registration and control be merely privatized, and such functions supplied by credit reference agencies? Are these the forces that are driving the current effacement of the distinctions between juridical persons, citizen, aliens and deviants, in the realm of identification that have subsisted for centuries? The price of freedom may be eternal vigilance but what if vigilance involves a level of identification and surveillance that itself curtails freedom? But such questions lie in the realm of choice, not of necessity.

Notes

NOTES TO CHAPTER 1: INTRODUCTION

1. 'Timeline: child benefits records loss', BBC News website: http://news.bbc.co.uk/1/hi/uk_politics/7104368.stm (Accessed on 27 March 2008). A good deal of use has been made of websites in the present work, and the web links given are to webpages as they existed at the time of consultation. Unfortunately, unlike the BBC website, many sites are not archived, and it may be difficult, therefore, always to use the links to identify the cited material. However, many of these pages may be retrieved from web archives such as the Internet Archive Wayback Machine at www.archive.org/web/web.php. This is yet another example of the transient nature of the digital archive I have discussed elsewhere, see Edward Higgs, 'The role of tomorrow's electronic archives', in Edward Higgs (ed.), *History and Electronic Artefacts* (Oxford: Clarendon Press, 1998), pp. 184–94.
2. Ross Anderson, Ian Brown, Terri Dowty, Philip Inglesant, William Heath and Angela Sasse, *Database State* (York: Joseph Rowntree Reform Trust, 2009), p. 8.
3. Edward Higgs, *The Information State in England: The Central Collection of Information on Citizens, 1500–2000* (London: Palgrave, 2004), pp. 99–193.
4. APACS website: www.apacs.org.uk/resources_publications/cards_facts_and_figures.html (Accessed on 26 March 2008).
5. Home Office Identity Fraud Steering Committee website: www.identity-theft.org.uk/faqs.html (Accessed on 23 March 2008); Cabinet Office, *Identity Fraud: A Study* (London: Cabinet Office, 2002), p. 13.
6. Kim Cohen, 'The laws of identity', p. 2. Available at www.identityblog.com/stories/2005/05/13/TheLawofIdentity.pdf (Accessed on 2 June 2010).
7. NO2ID website: www.no2id.net/ (Accessed on 2 April 2008).
8. Marc Garcelon, 'Colonizing the subject: the genealogy and legacy of the Soviet internal passport', in Jane Caplan and John Torpey (eds), *Documenting Individual Identity: The Development of State Practices in the Modern World* (Oxford: Princeton University Press, 2001), pp. 83–100; Götz Aly and Karl Heinz Roth, *The Nazi Census. Identification and Control in the Third Reich* (Philadelphia: Temple University Press, 2004).
9. Simon Szreter, 'The right of registration: development, identity registration and social security', History and Policy website: www.historyandpolicy.org/papers/policy-paper-53.html (Accessed 15 April 2008).
10. Commission on Legal Empowerment of the Poor, *Making the Law Work for Everyone* (New York: Commission on Legal Empowerment of the Poor, 2008), p. 32; 'Non-ID Palestinians in Lebanon Limbo', BBC News website: http://news.bbc.co.uk/1/hi/world/middle_east/7325147.stm (Accessed on 2 April 2008).

11. Jane Caplan and John Torpey (eds), *Documenting Individual Identity: The Development of State Practices in the Modern World* (Oxford: Princeton University Press, 2001).

12. John Torpey, *The Invention of the Passport: Surveillance, Citizenship and the State* (Cambridge: Cambridge University Press, 2000).

13. Simon A. Cole, *Suspect Identities. A History of Fingerprinting and Criminal Identification* (London: Harvard University Press, 2001); Chandak Sengoopta, *Imprint of the Raj. How Fingerprinting was Born in Colonial India* (London: Macmillan, 2003).

14. David Lyon, *Surveillance Society. Monitoring Everyday Life* (Buckingham: Open University Press, 2001); David Lyon, 'Surveillance as social sorting: computer codes and mobile bodies', in David Lyon (ed.), *Surveillance as Social Sorting: Privacy, Risk, and Digital Discrimination* (Abingdon: Routledge, 2003), pp. 13–30; David Lyon, *The Electronic Eye. The Rise of Surveillance Society* (Cambridge: Polity Press, 2004).

15. Cole, *Suspect Identities*, p. 8.

16. Sengoopta, *Imprint of the Raj*, p. 9.

17. Jane Caplan and John Torpey, 'Introduction', in Jane Caplan and John Torpey (eds), *Documenting Individual Identity: The Development of State Practices in the Modern World* (Oxford: Princeton University Press, 2001), p. 7.

18. For example, Rob Hamadi, *Identity Theft: What It is, How to Prevent It and What to Do If It Happens to You* (London: Vision, 2004), p. 1; Daniel J. Solove, *The Digital Person; Technology and Privacy in the Information Age* (London: New York University Press, 2004), p. 2.

19. Higgs, *The Information State in England*, pp. 11–13.

20. Michael Mann, *The Sources of Social Power, Vol. 1: A History of Power from the Beginning to AD 1760* (Cambridge: Cambridge University Press, 1986), pp. 31–2.

21. Ferdinand Tönnies, *Community and Association* (*Gemeinschaft und Gesellschaft*) (London: Routledge & Kegan Paul, 1955).

22. Georg Simmel, *The Stranger* (Chicago: Chicago University Press, 1971).

23. Didier Bigo, 'Frontiers and security in the European Union: the illusion of migration control', in Malcolm Anderson and Eberhard Bort (eds), *The Frontiers of Europe* (London: Pinter, 1998), pp. 148–64. See also, Malcolm Anderson, Didier Bigo and Ed Bort, 'Frontiers, identity and security in Europe, an agenda of research', in Martin Pratt and Janet Allison Brown (eds), *Borderlands under Stress* (London: Kluwer Law International, 2000), pp. 251–74.

24. Stephen Castles and Mark J. Miller, *The Age of Migration* (Basingstoke: Palgrave Macmillan, 2003), pp. 271–6.

25. Lyon, *Surveillance Society*, p. 19.

26. Lyon, *Surveillance Society*, p. 73. See also Lyon, *The Electronic Eye*, pp. 32–3.

27. Michel Foucault, 'The subject and power', in Hubert L. Dreyfus and Paul Rabinow (eds), *Michel Foucault: Beyond Structuralism and Hermeneutics, with an Afterword by Michel Foucault* (Brighton: Harvester, 1982), pp. 208–26; Michel Foucault, 'Governmentality', in Graham Burchell, Colin Gordon and Peter Miller (eds), *The Foucault Effect: Studies in Governmentality* (London: Harvester Wheatsheaf, 1991), pp. 87–104; Michel Foucault, *Discipline and Punish: The Birth of the Prison* (London: Allen Lane, 1977).

28. Bruce Curtis, *The Politics of Population. State Formation, Statistics and the Census of Canada, 1840–1875* (Toronto: University of Toronto Press, 2001), p. 26.

29. For example, Katja Franko Aas, '"The body does not lie": identity, risk and trust in technoculture', *Crime, Media, Culture*, 2 (2006), pp. 143–58.

30. Anthony Giddens, *The Nation-State and Violence: Volume Two of a Contemporary Critique of Historical Materialism* (Cambridge: Polity Press, 1987), pp. 172–97, 302–3.

31. James C. Scott, *Seeing Like a State: How Certain Schemes to Improve the Human Condition Have Failed* (London: Yale University Press, 1998).

32. Edward Higgs, 'Consumers, citizens and deviants – differing forms of personal identification in England since the Victorian period', in Kerstin Brückweh (ed.), *The Voice of the Citizen Consumer: A History of Market Research, Consumer Movements and the Political Public Sphere* (London: German Historical Institute, forthcoming).

33. Valentin Groebner, *Who are You? Identification, Deception and Surveillance in Early Modern Europe* (New York: Zone Books, 2007), pp. 22–3.

34. Valentin Groebner, 'Describing the person, reading the signs in late medieval and renaissance Europe: identity papers, vested figures, and the limits of identification, 1400–1600', in Jane Caplan and John Torpey (eds), *Documenting Individual Identity: The Development of State Practices in the Modern World* (Oxford: Princeton University Press, 2001), pp. 15–16.

35. Groebner, *Who are You?*, p. 225.

36. Scott, *Seeing Like a State*, p. 65.

37. Edward Higgs, *Life, Death and Statistics: Civil Registration, Censuses and the Work of the General Register Office, 1837–1952* (Hatfield: Local Population Studies, 2004), pp. 7–17.

38. Nick Vine Hall, *Tracing Your Family History in Australia* (Albert Park, Australia: Scriptorium Family History Centre, 1994), pp. 402–3.

39. Sengoopta, *Imprint of the Raj*, passim.

40. Cole, *Suspect Identities*, pp. 137–9.

41. John M. Butler, *Forensic DNA Typing: Biology, Technology and Genetics of STR Markers* (London: Elsevier Academic Press, 2005), pp. 1–16.

42. John Daugman, 'Introduction to Iris Recognition', John Daugman's webpage: www.cl.cam.ac.uk/users/jgd1000/iris_recognition.html (Accessed on 23 March 2005).

43. Clive Norris and Gary Armstrong, *The Maximum Surveillance Society: The Rise of CCTV* (Oxford: Berg, 1999).

44. 'Mary Poppins and Magna Carta', *The Economist*, 21 June 2008, pp.47–8.

45. Tadeusz Iwaszko, 'Die Haeftlinge' in *Auschwitz. Geschichte und Wirklichkeit des Lagers* (Reinbek: Rororo, 1980), pp. 57–8.

46. Groebner, *Who are You?*, p. 26.

47. Steve Hindle, 'Technologies of identification under the Old Poor Law', *The Local Historian*, 36 (2006), pp. 229–31.

48. See, for example, Henry French and Jonathan Barry (eds), *Identity and Agency in England, 1500–1800* (Basingstoke: Palgrave Macmillan, 2004).

49. Dror Wahrman, *The Making of the Modern Self* (London: Yale University Press, 2004).

50. C. B. Macpherson, *The Political Theory of Possessive Individualism: Hobbes to Locke* (Oxford: Clarendon Press, 1962); Keith Thomas, *The Ends of Life: Roads to Fulfillment in Early Modern England* (Oxford: Oxford University Press, 2009), pp. 37–43.

51. Alan Macfarlane, *The Origins of English Individualism: The Family, Property and Social Transition* (Oxford: Basil Blackwell, 1978).

52. Charles Taylor, *Sources of the Self: The Making of Modern Identity* (Cambridge: Cambridge University Press, 1989).

53. Erving Goffman, *The Presentation of Self in Everyday Life* (Harmondsworth: Penguin Books, 1971), p. 24.

54. Goffman, *The Presentation of Self in Everyday Life*, p. 241.

55. Goffman, *The Presentation of Self in Everyday Life*, pp. 244–5.

56. Alan Bennett, *Writing home* (London: Faber and Faber, 2005), p. 483.

57. Jane Caplan, '"This or that particular person"; protocols of identification in nineteenth-century Europe', in Jane Caplan and John Torpey (eds), *Documenting Individual Identity: The Development of State Practices in the Modern World* (Oxford: Princeton University Press, 2001), p. 51.

58. European Parliament Committee on Citizens' Freedoms and Rights, Justice and Home Affairs (LIBE), *Biometrics at the Frontiers: Assessing the Impact on Society* (2005). Available at http://ec.europa.eu/justice_home/doc_centre/freetravel/doc/biometrics_eur21585.pdf, pp. 11–12 (Accessed 30 April 2010).

59. European Parliament Committee on Citizens' Freedoms and Rights, Justice and Home Affairs (LIBE), p. 43.

60. Edward Higgs, 'Personal identification as information flows in England, 1500–2000', in Toni Weller (ed.), *Information History in the Modern World* (London: Palgrave Macmillan, forthcoming).

NOTES TO CHAPTER 2: THREE ROGUES

1. Goffman, *The Presentation of Self in Everyday Life*, pp. 66–7.

2. Tacitus, *The Histories, Book II*, The Internet Classics Archive website: http://classics.mit.edu?/Tacitus/histories.2.ii.html (Accessed on 3 April 2008).

3. Clive Cheesman and Jonathan Williams, *Rebels, Pretenders and Impostors* (London: British Museum Press, 2002), pp. 95–8.

4. Margaret Aston, *Lollards and Reformers: Images and Literacy in Late Medieval Religion* (London: Hambledon Press, 1984), p. 28.

5. Michael Bennett, *Lambert Simnel and the Battle of Stoke* (Stroud: Alan Sutton, 1987).

6. Cheeseman and Williams, *Rebels, Pretenders and Impostors*, pp. 137–9.

7. National Archives, London: Home Office: Registered Papers: HO 45/23607 ROYAL – OTHER MATTERS: Claim to throne by Anthony Hall: alleged descendant of Henry VIII 1931.

8. Sydney Anglo, *Images of Tudor Kingship* (London: Seaby, 1992), pp. 40–60.

9. Natalie Zemon Davis, *The Return of Martin Guerre* (London: Harvard University Press, 1983).

10. Geoff Hutchinson, *Grey Owl: The Incredible Story of Archie Belaney, 1888–1938* (Brede: G. Hutchinson, 1985).

11. S. J. Gunn, 'Warbeck, Perkin (*c.*1474–1499)', *Oxford Dictionary of National Biography*: www.oxforddnb.com/view/article/28669 (Accessed on 20 June 2008).

12. Ian Arthurson, *The Perkin Warbeck Conspiracy 1491–1499* (Stroud: Alan Sutton Publishing, 1997), p. 1.

13. Michael J. Bennett, 'Simnel, Lambert (*b.* 1476/7, *d.* after 1534)', *Oxford Dictionary of National Biography*: www.oxforddnb.com/view/article/25569 (Accessed on 20 June 2008).

14. Ann Wroe, *Perkin. A Story of Deception* (London: Vintage, 2003), pp. 361–420.

15. Francis Bacon, *The Reign of Henry VII* (London: C. and J. Rivington, 1826), p. 93.

16. Wroe, *Perkin. A Story of Deception*, pp. 516–18.

17. D. M. Kleyn, *Richard of England* (Oxford: Kensal Press, 1990).

18. Arthurson, *The Perkin Warbeck Conspiracy*, p. xii.

19. Wroe, *Perkin. A Story of Deception*, pp, 141–2.

20. Norbert Elias, *The Civilizing Process* (Oxford: Blackwell, 2000), pp. 47–142.

21. Arthurson, *The Perkin Warbeck Conspiracy*, p. xii.

22. Edward Hall, *Chronicle, Containing the History of England* . . . (London: J. Johnson; F. C. and J. Rivington, 1809), p. 462.

23. Arthurson, *The Perkin Warbeck Conspiracy*, p. 51.

24. Cited in Wroe, *Perkin. A Story of Deception*, p. 128.

25. Wroe, *Perkin. A Story of Deception*, pp. 132–4.

26. F. Madden, 'Documents relating to Perkin Warbeck, with remarks on his history', *Archaeologia*, 27 (1838), pp. 165–6, 202.

27. Wroe, *Perkin. A Story of Deception*, p. 469.

28. Davis, *The Return of Martin Guerre*, pp. 67–8.

29. Natalie Zemon Davis, 'On the lame', *The American Historical Review*, 93 (June 1988), p. 578.

30. Davis, *The Return of Martin Guerre*, pp. 69–70.

31. Davis, 'On the lame', pp. 576–7.

32. James Gairdner, *Memorials of Henry VII in the Rolls Series* (London: Longman, Brown, Green, Longmans, and Roberts, 1858), pp. 65–6.

33. Cited in Wroe, *Perkin. A Story of Deception*, p. 129.

34. Arthurson, *The Perkin Warbeck Conspiracy*, p. 190.

35. Rohan McWilliam, 'Tichborne claimant (*d.* 1898)', *Oxford Dictionary of National Biography*: www.oxforddnb.com/view/article/20855 (Accessed on 20 June 2008).

36. Kirsten McKenzie, *A Swindler's Progress: Nobles and Convicts in the Age of Liberty* (London: Harvard University Press, 2010).

37. Rohan McWilliam, *The Tichborne Claimant. A Victorian Sensation* (London: Hambledon Continuum, 2007), pp. 13–16.

38. Robyn Annear, *The Man Who Lost Himself. The Unbelievable Story of the Tichborne Claimant* (London: Robinson, 2003), p. 114; McWilliam, *The Tichborne Claimant*, pp. 190–1.

39. McWilliam, 'Tichborne claimant (*d.* 1898)'.

40. McWilliam, *The Tichborne Claimant*, pp. 35–52, 83–111.

41. Edward V. H. Kenealy, *The Book of God: The Apocalypse* (London: Trübner & Co, 1867).

42. McWilliam, 'Tichborne claimant (*d.* 1898)'; McWilliam, *The Tichborne Claimant*, pp. 113–69.

43. McWilliam, 'Tichborne claimant (*d.* 1898)'.

44. *The Pall Mall Gazette*, Saturday, 2 April 1898.

45. Maurice Edward Kenealy, *The Tichborne Tragedy, Being the Secret and Authentic History of the Extraordinary Facts and Circumstances Connected with the Claims, Personality, Identification, Conviction and Last Days of the Tichborne Claimant* (London: Francis Griffiths, 1913), pp. 35, 40.

46. Annear, *The Man Who Lost Himself*, pp. 11–13.

47. *The Pall Mall Gazette*, Saturday, 2 April 1898.

48. McWilliam, *The Tichborne Claimant*, p. 24.

49. Annear, *The Man Who Lost Himself*, p. 333.

50. McWilliam, *The Tichborne Claimant*, p. 23.

51. Annear, *The Man Who Lost Himself*, pp. 107, 112–16.

52. McWilliam, *The Tichborne Claimant*, pp. 113–69.

53. Ross McKibbin, 'Why was there no Marxism in Great Britain', *The English Historical Review*, 99 (1984), pp. 297–331.

54. Annear, *The Man Who Lost Himself*, p. 98.

55. Annear, *The Man Who Lost Himself*, pp. 353–5; Kenealy, *The Tichborne Tragedy*, p. 241; McWilliam, *The Tichborne Claimant*, p. 199.

56. McWilliam, *The Tichborne Claimant*, p. 226.

57. National Archives, London: Supreme Court of Judicature and Former Superior Courts: Central Office and Predecessors: Documents Exhibited or Deposited in Court: J 90/1225 Tichborne v Castro.

58. Cited in McWilliam, *The Tichborne Claimant*, p. 197.

59. C. P. Jones, 'Stigma and tattoo', in Jane Caplan (ed.), *Written on the Body. The Tattoo in European and American History* (London: Reaktion Books, 2000), pp. 1–16; Clare Anderson, 'Godna: Inscribing Indian convicts in the nineteenth century', in Jane Caplan (ed.), *Written on the Body. The Tattoo in European and American History* (London: Reaktion Books, 2000), pp. 103–4.

60. Jones, 'Stigma and tattoo', p. 13.

61. Hamish Maxwell-Stewart and Ian Duffield, 'Skin deep devotions: religious tattoos and convict transportation to Australia', in Jane Caplan (ed.), *Written on the Body. The Tattoo in European and American History* (London: Reaktion Books, 2000), pp. 118–35.

62. James Bradley, 'Body commodification? Class and tattoos in Victorian Britain', in Jane Caplan (ed.), *Written on the Body. The Tattoo in European and American History* (London: Reaktion Books, 2000), pp. 136–55.

63. McWilliam, *The Tichborne Claimant*, pp. 52, 96.

64. Kenealy, *The Tichborne Tragedy*, pp. 164–5; McWilliam, *The Tichborne Claimant*, p. 45.

65. Annear, *The Man Who Lost Himself*, p. 355.

66. Kenealy, *The Tichborne Tragedy*, photographs facing p. 97.

67. C. S. Nicholls and Tom McNally, 'Stonehouse, John Thomson (1925–1988)', *Oxford Dictionary of National Biography*: www.ixforddnb.com/view/article/39863 (Accessed on 24 January 2008).

68. John Stonehouse, *The Death of an Idealist* (London: W. H. Allen, 1975), pp. 96–114.

69. Stonehouse, *The Death of an Idealist*, pp. 128–9.

70. Ibid., p. 151.

71. *The Times*, Tuesday, 27 April 1976, p. 4; *The Times*, Thursday, 19 Apr 1976, p. 5.

72. Geoffrey Robertson, *The Justice Game* (London: Vintage, 1999), pp. 68–9.

73. Robertson, *The Justice Game*, pp. 69–70.

74. R. D. Laing, *The Divided Self* (London: Tavistock Publications, 1960).

75. Stonehouse, *The Death of an Idealist*, pp. 190–206.

76. Ibid., pp. 218–20.

77. John Stonehouse, *My Trial: My Blow-by-Blow Account and Psychological Reaction to the Trial and Verdict from the Old Bailey Dock* (London: Wyndham Publications, 1976), p. 44.

78. *The Times*, Tuesday, 27 April 1976, p. 4.

79. Stonehouse, *My Trial*, pp. 161, 168.

80. Stonehouse, *The Death of an Idealist*, p. 165.

81. Robertson, *The Justice Game*, pp. 63–4.

82. Ibid., pp. 66–7.

83. Ibid., p. 71.

84. *The Times*, Saturday, 7 August 1976, p. 1.

85. Nicholls and McNally, 'Stonehouse, John Thomson (1925–1988)'.

86. Roger Clarke, 'Human identification in information systems: management challenges and public policy issues', *Information Technology & People*, 7 (December 1994), pp. 6–37.

NOTES TO CHAPTER 3: EARLY MODERN ENGLAND – A FACE-TO-FACE SOCIETY?

1. See, for example, J. A. Sharpe, *Early Modern England: A Social History, 1550–1760* (London: Edward Arnold, 1987); John Rule, *Albion's People: English Society 1714–1815* (London: Longman, 1992); and Keith Wrightson, *English Society 1580–1680* (London: Hutchinson, 1982).

2. Tönnies, *Community and Association*, p. 68.

3. Ibid., p. 55.

4. Ibid., p. 48.

5. Henry Maine, *Ancient Law: Its Connection with the Early History of Society, and Its Relation to Modern Ideas* (London: John Murray, 1861).

6. R. M. Smith, '"Modernization" and the corporate medieval village community in England: some sceptical reflections', in A. R. H. Baker and D. Gregory (eds), *Explorations in Historical Geography: Interpretative Essays* (Cambridge: Cambridge University Press, 1984), pp. 140–79.

7. Groebner, *Who are You?*, pp. 22–5.

8. Macfarlane, *The Origins of English Individualism*, pp. 82–4.

9. Ibid., *passim*.

10. Peter Laslett, 'Clayworth and Cogenhoe', in Peter Laslett, *Family Life and Illicit Love in Earlier Generations* (Cambridge: Cambridge University Press, 1977), p. 66.

11. Ibid., pp. 64–7.

12. Alan Macfarlane, *Reconstructing Historical Communities* (Cambridge: Cambridge University Press, 1977), p. 9.

13. See, for example, Wrightson, *English Society 1580–1680*, p. 42; David Rollison, 'Exploding England: the dialectics of mobility and settlement in early modern England', *Social History*, 24 (1999), pp. 11–12.

14. Christopher Dyer, 'Were late medieval English villages "self-contained", in Christopher Dyer (ed.), *The Self-Contained Village? The Social History of Rural Communities 1250–1900* (Hatfield: University of Hertfordshire Press, 2007), p. 6.

15. Ibid., pp. 10–11.

16. Wrightson, *English Society 1580–1680*, p. 43.

17. Peter Clark, 'Migration in England during the late seventeenth and early eighteenth centuries', in Peter Clark and Dennis Souden (eds), *Migration and Society in Early Modern England* (London: Hutchinson, 1987), p. 215.

18. Patricia Fumerton, *Unsettled: The Culture of Mobility and the Working Poor in Early Modern England* (London: University of Chicago Press, 2006), pp. xiv–xv.

19. Ibid., p. 56.

20. Dave Postles, *Social Proprieties: Address and Naming in Early-modern England (1500–1640)* (Washington, DC: New Academia Publishing, 2006), pp. 46–8.

21. Ian D. Whyte, *Migration and Society in Britain 1550–1830* (Basingstoke: Macmillan, 2000), pp. 34–8, 65.

22. E. Anthony Wrigley, 'Urban growth and agricultural change: England and the Continent in the early modern period', in Roger S. Schofield and E. Anthony Wrigley (eds), *Population and History: From the Traditional to the Modern World* (Cambridge: Cambridge University Press, 1986), p. 150.

23. E. A. Wrigley, 'A simple model of London's importance in changing English society and economy 1650–1750', *Past and Present*, 37 (1967), pp. 44–70.

24. Whyte, *Migration and Society in Britain 1550–1830*, p. 64. For a recent article emphasizing the dynamic qualities of English society in this period, and of London in particular, see Richard Smith, 'Periods, structures and regimes in early modern demographic history', *History Workshop Journal*, 63 (2007), pp. 202–18.

25. Paul Griffiths, *Lost Londons: Change, Crime and Control in the Capital City, 1550–1660* (Cambridge: Cambridge University Press, 2008), pp. 27–42, 69–70.

26. Ibid., p. 41.

27. Thomas Harman, *A Caveat or Warening for Commen Cursetors Vulgarely Called Vagabones*, in Gamini Salgado (ed.), *Cony-Catchers and Bawdy Basket; an Anthology of Elizabethan Low Life* (Harmondsworth: Penguin Books, 1972), pp. 110–18.

28. Patricia Fumerton, 'Making vagrancy (in)visible: the economics of disguise in early modern rogue pamphlets', *English Literary Renaissance*, 33 (2003), pp, 211–27; Griffiths, *Lost Londons*, p. 140.

29. Cited in Philip Rawlings, *Drunks, Whores and Idle Apprentices: Criminal Biographies of the Eighteenth Century* (London: Routledge, 1992), p. 20.

30. Craig Muldrew, *The Economy of Obligation. The Culture of Credit and Social Relations in Early Modern England* (London: Macmillan, 1998), pp. 96–100.

31. Ibid., pp. 38–9.

32. Eric Kerridge, *Trade and Banking in Early-Modern England* (Manchester: Manchester University Press, 1988), pp. 39–42; Martin J. Daunton, *Progress and Poverty: An*

Economic and Social History of Britain, 1770–1850 (Oxford: Oxford University Press, 1995), pp. 248–9.

33. Muldrew, *The Economy of Obligation*, p. 174.

34. Julian Hoppit, 'The use and abuse of credit in eighteenth-century England', in Neil McKendrick and R. B. Outhwaite (eds), *Business Life and Public Policy: Essays in Honour of D. C. Coleman* (Cambridge: Cambridge University Press, 1986), p. 77.

35. Muldrew, *The Economy of Obligation*, pp. 174–7.

36. Craig Muldrew, 'Rural credit, market areas and legal institutions in the countryside in England, 1550–1700', in C. W. Brooks and Michael Lobban (eds), *Communities and Courts, Proceedings of the Twelfth Legal History Conference Held in Durham* (London: Hambledon Press, 1997), pp. 155–77.

37. Muldrew, *The Economy of Obligation*, p. 23.

38. William Shakespeare, *The Merchant of Venice*, Act I, Scene iii.

39. Lyon, *Surveillance Society*, pp. 15–16.

40. Cole, *Suspect Identities*, p. 9.

41. Muldrew, *The Economy of Obligation*, pp. 111–13.

42. L. R. Poos, *A Rural Society after the Black Death: Essex 1350–1525* (Cambridge: Cambridge University Press, 1991), p. 162.

43. Jane Whittle, 'Population mobility in rural Norfolk among landowners and others c.1440–c.1600', in Christopher Dyer (ed.), *The Self-Contained Village? The Social History of Rural Communities 1250–1900* (Hatfield: University of Hertfordshire Press, 2007), pp. 30–1; Ann Kussmaul, *Servants in Husbandry in Early Modern England* (Cambridge: Cambridge University Press, 1981), p. 57.

44. Kussmaul, *Servants in Husbandry*, pp. 31–4.

45. Ernest George Ravenstein, 'The laws of migration', *Journal of the Statistical Society of London*, 48 (1885), pp. 167–235; Ernest George Ravenstein, 'The laws of migration', *Journal of the Royal Statistical Society*, 52 (1889), pp. 241–305.

46. Ian Whyte, 'Cumbrian village communities: continuity and change, c.1750–c.1850', in Christopher Dyer (ed.), *The Self-Contained Village? The Social History of Rural Communities 1250–1900* (Hatfield: University of Hertfordshire Press, 2007), pp. 96–113.

47. Keith Wrightson and David Levine, *Poverty and Piety in an English Village: Terling, 1525–1700* (Oxford: Clarendon Press, 1995), p. 81.

48. E. A. Wrigley and R. S. Schofield, *The Population History of England 1541–1871: A Reconstruction* (London: Edward Arnold, 1981), pp. 207–15.

49. Clark, 'Migration in England during the late seventeenth and early eighteenth centuries', pp. 220–9; Whyte, *Migration and Society in Britain 1550–1830*, p. 33.

50. A notable exception being, Colin G. Pooley, Jean Turnbull and Mags Adams, *A Mobile Century?: Changes in Everyday Mobility in Britain in the Twentieth Century* (Aldershot: Ashgate, 2005).

51. K. D. M. Snell, *Parish and Belonging. Community, Identity and Welfare in England and Wales 1700–1950* (Cambridge: Cambridge University Press, 2006), pp. 28–80.

52. Colin Pooley, 'Mobility in the twentieth century: substituting commuting for migration', in D. Gilbert, D. Matless and B. Short (eds), *Geographies of British Modernity: Space and Society in the Twentieth Century* (Oxford: Blackwell, 2003), p. 87.

53. Richard Cobb, *Death in Paris 1795–1801* (Oxford: Oxford University Press, 1978), p. 34.

54. Ibid., p. 46.

55. Michael Anderson, *Family Structure in Nineteenth Century Lancashire* (Cambridge: Cambridge University Press, 1971), pp. 152–60.

56. Griffiths, *Lost Londons*, pp. 70–1.

57. Leslie Hannah, *The Rise of the Corporate Economy* (London: Methuen, 1976).

58. Higgs, *The Information State in England*, pp. 30–44.

59. See, for example, Steve Hindle, *On the Parish?: The Micro-Politics of Poor Relief in Rural England, c. 1550–1750* (Oxford: Clarendon Press, 2004); Lynn Hollen Lees, *The Solidarities of Strangers: The English Poor Laws and the People, 1700–1948* (Cambridge: Cambridge University Press, 1998); Geoffrey W. Oxley, *Poor Relief in England and Wales 1601–1834* (Newton Abbott: David & Charles, 1974);

60. K. D. M. Snell, 'Settlement, Poor Law, and the rural historian: new approaches and opportunities', *Rural History*, 3 (2) (1992), pp. 145–72.

61. Clive Emsley, *The English Police. A Political and Social History* (Hemel Hempstead: Harvester Wheatsheaf, 1991), pp. 8–9; T. A. Critchley, *A History of Police in England and Wales* (London: Constable, 1978), pp. 2–6.

62. Cynthia B. Herrup, 'New shoes and mutton pies: investigative responses to theft in seventeenth-century Sussex', *The Historical Journal*, 27 (1984), pp. 811–30; Sharon Howard, 'Investigating responses to theft in early modern Wales: communities, thieves and the courts', *Continuity and Change*, 19 (2004), pp. 409–30.

NOTES TO CHAPTER 4: IDENTIFYING THE GREAT AND THE GOOD IN EARLY MODERN ENGLAND

1. Ann Rosalind Jones and Peter Stallybrass, *Renaissance Clothing and the Materials of Memory* (Cambridge: Cambridge University Press, 2000), pp. 2–4; Groebner, *Who are You?*, pp. 31–42.

2. Alan Hunt, *Governance of the Consuming Passions: A History of Sumptuary Law* (Basingstoke: Macmillan, 1996), pp. 299–324; Susan Vincent, *Dressing the Elite. Clothes in Early Modern England* (Oxford: Berg, 2003), pp. 118–19.

3. Hunt, *Governance of the Consuming Passions*, p. 119.

4. Vincent, *Dressing the Elite*, p. 161.

5. Terry Castle, *Masquerade and Civilization: The Carnivalesque in Eighteenth-Century English Culture and Fiction* (London: Methuen, 1986).

6. Cited in Vic Gatrell, *City of Laughter. Sex and Satire in Eighteenth-Century London* (London: Atlantic Books, 2006), p. 130.

7. Daniel Defoe, *Moll Flanders* (London: Penguin Books, 1983), p. 78.

8. Jones and Stallybrass, *Renaissance Clothing*, pp. 184–7.

9. Vincent, *Dressing the Elite*, pp. 118–37.

10. Wrightson, *English Society 1580–1680*, pp. 48–50.

11. Daniel Woolf, *The Social Circulation of the Past. English Historical Culture 1500–1730* (Oxford: Oxford University Press, 2003), pp. 73–86.

12. Groebner, *Who are You?*, pp. 54–7.

13. Woolf, *The Social Circulation of the Past*, pp. 100–5.
14. Lawrence Stone, *The Crisis of the Aristocracy, 1558–1641* (Oxford: Clarendon Press, 1965), p. 25.
15. David Cressy, *Birth, Marriage and Death: Ritual, Religion, and the Life-Cycle in Tudor and Stuart England* (Oxford: Oxford University Press, 1997), pp. 450–1.
16. Jane Austen, *Persuasion* (London: Folio Society, 1975), pp. 103–4.
17. Ibid., p. 11.
18. Susan Foister, *Holbein in England* (London: Tate Publishing, 2006), pp. 30–1.
19. Anthony Richard Wagner, *Heralds and Heraldry in the Middle Ages. An Inquiry into the Growth of the Armorial Function of Heralds* (Oxford: Oxford University Press, 2000), 13–14.
20. Ibid., p. 17.
21. Sir Anthony Wagner, *Heralds of England. A History of the Office and College of Arms* (London: HMSO, 1967), p. 25.
22. Wagner, *Heralds and Heraldry in the Middle Ages*, p. 20.
23. Stephen Friar, *Heraldry for the Local Historian and Genealogist* (London: Grange Books, 1997), p. 4.
24. J. Horace Round, *Peerage and Pedigree. Studies in Peerage Law and Family History* (London: James Nisbet & Co., 1910), pp. 69–102.
25. Wagner, *Heralds of England*, p. 6.
26. Wagner, *Heralds and Heraldry in the Middle Ages*, pp. 25–6.
27. Ibid., pp. 63–4.
28. Ibid., pp. 1–10.
29. Wagner, *Heralds of England*, pp. 225–6.
30. Ibid., pp. 268–9.
31. Anthony Richard Wagner, *English Genealogy* (Oxford: Clarendon Press, 1972), p. 364.
32. Wagner, *Heralds of England*, p. 293; Wagner, *English Genealogy*, pp. 365–97.
33. Samuel Pepys, *Everybody's Pepys: The Diary of Samuel Pepys 1660–1669* (London: G. Bell and Sons, 1945), pp. 107–8.
34. Ibid., pp. 110, 189.
35. Friar, *Heraldry for the Local Historian*, p. 12.
36. Wagner, *Heralds of England*, p. 426.
37. Thomas, *The Ends of Life*, pp. 44–77.
38. Gatrell, *City of Laughter*, pp. 345–61.
39. See, for example, Mervyn Edward Wingfield, *Muniments of the Ancient Saxon Family of Wingfield* (London: Whitehall and Hughes, 1894), Preface.
40. John Prest, *Politics in the Age of Cobden* (London: Macmillan, 1977), pp. 1–2; Charles Seymour, *Electoral Reform in England and Wales: The Development and Operation of the Parliamentary Franchise 1832–1885* (Newton Abbott: David & Charles, 1970), p. 105.
41. Derek Hirst, *The Representative of the People?: Voters and Voting in England under the Early Stuarts* (Cambridge: Cambridge University Press, 1975), p. 38.
42. Prest, *Politics in the Age of Cobden*, pp. 3–4.
43. Hirst, *The Representative of the People?*, p. 38.
44. Prest, *Politics in the Age of Cobden*, p. 2.
45. See, for example, Barclays Group Archive: 03-56 Signature Book.

46. Georges Roux, *Ancient Iraq* (London: Penguin Books, 1992), pp. 51, 70–2.

47. David Mattingly, *An Imperial Possession: Britain in the Roman Empire* (London: Penguin Books, 2007), pp. 317, 498.

48. M. T. Clanchy, *From Memory to Written Record: England 1066–1307* (Oxford: Blackwell, 1993), p. 310.

49. Ibid., pp. 38–41, 77, 258–9.

50. P. D. A. Harvey and Andrew McGuinness, *A Guide to British Medieval Seals* (London: British Library and Public Record Office, 1996), pp. 3–20. National Archives, London: Chancery and Supreme Court of Judicature: Patent Rolls (C 66); Chancery and Supreme Court of Judicature: Close Rolls (C 54).

51. Clanchy, *From Memory to Written Record*, pp. 314–17.

52. Brigitte Miriam Bedos-Rezak, 'Medieval identity: a sign and a concept', *The American Historical Review*, 105 (December 2000), p. 1503.

53. Clanchy, *From Memory to Written Record*, pp. 314, 317.

54. Harvey and McGuinness, *A Guide to British Medieval Seals*, pp. 22–6; Sir Charles Hilary Jenkinson, *Guide to Seals in the Public Record Office* (London: HMSO, 1968), p. 2. The author's own training on seals as an archivist in the Public Record Office in the late 1970s was almost exclusively confined to their iconography.

55. Clanchy, *From Memory to Written Record*, p. 51.

56. Sir Charles Hilary Jenkinson, *Seals in Administration: (A Plea for Systematic Study)* (Naples: L'Arte Tipographica, 1959), p. 167.

57. Clanchy, *From Memory to Written Record*, pp. 48–51; Brigitte Bedos-Rezak, 'Les sceaux au temps de Philippe Auguste', *Form and Order in Medieval France. Studies in Social and Quantitative Sigillography* (Aldershot: Variorum, 1993), II, p. 731.

58. Jenkinson, *Guide to Seals in the Public Record Office*, p. 7.

59. Harvey and McGuinness, *A Guide to British Medieval Seals*, pp. 79–80, 91.

60. Alfred Hiatt, *The Making of Medieval Forgeries: False Documents in Fifteenth-Century England* (London: British Library, 2004), p. 27.

61. Clanchy, *From Memory to Written Record*, pp. 233, 295.

62. Ibid., p. 128.

63. Clanchy, *From Memory to Written Record*, p. 304.

64. Béatrice Fraenkel, *La Signature: Genèse d'un Signe* (Paris: Gallimard, 1992), pp. 26–9, 92–6.

65. John Stanley Purvis, *Notarial Signs from the York Archiepiscopal Records* (London: St Anthony's Press, 1957), pp. iii–vii.

66. Harvey and McGuinness, *A Guide to British Medieval Seals*, p. 2.

67. See, for example, the merchant's mark in Holbein's portrait of Cyriacus Kale of 1533 in Foister, *Holbein in England*, p. 66.

68. Groebner, *Who are You?*, pp. 60–4.

69. Harvey and McGuinness, *A Guide to British Medieval Seals*, p. 34.

70. Jenkinson, *Guide to Seals in the Public Record Office*, p. 5.

71. R. H. Hilton, *The Decline of Serfdom in Medieval England* (London: Macmillan, 1969), pp. 18–19.

72. Harvey and McGuinness, *A Guide to British Medieval Seals*, p. 91.

73. David Cressy, *Literacy and the Social Order: Reading and Writing in Tudor and Stuart England* (Cambridge: Cambridge University Press, 1980), p. 176.

74. *Seventy-Seventh Annual Report of the Registrar General* (1914), British Parliamentary Papers 1916 V [Cd 8206], p. xiv.

75. R. S. Schofield, 'The measurement of literacy in pre-industrial England', in Jack Goody (ed.), *Literacy in Traditional Societies* (Cambridge: Cambridge University Press, 1968), pp. 317–18.

76. Wrightson and Levine, *Poverty and Piety in an English Village*, p. 16.

77. Cressy, *Literacy and the Social Order*, pp. 120–1.

78. Macpherson, *The Political Theory of Possessive Individualism*, *passim*; Foucault, 'Governmentality'.

79. Fraenkel, *La Signature*, pp. 9–22.

80. Jane Caplan, 'Illegibility: reading and insecurity in history, law and government', *History Workshop Journal*, 68 (2009), pp. 109–10.

81. Fraenkel, *La Signature*, p. 158.

82. Sir William Holdsworth, *A History of English Law, Vol. VI* (London: Methuen, 1924), pp. 384–5.

83. Joseph T. Robertson, *Discussion Paper on the Statute of Frauds, 1677* (St John's, NL: Newfoundland Law Reform Commission, 1991).

84. Ibid., p. 37.

85. Philip Hamburger, 'The conveyancing purposes of the Statute of Frauds', *The American Journal of Legal History*, 27 (1983), pp. 355–65.

86. Robertson, *Discussion Paper*, pp. 37–8.

87. David Martin Jones, *Conscience and Allegiance in Seventeenth Century England: The Political Significance of Oaths and Engagements* (Rochester, NY: University of Rochester Press, 1999), pp. 272–3.

88. Samuel Rawson Gardiner, *The Constitutional Documents of the Puritan Revolution 1625–1660* (Oxford: Clarendon Press, 1906), pp. 267–71.

89. The author is grateful to Professor John Walter for guidance in this matter.

90. Jones, *Conscience and Allegiance in Seventeenth Century England*, p. 129.

91. Muldrew, *The Economy of Obligation*, pp. 41, 106.

92. Kerridge, *Trade and Banking*, pp. 39–42, 57.

93. Katherine Mainolfi Keppenhaver, *Forensic Document Examination. Principles and Practice* (Totowa, NJ: Humana Press, 2007), p. 47.

94. *Blackstone's Commentaries on the Laws of England*, The Avalon Project at Yale Law School website: www.yale.edu/lawweb/avalon/blackstone/bk4ch17.htm (Accessed on 18 September 2008).

95. Keppenhaver, *Forensic Document Examination*, p. 47.

96. *An Authentic Account of Forgeries and Frauds of Various Kinds Committed by that Most Consummate Adept in Deception, Charles Price, Otherwise Patch …, Who, to Avoid an Ignominious Death, Destroyed Himself . . . on the 24th of January, 1786.* London, 1786. Eighteenth Century Collections Online website. Gale Group: http://0-galenet.galegroup.com.serlib0.essex.ac.uk:80/servlet/ECCO (Accessed on 18 September 2008).

97. Randall McGowen, 'The Bank of England and the policing of forgery, 1797–1821', *Past and Present*, 186 (2005), pp. 81–116.

98. Keppenhaver, *Forensic Document Examination*, p. 47.

99. Proceedings of the Old Bailey website: www.oldbaileyonline.org/browse. jsp?ref+t17770409-17 (Accessed on 18 September 2008).

100. Proceedings of the Old Bailey website: www.oldbaileyonline.org/browse. jsp?ref+t17830910-47 (Accessed on 18 September 2008).

101. This is an insight gained from Ross Anderson: Identinet website: Position Paper: www.history.ox.ac.uk/identinet/documents/PositionPaperAnderson.pdf (Accessed on 24 September 2008).

102. James C. Scott, John Tehranian and Jeremy Mathias, 'Government surnames and legal entities', in Carl Watner and Wendy McElroy (eds), *National Identification Systems: Essays in Opposition* (London: MacFarlane & Company, 2004), p. 15.

103. Scott, *Seeing Like a State*, p. 65. See for his more general claims in this respect, James C. Scott, John Tehranian and Jeremy Mathias, 'The production of legal identities proper to states: the case of the permanent family surname', *Comparative Studies in Society and History*, 44 (2002), pp. 4–44.

104. Stephen Wilson, *The Means of Naming: A Social and Cultural History of Personal Naming in Western Europe* (London: UCL Press, 1998), p. 160.

105. Ibid., pp. 115–16.

106. Dave Postles, *Talking Ballocs: Nicknames and English Medieval Sociolinguistics* (Leicester: Centre for English Local History, University of Leicester, 2003), pp. 10–14.

107. Ibid., pp. 11–55.

108. R. A. McKinley, *A History of British Surnames* (London: Longman, 1990), pp. 32–4.

109. Scott Smith-Bannister, *Names and Naming Patterns in England, 1538–1700* (Oxford: Clarendon Press, 1997), pp. 99–102.

110. Postles, *Social Proprieties*, p. 20.

111. Ibid., p. 63.

112. Scott, Tehranian and Mathias, 'Government surnames and legal entities', p. 17.

113. Higgs, *The Information State in England*, pp. 30–40.

114. Proceedings of the Old Bailey website: www.oldbaileyonline.org/browse. jsp?ref=t16850116-9 (Accessed on 19 September 2008).

115. Griffiths, *Lost Londons*, pp. 186–7.

116. Postles, *Social Proprieties*, p. 62.

117. J. F. Josling, *Change of Name* (London: Longman, 1989), pp. 3–5. The optional nature if deed polls in change of name was something that the present author had to explain continually to surprised members of the public when he was responsible for running search rooms at the Public Record Office (now National Archives) in London in the 1980s.

118. Anne Lefebvre-Teillard, *Le Nom: Droit et Histoire* (Paris: Presses universitaires de France, 1990); Gérard Noiriel, 'The identification of the citizen: the birth of Republican civil status in France', in Jane Caplan and John Torpey (eds), *Documenting Individual Identity: The Development of State Practices in the Modern World* (Oxford: Princeton University Press, 2001), pp. 28–48.

119. Jeremy Gibson, *Bishop's Transcripts and Marriage Licences, Bands and Allegations. A Guide to Their Location and Indexes* (Birmingham: Federation of Family History Societies, 1997).

120. G. R. Elton, *Policy and Police. The Enforcement of the Reformation in the Age of Thomas Cromwell* (Cambridge: Cambridge University Press, 1972), pp. 254, 259–60.

121. *Report of the Select Committee Appointed to Consider and Report on the General State of Parochial Registration and the Laws Relating to Them, and on a General Registration of Births, Baptisms, Marriages, Deaths and Burials in England and Wales*, British Parliamentary Papers 1833 XIV [669], p. 145.

122. Higgs, *Life, Death and Statistics*, pp. 7–17.

123. Simon Szreter, 'The right of registration: development, identity registration, and social security – a historical perspective', *World Development*, 35 (2007), pp. 67–86.

124. *Report of the Select Committee . . . on the General State of Parochial Registries*, p. 145.

125. Wrigley and Schofield, *The Population History of England*, p. 19.

126. Groebner, *Who are You?*, pp. 200–1.

127. Jeremy Bentham, 'Principles of penal law', in John Bowring (ed.), *The Works of Jeremy Bentham* (Edinburgh: W. Tair, 1843), vol. 1, p. 557.

128. The author's father was also called Edward, although 'Edward Laurence' rather than 'Edward John'.

NOTES TO CHAPTER 5: IDENTIFYING THE POOR 'CITIZEN' AND THE DEVIANT IN EARLY MODERN ENGLAND

1. John Walter, *Understanding Popular Violence in the English Revolution: The Colchester Plunderers* (Cambridge: Cambridge University Press, 1999); John Walter, *Crowds and Popular Politics in Early Modern England* (Manchester: Manchester University Press, 2006).

2. Snell, *Parish and Belonging. Community*, pp. 93–114; Hindle, *On the Parish?*, pp. 398–432.

3. Snell, *Parish and Belonging*, pp. 85–6.

4. For a general introduction to the Poor Laws, see Paul Slack, *The English Poor Law, 1531–1782* (Basingstoke: Macmillan Education, 1990).

5. Hindle, *On the Parish?*, pp. 48–154.

6. Keith Wrightson, *Earthly Necessities: Economic Lives in Early Modern Britain* (New Haven, CT: London: Yale University Press, 2000), p. 216.

7. Torpey, *The Invention of the Passport*, pp. 66–9.

8. Hindle, *On the Parish?*, pp. 356–7.

9. Hindle, 'Technologies of identification under the Old Poor Law', p. 221.

10. Hindle, *On the Parish?*, pp. 358–9.

11. Lees, *The Solidarities of Strangers*, p. 32.

12. Richard Wall, Matthew Woollard and Beatrice Moring, *Census Schedules and Listings, 1801–1831: An Introduction and Guide*. Working Paper Series 5 (Colchester: University of Essex, Department of History, 2004), pp. 3–8.

13. Hindle, *On the Parish?*, pp. 258–60. See also, Oxley, *Poor Relief in England*, pp. 52–3.

14. W. E. Tate, *The Parish Chest: A Study of the Records of Parochial Administration in England* (Cambridge: Cambridge University Press, 1960), p. 202.

15. Szreter, 'The right of registration: development, identity registration, and social security', p. 76.

16. Hindle, 'Technologies of identification under the Old Poor Law', pp. 231–2.

17. Quoted in Snell, *Parish and Belonging*, p. 110.

18. Hindle, 'Technologies of identification under the Old Poor Law', pp. 228–9.

19. Thomas Sokoll (ed.), *Essex Pauper Letters 1731–1837* (Oxford: Oxford University Press, 2001), p. 307.

20. Hindle, 'Technologies of identification under the Old Poor Law', pp. 222–4.

21. Paul Slack, *Poverty and Policy in Tudor and Stuart England* (London: Longman, 1988), pp. 96–8.

22. A. L. Beier, *Masterless Men: The Vagrancy Problem in England 1560–1640* (London: Methuen, 1985), p. 154.

23. Hindle, 'Technologies of identification under the Old Poor Law', p. 224.

24. Ibid., p. 225.

25. Slack, *Poverty and Policy in Tudor and Stuart England*, p. 94.

26. Hindle, 'Technologies of identification under the Old Poor Law', p. 227.

27. Ibid.

28. Beier, *Masterless Men*, pp. 142–4.

29. Griffiths, *Lost Londons*, p. 121.

30. Groebner, *Who are You?*, pp. 203–17.

31. Harman, *A Caveat or Warening*, p. 109.

32. Ibid., p. 81.

33. 'Servant law among acts to be axed', BBC News website: http://news.bbc.co.uk/1/hi/uk_politics/7302566.stm (Accessed on 30 June 2010).

34. Steve Hindle, 'Dependency, shame and belonging: badging the deserving poor, c.1550–1750', *Cultural and Social History*, 1 (2004), pp. 6–10.

35. Groebner, *Who are You?*, pp. 48–53.

36. Hindle, 'Dependency, shame and belonging', pp. 11–19; Hindle, 'Technologies of identification under the Old Poor Law', pp. 229–30.

37. R. F. Hunnisett, *The Medieval Coroner* (Cambridge: Cambridge University Press, 1961), pp. 1–9; John Jervis, *A Practical Treatise on the Office and Duties of Coroners* (London: Sweet, Maxwell and Stevens & Norton, 1854), pp. 11–13.

38. Hunnisett, *The Medieval Coroner*, pp. 190–9.

39. John Jervis, *A Practical Treatise on the Office and Duties of Coroners* (London: Sweet, Maxwell and Stevens & Norton, 1854), pp. 11–13.

40. Ibid., pp. 27–9, 118–26.

41. Ibid., pp. 13–23.

42. Cressy, *Birth, Marriage and Death*, pp. 421–55.

43. Paul Matthews, 'Whose body? People as property', *Current Legal Problems*, 36 (1983), pp. 193–239.

44. R. F. Hunnisett, *Calendar of Nottinghamshire Coroners' Inquests 1485–1558* (Nottingham: Produced for the Thoroton Society by Derry and Sons, 1969), p. 148.

45. Leslie and Doreen Smith, *Sudden Deaths in Suffolk 1767–1858: A Survey of Coroners' Records in the Liberty of St Etheldreda* (Ipswich: Suffolk Family History Society, 1995).

46. R. F. Hunnisett, *Sussex Coroners' Inquests, 1603–1688* (Kew: Public Record Office, 1998), p. 52.

47. Foucault, *Discipline and Punish*, pp. 3–69.

48. Malcolm Gaskill, 'Witchcraft and evidence in early-modern England', *Past & Present*, 198 (2008), pp. 33–70; Heikki Pihlajamaki, 'Swimming the witch, pricking for the Devil's mark: ordeals in the early modern witchcraft trials', *The Journal of Legal History*, 21 (2000), pp. 43–4.

49. Beier, *Masterless Men*, pp. 159–60.

50. Griffiths, *Lost Londons*, p. 431.

51. William Lamont, 'Prynne, William (1600–1669)', *Oxford Dictionary of National Biography, Online Edition*, ed. Lawrence Goldman, January 2008: www.oxforddnb.com/view/article/22854 (Accessed on 9 November 2008).

52. Proceedings of the Old Bailey website: www.oldbaileyonline.org/static/Punishment.jsp#branding (Accessed on 10 October 2008).

53. Cole, *Suspect Identities*, pp. 7–8.

54. **Foucault,** *Discipline and Punish, passim*.

55. Proceedings of the Old Bailey website: www.oldbaileyonline.org/static/Punishment.jsp#branding (Accessed on 10 October 2008).

56. Henry T. F. Rhodes, *Alphonse Bertillon: Father of Scientific Detection* (London: Harrap, 1956), pp. 73–4.

57. Peter Becker, 'The standardized gaze: the standardization of the search warrant in nineteenth-century Germany', in Jane Caplan and John Torpey (eds), *Documenting Individual Identity: The Development of State Practices in the Modern World* (Oxford: Princeton University Press, 2001), p. 155.

58. Herrup, 'New shoes and mutton pies', p. 816. For the use of such warrants in criminal proceedings, see Alan Macfarlane, *The Justice and the Mare's Ale: Law and Disorder in Seventeenth-Century England* (Oxford: Basil Blackwell, 1981), pp. 87–8.

59. Griffiths, *Lost Londons*, pp. 255–7.

60. Herrup, 'New shoes and mutton pies', p. 817.

61. John Styles, 'Print and policing: crime advertising in eighteenth century England', in Douglas Hay and Francis Snyder (eds), *Policing and Prosecution in Britain 1750–1850* (Oxford: Clarendon Press, 1989), pp. 83–6.

62. Richard Burn, *The Justice of the Peace, and Parish Officer, Vol. II* (London: T. Cadell, 1770), pp. 439–40.

63. Keechang Kim, *Aliens in Medieval Law. The Origins of Modern Citizenship* (Cambridge: Cambridge University Press, 2000), pp. 32–3.

64. Ann Dummett and Andrew Nicol, *Subjects, Citizens, Aliens and Others: Nationality and Immigration Law* (London: Weidenfeld and Nicolson, 1990), p. 31.

65. Kim, *Aliens in Medieval Law*, pp. 37, 58.

66. Lien Luu, 'Natural-born versus stranger-born subjects: aliens and their status in Elizabethan London', in Nigel Goose and Lien Luu (eds), *Immigrants in Tudor and Early Stuart England* (Brighton: Sussex Academic Press, 2005), p. 59.

67. National Archives, London: Exchequer King's Remembrancer: Extents of Alien Priories, Aliens, etc., 1293–1483 (E106); Exchequer: King's Remembrancer: Particulars of Accounts and Other Records Relating to Lay and Clerical Taxation (E179).

68. William Durrant Cooper, *Lists of Foreign Protestants and Aliens Resident in England 1618–88; from Returns in the State Paper Office* (London: Camden Society, 1862), pp. x–xi.

69. Dummett and Nicol, *Subjects, Citizens, Aliens and Others*, p. 43; Cooper, *Lists of Foreign Protestants*, p. ix.

70. Cooper, *Lists of Foreign Protestants*, p. iii.

71. Groebner, *Who are You?*, pp. 156–75.

72. Stuart Clark, 'Inversion, misrule, and the meaning of witchcraft', *Past and Present*, 87 (1980), pp. 98–127.

73. Ibid.

74. Ronald Hutton, *The Rise and Fall of Merry England: The Ritual Year, 1400–1700* (Oxford: Oxford University Press, 1994), pp. 9–11, 90–1.

75. David Cressy, 'Gender trouble and cross-dressing in early modern England', *The Journal of British Studies*, 35 (4) (1996), pp. 459–63.

76. Hutton, *The Rise and Fall of Merry England*, pp. 8–9, 34–40, 61.

77. Griffiths, *Lost Londons*, p. 184.

78. E. P. Thompson, *Whigs and Hunters. The Origins of the Black Act* (Harmondsworth: Penguin, 1977).

79. Ibid., pp. 27, 82–3.

80. Ibid., p. 145.

81. Donald Grinde and Bruce Johansen, *Exemplar of Liberty: Native America and the Evolution of Democracy* (Los Angeles, CA: American Indian Studies Center, University of California, 1991), pp. 111–40. Grinde and Johansen's claim that the Indian disguise represented an identification with the Mohawks themselves as symbols of freedom has been much criticized: Philip A. Levy, 'Exemplars of taking liberties: the Iroquois influence thesis and the problem of evidence', *The William and Mary Quarterly, Third Series*, 53 (1996), pp. 588–604.

82. Robert Hughes, *The Fatal Shore. A History of the Transportation of Convicts to Australia, 1787–1868* (London: Guild Publishing, 1987), p. 227.

83. David Williams, *The Rebecca Riots. A Study in Agrarian Discontent* (Cardiff: University of Wales Press, 1955), pp. 187–207.

84. Lyon, *Surveillance Society*, p. 71.

85. Lyon, *The Electronic Eye*, pp. 18, 41, 71, 85.

NOTES TO CHAPTER 6: IDENTIFICATION IN THE FIRST INDUSTRIAL NATION, 1750–1850

1. N. F. R. Crafts, *British Economic Growth during the Industrial Revolution* (Oxford: Clarendon Press, 1985), p. 45.

2. Cambridge Group for the History of Population and Social Structure website: Leigh Shaw-Taylor and E. A. Wrigley, 'The occupational structure of England c.1750–1871: a

49. Simon Fowler and William Spencer, *Army Records for Family Historians* (Kew: Public Record Office, 1998), pp. 41–7.

50. Jeremy Gibson and Mervyn Medlycott, *Militia Lists and Musters, 1757–1876: A Directory of Holdings in the British Isles* (Bury: Federation of Family History Societies, 2000).

51. N. A. M. Rodger, *Naval Records for Genealogists* (Richmond: Public Record Office, 1998), p. 54.

52. National Archives, London: Admiralty: Royal Marines: Description Books: ADM 158/10 Chatham Division.

53. Bruno Pappalardo, *Tracing Your Naval Ancestors* (Kew: Public Record Office, 2002), pp. 8, 86–7, 117.

54. James Bradley and Hamish Maxwell-Stewart, 'Embodied explorations: investigating tattoos and the transportation system', in Ian Duffield and James Bradley (eds), *Representing Convicts: New Perspectives on Convict Forced Labour Migration* (London: Leicester University Press, 1997), p. 191.

55. Hughes, *The Fatal Shore*, pp. 347, 383–5.

56. Alastair Davidson, *The Invisible State: The Formation of the Australian State, 1788–1901* (Cambridge: Cambridge University Press, 1991), pp. 35–40.

57. Cited in Hughes, *The Fatal Shore*, p. 527.

58. National Archives, London, Moving Here website: www.movinghere.org.uk/galleries/roots/intro/migration/parliament2.htm (Accessed on 17 January 2008).

59. National Archives Moving Here website: www.movinghere.org.uk/galleries/roots/intro/migration/parliament3.htm (Accessed on 17 January 2008).

60. Torpey, *The Invention of the Passport*, pp. 69–71.

61. National Archives Moving Here website: www.movinghere.org.uk/galleries/roots/intro/migration/parliament3.htm (Accessed on 17 January 2008).

62. Bernard Gainer, *The Alien Invasion: The Origins of the Aliens Act of 1905* (London: Heinemann, 1972), pp. 8–9.

63. David Feldman, 'Was the nineteenth century a golden age for immigrants? The changing articulation of national, local and voluntary controls', in Andreas Fahrmeir, Olivier Faron and Patrick Weil (eds), *Migration Control in the North Atlantic World: The Evolution of State Practices in Europe and the United States from the French Revolution to the Inter-War Period* (Oxford: Berghahn Books, 2003), pp. 167–77.

64. Torpey, *The Invention of the Passport*, pp. 77–8.

65. Leo Lucassen, 'A many-headed monster: the evolution of the passport system in the Netherlands and Germany in the long nineteenth century', in Jane Caplan and John Torpey (eds), *Documenting Individual Identity: The Development of State Practices in the Modern World* (Oxford: Princeton University Press, 2001), pp. 235–55.

66. Torpey, *The Invention of the Passport*, pp. 1–2.

67. See, among an extensive literature: M. A. Crowther, *The Workhouse System, 1834–1929: The History of an English Social Institution* (London: Batsford, 1981); Felix Driver, *Power and Pauperism: The Workhouse System, 1834–1884* (Cambridge: Cambridge University Press, 1993).

68. Snell, 'Settlement, Poor Law, and the rural historian', p. 159.

69. Snell, *Parish and Belonging*, pp. 17–18, 217–18, 231–3.

70. Cited in Snell, *Parish and Belonging*, pp. 254–5.

71. R. M. Gutchen, 'Paupers in union workhouses: computer analysis of admissions and discharges', *The Local Historian*, 11 (1974–75), pp. 452–6.

72. See, for example, the advertisement in *The Northern Star and Leeds General Advertiser* of Saturday, 22 December 1838 for a runaway apprentice 'about fifteen years of age, of a fair complexion. Light blue eyes, stands about five foot high'.

73. Prest, *Politics in the Age of Cobden*, pp. 19–21; J. A. Thomas, 'The system of registration and the development of party organisation, 1832–70', *History*, 35 (1950), pp. 82–3.

74. 2 & 3 Will. IV, c.45, s. 58.

75. National Archives, London: Central Criminal Court Depositions: CRIM 1/24/4 Defendant: Stubley, Benjamin Charge: Personation 1886.

76. Seymour, *Electoral Reform*, pp. 122–30.

77. John Jervis, *A Practical Treatise on the Office and Duties of Coroners* (London: Sweet, Maxwell and Stevens & Norton, 1854), pp. 277–8.

78. M. A. Crowther and Brenda M. White, *On Soul and Conscience: The Medical Expert and Crime. 150 years of Forensic Medicine in Glasgow* (Aberdeen: Aberdeen University Press, 1988), pp. 7; Kenneth C. Saunders, *The Medical Detectives: A Study of Forensic Pathologists* (London: Middlesex University Press, 2001), p. 52.

79. Margaret M. Stark, *A Physician's Guide to Clinical Forensic Medicine* (New Jersey: Humana Press, 2000), p. 5.

80. Aletha Kowitz, 'The earliest use of dental evidence in a courtroom', *Bulletin of the History of Dentistry*, 29 (1981), pp. 82–7.

81. Alfred Swaine Taylor, *Elements of Medical Jurisprudence* (London: Deacon, 1836); Alfred Swaine Taylor, *Medical Jurisprudence* (London: John Churchill, 1852, 4th edn), pp. 317, 398.

82. *The Morning Chronicle*, Wednesday, 10 September 1828.

83. Ibid.

84. Charles Dickens, *Bleak House* (Boston: James R. Osgood and Company, 1873), p. 86.

85. Ruth Richardson, *Death, Dissection and the Destitute* (London: Routledge & Kegan Paul, 1987), pp. 65, 370.

86. J. Neville Porter, 'Mortuary reform', *The Sanitary Record*, 12 (1890–91), p. 57.

87. Richardson, *Death, Dissection and the Destitute*, pp. 219–38.

88. Jeffery Grey, *A Military History of Australia* (Cambridge: Cambridge University Press, 1999), pp. 5–24.

89. Higgs, *The Information State in England*, pp. 10–27.

NOTES TO CHAPTER 7: TOWARDS THE 'DOSSIER SOCIETY': IDENTIFYING DEVIANTS IN ENGLAND, 1850 TO 1970

1. Richard V. Ericson and Clifford D. Shearing, 'The scientification of police work', in Gernot Bohme and Nico Stehr (eds), *The Knowledge Society: The Growing Impact of Scientific Knowledge on Social Relations* (Dordrecht: D. Reidel, 1986), pp. 129–59.

2. K. D. Haggerty and Richard V. Ericson, 'The surveillant assemblage', *British Journal of Sociology*, 51 (2000), p. 613.

3. Martin J. Weiner, *Reconstructing the Criminal: Culture, Law and Policy in England, 1830–1914* (Cambridge: Cambridge University Press,1990), p. 150.

4. Mathew Thomson, *The Problem of Mental Deficiency: Eugenics, Democracy and Social Policy in Britain, c.1870–1959* (Oxford: Oxford University Press, 1998), p. 54.

5. Neil Davie, *Tracing the Criminal: The Rise of Scientific Criminology in Britain 1860–1918* (Oxford: Bardwell Press, 2005), p. 27.

6. Ibid., p. 48.

7. Hughes, *The Fatal Shore*, pp. 160–1.

8. Keith McClelland, 'England's greatness, the working man', in Catherine Hall, Keith McClelland and Jane Rendall (eds), *Defining the Nation: Class, Race, Gender and the Reform Act of 1867* (Cambridge: Cambridge University Press, 2000), p. 101; José Harris, 'Between civic virtue and social Darwinism: the concept of the residuum', in David Englander and Rosemary O'Day (eds), *Retrieved Riches: Social Investigation in England 1840–1914* (Aldershot: Scolar Press, 1995), pp. 74–5.

9. Cited in McClelland, 'England's greatness, the working man', pp. 97–8.

10. Cited in Davie, *Tracing the Criminal*, p. 131.

11. David G. Horn, *The Criminal Body: Lombroso and the Anatomy of Deviance* (London: Routledge, 2003), p. 40.

12. Robert J. Richards, *The Tragic Sense of Life: Ernst Haeckel and the Struggle over Evolutionary Thought* (London: University of Chicago Press, 2008), pp. 148–56.

13. Davie, *Tracing the Criminal*, p. 89.

14. Colin Beavan, *Fingerprints: Murder and the Race to Uncover the Science of Identity* (London: Fourth Estate, 2002), p. 54.

15. Clare Anderson, *Legible Bodies Race, Criminality, and Colonialism in South Asia* (Oxford: Berg, 2004); C. A. Bayly, *Empire and Information: Intelligence Gathering and Social Communication in India, 1780–1870* (Cambridge: Cambridge University Press, 1996), pp. 49–54, 144–79, 215–24; Bernard S. Cohn, *An Anthropologist among the Historians and Other Essays* (Oxford: Oxford University Press, 2004), pp. 141–58.

16. Davie, *Tracing the Criminal*, pp. 182–7, 273–4.

17. *Identification of Habitual Criminals*, British Parliamentary Papers 1893–94 LXXII [C 7263], p. 6.

18. Charles Booth, *Life and Labour of the People in London, Volume 1* (London: Macmillan, 1902), pp. 33–62.

19. See, for example, the debates in Richard Wetzell, *Inventing the Criminal: A History of German Criminology, 1880–1945* (London: University of North Carolina Press, 2000); Daniel Mark Vyleta, 'Was early twentieth-century criminology a science of the 'Other'? A re-evaluation of Austro-German criminological debates', *Cultural and Social History*, 3 (2006), pp. 406–23.

20. *Report of the Royal Commission on Penal Servitude*, British Parliamentary Papers 1863 XXI [3190], Evidence, pp. 140, 427, 450; *Report from the Select Committee of the House of Lords on the Present State of Discipline in Gaols and Houses of Correction*, British Parliamentary Papers 1863 IX [499], Evidence, pp. 128, 221, 290.

21. Michel Foucault, *Naissance de la clinique – une archéologie du regard médical* (Paris: Presses universitaires de France, 1963); Michel Foucault, *Les mots et les choses – une archéologie des sciences humaines* (Paris: Gallimard, 1966).

22. Higgs, *The Information State in England*, pp. 95–7.

23. Davie, *Tracing the Criminal*, p. 92.

24. Hawkings, *Criminal Ancestors*, pp. 250–60.

25. National Archives, London: Home Office: Registered Papers: HO 45/9320/16629C, Prisons and Prisoners: (4) Other: Prevention of Crimes Act, 1871. Regulations for photographing prisoners; Report . . . into . . . identifying habitual criminals, pp. 12–19.

26. Martine Kaluszynski, 'Republican identity: Bertillonage as government technique', in Jane Caplan and John Torpey (eds), *Documenting Individual Identity. The Development of State Practices in the Modern World* (Princeton: Princeton University Press, 2001), p. 124; Becker, 'The standardized gaze', pp. 153–63.

27. William Matthews, *From Chili to Piccadilly with Sir Roger Tichborne. The Santiago Daguerreo-types and the London Photographs Compared, Identity Demonstrated Geometrically, etc.* (Bristol: J Wright and Co., 1876).

28. Nicholas Wright Gillham, *A Life of Sir Francis Galton. From African Exploration to the Birth of Eugenics* (Oxford: Oxford University Press, 2001), pp. 215–20.

29. *Report of a Committee Appointed by the Secretary of State to Inquire into the Best Means Available for Identifying Habitual Criminals ...*, British Parliamentary Papers 1893–94 LXXII [C 7263], pp. 7–8; National Archives, London: Metropolitan Police; Criminal Record Office: Habitual Criminals Registers and Miscellaneous Papers: MEPO 6/90 Pt 2; Registry of criminals, p. 8; National Archives, London: Home Office Registered Papers, Supplementary: HO 144/184/A45507, p. 4.

30. National Archives, London: Home Office: Registered Papers: HO 45/9320/16629C, Prisons and Prisoners: (4) Other: Prevention of Crimes Act, 1871. Regulations for photographing prisoners; Report . . . into . . . identifying habitual criminals, pp. 12–19; Original photographs can be found in PRO: Home Office and Prison Commission: Prisons Records, Series I (PCOM 2); Davie, *Tracing the Criminal*, p. 94.

31. Sengoopta, *Imprint of the Raj*, p. 16; Cole, *Suspect Identities*, p. 19.

32. Sengoopta, *Imprint of the Raj*, pp. 13–14; Beavan, *Fingerprints*, pp. 157–66.

33. Jean Robins, *Rebel Queen: How the Trial of Caroline Brought England to the Brink of Revolution* (London: Pocket, 2007).

34. National Archives, London: Home Office: Domestic Correspondence from 1773 to 1860: HO 44/9 ff. 88–89. Disturbances at Queen Caroline's funeral: correspondence relating to the identification parade of Life Guards allegedly involved in the shooting of Richard Honey or Hannay, August 1821; Alan Moss and Keith Skinner, *The Scotland Yard Files. Milestones in Crime Detection* (Kew: National Archives, 2006), pp. 58–9.

35. *Report of the [Devlin] Committee on Evidence of Identification in Criminal Cases*, British Parliamentary Papers 1975–76 XIX [338], p. 112.

36. Ibid., pp. 9–66, 72–84, 108; National Archives, London: Committee on Evidence of Identity in Criminal Cases: Evidence and Papers: HO 280/58 Dock Identification 1974–75.

37. David Frank Ross, J. Don Read and Michael P. Toglia (eds), *Adult Eyewitness Testimony: Current Trends and Developments* (Cambridge: Cambridge University Press, 1994); Brian L. Cutler and Steven D. Penrod, *Mistaken Identification: The Eyewitness, Psychology and the Law* (Cambridge: Cambridge University Press, 1995).

38. National Archives, London: Committee on Evidence of Identity in Criminal Cases: Evidence and Papers: HO 280/65 Use of photographs and Photofit 1974–75; Jacques

Penry, *Looking at Faces and Remembering Them. A Guide to Facial Identification* (London: Elek, 1971).

39. Moss and Skinner, *The Scotland Yard Files*, pp. 163–70.

40. National Archives, London: Home Office: Police Research and Planning Branch and Successors: Reports: HO 377/73 Use of identikits: a note on facial identification techniques 1969.

41. National Archives, London: HO 280/65.

42. See the excellent website of the Project Bertillon: www.criminocorpus.cnrs.fr/bertillon/entree.html (Accessed on 18 May 2010).

43. Sengoopta, *Imprint of the Raj*, p. 19; Cole, *Suspect Identities*, pp. 20, 33–4, 57.

44. Sengoopta, *Imprint of the Raj*, pp. 121–4.

45. Rhodes, *Alphonse Bertillon*, p. 49.

46. Becker, 'The standardized gaze', p. 155.

47. Kaluszynski, 'Republican identity', p. 124.

48. Alphonse Bertillon, *Identification Anthropometrique: Instructions Signaletiques* (Melun: Imprimerie Administrative, 1893), p. xiv.

49. Rhodes, *Alphonse Bertillon*, p. 75.

50. Cole, *Suspect Identities*, p. 45.

51. Bertillon, *Identification Anthropometrique*, pp. 137–44; Cole, *Suspect Identities*, pp. 46–7; Becker, 'The standardized gaze', pp. 148–51.

52. Anthony Giddens, *The Constitution of Society* (Cambridge: Polity Press, 1986), pp. 64–73, 123–4.

53. Rhodes, *Alphonse Bertillon*, pp. 130–8.

54. Anne M. Joseph, 'Anthropometry, the police expert, and the Deptford Murders: the contested introduction of fingerprinting for the identification of criminals in late Victorian and Edwardian Britain', in Jane Caplan and John Torpey (eds), *Documenting Individual Identity: The Development of State Practices in the Modern World* (Oxford: Princeton University Press, 2001), pp. 170–1; Cole, *Suspect Identities*, pp. 35–6.

55. Francis Galton, 'Personal identification and description', *Proceedings of the Royal Institution*, 12 (1888), pp. 346–60.

56. Cole, *Suspect Identities*, pp. 60–1.

57. Beavan, *Fingerprints*, pp. 36–7.

58. Kristin Ruggiero, 'Fingerprinting and the Argentine plan for universal identification in the late nineteenth and early twentieth centuries', in Jane Caplan and John Torpey (eds), *Documenting Individual Identity: The Development of State Practices in the Modern World* (Oxford: Princeton University Press, 2001), pp. 184–96.

59. Sengoopta, *Imprint of the Raj*, pp. 53–78.

60. Henry Faulds, 'On the skin-furrows of the hand', *Nature*, 22 (1880), p. 605.

61. Sengoopta, *Imprint of the Raj*, pp. 84–5.

62. Francis Galton, *Finger Prints* (London: Macmillan, 1892).

63. Stephen M. Stigler, 'Galton and identification by fingerprints', *Genetics*, 140 (1995), pp. 857–60.

64. Cole, *Suspect Identities*, pp. 80–1.

65. E .R. Henry, *Bengal Police: Instructions for Classifying and Deciphering Finger Impressions and for Describing Them with Sufficient Exactness to Enable Comparison*

of the Description with the Original Impression to Be Satisfactorily Made (India: Bengal Police, 1896).

66. Sengoopta, *Imprint of the Raj*, pp. 171–83.

67. Higgs, *The Information State in England*, p. 114.

68. Cole, *Suspect Identities*, pp. 233–4.

69. Jennifer Ward, 'Origins and development of forensic medicine and forensic science in England 1823–1946', Open University Doctoral Thesis, 1993, pp. 226–7.

70. Neil Gerlach, *Genetic Imaginary: DNA in the Canadian Criminal Justice System* (Toronto: University of Toronto Press, 2004), p. 37.

71. Cole, *Suspect Identities*, pp. 137–9.

72. Sengoopta, *Imprint of the Raj*, pp. 84–5.

73. Cole, *Suspect Identities*, pp. 171–4.

74. Simon Cole, 'What counts for identity?: the historical origins of the methodology of latent fingerprint identification', *Science in Context*, 12 (1) (1999), pp. 139–72.

75. Cole, *Suspect Identities*, pp. 194–205.

76. David Welsh, 'The growth of towns', in Monica Wilson and Leonard Thompson (eds), *The Oxford History of South Africa: II South Africa 1870–1966* (Oxford: Clarendon Press, 1975), pp. 196–7.

77. B. Pachai, *The International Aspects of the South African Indian Question 1860–1971* (Cape Town: C. Struik, 1971), p. 14.

78. J. Rowland, *The Finger-Print Man: The Story of Sir Edward Henry* (London: Lutterworth Press, 1959), p. 96. This is a rather suspect book, 'part an imaginative tale', but the author seems to have had information from Henry's daughters.

79. Keith Breckenridge, 'Verwoerd's Bureau of Proof: total information in the making of Apartheid', *History Workshop Journal*, 59 (2005), pp. 83–108; Keith Breckenridge, 'The elusive panopticon: the HANIS project and the politics of standards in South Africa', in Colin J. Bennett and David Lyon (eds), *Playing the Identity Card: Surveillance, Security and Identification in Global Perspective* (London: Routledge, 2008), pp. 39–42.

80. Pachai, *The International Aspects*, pp. 25,33.

81. Keith Breckenridge, 'Fingers and thumbs: Gandhi, Smuts and the origins of Satyagraha'. Roskilde University website: www.ruc.dk/upload/application/pdf/fd8a6900/Keith_Breckenridge.pdf (Accessed on 18 May 2009).

82. Maureen Swan, *Gandhi: The South African Experience* (Johannesburg: Ravan Press, 1985), pp. 111–23.

83. Pachai, *The International Aspects*, pp. 39–41, 66.

84. Ward, 'Origins and development', *passim*.

85. Norman Vincent Ambage, 'The origins and development of the Home Office Forensic Science Service, 1931–1967', University of Lancaster Doctoral Thesis, 1987, pp. 31–87.

86. National Archives, London: Home Office: Registered Papers: HO 45/18103 POLICE: East Midlands Forensic Science Laboratory, Nottingham 1935–36.

87. National Archives, London: Home Office: Registered Papers: HO 45/24185 POLICE: Scientific aids to criminal investigation: forensic science circulars 1936–50.

88. Ambage, 'The origins and development', pp. 92–286.

89. A. D. Farr, 'Blood group serology – the first four decades (1900–1939)', *Medical History*, 23 (2) (1979), pp. 215–26.

90. National Archives, London: Home Office: Registered Papers: HO 45/18105 POLICE: West Midlands Forensic Science Laboratory, Birmingham 1936–39.

91. Ibid.

92. Registers of deportations orders from 1906–63 are at National Archives in the record series HO 372.

93. Dummett and Nicol, *Subjects, Citizens, Aliens and Others*, pp. 104, 161.

94. Gainer, *The Alien Invasion*, pp. 67–73, 166–200: Higgs, *The Information State in England*, pp. 99–108.

95. Gerard Noiriel, *The French Melting Pot: Immigration, Citizenship, and National Identity* (Minneapolis: University of Minnesota Press, 1996), pp. 51–62.

96. Adam McKeown, *Melancholy Order: Asian Migration and the Globalization of Borders* (New York: Columbia University Press, 2008). See also, Uma Dhupelia-Mesthrie, 'The passenger Indian as worker: Indian immigrants in Cape Town in the early twentieth century', *African Studies*, 68 (1) (April 2009), pp. 111–34.

97. National Archives Moving Here website: www.movinghere.org.uk/galleries/roots/intro/migration/parliament4.htm (Accessed on 17 January 2008). No central register of people survive but the series of records from the Metropolitan Police held in the National Archives, London in MEPO 35 contains the surviving registration cards for the London area. See also, Scott Thompson, 'Separating the sheep from the goats: the United Kingdom's National Registration programme and social sorting in the pre-electronic era', in Colin J. Bennet and David Lyon (eds), *Playing the Identity Card: Surveillance, Security and Identification in Global Perspective* (London: Routledge, 2008), p. 154.

NOTES TO CHAPTER 8: TOWARDS THE 'DOSSIER SOCIETY': IDENTIFYING CITIZENS AND CUSTOMERS IN ENGLAND, 1850 TO 1970

1. Higgs, *The Information State in England*, pp. 99–108.

2. Harris, *The Origins of the British Welfare State*, pp. 150–65.

3. Paul Johnson, 'The role of the State in twentieth-century Britain', in Paul Johnson (ed.), *Twentieth-Century Britain: Economic, Social and Cultural Change* (Harlow: Longman, 1994), pp. 476–91.

4. Hannah, *The Rise of the Corporate Economy, passim*.

5. Michael J. Winstanley, *The Shopkeeper's World, 1830–1914* (Manchester: Manchester University Press, 1983), pp. 33–9.

6. JoAnne Yates, *Control through Communication: The Rise of System in American Management* (Baltimore: Johns Hopkins University Press, 1989), p. 271. See also: James R. Beniger, *The Control Revolution. Technology and the Economic Origins of the Information Society* (London: Harvard University Press, 1986).

7. Yates, *Control through Communication*, pp. 10, 21–64. The period also saw the development of early systems of record/information management within organizations: Edward Higgs, 'From medieval erudition to information management: the evolution of the archival profession', *Archivum (Proceedings of the XIII International Congress on Archives, Beijing, 2–7 September 1996)* 43 (1997), pp. 136–44.

8. An earlier version of this section can be found in Edward Higgs, 'Fingerprints and citizenship: the British State and the identification of pensioners in the inter-war period', *History Workshop Journal*, 69 (2010), pp. 52–67.

9. National Archives, London: Treasury Board Papers: T1/11665/17893 Committee on Periodical Identification of Government Pensioners. Selection of departmental delegates. Report. 1914.

10. National Archives, London: Treasury Supply Department: Registered Files (S Series): T161/1307 PENSIONS. Identification: Identification of pensioners 1919–1929: Memo on the 'Identification of Pensioners'.

11. National Archives, London: Treasury Board Papers: T1/12181 Ministry of National Service. Use of finger prints as a means of identification of discharged military personnel: letter of 17 April 1918.

12. National Archives, London: T1/12181, letter of 4 May 1918.

13. Higgs, *The Information State in England*, pp. 134–5.

14. National Archives, London: T161/1307, Memorandum on 'Identification of prisoners'.

15. National Archives, London: Treasury Board Papers: T1/12500/10570/1920. Method of identification of pensioners: observations by various government departments on proposals to revise the system. 1920.

16. National Archives, London: Supply Department: Registered Files (S Series): T161/101 PENSIONS: Identification: Identification of pensioners. Prosecution in cases of fraud 1921.

17. National Archives, London: Supply Department: Registered Files (S Series): T161/101 PENSIONS: Identification: Identification of Pensioners. Audit of pension payments 1923–5.

18. Cited in Beavan, *Fingerprints*, p. 60.

19. Francis Galton, 'Identification by finger tips', *Nineteenth Century*, 30 (1891), p. 304.

20. Cited in Sengoopta, *Imprint of the Raj*, p. 77.

21. Ibid., pp. 152–4.

22. Ruggiero, 'Fingerprinting and the Argentine plan', *passim*.

23. National Archives, London: Treasury Board Papers: T1/12181, memorandum p. 6.

24. National Archives, London: T1/12181, memorandum p. 6.

25. National Archives, London: T1/12500/10570/1920.

26. National Archives, London: War Office and Successors: Registered Files (General Series): WO32/8708 ENLISTMENTS AND EXTENSIONS OF SERVICE: General (Code 26 (A)): Methods for preventing fraudulent enlistment: Proposals for more stringent check on previous history of candidates for enlistment: Précis for the Army Council No. 476, 'Adoption of the finger-print system in the Army to prevent fraudulent enlistment, October 1910'.

27. National Archives, London: War Office: Reports, Memoranda and Papers (O and A Series): WO33/229 Report of Committee on identification by fingerprints 1902.

28. Sengoopta, *Imprint of the Raj*, pp. 48–50.

29. T. B. Macaulay, *The Works of Lord Macaulay, Vol. VI* (London: Spottiswoode and Co., 1866), p. 556.

30. Gillham, *A Life of Sir Francis Galton*, pp. 242–3.

31. Galton, 'Identification by finger tips', p. 303.

32. Pierre Piazza and Laurent Laniel, 'The INES biometric card and the politics of national identity assignment in France', in Colin J. Bennet and David Lyon (eds), *Playing the Identity Card: Surveillance, Security and Identification in Global Perspective* (London: Routledge, 2008), p. 200.

33. National Archives, London: Board of Inland Revenue and Board of Customs and Excise: Non Contributory Old Age Pensions, Registered Files: AST 15/64 Old Age Pensions Acts 1908 and 1911: Instructions to Pension Officers; proofs 1911–1913.

34. National Archives, London: National Assistance Board and Successor: Codes of Instructions and Circulars: AST 13/71 National Insurance Act, 1911: departmental instructions concerning application for, and payment of benefit 1912.

35. National Archives, London: Ministry of Pensions and Successors: War Pensions, Registered Files (GEN Series) and Other Records: PIN 15/1352 Identification of Pensioners 1917–1919.

36. National Archives, London: Ministry of Pensions and Successors: War Pensions, Registered Files (GEN Series) and Other Records: PIN 15/2594 Identification of Pensioners 1929–39.

37. National Archives, London: War Office and Successors: Registered Files (General Series): WO32/6503 PENSIONS: General (Code 4(A)): Pledging of pensioners' identity and life certificates 1885–1890.

38. National Archives, London: Ministry of Pensions and successors: War Pensions, Registered Files (GEN Series) and Other Records: PIN 15/3703 Identification of pensioners: modification of procedure for examination of life certificates 1949–73.

39. National Archives, London: Foreign Office and Foreign and Commonwealth Office: Chief Clerk's Department and Passport Office: Correspondence: FO612/134 Recommenders on passport applications: question of what constitutes 'personal knowledge' 1924–1937.

40. National Archives, London: WO32/6503.

41. National Archives, London: War Office and successors: Registered Files (General Series): WO32/2580 PENSIONS: General (Code 4(A)): Review of identification procedures of Pensioners 1919–21.

42. National Archives, London: AST 15/64.

43. National Archives, London: Treasury Board Papers: T1/11491 London County Local Pension Committee. Verification of ages of claimants to old-age pensions by making available for public examination of records, primarily Census Enumeration Books, at the Public Record Office. 1912.

44. National Archives, London: Ministry of Pensions and National Insurance and Predecessors: Specimens of Series of Documents Destroyed: PIN 900/2 Forms and records: national insurance pensions 1939–1963.

45. National Archives, London: Treasury: Organisation and Methods Division: Registered Files (OM and 2OM Series): T222/246 Procedures for established identity and nationality on abolition of national registration, 1952.

46. Social Security Office, *How to Prove Your Identity for Social Security* (Leeds: Social Security Office, 2003).

47. National Archives, London: Board of Inland Revenue: Stamps and Taxes Division: Registered Files: IR 40/14801 Chief Inspector's Memo: verification of identity for

repayment 1962; IR 40/17319 Review of arrangements for verifying the identity of a claimant with no fixed address 1968.

48. General Register Office, *Thirty-Eighth Annual Report of the Registrar General for 1875* (London: HMSO, 1877), p. liii.

49. Ibid., p. viii.

50. General Register Office, *Seventy-Seventh Annual Report of the Registrar General for 1914* (London: HMSO, 1916), p. viii; General Register Office, *Seventy-Ninth Annual Report of the Registrar General for 1916* (London: HMSO, 1918), p. lxxxvii.

51. *Report of the Committee on Electoral Registration*, British Parliamentary Papers 1946–47 XI [Cmd 7004], pp. 5–8.

52. Sylvanus Vivian, *History of National Registration* (London: Cabinet Office Historical Branch, 1951), pp. 207–19.

53. Higgs, *The Information State in England*, pp. 135–6.

54. Rosemary Elliot, 'An early experiment in national identity cards: the battle over registration in the First World War', *Twentieth Century British History*, 17 (2) (2006), pp. 145–76; National Archives, London: General Register Office: Specimens of Documents Destroyed: RG 900/1 Specimen documents National Registration Acts 1915 and 1918; National Archives, London: General Register Office: National Registration: Correspondence and Papers: RG 28/13 Miscellaneous memoranda and instructions 1915–18.

55. Higgs, *The Information State in England*, pp. 137–9.

56. National Archives, London: General Register Office: National Registration: Correspondence and Papers: RG 28/1, Bill and policy file. Part I Memorandum by the General Register Office on the working of the Register. Part II. Memorandum on the National Registration system 1915.

57. Jon Agar, 'Modern horrors: British identity and identity cards', in Jane Caplan and John Torpey (eds), *Documenting Individual Identity: The Development of State Practices in the Modern World* (Oxford: Princeton University Press, 2001), p. 113.

58. Higgs, *Life, Death and Statistics*, pp. 188–202.

59. National Archives, London: General Register Office: National Registration: Correspondence and Papers: RG 28/146 Ration books and identity cards: original issue, 1939–41.

60. Aly and Roth, *The Nazi Census*, pp. 52–3, 119–20, 140–7.

61. Thompson, 'Separating the sheep from the goats', pp. 150–4; Vivian, *History of National Registration*, pp. 163–71.

62. Vivian, *History of National Registration*, p. 93.

63. Thompson, 'Separating the sheep from the goats', pp. 150–4.

64. Vivian, *History of National Registration*, p. 93.

65. Ibid., p. 160.

66. National Archives, London: Home Office: Aliens, General Matters (ALG Symbol Series) Files: HO 352/60 Working Party on Change of Name (Home Office) 1950–65; RG 28/68 Change of Name: Departmental Correspondence (Legal View).

67. Higgs, *The Information State in England*, pp. 142–3.

68. Cited in Agar, 'Modern horrors', p. 110.

69. Ibid.

70. Higgs, *The Information State in England*, pp. 137–44.

71. Thompson, 'Separating the sheep from the goats', p. 157.
72. National Archives, London: Domestic Records Information 60: Passport Records: www.nationalarchives.gov.uk/catalogue/RDleaflet.asp?sLeafletID=109 (Accessed on 30 June 2009).
73. Andreas Fahrmeir, 'Governments and forgers: passports in nineteenth-century Europe', in Jane Caplan and John Torpey (eds), *Documenting Individual Identity: The Development of State Practices in the Modern World* (Oxford: Princeton University Press, 2001), pp. 228–9.
74. National Archives, London: History of Passports. http://yourarchives.nationalarchives.gov.uk/index.php?title=History_of_Passports (Accessed on 30 June 2009).
75. National Archives, London: Domestic Records Information 60: Passport Records: www.nationalarchives.gov.uk/catalogue/RDleaflet.asp?sLeafletID=109&j=1 (Accessed on 30 June 2009).
76. National Archives, London: History of Passports. http://yourarchives.nationalarchives.gov.uk/index.php?title=History_of_Passports (Accessed on 30 June 2009).
77. Cited in Torpey, *The Invention of the Passport*, p. 146.
78. Garcelon, 'Colonizing the subject', pp. 83–100.
79. For a general consideration of the genesis and significance of the Act, see: Clive Emsley, '"Mother, what *did* policemen do when there weren't any motors?" The law, the police and the regulation of motor traffic in England, 1900–1939', *Historical Journal*, 36 (1993), pp. 357–81.
80. *Hansard, Fourth Series* 122, 7 May to 26 May 1903, cols 1060–1; *Hansard, Fourth Series* 125, 8 July to 22 July 1903, cols 529–30; *Hansard, Fourth Series* 127, 6 August to 14 August 1903, col. 416.
81. *Hansard, Fourth Series* 125, 8 July to 22 July 1903, col. 977; *Hansard, Fourth Series* 127, 6 August to 14 August 1903, col. 471.
82. Derek Hudson, *Munby: Man of Two Worlds. The Life and Diaries of Arthur J. Munby 1828–1910* (London: Sphere Books, 1974), p. 449.
83. Higgs, *The Information State in England*, pp. 178–9.
84. David Anderson, *The Exeter Theatre Fire* (Royston: Entertainment Technology Press, 2002), pp. 92, 98–109.
85. Ian A. Burney, *Bodies of Evidence. Medicine and the Politics of the English Inquest, 1830–1926* (Baltimore: Johns Hopkins University Press, 2000), pp. 165–72.
86. National Archives, London: Air Ministry and Ministry of Defence: Registered Files: AIR2/18242 Forensic odontology 1964–1970: 'The role of the RAF Dental Branch in major aircraft accident investigations', p. 2.
87. National Archives, London: Home Office: Police (POL Symbol Series) Files: HO 287/622 Identification of bodies: Stockport air disaster June 1967; includes report and booklet; future police training 1967–72.
88. National Archives, London: Health and Safety Executive: Inquiry into the Disaster which Occurred at Nypro (UK) Ltd, Flixborough: Unregistered Records: EF12/4 Statements by Humberside Police and relatives of the deceased in relation to identification of bodies: forensic evidence 1974.
89. *Report of the Committee on Death Certification and Coroners*, British Parliamentary Papers 1971–72 XXI [Cmnd 4810], pp. 126–7.

90. Alfred Swaine Taylor, *Medical Jurisprudence* (London: John Churchill, 1852, 4th edn), pp. 317, 398; Alfred Swaine Taylor, *The Principles and Practice of Medical Jurisprudence* (London: John Churchill, 1865, 1st edn), 103–15; Alfred Swaine Taylor *The Principles and Practice of Medical Jurisprudence* (ed. Thomas Stevenson) (London: John Churchill, 1883, 3rd edn, vol. 1), p. 626; Fred J. Smith, *Taylor's Principles and Practice of Medical Jurisprudence* (London: John Churchill, 1910, 6th edn, vol. 1), pp. 121–241.

91. Crowther and White, *On Soul and Conscience*, p. 90.

92. John Glaister (ed.), *Glaister's Medical Jurisprudence and Toxicology* (Edinburgh: E. & S. Livingstone, 1938, 6th edn), pp. 99–107.

93. Personal recollection of the author.

94. National Archives, London: Home Office: Registered Papers: HO 45/9989/X78999 CORONERS AND INQUESTS: Two skeletons found buried outside a cottage. Inquest not necessary. 1900.

95. *Report of the Departmental Committee on Coroners*, British Parliamentary Papers 1935–36 VIII [Cmd 5070], p. 4.

96. W. B. Purchase, *Jervis on the Office and Duties of Coroners* (London: Sweet and Maxwell, 1957).

97. Paul Matthews and J. C. Foreman, *Jervis on the Office and Duties of Coroners* (London: Sweet and Maxwell, 1986), pp. 116–18.

98. Caroline Wilkinson, *Forensic Facial Reconstruction* (Cambridge: Cambridge University Press, 2004), pp. 55–61.

99. *Hansard, Third Series* 355, 1 July 1891 to 21 July 1891, col. 533.

100. National Archives, London: Home Office: Registered Papers: HO 45/10483/X83466 Law Officers Opinion: use of mortuaries, 1901–1914, p. 2.

101. Porter, 'Mortuary reform', pp. 6–7.

102. Burney, *Bodies of Evidence*, p. 86.

103. Porter, 'Mortuary reform', p. 9; *Report of the Committee on Death Certification and Coroners*, p. 270.

104. *Report of the Departmental Committee on Coroners*, p. 50.

105. *Report of the Committee on Death Certification and Coroners*, pp. 270–1.

106. Nina Biehal, Fiona Mitchell and Jim Wade, *Lost from View: Missing Persons in the UK* (Bristol: Policy Press, 2003), pp. 3–4, 14.

107. International Committee of the Red Cross, *Missing Persons: A Hidden Tragedy* (Geneva: International Committee of the Red Cross, 2007).

108. National Archives, London: Metropolitan Police: Office of the Commissioner: Correspondence and Papers: MEPO 2/335 Missing persons: enquiry procedure 1894–1896.

109. National Archives, London: Metropolitan Police: Office of the Commissioner: Correspondence and Papers: MEPO 2/1247 Lost property and missing persons: revised forms 1908–1909.

110. National Archives, London: Metropolitan Police: Office of the Commissioner: Correspondence and Papers: MEPO 2/596 Dead bodies: identification 1902–1917.

111. National Archives, London: Metropolitan Police: Office of the Commissioner: Correspondence and Papers: MEPO 2/1328 Dead bodies: photographing for identification purposes 1909–1910.

112. National Archives, London: MEPO 2/596.

113. National Archives, London: Metropolitan Police: Office of the Commissioner: Correspondence and Papers: MEPO 2/6876 Missing persons and bodies found indices: proposed amalgamation to increase efficiency 1935–1953.

114. National Archives, London: Home Office: Police (POL Symbol Series) Files: HO 287/135 Missing persons: report on the tracing of missing persons and a suggestion for a national register 1961–1962; National Archives, London: Metropolitan Police: Office of the Commissioner: Correspondence and Papers: MEPO 2/10264 Suggestion by Dr Gordon Davies, HM Coroner, for establishment of a national bureau of missing persons; adoption of new recording and reporting procedure by Metropolitan Police 1963–1968; *The Times*, 19 March 1994.

115. Geoff Newiss, *Missing Presumed …?: The Police Response to Missing Persons* (London: Home Office, Policing and Reducing Crime Unit, 1999), pp. 3–15.

116. US Department of Defense DNA Registry website: www.afip.org/Departments/oafme/dna/ (Accessed on 21 January 2008).

117. National Archives, London: Ministry of Defence and Predecessors: Army Circulars, Memoranda, Orders and Regulations: WO 123/55 Army Orders 1913.

118. National Archives, London: Metropolitan Police: Office of the Commissioner: Correspondence and Papers: MEPO 2/6580 Difficulties in identification of air raid victims: appointment of police casualty officers.

119. National Archives, London: Ministry of Home Security: Air Raid Precautions (ARP GEN) Registered Files: HO 186/629 CASUALTY SERVICES, Identification of air raid casualties 1940–1941; National Archives, London: Home Office: Civil Defence (Various Symbol Series) Files: HO 322/142 Identity disks for civilians: consideration of possible introduction in wartime 1951–57.

120. National Archives, London: HO 322/142.

121. Ibid.

122. Margaret Ackrill and Leslie Hannah, *Barclays: The Business of Banking 1690–1996* (Cambridge: Cambridge University Press, 2001), p. 165.

123. Cited in Finn, *The Character of Credit*, p. 80.

124. Avram Taylor, *Working Class Credit and Community since1918* (Basingstoke: Palgrave, 2002), pp. 46–178.

NOTES TO CHAPTER 9: TOWARDS THE 'DIGITAL PERSON': IDENTIFYING THE CONSUMER IN ENGLAND, 1970 TO THE PRESENT

1. Edward Higgs, 'The statistical Big Bang of 1911: ideology, technological innovation and the production of medical statistics', *Social History of Medicine*, 9 (3) (1996), pp. 409–26.

2. Christine Bellamy and John A. Taylor, *Governing in the Information Age* (Buckingham: Open University Press, 1998), pp. 8–9, 39.

3. Ulrich Beck, *World Risk Society* (Cambridge: Polity Press, 1999), pp. 3–4.

4. Avner Offer, *The Challenge of Affluence: Self-Control and Well-Being in the United States and Britain since 1950* (Oxford: Oxford University Press, 2006), pp. 126–9.

5. Lars Svendsen, *A Philosophy of Fear* (London: Reaktion Books, 2008), pp. 95–6.

6. Frank Furedi, *Culture of Fear: Risk-Taking and the Morality of Low Expectation* (London: Continuum, 2005), pp. 173–8.

7. Svendsen, *A Philosophy of Fear*, pp. 104–8.

8. Nikolas Rose, *Powers of Freedom: Reframing Political Thought* (Cambridge: Cambridge University Press, 1999), p. 234.

9. Ibid.

10. Dan Schiller, *How to Think about Information* (Urbana: University of Illinois Press, 2007), pp. 40–8.

11. Shoshana Zuboff, *In the Age of the Smart Machine: The Future of Work and Power* (London: Heinemann Professional, 1988).

12. Higgs, *The Information State in England, passim*.

13. Ackrill and Hannah, *Barclays*, pp. 165, 206–67; Mark St J. Carrington, Philip W. Langguth and Thomas D. Steiner, *The Banking Revolution: Salvation or Slaughter? How Technology is Creating Winners and Losers* (London: Pitman, 1997), p. 18.

14. John Thomson, 'The case for credit cards', *The Banker*, 116 (July 1966), p. 444; Roy Vine, 'Why the banks have gone in for automation', *The Banker*, 117 (1967), p. 503; Tim Hindle, 'The customer comes first', *The Banker*, 130 (March 1980), p. 89.

15. 'Why Giro is worrying the banks', *The Times*, Friday, 19 August 1966, p. 15; 'New banking moves to counter Giro', *The Times*, Tuesday, 17 January 1967, p. 14.

16. Vine, 'Why the banks', pp. 501–7.

17. [Anon.], 'The banking year', *The Banker's Magazine*, 205 (January to June 1968), pp. 12–13.

18. *Monopolies and Mergers Commission: Credit Card Franchise Services* British Parliamentary Papers 1979–80 LXXVIII [Cmnd 8034], pp. 6–8.

19. Ibid., p. 28.

20. [Anon.], 'A financial notebook', *The Banker*, 115 (November 1965), p. 706.

21. Davide Consoli, *The Evolution of Retail Banking Services in United Kingdom: A Retrospective Analysis* (Manchester: Centre for Research on Innovation and Competition, University of Manchester, 2003), p. 8.

22. E. Schoeters, 'The "dematerialisation" of payment systems', *The Banker*, 130 (March 1980), pp. 101–5.

23. 'The man who invented the cash machine', BBC News website: http://news.bbc.co.uk/1/hi/business/6230194.stm (Accessed on 27 July 2009).

24. [Anon.], 'The phantom at the ATM', *The Banker*, 135 (October 1985), p. 73.

25. Ackrill and Hannah, *Barclays*, pp. 185–90.

26. Carrington, Langguth, Steiner, *The Banking Revolution*, pp. 144–6.

27. *The Monopolies and Mergers Commission: Credit Card Service*, British Parliamentary Papers 1988–89 LIV [Cm 718], pp. 228–9.

28. 'Cheques to be phased out in 2018', BBC News website: http://news.bbc.co.uk/1/hi/business/8414341.stm (Accessed on 19 May 2010).

29. 'The History of the Nottingham', Nottingham Building Society website: http://thenottingham.com/main.asp?p=1710 (Accessed on 5 August 2009).

30. [Anon.], 'Fraud-free credit card', *The Banker*, 118 (1968), p. 175.

31. [Anon.], 'Cashpoint – the world outside', *The Banker*, 124 (1974), p. 1460.

32. [Anon.], 'The decline of the cheque', *The Banker*, 123 (1973), p. 1411.

33. [Anon.], 'Counterfeit and counter measures', *The Banker*, 134 (March 1984), pp. 79–82.

34. London School of Economics, *The Identity Project: An Assessment of the UK Identity Cards Bill & Its Implications. Interim Report* (London: LSE, 2005), pp. 33–4.

35. Solove, *The Digital Person*, p. 110.

36. Cabinet Office, *Identity Fraud*, pp. 13–14.

37. 'Waste bins "an ID theft goldmine", BBC News website: http://news.bbc.co.uk/1/hi/business/6044698.stm (Accessed on 24 July 2009).

38. Cabinet Office, *Identity Fraud*, p. 13.

39. 'UK bank details "for sale for £5"', BBC News website: http://news.bbc.co.uk/1/hi/uk/7335844.stm (Accessed on 19 May 2010).

40. 'Fraudsters' website shut in swoop', BBC News website: news.bbc.co.uk/1/hi/uk/7675191.stm (Accessed on 28 July 2009).

41. [Anon.], 'More thefts, bigger sums', *The Banker*, 137 (February 1987), p. 65.

42. S. Dixon-Childe, 'The future', *The Banker*, 117 (1967), pp. 516–17.

43. [Anon.], 'Photo-finish', *The Banker*, 133 (March 1983), p. 84.

44. 'Now the PIN is mightier than the pen', BBC News website: http://news.bbc.co.uk/ 1/hi/uk/3039619.stm (Accessed on 24 July 2009).

45. [Anon.], 'First admit there is a problem', *The Banker*, 136 (December 1986), p. 69.

46. 'Now the PIN is mightier than the pen'.

47. National Archives, London: Department of Trade and Industry and Successors: Consumer Credit Branch: Registered Files (CCB Series): FV 82/6 Report of the Committee on Privacy (Younger Committee): credit reference bureaux; views from trade and consumer interests, 1973, pp. 1, 5.

48. National Archives, London: Board of Trade: Committee on Consumer Credit: Files: BT 250/108 credit reference bureaux, p. 2.

49. Ibid., pp. 2–3; *Report of the Committee on Consumer Credit*, British Parliamentary Papers 1970–71 IX [Cmnd 4596], p. 103.

50. National Archives, London: Records Created or Inherited by the Department of Trade and Industry, 1970–1974, and Successors: FV 62/140 Consumer Credit: Report of the Committee (Cmnd 4596) (The Crowther Report); Implementation in the Proposed Consumer Credit Bill of the Report's Recommendations: Licensing: special issues raised by credit intermediaries: credit reference bureaux, 1972–1974.

51. 'Equifax Ltd', Funding Universe website: www.fundinguniverse.com/company-histories/Equifax-Inc-Company-History.html (Accessed on 5 August 2009).

52. Sean O'Connell, *Credit and Community: Working-Class Debt in the UK since 1880* (Oxford: Oxford University Press, 2009), pp. 89–90, 115.

53. Ibid., p. 114.

54. 'Consumer Information', Experian website: www.experian.co.uk/www/pages/why_experian/our_information_source/ our_information_source_consumer_information.html (Accessed on 5 August 2009).

55. 'Death records used to fight fraud', BBC News website: http://news.bbc.co.uk/ 1/hi/uk/7796720.stm (Accessed on 5 August 2009).

56. 'We are Experian', Experian website: www.experian.co.uk/www/pages/about_us/about_experian/index_continued.html (Accessed on 6 August 2009).

57. 'Consumer information solutions', Equifax website: www.equifax.co.uk/Consumer-Credit-Services/consumer_solutions.html (Accessed on 6 August 2009).

58. 'Our core capabilities', Experian website: www.experian.co.uk/www/pages/about_us/index.html (Accessed on 6 August 2009); 'Take charge of your credit', Equifax website: www.experian.co.uk/ (Accessed on 6 August 2009).

59. 'New customer information', Equifax website: www.econsumer.equifax.co.uk/consumer/uk/order.ehtml?prod_cd=UKESNGO (Accessed on 6 August 2009).

60. Director General of Fair Trading, *Credit Scoring: A Report* (London: Office of Fair Trading, 1992), pp. 28–30.

61. David Lyon, 'Surveillance as social sorting: computer codes and mobile bodies', *passim*.

62. 'Consumer risk solutions', Equifax website: www.equifax.co.uk/efx_pdf/Risk_Navigator_af.pdf (Accessed on 6 August 2009); 'What can it do for me', Experian website: www.experian.co.uk/www/pages/what_we_offer/prodcuts/mosaic_uk.html (Accessed on 6 August 2009).

63. John A. Dawson and Leigh Sparks, *Information Sources and Retail Planning* (Stirling: University of Stirling, Department of Business Studies, 1985), pp. 3–12.

64. Tell us a little bit about yourself …', Nectar website: www.nectar.com/join/takeoneYourdetails.snectar (Accessed on 6 August 2009).

65. Dawson and Sparks, *Information Sources and Retail Planning*, pp. 3–13.

66. Devon Wylie, 'Tesco has links with the corner shops of England's past', Sekelemian/Newell International Marketing Consultants website: www.loyalty.vg/pages/CRM/case_study_14_Tesco.htm (Accessed on 10 July 2008).

67. Wylie, 'Tesco has links'; Martin Evans, 'Food retailing loyalty schemes and the Orwellian Millennium', *British Food Journal*, 101 (1999), p. 135.

68. Ibid.

69. James Runcie, *The Future of Global Markets for Personal Identification: Strategic Five-Year Forecasts* (Leatherhead: Pira International, 2003), p. 78.

70. Andrew Smith and Leigh Sparks, 'Making tracks: loyalty cards as consumer surveillance', in Darach Turley and Stephen Brown (eds), *European Advances in Consumer Research, Volume 6* (Valdosta, GA: Association for Consumer Research, 2003), pp. 368–73.

71. Solove, *The Digital Person*, pp. 16–19.

72. Whichlist.com website: www.whichlist.com/products/consumer_master_file.php (Accessed on 2 June 2008).

73. Solove, *The Digital Person*, pp. 24–5.

74. 'Are Facebook privacy settings good enough?', Equifax website: www.equifax.co.uk/About-us/Press_releases/2008/ARE_FACEBOOK_PRIVACY_SETTINGS_GOOD_ENOUGH.htm (Accessed on 31 December 2008).

NOTES TO CHAPTER 10: TOWARDS THE 'DIGITAL PERSON': IDENTIFICATION IN THE DIGITAL DATABASE STATE, 1970 TO 2010

1. Higgs, *The Information State in England*, pp. 5–6.

2. *Report of the [Lindop] Committee on Data Protection*, British Parliamentary Papers 1978–79 V [Cmnd 7341], Appendix 6; Duncan Campbell and Steve Connor, *On the Record. Surveillance, Computers and Privacy – the Inside Story* (London: Michael Joseph, 1986), pp. 62–5.

3. Bellamy and Taylor, *Governing in the Information Age*, pp. 64–89; Campbell and Connor, *On the Record*, p. 87.

4. Anderson, Brown, Dowty, Inglesant, Heath and Sasse, *Database State, passim*.

5. Ibid., p. 20.

6. Campbell and Connor, *On the Record*, p. 90.

7. Bellamy and Taylor, *Governing in the Information Age*, p. 85.

8. *Third Annual Report of the Data Protection Registrar* (hereafter *ARDPR*) *June 1987*, British Parliamentary Papers 1987–88 [HC 33], p. 5; *Fourth ARDPR June 1988*, British Parliamentary Papers 1987–88 [HC 570], pp. 13–14.

9. 'DSS registration', Information Commissioner's Office website: www.dpr.gov.uk/cgi-bin/dpr98-fetch.pl?source=DPR&dcid=155219 (Accessed on 12 September 2001).

10. Cabinet Office Performance and Innovation Unit, *Privacy and Data-Sharing: The Way Forward for Public Services* (London: Cabinet Office, 2002), p. 7.

11. *Sixth ARDPR June 1990*, British Parliamentary Papers 1989–90 [HC 472], pp. 3–4; *Tenth ARDPR June 1994*, British Parliamentary Papers 1993–94 [HC 453], p. 8.

12. *Fourteenth ARDPR June 1998*, British Parliamentary Papers 1997–98 [HC 910], p. 38.

13. James L. Wayman, 'The scientific development of biometrics over the last 40 years', in Karl de Leeuw and Jan Bergstra (eds), *The History of Information Security: A Comprehensive Handbook* (Amsterdam: Elsevier B. V., 2007), pp. 264–8.

14. Ibid.

15. Lyon, *Surveillance Society*, p. 79.

16. 'Smartgate reaches milestone of 150,000 passages in Australia', Morpho website: www.morpho.com/spip.php?article561 (Accessed on 10 August 2009).

17. Wayman, 'The scientific development of biometrics', pp. 265–6; Lyon, *Surveillance Society*, p. 79.

18. Wayman, 'The scientific development of biometrics', pp. 269–71.

19. Zeinab Karake-Shalhoub, 'Population ID card systems in the Middle East: the case of the UAE', in Colin J. Bennet and David Lyon (eds), *Playing the Identity Card: Surveillance, Security and Identification in Global Perspective* (London: Routledge, 2008), p. 135.

20. Ibid., pp. 269–71.

21. Valerio Cusimano, 'Market trends for biometric systems', *Dialogue: The Newsletter of HIDE*, 1 (July 2008). Hide Project website: www.hideproject.org/downloads/newsletter/HIDE_Newsletter1_200807.pdf (Accessed on 10 August 2009).

22. Zoë Corbyn, 'The small scientist', *Times Higher Education*, 1912 (3 September 2009), p. 36; Shari Rudavsky, 'Blood will tell: the role of science and culture in twentieth century paternity disputes', Doctoral Thesis, University of Pennsylvania, 1996, p. 374.

23. Peter Gill, Alec Jeffreys and David Werrett, 'Forensic application of DNA "fingerprints"', *Nature* (December 1985), pp. 577–9.

24. Robin Williams and Paul Johnson, *Genetic Policing. The Use of DNA in Criminal Investigations* (Cullompton, Devon: Willan Publishing, 2008), pp. 51–3.

25. Michael Lynch, Simon A. Cole, Ruth McNally and Kathleen Jordan, *Truth Machine. The Contentious History of DNA Fingerprinting* (London: University of Chicago Press, 2008), p. 345.

26. Prison Reform Trust, *Electronic Tagging: Viable Option or Expensive Diversion?* (London: Prison Reform Trust, 1997), *passim.*

27. Robin Williams, Paul Johnson and Paul Martin, *Genetic Information & Crime Investigation: Social, Ethical and Public Policy Aspects of the Establishment, Expansion and Police Use of the National DNA Database* (Durham: School of Applied Social Sciences, University of Durham, 2004), p. 111.

28. Andrew Grubb and David S. Pearl, *Blood Testing, AIDS, and DNA Profiling: Law and Policy* (Bristol: Family Law, 1990), p. 161.

29. Williams, Johnson and Martin, *Genetic Information*, pp. 17–19.

30. *Report of the Royal Commission on Criminal Procedure*, British Parliamentary Papers 1980–81 XLI [Cmnd 8092], p. 68.

31. National Archives, London: Law Society: Legal Aid Administration: Registered Files (Numeric Series 2): FR 6/176 DNA analysis/genetic fingerprinting: policy guidelines; correspondence between Area Offices, The Law Society and the Home Office, 1987–88.

32. Williams and Johnson, *Genetic Policing*, pp. 47, 105.

33. Williams, Johnson and Martin, *Genetic Information*, pp. 29–34.

34. Williams and Johnson, *Genetic Policing*, pp. 83–7.

35. Robin Williams and Paul Johnson, *Forensic DNA Databasing: A European Perspective Interim Report* (Durham: School of Applied Social Science, University of Durham, 2005), p. 92.

36. Williams and Johnson, *Genetic Policing*, pp. 4–6.

37. Dorothy Nelkin and Lori Andrews, 'Surveillance creep in the genetic age', in David Lyon (ed.), *Surveillance as Social Sorting: Privacy, Risk, and Digital Discrimination* (London: Routledge, 2003), p. 101.

38. Ibid., p. 96.

39. European Parliament Committee on Citizens' Freedoms and Rights, Justice and Home Affairs (LIBE), *Biometrics at the Frontiers: Assessing the Impact on Society* (2005), European Commission, Justice and Home Affairs website: http://ec.europa.eu/justice_home/doc_centre/freetravel/doc/biometrics_eur21585_en.pdf (Accessed on 20 May 2010).

40. 'The national DNA database', Home Office website: www.homeoffice.gov.uk/science-research/using-science/dna-database/ (Accessed on 1 February 2008).

41. Williams, Johnson and Martin, *Genetic Information*, p. 37.

42. Home Office website, 'The national DNA database'.

43. Williams and Johnson, *Genetic Policing*, pp. 150–1.

44. Ibid., p. 150.

45. DNA database 'breach of rights', BBC News website: http://news.bbc.co.uk/1/hi/uk/7764069.stm (Accessed on 28 July 2009).

46. Williams and Johnson, *Genetic Policing*, pp. 147–8.

47. Anderson, Brown, Dowty, Inglesant, Heath and Sasse, *Database State*, p. 23.

48. 'All UK "must be on DNA database"', BBC News website: http://news.bbc.co.uk/ 1/hi/uk/6979138.stm (Accessed on 24 July 2009); 'Panorama: two thirds polled in favour of compulsory national DNA database', BBC News website: www.bbc.co.uk/pressoffice/pressreleases/stories/2007/09_september/24/dna.shtml (Accessed on 24 July 2009).

49. Williams, Johnson and Martin, *Genetic Information*, pp. 2–3.

50. Lynch, Cole, McNally and Jordan, *Truth Machine*, pp. ix–xiii.

51. [Anon.], 'The "CSI effect"', *The Economist*, 395, 24 April 2010, pp. 77–8. But see also, Lynch, Cole, McNally and Jordan, *Truth Machine*, p. x.

52. Williams, Johnson and Martin, *Genetic Information*, p. 117; Williams and Johnson, *Forensic DNA Databasing*, p. 108.

53. Examples can be found on the Council of the European Union PRADO website: www. consilium.europa.eu/prado/EN/1980/docHome.html (Accessed on 1 October 2009).

54. 'Identity cards for foreign nationals', UK Border Agency website: www.ukba.homeoffice. gov.uk/managingborders/idcardsforforeignnationals/ (Accessed on 1 October 2009).

55. 'UK drivers face new photocard licence', BBC News website: http://news.bbc.co.uk/1/ hi/uk/137238.stm (Accessed on 23 June 2010).

56. Council Directive 91/439/EEC of 29 July 1991 on driving licences, *Official Journal L 237, 24 August 1991, pp. 1–24.*

57. Directgov website: www.direct.gov.uk/en/TravelandTransport/Passports/ Applicationinformation/DG_174153 (Accessed on 20 July 2010).

58. 'Ifyournamehaschangedorisabouttochange–firstadultpassport',Directgovwebsite:www. direct.gov.uk/en/TravelAndTransport/Passport/Applyingforyourfirstadultpassport/ DG_174104 (Accessed on 1 October 2009).

59. London School of Economics, *The Identity Project*, p. 161.

60. European Parliament Committee on Citizens' Freedoms and Rights, Justice and Home Affairs (LIBE), pp. 21–2.

61. Border and Immigration Agency, *Prevention of Illegal Working. Immigration Asylum and Nationality Act 2006. Comprehensive Guidance for Employers in Preventing Illegal Working* (London: Border and Immigration Agency Communications Directorate, 2008), p. 5.

62. Ibid., p. 12.

63. Ibid., p. 43.

64. Ibid., p. 9.

65. David Wills, 'The United Kingdom identity card scheme: shifting motivations, static technologies', in Colin J. Bennet and David Lyon (eds), *Playing the Identity Card: Surveillance, Security and Identification in Global Perspective* (London: Routledge, 2008), pp. 173–6.

66. Higgs, *The Information State in England*, pp. 134–44.

67. Ibid., pp. 184–5.

68. 'Conservative backing for ID cards', BBC News website: http://news.bbc.co.uk1/hi/ uk_politics/4093583.stm (Accessed on 5 October 2009).

69. London School of Economics, *The Identity Project*, pp. 48–90; Colin J. Bennet and David Lyon (eds), *Playing the Identity Card: Surveillance, Security and Identification in Global Perspective* (London: Routledge, 2008), *passim*.

70. 'Benefit fraud: Cameron defends use of credit rate firms', BBC News website: www.bbc. co.uk/news/uk-10922261 (Accessed on 23 August 2010).

71. 'Why we need ID cards', Home Office website: www.homeoffice.gov.uk/passports- and-immigration/id-cards/why-we-need-id-cards/ (Accessed on 14 August 2009).

72. *Pursue Prevent Protect Prepare. The United Kingdom's Strategy for Countering International Terrorism*, British Parliamentary Papers 2009 [Cm 7547], pp. 111–15.

73. Cabinet Office, *Identity Fraud*, p. 12.

74. Bigo, 'Frontiers and security in the European Union', *passim*.

75. 'Immigration: UKIP Policy 2009', UK Independence Party website: www.ukip.org/content/ukip-policies/226-immigration-ukip-policy-2009 (Accessed on 3 August 2009).

76. *Beating Fraud is Everyone's Business: Securing the Future*, British Parliamentary Papers 1997–98 [Cm 4012], p. 12; *A New Contract for Welfare: Safeguarding Social Security*, British Parliamentary Papers 1997–98 [Cm 4276], p. 7–9.

77. *Housing Benefit Fraud: Third Report, House of Commons, Social Security Committee, Session 1995–96, V.I. Report, together with Proceedings. – V.II. Minutes of Evidence and Appendices to the Minutes of Evidence*, British Parliamentary Papers 1995–96 [HC 90-I, II], pp. lv–lvi; *Child Benefit Fraud: Second Report, House of Commons, Social Security Committee, Session 1996–97*, British Parliamentary Papers 1996–97 [HC 56], p. xi.

78. Department of Social Security, *Safeguarding Social Security: Getting the Information We Need* (London: Department of Social Security, 2000), pp. 1–5.

79. Cabinet Office, *Identity Fraud*, pp. 20–9.

80. Higgs, *The Information State in England*, pp. 172–3.

81. Stuart Wilks-Heeg, *Purity of Elections in the UK: Causes for Concern* (York: Joseph Rowntree Trust, 2008), pp. 10, 65.

82. 'Individual voter ID plan brought forward to 2014', BBC News website: www.bbc.co.uk/news/uk_politics_11312362 (Accessed on 14 September 2010).

83. *Transformational Government Enabled through Technology*, British Parliamentary Papers 2005 [Cm 6683], p. 1.

84. Ibid., p. 13.

85. C. A. R. Crosland, *The Future of Socialism* (London: Jonathan Cape, 1956).

NOTES TO CHAPTER 11: CONCLUSION

1. Scott, Tehranian and Mathias, 'Government surnames and legal entities', p. 48.

2. The term is taken from Peter Mathias's seminal book on the Industrial Revolution, *The First Industrial Nation: An Economic History of Britain, 1700–1914* (London: Methuen, 1969).

3. Karl Marx, *Capital: A Critique of Political Economy, Volume 1* (Harmondsworth: Penguin Books, 1976), pp. 873–926.

4. See, for example, W. W. Rostow, *The Stages of Economic Growth: A Non-Communist Manifesto* (Cambridge: Cambridge University Press, 1960).

5. Higgs, 'Fingerprints and citizenship', *passim*.

6. 'Gordon Brown "bigoted woman" comment caught on tape', BBC News website: http://news.bbc.co.uk/1/hi/uk_politics/election_2010/864901.stm (Accessed on 23 August 2010).

7. Foucault, *Discipline and Punish*, *passim*.

8. Jürgen Habermas, *The Philosophical Discourse of Modernity* (Cambridge: Polity Press, 1990), pp. 238–65.

Bibliography

BRITISH PARLIAMENTARY PAPERS

Beating Fraud is Everyone's Business: Securing the Future, British Parliamentary Papers 1997–98 [Cm 4012].

Census of England and Wales, 1861, Population Tables. Ages, Civil Condition, Occupations, and Birthplaces of the People, British Parliamentary Papers 1863 LIII [3221].

Child Benefit Fraud: Second Report, House of Commons, Social Security Committee, Session 1996–97, British Parliamentary Papers 1996–97 [HC 56].

Fourteenth Annual Report of the Data Protection Registrar June 1998, British Parliamentary Papers 1997–98 [HC 910].

Fourth Annual Report of the Data Protection Registrar June 1988, British Parliamentary Papers 1987–88 [HC 570].

Hansard, Fourth Series.

Hansard, Third Series.

Housing Benefit Fraud: Third Report, House of Commons, Social Security Committee, Session 1995–96, V.I. Report, together with Proceedings. – V.II. Minutes of Evidence and Appendices to the Minutes of Evidence, British Parliamentary Papers 1995–96 [HC 90-I, II].

Identification of Habitual Criminals, British Parliamentary Papers 1893–94 LXXII [C 7263].

Monopolies and Mergers Commission: Credit Card Franchise Services, British Parliamentary Papers 1979–80 LXXVIII [Cmnd 8034].

Monopolies and Mergers Commission: Credit Card Service, British Parliamentary Papers 1988–89 LIV [Cm 718].

A New Contract for Welfare: Safeguarding Social Security, British Parliamentary Papers 1997–98 [Cm 4276].

Pursue Prevent Protect Prepare. The United Kingdom's Strategy for Countering International Terrorism, British Parliamentary Papers 2009 [Cm 7547].

Report from the Select Committee of the House of Lords on the Present State of Discipline in Gaols and Houses of Correction, British Parliamentary Papers 1863 IX [499].

Report of a Committee Appointed by the Secretary of State to Inquire into the Best Means Available for Identifying Habitual Criminals ..., British Parliamentary Papers 1893–94 LXXII [C 7263].`

Report of the Committee on Consumer Credit, British Parliamentary Papers 1970–71 IX [Cmnd 4596].

Report of the Committee on Death Certification and Coroners, British Parliamentary Papers 1971–72 XXI [Cmnd 4810].

Report of the Committee on Electoral Registration, British Parliamentary Papers 1946–47 XI [Cmd 7004].*Report of the Departmental Committee on Coroners*, British Parliamentary Papers 1935–36 VIII [Cmd 5070].

Report of the [Devlin] Committee on Evidence of identification in Criminal Cases, British Parliamentary Papers 1975–76 XIX [338].

Report of the [Lindop] Committee on Data Protection, British Parliamentary Papers 1978–79 V [Cmnd 7341].

Report of the Royal Commission on Criminal Procedure, British Parliamentary Papers 1980–81 XLI [Cmnd 8092].

Report of the Royal Commission on Penal Servitude, British Parliamentary Papers 1863 XXI [3190].

Report of the Select Committee Appointed to Consider and Report on the General State of Parochial Registration and the Laws Relating to Them, and on a General Registration of Births, Baptisms, Marriages, Deaths and Burials in England and Wales, British Parliamentary Papers 1833 XIV [669].

Seventy-Seventh Annual Report of the Registrar General (1914), British Parliamentary Papers 1916 V [Cd 8206].

Sixth Annual Report of the Data Protection Registrar June 1990, British Parliamentary Papers 1989–90 [HC 472].

Tenth Annual Report of the Data Protection Registrar June 1994, British Parliamentary Papers 1993–94 [HC 453].

Third Annual Report of the Data Protection Registrar June 1987, British Parliamentary Papers 1987–88 [HC 33].

Transformational Government Enabled through Technology, British Parliamentary Papers 2005 [Cm 6683].

ARTICLES, BOOKS, CONTRIBUTIONS TO EDITED COLLECTIONS, THESES

Aas, Katja Franko, '"The body does not lie": identity, risk and trust in technoculture', *Crime, Media, Culture*, 2 (2006), pp. 143–58.

Ackrill, Margaret and Hannah, Leslie, *Barclays: The Business of Banking 1690–1996* (Cambridge: Cambridge University Press, 2001).

Agar, Jon, 'Modern horrors: British identity and identity cards', in Jane Caplan and John Torpey (eds), *Documenting Individual Identity: The Development of State Practices in the Modern World* (Oxford: Princeton University Press, 2001), pp. 101–20.

Aly, Götz and Roth, Karl Heinz, *The Nazi Census. Identification and Control in the Third Reich* (Philadelphia: Temple University Press, 2004).

Ambage, Norman Vincent, 'The origins and development of the Home Office Forensic Science Service, 1931–1967', University of Lancaster Doctoral Thesis, 1987.

Anderson, Clare, 'Godna: Inscribing Indian convicts in the nineteenth century', in Jane Caplan (ed.), *Written on the Body. The Tattoo in European and American History* (London: Reaktion Books, 2000), pp. 102–17.

— *Legible Bodies Race, Criminality, and Colonialism in South Asia* (Oxford: Berg, 2004).

Anderson, David, *The Exeter Theatre Fire* (Royston: Entertainment Technology Press, 2002).

Anderson, Malcolm, Bigo, Didier and Bort, Ed, 'Frontiers, identity and security in Europe, an agenda of research', in Martin Pratt and Janet Allison Brown (eds), *Borderlands under Stress* (London: Kluwer Law International, 2000), pp. 251–74.

Anderson, Michael, *Family structure in Nineteenth Century Lancashire* (Cambridge: Cambridge University Press, 1971).

Anderson, Ross, Brown, Ian, Dowty, Terri, Inglesant, Philip, Heath, William and Sasse, Angela, *Database State* (York: Joseph Rowntree Reform Trust, 2009).

Anglo, Sydney, *Images of Tudor Kingship* (London: Seaby, 1992).

Annear, Robyn, *The Man Who Lost himself. The Unbelievable Story of the Tichborne Claimant* (London: Robinson, 2003).

[Anon.], 'The banking year', *The Banker's Magazine*, 205 (January to June 1968), pp. 8–13.

— 'Cashpoint – the world outside', *The Banker*, 124 (1974), p. 1460.

— 'Counterfeit and counter measures', *The Banker*, 134 (March 1984), pp. 79–82.

— 'The "CSI effect"', *The Economist*, 395 (24) (April 2010), pp. 77–8.

— 'The decline of the cheque', *The Banker*, 123 (1973), p. 1411.

— 'A financial notebook', *The Banker*, 115 (November 1965), pp. 701–6.

— 'First admit there is a problem', *The Banker*, 136 (December 1986), pp. 69–70.

— 'Fraud-free credit card', *The Banker*, 118 (1968), p. 175.

— *A Hue and Cry. Run Away from His Master's Service in the Night-Time, . . .* [Dublin?], [1755?].

— 'More thefts, bigger sums', *The Banker*, 137 (February 1987), p. 65.

— 'The phantom at the ATM', *The Banker*, 135 (October 1985), pp. 71–3.

— 'Photo-finish', *The Banker*, 133 (March 1983), pp. 82–4.

Arthurson, Ian, *The Perkin Warbeck Conspiracy 1491–1499* (Stroud: Alan Sutton Publishing, 1997).

Ashton, Rosemary, *Little Germany: Exile and Asylum in Victorian England* (Oxford: Oxford University Press, 1986).

Aston, Margaret, *Lollards and Reformers: Images and Literacy in Late Medieval Religion* (London: Hambledon Press, 1984).

Austen, Jane, *Persuasion* (London: Folio Society, 1975).

Bacon, Francis, *The Reign of Henry VII* (London: C. and J. Rivington, 1826).

Basten, Stuart, 'From Rose's Bill to Rose's Act: a reappraisal of the 1812 Parish Register Act', *Local Population Studies*, 76 (Spring 2006), pp. 43–62.

Bayly, C. A., *Empire and Information: Intelligence Gathering and Social Communication in India, 1780–1870* (Cambridge: Cambridge University Press, 1996).

Beavan, Colin, *Fingerprints: Murder and the Race to Uncover the Science of Identity* (London: Fourth Estate, 2002).

Beck, Ulrich, *World Risk Society* (Cambridge: Polity Press, 1999).

Becker, Peter, 'The standardized gaze: the standardization of the search warrant in nineteenth-century Germany', in Jane Caplan and John Torpey (eds), *Documenting Individual Identity: The Development of State Practices in the Modern World* (Oxford: Princeton University Press, 2001), pp. 139–63.

Bedos-Rezak, Brigitte, 'Les sceaux au temps de Philippe Auguste', in Brigitte Bedos-Rezak, *Form and Order in Medieval France. Studies in Social and Quantitative Sigillography* (Aldershot: Variorum, 1993), II, pp. 721–73.

— 'Medieval identity: a sign and a concept', *The American Historical Review*, 105 (December 2000), pp. 1489–533.

Beier, A. L., *Masterless Men: The Vagrancy Problem in England 1560–1640* (London: Methuen, 1985).

Bellamy, Christine and Taylor, John A., *Governing in the Information Age* (Buckingham: Open University Press, 1998).

Beniger, James R., *The Control Revolution. Technology and the Economic Origins of the Information Society* (London: Harvard University Press, 1986).

Bentham, Jeremy, 'Principles of penal law', in John Bowring (ed.), *The Works of Jeremy Bentham* (Edinburgh: W. Tair, 1843), vol. 1, p. 557.

Bennet, Colin J. and Lyon, David (eds), *Playing the Identity Card: Surveillance, Security and Identification in Global Perspective* (London: Routledge, 2008).

Bennett, Alan, *Writing home* (London: Faber and Faber, 2005).

Bennett, Michael, *Lambert Simnel and the Battle of Stoke* (Stroud: Alan Sutton, 1987).

Bertillon, Alphonse, *Identification Anthropometrique: Instructions Signaletiques* (Melun: Imprimerie Administrative, 1893).

Biehal, Nina, Mitchell, Fiona and Wade, Jim, *Lost from View: Missing Persons in the UK* (Bristol: Policy Press, 2003).

Bigo, Didier, 'Frontiers and security in the European Union: the illusion of migration control', in Malcolm Anderson and Eberhard Bort (eds), *The Frontiers of Europe* (London: Pinter, 1998), pp. 148–64.

Booth, Charles, *Life and Labour of the People in London, Volume 1* (London: Macmillan, 1902).

Border and Immigration Agency, *Prevention of Illegal Working. Immigration Asylum and Nationality Act 2006. Comprehensive Guidance for Employers in Preventing Illegal Working* (London: Border and Immigration Agency Communications Directorate, 2008).

Bradley, James, 'Body commodification? Class and tattoos in Victorian Britain', in Jane Caplan (ed.), *Written on the Body. The Tattoo in European and American History* (London: Reaktion Books, 2000), pp. 136–55.

Bradley, James and Maxwell-Stewart, Hamish, 'Embodied explorations: investigating tattoos and the transportation system', in Ian Duffield and James Bradley (eds), *Representing Convicts: New Perspectives on Convict Forced Labour Migration* (London: Leicester University Press, 1997), pp. 183–203.

Breckenridge, Keith, 'The elusive panopticon: the HANIS project and the politics of standards in South Africa', in Colin J. Bennett and David Lyon (eds), *Playing the Identity Card: Surveillance, Security and Identification in Global Perspective* (London: Routledge, 2008), pp. 39–56.

— 'Verwoerd's Bureau of Proof: total information in the making of Apartheid', *History Workshop Journal*, 59 (2005), pp. 83–108.

Bromwell, Anne, *Tracing Family History in New Zealand* (Auckland: Godwit, 1996).

Burn, Richard, *The Justice of the Peace, and Parish Officer, Vol. II* (London: T. Cadell, 1770).

Burney, Ian A., *Bodies of Evidence. Medicine and the Politics of the English Inquest, 1830–1926* (Baltimore: Johns Hopkins University Press, 2000).

Butler, John M., *Forensic DNA Typing: Biology, Technology and Genetics of STR Markers* (London: Elsevier Academic Press, 2005).

Cabinet Office, *Identity Fraud: A Study* (London: Cabinet Office, 2002).

Cabinet Office Performance and Innovation Unit, *Privacy and Data-Sharing: The Way Forward for Public Services* (London: Cabinet Office, 2002).

Cameron, Anne, 'The establishment of civil registration in Scotland', *Historical Journal*, 50 (2007), pp. 377–95.

Campbell, Duncan and Connor, Steve, *On the Record. Surveillance, Computers and Privacy – the Inside Story* (London: Michael Joseph, 1986).

Caplan, Jane, 'Illegibility: reading and insecurity in history, law and government', *History Workshop Journal*, 68 (2009), pp. 99–121.

— '"This or That Particular Person"; Protocols of Identification in Nineteenth-Century Europe', in Jane Caplan and John Torpey (eds), *Documenting Individual Identity: The Development of State Practices in the Modern World* (Oxford: Princeton University Press, 2001), pp. 49–66.

Caplan, Jane and Torpey, John (eds), *Documenting Individual Identity: The Development of State Practices in the Modern World* (Oxford: Princeton University Press, 2001).

— 'Introduction', in Jane Caplan and John Torpey (eds), *Documenting Individual Identity: The Development of State Practices in the Modern World* (Oxford: Princeton University Press, 2001), pp. 1–12.

Carrington, Mark St J., Langguth, Philip W. and Steiner, Thomas D., *The Banking Revolution: Salvation or Slaughter? How Technology is Creating Winners and Losers* (London: Pitman, 1997).

Castle, Terry, *Masquerade and Civilization: The Carnivalesque in Eighteenth-Century English Culture and Fiction* (London: Methuen, 1986).

Castles, Stephen and Miller, Mark J, *The Age of Migration* (Basingstoke: Palgrave Macmillan, 2003).

Cheesman, Clive and Williams, Jonathan, *Rebels, Pretenders and Impostors* (London: British Museum Press, 2002).

Clanchy, M. T., *From Memory to Written Record: England 1066–1307* (Oxford: Blackwell, 1993).

Clark, Peter, 'Migration in England during the late seventeenth and early eighteenth centuries', in Peter Clark and Dennis Souden (eds), *Migration and Society in Early Modern England* (London: Hutchinson, 1987), pp. 213–52.

Clark, Stuart, 'Inversion, misrule, and the meaning of witchcraft', *Past and Present*, 87 (1980), pp. 98–127.

Clarke, Roger, 'Human identification in information systems: management challenges and public policy issues', *Information Technology & People*, 7 (December 1994), pp. 6–37.

Cobb, Richard, *Death in Paris 1795–1801* (Oxford: Oxford University Press, 1978).

Cohn, Bernard S., *An Anthropologist among the Historians and Other Essays* (Oxford: Oxford University Press, 2004).

Cole, Simon A., *Suspect Identities. A History of Fingerprinting and Criminal Identification* (London: Harvard University Press, 2001).

— 'What counts for identity?: the historical origins of the methodology of latent fingerprint identification', *Science in Context*, 12 (1) (1999), pp. 139–72.

Commission on Legal Empowerment of the Poor, *Making the Law Work for Everyone* (New York: Commission on Legal Empowerment of the Poor, 2008).

Consoli, Davide, *The Evolution of Retail Banking Services in United Kingdom: A Retrospective Analysis* (Manchester: Centre for Research on Innovation and Competition, University of Manchester, 2003).

Cook, Chris and Keith, Brendan, *British Political Facts 1830–1900* (New York: St Martin's Press, 1975).

Cooper, William Durrant, *Lists of Foreign Protestants and Aliens Resident in England 1618–88; from Returns in the State Paper Office* (London: Camden Society, 1862).

Corbyn, Zoë, 'The small scientist', *Times Higher Education*, 1912 (3 September 2009), p. 36.

Crafts, N. F. R., *British Economic Growth during the Industrial Revolution* (Oxford: Clarendon Press, 1985).

Cressy, David, *Birth, Marriage and Death: Ritual, Religion, and the Life-Cycle in Tudor and Stuart England* (Oxford: Oxford University Press, 1997).

— 'Gender trouble and cross-dressing in early modern England', *The Journal of British Studies*, 35 (4) (1996), pp. 438–65.

— *Literacy and the Social Order: Reading and Writing in Tudor and Stuart England* (Cambridge: Cambridge University Press, 1980).

Critchley, T. A., *A History of Police in England and Wales* (London: Constable, 1978).

Crosland, C. A. R., *The Future of Socialism* (London: Jonathan Cape, 1956).

Crowther, M. A., *The Workhouse System, 1834–1929: The History of an English Social Institution* (London: Batsford, 1981).

Crowther, M. A. and White, Brenda M., *On Soul and Conscience: The Medical Expert and Crime. 150 years of Forensic Medicine in Glasgow* (Aberdeen: Aberdeen University Press, 1988).

Curtis, Bruce, *The Politics of Population. State Formation, Statistics and the Census of Canada, 1840–1875* (Toronto: University of Toronto Press, 2001).

Cutler, Brian L. and Penrod, Steven D., *Mistaken Identification: The Eyewitness, Psychology and the Law* (Cambridge: Cambridge University Press, 1995).

Daunton, Martin J., *Progress and Poverty: An Economic and Social History of Britain, 1770–1850* (Oxford: Oxford University Press, 1995).

Davidson, Alastair, *The Invisible State: The Formation of the Australian State, 1788–1901* (Cambridge: Cambridge University Press, 1991).

Davie, Neil, *Tracing the Criminal: The Rise of Scientific Criminology in Britain 1860–1918* (Oxford: Bardwell Press, 2005.

Davis, Natalie Zemon, 'On the lame', *The American Historical Review*, 93 (June 1988), pp. 572–603.

— *The Return of Martin Guerre* (London: Harvard University Press, 1983).

Dawson John A. and Sparks, Leigh, *Information Sources and Retail Planning* (Stirling: University of Stirling, Department of Business Studies, 1985).

Deane, Phyllis and Cole, W. A., *British Economic Growth 1688–1959* (Cambridge: Cambridge University Press, 1967).

Defoe, Daniel, *Moll Flanders* (London: Penguin Books, 1983).

Department of Social Security, *Safeguarding Social Security: Getting the Information We Need* (London: Department of Social Security, 2000).

Dhupelia-Mesthrie, Uma, 'The passenger Indian as worker: Indian immigrants in Cape Town in the early twentieth century', *African Studies*, 68 (1) (April 2009), pp. 111–34.

Dickens, Charles, *Bleak House* (Boston: James R. Osgood and Company, 1873).

Director General of Fair Trading, *Credit Scoring: A Report* (London: Office of Fair Trading, 1992).

Dixon-Childe, S., 'The future', *The Banker*, 117 (1967), pp. 514–17.

Driver, Felix, *Power and Pauperism: The Workhouse System, 1834–1884* (Cambridge: Cambridge University Press, 1993).

Dummett, Ann and Nicol, Andrew, *Subjects, Citizens, Aliens and Others: Nationality and Immigration Law* (London: Weidenfeld and Nicolson, 1990).

Dyer, Christopher, 'Were late medieval English villages "self-contained", in Christopher Dyer (ed.), *The Self-contained Village? The Social History of Rural Communities 1250–1900* (Hatfield: University of Hertfordshire Press, 2007), pp. 6–27.

Elias, Norbert, *The Civilizing Process* (Oxford: Blackwell, 2000).

Elliot, Rosemary, 'An early experiment in national identity cards: the battle over registration in the First World War', *Twentieth Century British History*, 17 (2) (2006), pp. 145–76.

Elton, G. R., *Policy and Police. The Enforcement of the Reformation in the Age of Thomas Cromwell* (Cambridge: Cambridge University Press, 1972).

Emsley, Clive, *The English Police. A Political and Social History* (Hemel Hempstead: Harvester Wheatsheaf, 1991).

— '"Mother, what *did* policemen do when there weren't any motors?" The law, the police and the regulation of motor traffic in England, 1900–1939', *Historical Journal*, 36 (1993), pp. 357–81.

Engels, Friedrich, *The Condition of the Working-Class in England* (Moscow: Progress Publishers, 1973).

Ericson, Richard V. and Shearing, Clifford D., 'The scientification of police work' in Gernot Bohme and Nico Stehr (eds), *The Knowledge Society: The Growing Impact of Scientific Knowledge on Social Relations* (Dordrecht: D. Reidel, 1986), pp. 129–59.

European Parliament Committee on Citizens' Freedoms and Rights, Justice and Home Affairs (LIBE), *Biometrics at the Frontiers: Assessing the Impact on Society* (2005).

Evans, Martin, 'Food retailing loyalty schemes and the Orwellian Millennium', *British Food Journal*, 101 (1999), pp. 132–47.

Fahrmeir, Andreas, 'Governments and forgers: passports in nineteenth-century Europe', in Jane Caplan and John Torpey (eds), *Documenting Individual Identity: The Development of State Practices in the Modern World* (Oxford: Princeton University Press, 2001), pp. 218–34.

Farr, A. D., 'Blood group serology – the first four decades (1900–1939)', *Medical History*, 23 (2) (1979), pp. 215–26.

Faulds, Henry, 'On the skin-furrows of the hand', *Nature*, 22 (1880), p. 605.

Feldman, David, 'Was the nineteenth century a golden age for immigrants? The changing articulation of national, local and voluntary controls', in Andreas Fahrmeir, Olivier Faron and Patrick Weil (eds), *Migration Control in the North Atlantic World: The Evolution of State Practices in Europe and the United States from the French Revolution to the Inter-War Period* (Oxford: Berghahn Books, 2003), pp. 167–77.

Finn, Margo C., *The Character of Credit. Personal Debt in English Culture, 1740–1914* (Cambridge: Cambridge University Press, 2003).

— 'Scotch drapers and the politics of modernity: gender, class and national identity in Victorian tally trade', in Martin Daunton and Matthew Hilton (eds), *The Politics of Consumption. Material Culture and Citizenship in Europe and America* (Oxford: Berg, 2001), pp. 89–108.

Fletcher, Joseph, 'Moral and educational statistics of England and Wales', *Journal of the London Statistical Society*, 10 (1847), pp. 193–233.

Foister, Susan, *Holbein in England* (London: Tate Publishing, 2006).

Foucault, Michel, *Discipline and Punish: The Birth of the Prison* (London: Allen Lane, 1977).

— 'Governmentality', in Graham Burchell, Colin Gordon and Peter Miller (eds), *The Foucault Effect: Studies in Governmentality* (London: Harvester Wheatsheaf, 1991), pp. 87–104.

— *Les mots et les choses – une archéologie des sciences humaines* (Paris: Gallimard, 1966).

— *Naissance de la clinique – une archéologie du regard médical* (Paris: Presses universitaires de France, 1963).

— 'The subject and power', in Hubert L. Dreyfus and Paul Rabinow (eds), *Michel Foucault: Beyond Structuralism and Hermeneutics, with an Afterword by Michel Foucault* (Brighton: Harvester, 1982), pp. 208–26.

Fowler, Simon and Spencer, William, *Army Records for Family Historians* (Kew: Public Record Office, 1998).

Fraenkel, Béatrice, *La Signature: Genèse d'un Signe* (Paris: Gallimard, 1992).

French, Henry and Barry, Jonathan (eds), *Identity and Agency in England, 1500–1800* (Basingstoke: Palgrave Macmillan, 2004).

Friar, Stephen, *Heraldry for the Local Historian and Genealogist* (London: Grange Books, 1997).

Fumerton, Patricia, 'Making vagrancy (in)visible: the economics of disguise in early modern rogue pamphlets', *English Literary Renaissance*, 33 (2003), pp, 211–27.

— *Unsettled: The Culture of Mobility and the Working Poor in Early Modern England* (London: University of Chicago Press, 2006).

Furedi, Frank, *Culture of Fear: Risk-Taking and the Morality of Low Expectation* (London: Continuum, 2005).

Gainer, Bernard, *The Alien Invasion: The Origins of the Aliens Act of 1905* (London: Heinemann, 1972).

Gairdner, James, *Memorials of Henry VII in the Rolls Series* (London: Longman, Brown, Green, Longmans, and Roberts, 1858).

Galton, Francis, *Finger Prints* (London: Macmillan, 1892).

— 'Identification by finger tips', *Nineteenth Century*, 30 (1891), pp. 303–11.

— 'Personal identification and description', *Proceedings of the Royal Institution*, 12 (1888), pp. 346–60.

Garcelon, Marc, 'Colonizing the subject: the genealogy and legacy of the Soviet internal passport', in Jane Caplan and John Torpey (eds), *Documenting Individual Identity: The Development of State Practices in the Modern World* (Oxford: Princeton University Press, 2001), pp. 83–100.

Gardiner, Samuel Rawson, *The Constitutional Documents of the Puritan Revolution 1625–1660* (Oxford: Clarendon Press, 1906).

Gaskill, Malcolm, 'Witchcraft and evidence in early-modern England', *Past & Present*, 198 (2008), pp. 33–70.

Gatrell, V. A. C. and Hadden, T. B., 'Criminal statistics and their interpretation', in E. A. Wrigley (ed.), *Nineteenth-Century Society: Essays in the Use of Quantitative Methods for the Study of Social Data* (Cambridge: Cambridge University Press, 1972), pp. 336–96.

Gatrell, Vic, *City of Laughter. Sex and Satire in Eighteenth-Century London* (London: Atlantic Books, 2006).

General Register Office, *Fifty-Ninth Annual Report of the Registrar General for 1896* (London: HMSO, 1897).

— *Seventy-Ninth Annual Report of the Registrar General for 1916* (London: HMSO, 1918).

— *Seventy-Seventh Annual Report of the Registrar General for 1914* (London: HMSO, 1916).

— *Thirty-Eighth Annual Report of the Registrar General for 1875* (London: HMSO, 1877).

— *Twenty-Second Annual Report of the Registrar General for 1859* (London: HMSO, 1861).

Gerlach, Neil, *Genetic Imaginary: DNA in the Canadian Criminal Justice System* (Toronto: University of Toronto Press, 2004).

Gibson, Jeremy, *Bishop's Transcripts and Marriage Licences, Bands and Allegations. A Guide to Their Location and Indexes* (Birmingham: Federation of Family History Societies, 1997).

Gibson, Jeremy and Medlycott, Mervyn, *Militia Lists and Musters, 1757–1876: A Directory of Holdings in the British Isles* (Bury: Federation of Family History Societies, 2000).

Giddens, Anthony, *The Constitution of Society* (Cambridge: Polity Press, 1986).

— *The Nation-State and Violence: Volume Two of a Contemporary Critique of Historical Materialism* (Cambridge: Polity Press, 1987).

Gill, Peter, Jeffreys, Alec and Werrett, David, 'Forensic application of DNA "fingerprints"', *Nature* (December 1985), pp. 577–9.

Gillham, Nicholas Wright, *A Life of Sir Francis Galton. From African Exploration to the Birth of Eugenics* (Oxford: Oxford University Press, 2001).

Glaister, John (ed.), *Glaister's Medical Jurisprudence and Toxicology* (Edinburgh: E. & S. Livingstone, 1938, 6th edn).

Goffman, Erving, *The Presentation of Self in Everyday Life* (Harmondsworth: Penguin Books, 1971).

Grey, Jeffery, *A Military History of Australia* (Cambridge: Cambridge University Press, 1999).

Griffiths, Paul, *Lost Londons: Change, Crime and Control in the Capital City, 1550–1660* (Cambridge: Cambridge University Press, 2008).

Grinde, Donald and Johansen, Bruce, *Exemplar of Liberty: Native America and the Evolution of Democracy* (Los Angeles, CA: American Indian Studies Center, University of California, 1991).

Groebner, Valentin, 'Describing the person, reading the signs in late medieval and renaissance Europe: identity paper, vested figures, and the limits of identification, 1400–1600', in Jane Caplan and John Torpey (eds), *Documenting Individual Identity: The Development of State Practices in the Modern World* (Oxford: Princeton University Press, 2001), pp. 15–27.

— *Who are You? Identification, Deception and Surveillance in Early Modern Europe* (New York: Zone Books, 2007).

Grubb, Andrew and Pearl, David S., *Blood Testing, AIDS, and DNA Profiling: Law and Policy* (Bristol: Family Law, 1990).

Gutchen, R. M., 'Paupers in union workhouses: computer analysis of admissions and discharges', *The Local Historian*, 11 (1974–75), pp. 452–6.

Habermas, Jürgen, *The Philosophical Discourse of Modernity* (Cambridge: Polity Press, 1990).

Haggerty, K. D. and Ericson, Richard V., 'The surveillant assemblage', *British Journal of Sociology*, 51 (2000), pp. 605–22.

Hall, Edward, *Chronicle, Containing the History of England . . .* (London: J. Johnson; F. C. and J. Rivington, 1809).

Hall, Nick Vine, *Tracing Your Family History in Australia* (Albert Park, Australia: Scriptorium Family History Centre, 1994).

Hamadi, Rob, *Identity Theft: What It is, How to Prevent It and What to Do If It Happens to You* (London: Vision, 2004).

Hamburger, Philip, 'The conveyancing purposes of the Statute of Frauds', *The American Journal of Legal History*, 27 (1983), pp. 354–85.

Hannah, Leslie, *The Rise of the Corporate Economy* (London: Methuen, 1976).

Harman, Thomas, *A Caveat or Warening for Commen Cursetors Vulgarely Called Vagabones*, in Gamini Salgado (ed.), *Cony-Catchers and Bawdy Basket; an Anthology of Elizabethan Low Life* (Harmondsworth: Penguin Books, 1972), pp. 79–154.

Harris, Bernard, *The Origins of the British Welfare State: Society, State and Social Welfare in England and Wales, 1800–1945* (Basingstoke: Palgrave Macmillan, 2004).

Harris, José, 'Between civic virtue and social Darwinism: the concept of the residuum', in David Englander and Rosemary O'Day (eds), *Retrieved Riches: Social Investigation in England 1840–1914* (Aldershot: Scolar Press, 1995), pp. 67–88.

Harrison, Jennifer, *Australian Birth, Death and Marriage Registration* (Brisbane: Library Board of Queensland, 1989).

Harvey, P. D. A. and McGuinness, Andrew, *A Guide to British Medieval Seals* (London: British Library and Public Record Office, 1996).

Hawkings, David T., *Criminal Ancestors: A Guide to Historical Criminal Records in England and Wales* (Stroud: History Press, 2009).

Henry, E. R., *Bengal Police: Instructions for Classifying and Deciphering Finger Impressions and for Describing Them with Sufficient Exactness to Enable Comparison of the Description with the Original Impression to Be Satisfactorily Made* (India: Bengal Police, 1896).

Herrup, Cynthia B., 'New shoes and mutton pies: investigative responses to theft in seventeenth-century Sussex', *The Historical Journal*, 27 (1984), pp. 811–30.

Hiatt, Alfred, *The Making of Medieval Forgeries: False Documents in Fifteenth-Century England* (London: British Library, 2004).

Higgs, Edward, 'Consumers, citizens and deviants – differing forms of personal identification in England since the Victorian period', in Kerstin Brückweh (ed.), *The Voice of the Citizen Consumer: A History of Market Research, Consumer Movements and the Political Public Sphere* (London: German Historical Institute, forthcoming).

— 'Fingerprints and citizenship: the British State and the identification of pensioners in the inter-war period', *History Workshop Journal*, 69 (2010), pp. 52–67.

— 'From medieval erudition to information management: the evolution of the archival profession', *Archivum (Proceedings of the XIII International Congress on Archives, Beijing, 2–7 September 1996)* 43 (1997), pp. 136–44.

— *The Information State in England: The Central Collection of Information on Citizens, 1500–2000* (London: Palgrave, 2004).

— *Life, Death and Statistics: Civil Registration, Censuses and the Work of the General Register Office, 1837–1952* (Hatfield: Local Population Studies, 2004).

— *Making Senses of the Census* (London: HMSO, 1989).

— 'Personal identification as information flows in England, 1500–2000', in Toni Weller (ed.), *Information History in the Modern World* (London: Palgrave Macmillan, forthcoming).

— 'The role of tomorrow's electronic archives', in Edward Higgs (ed.), *History and Electronic Artefacts* (Oxford: Clarendon Press, 1998), pp. 184–94.

— 'The statistical Big Bang of 1911: ideology, technological innovation and the production of medical statistics', *Social History of Medicine*, 9 (3) (1996), pp. 409–26.

Hilton, R. H., *The Decline of Serfdom in Medieval England* (London: Macmillan, 1969).

Hindle, Steve, 'Dependency, shame and belonging: badging the deserving poor, c.1550–1750', *Cultural and Social History*, 1 (2004), pp. 6–35.

— *On the Parish?: The Micro-Politics of Poor Relief in Rural England, c.1550–1750* (Oxford: Clarendon Press, 2004).

— 'Technologies of identification under the Old Poor Law', *The Local Historian*, 36 (2006), pp. 220–36.

Hindle, Tim, 'The customer comes first', *The Banker*, 130 (March 1980), pp. 89–93.

Hirst, Derek, *The Representative of the People?: Voters and Voting in England under the early Stuarts* (Cambridge: Cambridge University Press, 1975).

Holdsworth, William, *A History of English Law, Vol. VI* (London: Methuen, 1924).

Hoppit, Julian, 'The use and abuse of credit in eighteenth-century England', in Neil McKendrick and R. B. Outhwaite (eds), *Business Life and Public Policy: Essays in Honour of D. C. Coleman* (Cambridge: Cambridge University Press, 1986), pp. 64–78.

Horn, David G., *The Criminal Body: Lombroso and the Anatomy of Deviance* (London: Routledge, 2003).

Howard, Sharon, 'Investigating responses to theft in early modern Wales: communities, thieves and the courts', *Continuity and Change*, 19 (2004), pp. 409–30.

Hudson, Derek, *Munby: Man of Two Worlds. The Life and Diaries of Arthur J. Munby 1828–1910* (London: Sphere Books, 1974).

Hughes, Robert, *The Fatal Shore. A History of the Transportation of Convicts to Australia, 1787–1868* (London: Guild Publishing, 1987).

Hunnisett, R. F., *Calendar of Nottinghamshire Coroners' Inquests 1485–1558* (Nottingham: Produced for the Thoroton Society by Derry and Sons, 1969).

— *The Medieval Coroner* (Cambridge: Cambridge University Press, 1961).

— *Sussex Coroners' Inquests, 1603–1688* (Kew: Public Record Office, 1998).

Hunt, Alan, *Governance of the Consuming Passions: A History of Sumptuary Law* (Basingstoke: Macmillan, 1996).

Hutchinson, Geoff, *Grey Owl: The Incredible Story of Archie Belaney, 1888–1938* (Brede: G. Hutchinson, 1985).

Hutton, Ronald, *The Rise and Fall of Merry England: The Ritual Year, 1400–1700* (Oxford: Oxford University Press, 1994).

International Committee of the Red Cross, *Missing Persons: A Hidden Tragedy* (Geneva: International Committee of the Red Cross, 2007).

Iwaszko, Tadeusz, 'Die Haeftlinge', in *Auschwitz. Geschichte und Wirklichkeit des Lagers* (Reinbek: Rororo, 1980).

Jenkinson, Charles Hilary, *Guide to Seals in the Public Record Office* (London: HMSO, 1968).

— *Seals in Administration: (A Plea for Systematic Study)* (Naples: L'Arte Tipographica, 1959).

Jervis, John, *A Practical Treatise on the Office and Duties of Coroners* (London: Sweet, Maxwell and Stevens & Norton, 1854).

Johnson, Paul, 'The role of the State in twentieth-century Britain', in Paul Johnson (ed.), *Twentieth-Century Britain: Economic, Social and Cultural Change* (Harlow: Longman, 1994), pp. 476–91.

Jones, Ann Rosalind and Stallybrass, Peter, *Renaissance Clothing and the Materials of Memory* (Cambridge: Cambridge University Press, 2000).

Jones, C. P., 'Stigma and tattoo', in Jane Caplan (ed.), *Written on the Body. The Tattoo in European and American History* (London: Reaktion Books, 2000), pp. 1–16.

Jones, David Martin, *Conscience and Allegiance in Seventeenth Century England: The Political Significance of Oaths and Engagements* (Rochester, NY: University of Rochester Press, 1999).

Joseph, Anne M., 'Anthropometry, the police expert, and the Deptford Murders: the contested introduction of fingerprinting for the identification of criminals in late Victorian and Edwardian Britain', in Jane Caplan and John Torpey (eds), *Documenting Individual Identity: The Development of State Practices in the Modern World* (Oxford: Princeton University Press, 2001), pp. 163–83.

Josling, J. F., *Change of Name* (London: Longman, 1989).

Kaluszynski, Martine, ' Republican identity: Bertillonage as government technique', in Jane Caplan and John Torpey (eds), *Documenting Individual Identity. The Development of State Practices in the Modern World* (Princeton: Princeton University Press, 2001), pp. 123–38.

Karake-Shalhoub, Zeinab, 'Population ID card systems in the Middle East: the case of the UAE', in Colin J. Bennet and David Lyon (eds), *Playing the Identity Card: Surveillance, Security and Identification in Global Perspective* (London: Routledge, 2008), pp. 128–41.

Kenealy, Edward V. H., *The Book of God: The Apocalypse* (London: Trübner & Co, 1867).

Kenealy, Maurice Edward, *The Tichborne Tragedy, Being the Secret and Authentic History of the Extraordinary Facts and Circumstances Connected with the Claims, Personality, Identification, Conviction and Last Days of the Tichborne Claimant* (London: Francis Griffiths, 1913).

Keppenhaver, Katherine Mainolfi, *Forensic Document Examination. Principles and Practice* (Totowa, NJ: Humana Press, 2007).

Kerridge, Eric, *Trade and Banking in Early-Modern England* (Manchester: Manchester University Press, 1988).

Kim, Keechang, *Aliens in Medieval Law. The Origins of Modern Citizenship* (Cambridge: Cambridge University Press, 2000).

Kipling, Rudyard, *Kim* (London: Penguin Books, 2000).

Kleyn, D. M., *Richard of England* (Oxford: Kensal Press, 1990).

Kowitz, Aletha, 'The earliest use of dental evidence in a courtroom', *Bulletin of the History of Dentistry*, 29 (1981), pp. 82–7.

Kussmaul, Ann, *Servants in Husbandry in Early Modern England* (Cambridge: Cambridge University Press, 1981).

Laing, R. D., *The Divided Self* (London: Tavistock Publications, 1960).

Lampard, Eric E., 'The urbanizing world', in H. J. Dyos and Michael Wolff (eds), *The Victorian City: Images and Realities, Volume I* (London: Routledge & Kegan Paul, 1976), pp. 3–58.

Laslett, Peter, *Family Life and Illicit Love in Earlier Generations* (Cambridge: Cambridge University Press, 1977).

Lees, Lynn Hollen, *The Solidarities of Strangers: The English Poor Laws and the People, 1700–1948* (Cambridge: Cambridge University Press, 1998).

Lefebvre-Teillard, Anne, *Le Nom: Droit et Histoire* (Paris: Presses universitaires de France, 1990).

Levy, Philip A., 'Exemplars of taking liberties: the Iroquois influence thesis and the problem of evidence', *The William and Mary Quarterly, Third Series*, 53 (1996), pp. 588–604.

London School of Economics, *The Identity Project: An Assessment of the UK Identity Cards Bill & Its Implications. Interim Report* (London: LSE, 2005).

Lucassen, Leo, 'A many-headed monster: the evolution of the passport system in the Netherlands and Germany in the long nineteenth century', in Jane Caplan and John Torpey (eds), *Documenting Individual Identity: The Development of State Practices in the Modern World* (Oxford: Princeton University Press, 2001), pp. 235–55.

Luu, Lien, 'Natural-born versus stranger-born subjects: aliens and their status in Elizabethan London', in Nigel Goose and Lien Luu (eds), *Immigrants in Tudor and Early Stuart England* (Brighton: Sussex Academic Press, 2005), pp. 57–75.

Lynch, Michael, Cole, Simon A., McNally, Ruth and Jordan, Kathleen, *Truth Machine. The Contentious History of DNA Fingerprinting* (London: University of Chicago Press, 2008).

Lyon, David, *The Electronic Eye. The Rise of Surveillance Society* (Cambridge: Polity Press, 2004).

— 'Surveillance as social sorting: computer codes and mobile bodies', in David Lyon (ed.), *Surveillance as Social Sorting: Privacy, Risk, and Digital Discrimination* (Abingdon: Routledge, 2003), pp. 13–30.

— *Surveillance Society. Monitoring Everyday Life* (Buckingham: Open University Press, 2001).

Macaulay, T. B., *The Works of Lord Macaulay, Vol. VI* (London: Spottiswoode and Co., 1866).

McClelland, Keith, 'England's greatness, the working man', in Catherine Hall, Keith McClelland and Jane Rendall (eds), *Defining the Nation: Class, Race, Gender and the Reform Act of 1867* (Cambridge: Cambridge University Press, 2000), pp. 71–118.

Macfarlane, Alan, *The Justice and the Mare's Ale: Law and Disorder in Seventeenth-Century England* (Oxford: Basil Blackwell, 1981).

— *The Origins of English Individualism: The Family, Property and Social Transition* (Oxford: Basil Blackwell, 1978).

— *Reconstructing Historical Communities* (Cambridge: Cambridge University Press, 1977).

McGowen, Randall, 'The Bank of England and the policing of forgery, 1797–1821', *Past and Present*, 186 (2005), pp. 81–116.

McKenzie, Kirsten, *A Swindler's Progress: Nobles and Convicts in the Age of Liberty* (London: Harvard University Press, 2010).

McKeown, Adam, *Melancholy Order: Asian Migration and the Globalization of Borders* (New York: Columbia University Press, 2008).

McKibbin, Ross, 'Why Was There No Marxism in Great Britain', *The English Historical Review*, 99 (1984), pp. 297–331.

McKinley, R. A., *A History of British Surnames* (London: Longman, 1990).

Macpherson, C. B., *The Political Theory of Possessive Individualism: Hobbes to Locke* (Oxford: Clarendon Press, 1962).

McWilliam, Rohan, *The Tichborne Claimant. A Victorian Sensation* (London: Hambledon Continuum, 2007).

Madden, F., 'Documents relating to Perkin Warbeck, with remarks on his history', *Archaeologia*, 27 (1838), pp. 165–6, 202.

Maine, Henry, *Ancient Law: Its Connection with the Early History of Society, and Its Relation to Modern Ideas* (London: John Murray, 1861).

Mann, Michael, *The Sources of Social Power, Volume 1: A History of Power from the Beginning to AD 1760* (Cambridge: Cambridge University Press, 1986).

Marx, Karl, *Capital: A Critique of Political Economy, Volume 1* (Harmondsworth: Penguin Books, 1976).

Mathias, Peter, *The First Industrial Nation: An Economic History of Britain, 1700–1914* (London: Methuen, 1969).

Matthews, Paul, 'Whose body? People as property', *Current Legal Problems*, 36 (1983), pp. 193–239.

Matthews, Paul and Foreman, J. C., *Jervis on the Office and Duties of Coroners* (London: Sweet and Maxwell, 1986).

Matthews, William, *From Chili to Piccadilly with Sir Roger Tichborne. The Santiago Daguerreo-Types and the London Photographs Compared, Identity Demonstrated Geometrically, etc.* (Bristol: J Wright and Co., 1876).

Mattingly, David, *An Imperial Possession: Britain in the Roman Empire* (London: Penguin Books, 2007).

Maxwell-Stewart, Hamish and Duffield, Ian, 'Skin deep devotions: religious tattoos and convict transportation to Australia', in Jane Caplan (ed.), *Written on the Body. The Tattoo in European and American History* (London: Reaktion Books, 2000), pp. 118–35.

Moss, Alan and Skinner, Keith, *The Scotland Yard Files. Milestones in Crime Detection* (Kew: The National Archives, 2006).

Muldrew, Craig, *The Economy of Obligation. The Culture of Credit and Social Relations in Early Modern England* (London: Macmillan, 1998).

— 'Rural credit, market areas and legal institutions in the countryside in England, 1550–1700', in C. W. Brooks and Michael Lobban (eds), *Communities and Courts, Proceedings of the Twelfth Legal History Conference Held in Durham* (London: Hambledon Press, 1997), pp. 155–77.

Nelkin, Dorothy and Andrews, Lori, 'Surveillance creep in the genetic age', in David Lyon (ed.), *Surveillance as Social Sorting: Privacy, Risk, and Digital Discrimination* (London: Routledge, 2003), pp. 94–110.

Newiss, Geoff, *Missing Presumed ...?: The Police Response to Missing Persons* (London: Home Office, Policing and Reducing Crime Unit, 1999).

Noiriel, Gérard, *The French Melting Pot: Immigration, Citizenship, and National Identity* (Minneapolis: University of Minnesota Press, 1996).

— 'The identification of the citizen: the birth of Republican civil status in France', in Jane Caplan and John Torpey (eds), *Documenting Individual Identity: The Development of State Practices in the Modern World* (Oxford: Princeton University Press, 2001), pp. 28–48.

Norris, Clive and Armstrong, Gary, *The Maximum Surveillance Society: The Rise of CCTV* (Oxford: Berg, 1999).

O'Connell, Sean, *Credit and Community: Working-Class Debt in the UK since 1880* (Oxford: Oxford University Press, 2009).

Offer, Avner, *The Challenge of Affluence: Self-Control and Well-Being in the United States and Britain since 1950* (Oxford: Oxford University Press, 2006).

Oxley, Geoffrey W., *Poor Relief in England and Wales 1601–1834* (Newton Abbott: David & Charles, 1974).

Pachai, B., *The International Aspects of the South African Indian Question 1860–1971* (Cape Town: C. Struik, 1971).

Pappalardo, Bruno, *Tracing Your Naval Ancestors* (Kew: Public Record Office, 2002).

Penry, Jacques, *Looking at Faces and Remembering Them. A Guide to Facial Identification* (London: Elek, 1971).

Pepys, Samuel, *Everybody's Pepys: The Diary of Samuel Pepys 1660–1669* (London: G. Bell and Sons, 1945).

Piazza, Pierre and Laniel, Laurent, 'The INES biometric card and the politics of national identity assignment in France', in Colin J. Bennet and David Lyon (eds), *Playing the Identity Card: Surveillance, Security and Identification in Global Perspective* (London: Routledge, 2008), pp. 198–217.

Pihlajamaki, Heikki, 'Swimming the witch, pricking for the Devil's mark: ordeals in the early modern witchcraft trials', *The Journal of Legal History*, 21 (2000), pp. 35–58.

Pooley, Colin, 'Mobility in the twentieth century: substituting commuting for migration', in D. Gilbert, D. Matless and B. Short (eds), *Geographies of British Modernity: Space and Society in the Twentieth Century* (Oxford: Blackwell, 2003), pp. 80–96.

Pooley, Colin G., Turnbull, Jean and Adams, Mags, *A Mobile Century?: Changes in Everyday Mobility in Britain in the Twentieth Century* (Aldershot: Ashgate, 2005).

Poos, L. R., *A Rural Society after the Black Death: Essex 1350–1525* (Cambridge, Cambridge University Press, 1991).

Porter, J. Neville, 'Mortuary reform', *The Sanitary Record*, 12 (1890–91), pp. 5–9, 57–60.

Postles, Dave, *Social Proprieties: Address and Naming in Early-Modern England (1500–1640)* (Washington, DC: New Academia Publishing, 2006).

— *Talking Ballocs: Nicknames and English Medieval Sociolinguistics* (Leicester: Centre for English Local History, University of Leicester, 2003).

Prest, John, *Politics in the Age of Cobden* (London: Macmillan, 1977).

Pringle, Patrick, *Hue and Cry: The Birth of the British Police* (London: Museum Press, 1955).

Prison Reform Trust, *Electronic Tagging: Viable Option or Expensive Diversion?* (London: Prison Reform Trust, 1997).

Purchase, W. B., *Jervis on the Office and Duties of Coroners* (London: Sweet and Maxwell, 1957).

Purvis, John Stanley, *Notarial Signs from the York Archiepiscopal Records* (London: St Anthony's Press, 1957).

Ravenstein, Ernest George, 'The laws of migration', *Journal of the Statistical Society of London*, 48 (1885), pp. 167–235.

— 'The laws of migration', *Journal of the Royal Statistical Society*, 52 (1889), pp. 241–305.

Rawlings, Philip, *Drunks, Whores and Idle Apprentices: Criminal Biographies of the Eighteenth Century* (London: Routledge, 1992).

Richards, Robert J., *The Tragic Sense of Life: Ernst Haeckel and the Struggle over Evolutionary Thought* (London: University of Chicago Press, 2008).

Richardson, Ruth, *Death, Dissection and the Destitute* (London: Routledge & Kegan Paul, 1987).

Rhodes, Henry T. F., *Alphonse Bertillon: Father of Scientific Detection* (London: Harrap, 1956).

Robertson, Geoffrey, *The Justice Game* (London: Vintage, 1999).

Robertson, Joseph T., *Discussion Paper on the Statute of Frauds, 1677* (St John's, NL: Newfoundland Law Reform Commission, 1991).

Robins, Jean, *Rebel Queen: How the Trial of Caroline Brought England to the Brink of Revolution* (London: Pocket, 2007).

Rodger, N. A. M., *Naval Records for Genealogists* (Richmond: Public Record Office, 1998).

Rollison, David, 'Exploding England: the dialectics of mobility and settlement in early modern England', *Social History*, 24 (1999), pp. 1–16.

Rose, Nikolas, *Powers of Freedom: Reframing Political Thought* (Cambridge: Cambridge University Press, 1999).

Ross, David Frank, Read, J. Don and Toglia, Michael P. (eds), *Adult Eyewitness Testimony: Current Trends and Developments* (Cambridge: Cambridge University Press, 1994).

Rostow, W. W., *The Stages of Economic Growth: A Non-Communist Manifesto* (Cambridge: Cambridge University Press, 1960).

Round, J. Horace, *Peerage and Pedigree. Studies in Peerage Law and Family History* (London: James Nisbet & Co., 1910).

Roux, Georges, *Ancient Iraq* (London: Penguin Books, 1992).

Rowland, J., *The Finger-Print Man: The Story of Sir Edward Henry* (London: Lutterworth Press, 1959).

Rudavsky, Shari, 'Blood will tell: the role of science and culture in twentieth century paternity disputes', Doctoral Thesis, University of Pennsylvania, 1996.

Ruggiero, Kristin, 'Fingerprinting and the Argentine plan for universal identification in the late nineteenth and early twentieth centuries', in Jane Caplan and John Torpey (eds), *Documenting Individual Identity: The Development of State Practices in the Modern World* (Oxford: Princeton University Press, 2001), pp. 184–96.

Rule, John, *Albion's People: English Society 1714–1815* (London: Longman, 1992).

Runcie, James, *The Future of Global Markets for Personal Identification: Strategic Five-Year Forecasts* (Leatherhead: Pira International, 2003).

Sandage, Scott A., *Born Losers: A History of Failure in America* (Cambridge, MA: Harvard University Press, 2005).

Saunders, Kenneth C., *The Medical Detectives: A Study of Forensic Pathologists* (London: Middlesex University Press, 2001).

Schiller, Dan, *How to Think about Information* (Urbana: University of Illinois Press, 2007).

Schoeters, E., 'The "dematerialisation" of payment systems', *The Banker*, 130 (March 1980), pp. 101–5.

Schofield, R. S., 'The measurement of literacy in pre-industrial England', in Jack Goody (ed.), *Literacy in Traditional Societies* (Cambridge: Cambridge University Press, 1968), pp. 311–25.

Scott, James C., *Seeing Like a State: How Certain Schemes to Improve the Human Condition Have Failed* (London: Yale University Press, 1998).

Scott, James C., Tehranian, John and Mathias, Jeremy, 'Government surnames and legal entities', in Carl Watner and Wendy McElroy (eds), *National Identification Systems: Essays in Opposition* (London: MacFarlane, 2004), pp. 11–54.

— 'The production of legal identities proper to states: the case of the permanent family surname', *Comparative Studies in Society and History*, 44 (2002), pp. 4–44.

Sengoopta, Chandak, *Imprint of the Raj. How Fingerprinting was Born in Colonial India* (London: Macmillan, 2003).

Seymour, Charles, *Electoral Reform in England and Wales: The Development and Operation of the Parliamentary Franchise 1832–1885* (Newton Abbott: David & Charles, 1970).

Sharpe, J. A., *Early Modern England: A Social History, 1550–1760* (London: Edward Arnold, 1987).

Slack, Paul, *The English Poor Law, 1531–1782* (Basingstoke: Macmillan Education, 1990).

— *Poverty and Policy in Tudor and Stuart England* (London: Longman, 1988).

Simmel, Georg, *The Stranger* (Chicago: Chicago University Press, 1971).

Smith, Andrew and Sparks, Leigh, 'Making tracks: loyalty cards as consumer surveillance', in Darach Turley and Stephen Brown (eds), *European Advances in Consumer Research, Volume 6* (Valdosta, GA: Association for Consumer Research, 2003), pp. 368–73.

Smith, Fred J., *Taylor's Principles and Practice of Medical Jurisprudence* (London: John Churchill, 1910, 6th edn, vol. 1).

Smith, Leslie and Doreen, *Sudden Deaths in Suffolk 1767–1858: A Survey of Coroners' Records in the Liberty of St Etheldreda* (Ipswich: Suffolk Family History Society, 1995).

Smith, Richard M., '"Modernization' and the corporate medieval village community in England: some sceptical reflections', in A. R. H. Baker and D. Gregory (eds), *Explorations in Historical Geography: Interpretative Essays* (Cambridge: Cambridge University Press, 1984), pp. 140–79.

— 'Periods, structures and regimes in early modern demographic history', *History Workshop Journal*, 63 (2007), pp. 202–18.

Smith-Bannister, Scott, *Names and Naming Patterns in England, 1538–1700* (Oxford: Clarendon Press, 1997).

Snell, K. D. M., *Parish and Belonging. Community, Identity and Welfare in England and Wales 1700–1950* (Cambridge: Cambridge University Press, 2006).

— 'Settlement, Poor Law, and the rural historian: new approaches and opportunities', *Rural History*, 3 (2) (1992), pp. 145–72.

Social Security Office, *How to Prove Your Identity for Social Security* (Leeds: Social Security Office, 2003).

Sokoll, Thomas (ed.), *Essex Pauper Letters 1731–1837* (Oxford: Oxford University Press, 2001).

Solove, Daniel J., *The Digital Person; Technology and Privacy in the Information Age* (London: New York University Press, 2004).

Stark, Margaret M., *A Physician's Guide to Clinical Forensic Medicine* (New Jersey: Humana Press, 2000).

Stigler, Stephen M,. 'Galton and identification by fingerprints', *Genetics*, 140 (1995), pp. 857–60.

Stonehouse, John, *The Death of an Idealist* (London: W. H. Allen, 1975).

— *My Trial: My Blow-by-Blow Account and Psychological Reaction to the Trial and Verdict from the Old Bailey Dock* (London: Wyndham Publications, 1976).

Styles, John, 'Print and policing: crime advertising in eighteenth century England', in Douglas Hay and Francis Snyder (eds), *Policing and Prosecution in Britain 1750–1850* (Oxford: Clarendon Press, 1989), pp. 55–112.

Svendsen, Lars, *A Philosophy of Fear* (London: Reaktion Books, 2008).

Swan, Maureen, *Gandhi: The South African experience* (Johannesburg: Ravan Press, 1985).

Szreter, Simon, 'The right of registration: development, identity registration, and social security – a historical perspective', *World Development*, 35 (2007), pp. 67–86.

Tate, W. E., *The Parish Chest: A Study of the Records of Parochial Administration in England* (Cambridge: Cambridge University Press, 1960).

Taylor, Alfred Swaine, *Elements of Medical Jurisprudence* (London: Deacon, 1836).

— *Medical Jurisprudence* (London: John Churchill, 1852, 4th edn).

— *The Principles and Practice of Medical Jurisprudence* (London: John Churchill, 1865, 1st edn).

— *The Principles and Practice of Medical Jurisprudence* (ed. Thomas Stevenson) (London: John Churchill, 1883, 3rd edn, vol. 1).

Taylor, Avram, *Working Class Credit and Community since 1918* (Basingstoke: Palgrave, 2002).

Taylor, Charles, *Sources of the Self: The Making of Modern Identity* (Cambridge: Cambridge University Press, 1989).

Thomas, J. A., 'The system of registration and the development of party organisation, 1832–70',. *History*, 35 (1950), pp. 81–98.

Thomas, Keith, *The Ends of Life: Roads to Fulfilment in Early Modern England* (Oxford: Oxford University Press, 2009).

Thompson, E. P., *The Making of the English Working Class* (Harmondsworth: Penguin Books, 1968).

— *Whigs and Hunters. The Origins of the Black Act* (Harmondsworth: Penguin, 1977).

Thompson, Scott, 'Separating the sheep from the goats: the United Kingdom's National Registration programme and social sorting in the pre-electronic era', in Colin J. Bennet and David Lyon (eds), *Playing the Identity Card: Surveillance, Security and Identification in Global Perspective* (London: Routledge, 2008), pp. 145–62.

Thomson, John, 'The case for credit cards', *The Banker*, 116 (July 1966), pp. 444–6.

Thomson, Mathew, *The Problem of Mental Deficiency: Eugenics, Democracy and Social Policy in Britain, c.1870–1959* (Oxford: Oxford University Press, 1998).

Tönnies, Ferdinand, *Community and Association (Gemeinschaft und Gesellschaft)* (London: Routledge & Kegan Paul, 1955).

Torpey, John, *The Invention of the Passport: Surveillance, Citizenship and the State* (Cambridge: Cambridge University Press, 2000).

Vincent, Susan, *Dressing the Elite. Clothes in Early Modern England* (Oxford: Berg, 2003).

Vine, Roy, 'Why the banks have gone in for automation', *The Banker*, 117 (1967), pp. 501–7.

Vivian, Sylvanus, *History of National Registration* (London: Cabinet Office Historical Branch, 1951).

Vyleta, Daniel Mark, 'Was early twentieth-century criminology a science of the 'Other'? A re-evaluation of Austro-German criminological debates', *Cultural and Social History*, 3 (2006), pp. 406–23.

Wagner, Anthony Richard, *English Genealogy* (Oxford: Clarendon Press, 1972).

—— *Heralds and Heraldry in the Middle Ages. An Inquiry into the Growth of the Armorial Function of Heralds* (Oxford: Oxford University Press, 2000).

—— *Heralds of England. A History of the Office and College of Arms* (London: HMSO, 1967).

Wahrman, Dror, *The Making of the Modern Self* (London: Yale University Press, 2004).

Wall, Richard, Woollard, Matthew and Moring, Beatrice, *Census Schedules and Listings, 1801–1831: An Introduction and Guide*. Working Paper Series 5 (Colchester: University of Essex, Department of History, 2004).

Walter, John, *Crowds and Popular Politics in Early Modern England* (Manchester: Manchester University Press, 2006).

—— *Understanding Popular Violence in the English Revolution: The Colchester Plunderers* (Cambridge: Cambridge University Press, 1999).

Ward, Jennifer, 'Origins and development of forensic medicine and forensic science in England 1823–1946', Open University Doctoral Thesis, 1993.

Wayman, James L., 'The scientific development of biometrics over the last 40 years', in Karl de Leeuw and Jan Bergstra (eds), *The History of Information Security: A Comprehensive Handbook* (Amsterdam: Elsevier B. V., 2007), pp. 263–76.

Weiner, Martin J., *Reconstructing the Criminal: Culture, Law and Policy in England, 1830–1914* (Cambridge: Cambridge University Press, 1990).

Welsh, David, 'The growth of towns', in Monica Wilson and Leonard Thompson (eds), *The Oxford History of South Africa: II South Africa 1870–1966* (Oxford: Clarendon Press, 1975), pp. 188–210.

Wetzell, Richard, *Inventing the Criminal: A History of German Criminology, 1880–1945* (London: University of North Carolina Press, 2000).

Whittle, Jane, 'Population mobility in rural Norfolk among landowners and others c.1440–c.1600', in Christopher Dyer (ed.), *The Self-Contained Village? The Social History of Rural Communities 1250–1900* (Hatfield: University of Hertfordshire Press, 2007), pp. 28–45.

Whyte, Ian, 'Cumbrian village communities: continuity and change, c.1750–c.1850', in Christopher Dyer (ed.), *The Self-Contained Village? The Social History of Rural Communities 1250–1900* (Hatfield: University of Hertfordshire Press, 2007), pp. 96–113.

— *Migration and Society in Britain 1550–1830* (Basingstoke: Macmillan, 2000).

Wilkinson, Caroline, *Forensic Facial Reconstruction* (Cambridge: Cambridge University Press, 2004).

Wilks-Heeg, Stuart, *Purity of Elections in the UK: Causes for Concern* (York: Joseph Rowntree Trust, 2008).

Williams, David, *The Rebecca Riots. A Study in Agrarian Discontent* (Cardiff: University of Wales Press, 1955).

Williams, Robin and Johnson, Paul, *Forensic DNA Databasing: A European Perspective Interim Report* (Durham: School of Applied Social Science, University of Durham, 2005).

— *Genetic Policing. The Use of DNA in Criminal Investigations* (Cullompton, Devon: Willan Publishing, 2008).

Williams, Robin, Johnson, Paul and Martin, Paul, *Genetic Information & Crime Investigation: Social, Ethical and Public Policy Aspects of the Establishment, Expansion and Police Use of the National DNA Database* (Durham: School of Applied Social Sciences, University of Durham, 2004).

Wills, David, 'The United Kingdom identity card scheme: shifting motivations, static technologies', in Colin J. Bennet and David Lyon (eds), *Playing the Identity Card: Surveillance, Security and Identification in Global Perspective* (London: Routledge, 2008), pp. 163–79.

Wilson, Stephen, *The Means of Naming: A Social and Cultural History of Personal Naming in Western Europe* (London: UCL Press, 1998).

Wingfield, Mervyn Edward, *Muniments of the Ancient Saxon Family of Wingfield* (London: Whitehall and Hughes, 1894).

Winstanley, Michael J, *The Shopkeeper's World, 1830–1914* (Manchester: Manchester University Press, 1983).

Woolf, Daniel, *The Social Circulation of the Past. English Historical Culture 1500–1730* (Oxford: Oxford University Press, 2003).

Wrightson Keith, *Earthly Necessities: Economic Lives in early modern Britain* (New Haven, CT; London: Yale University Press, 2000),

— *English Society 1580–1680* (London: Hutchinson, 1982).

Wrightson, Keith and Levine, David, *Poverty and Piety in an English Village: Terling, 1525–1700* (Oxford: Clarendon Press, 1995).

Wrigley, E. A., 'A simple model of London's importance in changing English society and economy 1650–1750', *Past and Present*, 37 (1967), pp. 44–70.

— 'Urban growth and agricultural change: England and the Continent in the early modern period', in Roger S. Schofield and E. Anthony Wrigley (eds), *Population and History: From the Traditional to the Modern World* (Cambridge: Cambridge University Press, 1986), pp. 123–68.

Wrigley, E. A. and Schofield, R. S., *The Population History of England 1541–1871: A Reconstruction* (London: Edward Arnold, 1981).

Wroe, Ann, *Perkin. A Story of Deception* (London: Vintage, 2003).

Yates, JoAnne, *Control through Communication: The Rise of System in American Management* (Baltimore: Johns Hopkins University Press, 1989).

Zuboff, Shoshana, *In the Age of the Smart Machine: The Future of Work and Power* (London: Heinemann Professional, 1988).

NEWSPAPERS AND JOURNALS

The Economist
The Hull Packet and Humber Mercury
The Liverpool Mercury
The Morning Chronicle
The Northern Star and Leeds General Advertiser
The Pall Mall Gazette
The Preston Guardian
The Times

OFFICIAL RECORDS SERIES IN THE NATIONAL ARCHIVES, LONDON

Admiralty: Royal Marines: Description Books (ADM 158).

Air Ministry and Ministry of Defence: Registered Files (AIR 2).

Board of Inland Revenue and Board of Customs and Excise: Non Contributory Old Age Pensions, Registered Files (AST 15).Board of Inland Revenue: Stamps and Taxes Division: Registered Files (IR 40).

Board of Trade: Committee on Consumer Credit: Files (BT 250).

Central Criminal Court Depositions (CRIM 1).

Chancery and Supreme Court of Judicature: Close Rolls (C 54).Chancery and Supreme Court of Judicature: Patent Rolls (C 66).

Committee on Evidence of Identity in Criminal Cases: Evidence and Papers (HO 280).

Department of Trade and Industry and Successors: Consumer Credit Branch: Registered Files (CCB Series) (FV 82).

Exchequer King's Remembrancer: Extents of Alien Priories, Aliens, etc., 1293–1483 (E106).

Exchequer: King's Remembrancer: Particulars of Accounts and Other Records Relating to Lay and Clerical Taxation (E179).

Foreign Office and Foreign and Commonwealth Office: Chief Clerk's Department and Passport Office: Correspondence (FO 612).

General Register Office: National Registration: Correspondence and Papers (RG 28).

General Register Office: Specimens of Documents Destroyed (RG 900).

Health and Safety Executive: Inquiry into the Disaster which Occurred at Nypro (UK) Ltd, Flixborough: Unregistered Records (EF12).

Home Office: Aliens, General Matters (ALG Symbol Series) Files (HO 352).

Home Office and Prison Commission: Prisons Records, Series I (PCOM 2).

Home Office: Civil Defence (Various Symbol Series) Files (HO 322).

Home Office: Criminal Registers, Middlesex (HO 26).

Home Office: Domestic Correspondence from 1773 to 1860 (HO 44).

Home Office: Immigration and Nationality Department and Predecessors: Registers of Deportees (HO 372).

Home Office: Police (POL Symbol Series) Files (HO 287).

Home Office: Registered Papers (HO 45).

Home Office Registered Papers, Supplementary (HO 144).

Law Society: Legal Aid Administration: Registered Files (Numeric Series 2) (FR 6).

Metropolitan Police; Criminal Record Office: Habitual Criminals Registers and Miscellaneous Papers (MEPO 6).

Metropolitan Police: Office of the Commissioner: Correspondence and Papers (MEPO 2).

Ministry of Defence and Predecessors: Army Circulars, Memoranda, Orders and Regulations (WO 123).

Ministry of Home Security: Air Raid Precautions (ARP GEN) Registered Files (HO 186).

Ministry of Pensions and National Insurance and Predecessors: Specimens of Series of Documents Destroyed (PIN 900).

Ministry of Pensions and Successors: War Pensions, Registered Files (GEN Series) and Other Records (PIN 15).

National Assistance Board and Successor: Codes of Instructions and Circulars (AST 13).

Police Research and Planning Branch and Successors: Reports (HO 377).

Records Created or Inherited by the Department of Trade and Industry, 1970–1974, and Successors (FV 62).

Supreme Court of Judicature and Former Superior Courts: Central Office and Predecessors: Documents Exhibited or Deposited in Court (J 90).

Treasury: Board Papers (T1).

Treasury: Organisation and Methods Division: Registered Files (OM and 2OM Series) (T222).Treasury: Supply Department: Registered Files (S Series) (T161).

War Office and Successors: Registered Files (General Series) (WO32).

War Office: Reports, Memoranda and Papers (O and A Series) (WO33).

OTHER ARCHIVAL MATERIAL

Barclays Group Archive: 03–56 Signature Books

WEBSITES

APACS website: www.apacs.org.uk/

Avalon Project at Yale Law School website: www.yale.edu/lawweb/avalon/

BBC News website: http://news.bbc.co.uk/

Cambridge Group for the History of Population and Social Structure website: www.hpss. geog.cam.ac.uk/

Directgov website: www.direct.gov.uk/

Eighteenth Century Collections Online website. Gale Group: http://0-galenet.galegroup.com.

Equifax website: www.equifax.co.uk/

European Commission, Justice and Home Affairs website: http://ec.europa.eu/justice_home/

European Union PRADO website: www.consilium.europa.eu/prado/

Experian website: www.experian.co.uk/

Funding Universe website: www.fundinguniverse.com/

Hide Project website: www.hideproject.org/

History and Policy website: www.historyandpolicy.org/

Home Office Identity Fraud Steering Committee website: www.identity-theft.org.uk/

Identinet website: www.history.ox.ac.uk/identinet/

Identity Blog website: www.identityblog.com/

Information Commissioner's Office website: www.dpr.gov.uk/

Internet Classics Archive website: http://classics.mit.edu?/

Irish General Register Office website: www.groireland.ie/

John Daugman's webpage: www.cl.cam.ac.uk/users/jgd1000/

Law Reform Commission New South Wales Lawlink website: www.lawlink.nsw.gov.au/

Library and Archives Canada, Canadian Genealogy Centre website: www.collectionscanada.gc.ca/

Liverpool Maritime Archives & Library website: www.liverpoolmuseums.org.uk/

Manchester's Ancoats Little Italy website: www.ancoatslittleitaly.com/

Morpho website: www.morpho.com/

National Archives, London: History of Passports website: http://yourarchives.nationalarchives.gov.uk/

National Archives, London, Moving Here website: www.movinghere.org.uk/National Archives, London, website: www.nationalarchives.gov.uk/

Nectar website: www.nectar.com/

NO2ID website: www.no2id.net/

Nottingham Building Society website: http://thenottingham.com/

Oxford Dictionary of National Biography website: www.oxforddnb.com/

Proceedings of the Old Bailey website: www.oldbaileyonline.org/

Project Bertillon website: www.criminocorpus.cnrs.fr/bertillon/

Roskilde University website: www.ruc.dk/

Sekelemian/Newell International Marketing Consultants website: www.loyalty.vg/

UK Border Agency website: www.ukba.homeoffice.gov.uk/

UK Independence Party website: www.ukip.org/

US Department of Defense DNA Registry website: www.afip.org/

Whichlist.com website: www.whichlist.com/

Index